EMINENT ASIANS

PRINCE ITO

EMINENT ASIANS

Six Great Personalities of the New East

BY

JOSEF WASHINGTON HALL

("UPTON CLOSE")

PORTRAIT DRAWINGS BY
ORRÉ NOBLES

KENNIKAT PRESS
Port Washington, N. Y./London

DEDICATED

TO THAT INNER GLOW OF ESSENTIAL HUMANNESS
WHICH SHINES WITH THE SAME WARMTH THROUGH
ANY PIGMENT. . . . FOR THEY, ALSO, ARE MEN.

CONTENTS

ILLUSTRATIONS

PROLOGUE
Personality in Asia

INDIVIDUALISM is subdued in the East. There is no word for "personality" in the Chinese language. Asia's lack of emphasis upon this fetish of the Occidental world reveals one of the profound divergencies in spirit between East and West.

The Western poet egoistically explains the universe in terms of himself. His Oriental brother fulfills the craving for self-revelation only as he can insinuate personal moods into the repose or mutation of Nature. Hence arises the ethereal delicacy of Eastern lyricism. But, as beauty is often attended by weakness, the Oriental subduing of egoism results in a rarity of forceful leadership among Asian peoples.

The emphasis the West has put upon personality is most obvious in religious thought. While China and India worshiped impersonal forces, personality became the prime attribute of the Occidental's God—evidenced not merely in crude anthropomorphism but more profoundly in the Deity's way of speaking to his people. "Thus saith the Lord, Thou shalt not" represents God as the very essence of Personality. This god spoke to his servants and commissioned them to launch causes for him. Their personalities were made the more rugged under the sense of a Supreme Personality directing them.

The effect might be either for good or evil, but it has

[3]

lent a definiteness and certain awfulness to most great men of the West. He who conceives that God is with him (or he is with God—it is the same in the outworking) speaks with a conviction and fights with a ruthlessness denied to the man who relies for sanction merely upon his own reason, altruism or ambition, or the wisdom of his fathers. Thus, leaders of the West, speaking generally, have wrought either greater misery or more drastic good for their societies than have their contemporaries of the East.

I use the terms East and West in a philosophic sense, in which I would set down Judaism and Muhammadanism as Western—is not the former one of the roots of European thought? And I must crave exception for individuals like Genghis Khan who were purely primitive minds uninfluenced by either Eastern or Western philosophic thought. But as regards cultured societies history bears out my generalization. On the debit side China or India have never produced a Xavier or a Luther or a Cromwell or a Lincoln; on the credit side neither have they produced an Inquisitor nor a Richelieu nor a Kaiser Wilhelm—nor yet an Anthony Comstock nor a Grand Cyclops.

"Not peace, but a sword," attended the teachings of the rather Oriental Jesus when fitted to the psychology of vigorous and intolerant Western civilization. In so far as we can catch its nuances, the spirit of Jesus sounds more in tune with those of harmony-seeking Confucius or pitying, frailty-excusing Gautama, or Mo

Dee (Meh Ti), Chinese advocate of the doctrine of love, than with the spirits of the fanatical Jews from which he sprang or the driving, organizing Paul or the dialectical St. Augustine. Christ had a sublime optimism and emotional quality lacked by the Oriental sages—more "personality," perhaps, yet he also lacked the militancy and "no compromise" which is the strength of our Western heroes.

Asian leaders for the most part have been mellowed, and therefore weakened by a sense of their own insignificance and fallibility. They have largely lacked the sublime but fortifying arrogance to appropriate God as founder of their causes and justifier of their methods. They have humbly accepted the assumption, basis of all Oriental philosophy, that mankind, in the whole, knows more than the most brilliant teacher. They have told their audiences not: "The Lord spake unto me," but: "Thus and so do the lives of men indicate. Look in your own hearts." The individual lacked sanction to transform society. Society, idealized, was to conform him.

Such is the tradition of Asian leadership. Looking backward through five millenniums of Asian history, we discern a few towering men who have either triumphed over this handicap and built their prestige upon their very ability to flout it, or, on the other hand, have assented to it, incorporated it in their appeal and made it the pillar of their eminence. Of the first group is Chin Shih Huang Ti, who, emulating, a century later,

[5]

Alexander the Great, apostatized from Chinese scholar-worship and crushed Chinese group independence, leaving a "fame" indicated by the desire of every Chinese passer-by to share the pleasure of befouling his grave. But he built the longest-lived empire in history. Of the first group in another realm is the heterodox philosopher Hsün-tzu, who considered it betrayal of his being to give one hair of his head to save civilization. Of the same also are Hideyoshi, who built the Japanese nation against its will, and Muhammad, who triumphed not only in accomplishment but in the hearts of his people. Of the second group are Confucius the ethical teacher, Mencius the political constitutionalist, and Gautama the Buddha or Enlightened One. Leaders of the latter type, I would have it understood, did not escape opposition and even persecution. But their conflict was with individuals and perverted interpretations, not with the Spirit of Asia.

Out of the Eastern soil producing such leadership, but blown upon by terrific new winds from the West, have grown the personalities of modern Asia which we here view. They have been warped by the strange gales, but they have also acquired a strength and a vigor not possessed by their predecessors. This is notably the case with Mustapha Kemal. Sun Yat-sen, viewed from old China, is indeed warped by a foreign pragmatism, but he gained an unconquerable confidence therefrom. Yamagata and Ito, the temporary compromises in whose perpetual feud determined modern Japan, escaped to greater degree than the others the stress of conflict between the Eastern and Western minds, because they belonged to that Oriental people which in its direct attack upon problems and its literal-mindedness is semi-Occidental. Mahatma Gandhi stands upon a spiritual base so eternal that storms of criticism scarcely do more than refresh his countenance. Yet there is clearly revealed in him a composite of two influences. He provides an impressive evidence that the peace and fortitude of the East can unite with the vigor and hokum-killing directness of the West. If enough men arise, in both East and West, who can thus unite the best from both (it need not always be the *same* best) we shall have hope of a new civilization.

In the wide view of ultimate effect upon the thought and environment of humanity the makers of new Asia are probably the most important figures of this age. Theirs is, from the West's own standpoint, the greatest synchrony of political movements since the establishment of democracy, and of cultural movements since the Renaissance. They are transforming Asia from an idyl into a force. They are leading the world's largest continent and some of its most gifted races from what we Westerners, at least, have chosen to regard as a side show into the main ring of the world's circus.

And as these unadorned sketches, written from sources in a half dozen of the world's obscure languages [1] and

---

[1] —which, however, are yet to become as frequently taught among us as German and French.

out of table talk and anecdotes of the road in every country of Asia, will show, they also are men.

I have seen the reading of a Chinese lyric do more to remove the blindness that threatens to destroy our world than an entire course of sermons against race prejudice. Lyrics and lives—these lift the hood off the lamp of the human spirit within all men. The inconsequential pigment of their skins is not enough to so much as tint its glow.

SUN YAT-SEN

1866–1925

孫中山

SUN YAT-SEN

I

THOSE of us who saw Sun Yat-sen's quixotic struggles, reported his bombastic statements for a supercilious press, and felt, in our little pride, embarrassed at his puerilities, now begin to realize that one of those life dramas which bring into being the world's demigods was playing before our eyes.

A peasant boy goes to far islands where he learns the wisdom and magic of a strange and ruthless people. A dreaming youth conceives a crusade against a powerful and wicked throne. From behind a surgeon's apron, a young revolutionist strikes at the earth's oldest monarchy. An unknown student invades a palace to point the way of righteousness to the mightiest satrap in the empire. Outlawed, he drifts around and around the globe, a price of a half million dollars, the largest ever offered for a man, on his head. With suddenly recruited cohorts he descends to wreak vengeance upon tyrants—disappearing mysteriously as they rally against him. Still he is captured once and again. He gains his freedom with no other weapons than his earnest voice and compelling logic. . . . Suddenly the outlaw is called back by an acclaiming nation to be its First Citizen. With impressive ceremony he announces to the spirits of the ancient heroes that he has liberated the ancestral land.

But fame and power are not the end of this story. As the true drama must, it continues into heroic frustration. For the good of his people, the "Great Soul" abdicates his place in favor of a contemporary. But he discovers that himself and the people have been betrayed and rises in wrath to annihilate the offender. He fails, and is left tragically struggling against treachery in his own ranks and ridicule from the world.

At the lowest ebb of fortune his lonely heart is strengthened by union with one of the most beautiful and gifted women of his race. She inspires his appeal to his people and comforts his life. Once more, and once more again, he gains a foothold and reëstablishes his power in his native district, only to come into disfavor there. Whereupon he progresses to the scornful enemy capital which for thirty years had sought his life, and enters it a triumphal hero—to succumb immediately, just in time to escape a tragic reverse, to a long-flouted disease and die quietly among worshiping disciples. And his cause marches on amid the scoffing of a supercilious world to consummation.

Sun was summoned from life's stage at the right moment to insure fame. Fate grants to few such favor. President Harding was most fortunate; Presidents Wilson and Roosevelt were not. Two weeks more of life would have left Sun Yat-sen an inglorious victim upon the altar of his opportunistic trust of rogues. Death brought suspension of popular judgment. Then the hot-headed act of a British police inspector in Shanghai set all China aflame, rallying support to an obscure and erstwhile hopeless military movement launched by the crusader as one of his last experiments. The Nationalist army swept the country, carrying as conquering ensign the enlarged photograph of the "Sainted Doctor."

Sun Yat-sen is thus made the father of a renewed nation. He becomes its Lenin, its George Washington, its Napoleon. In China's pantheon he already ranks with Chu Yuan-chang, who overthrew the Mongol tyranny five hundred years ago. He did not have to await the approval of generations of scholars for beatification as did that first Ming emperor, for in his new age such honor is bestowed, as with us in the West, by publicity.

Since it so happened that the spectacular uprising of China marked the arrival of all Asia at consciousness of revolt against the hitherto dominant race, Sun Yat-sen becomes the inspirer of a continent. He is the model rebel, the ideal expression in an individual life of the resentment and aspiration of the colored races. To-day his name is used as a spur in Japan, Indo-China, the Dutch East Indies, Siam, India, Iraq, and Egypt. Russia eulogizes him, and the Third Internationale founds a university for education of Asiatics named with his famous alias, "Chung Shan." This may be chiefly "for export," but it is sincere in so far as Russia feels herself a member of the confraternity of the snubbed. With divergencies suitable to another time and continent, Sun becomes the Bolivar of Asia.

Indeed a story for saga-singers and dramatists!

Sun died March 12, 1925. Already the myths are gathering about him, particularly furthered by the new intelligentsia of China, a class which had boasted itself impervious to hero worship. It is so with Lenin. We read in the pamphlets of the Kuomintang Party—which was critical enough during his life, yet, like many a widow, now permits no hint of imperfection in the lamented one—that he failed ten times, but was never wrong. We are told of a prodigy who before the age often had set himself to overthrow not only the Manchu Dynasty, but Superstition and Inequality as well. We see a boy hero in turned-up shoes leading a family rebellion against the binding of his sister's feet. He then named himself, say these unsophisticated eulogies, the second Hung Hsiu-chuan—the rebel who started out to establish the reign of Taiping (Eternal Peace) but ended by causing the death of two million fellow countrymen. The youthful Sun's idol-smashing exploit in the village temple is as much elaborated upon as George Washington's cherry tree adventure. In place of the crossing of the Delaware we have the revolutionary doctor being let down over the walls of Canton in a coolie's carrying-basket. His escape from his kidnapers in Lond ranks with Napoleon's flight from Elba as material for romancers. One thing will hinder the saga-singers. It is difficult to spin the golden web of fancy about the humorless, heavy portraits scattered like the leaves of autumn which probably outnumber even those of Lenin and Mussolini. One wonders if— had there been illustrated sections and publicity bureaus in the days of Washington and Napoleon—these heroes would have inspired such reverence.

Sun Yat-sen's life was a reversal of traditional Chinese philosophic attitude; his deification is a reversal of the too common Chinese trait of amiably doubting all human excellence. Only a career more dramatic than fiction could have induced the earth's most experienced and sophisticated nation to give way to this unrestrained adulation.

But there is an element in Sun's career more significant than his dizzying shifts of fortune or spectacular arrival at fame. His development provides the most arresting warning yet given us of the paradoxical effects of the impact of West upon East. No life ever ran a greater gamut. Sun Yat-sen was begotten by a Christian father, an employee of the London Missionary Society which, as things went in China of the past century, meant a protégé of Great Britain. Yet Sun died a bitter enemy of "missionary" Christianity, and wrought as much damage to the British Empire as any individual who ever lived. He was brought up under the influence of Western civilization and was one of its most effective champions in China, but came to rebel against its present social inequalities as vigorously as against dynastic tyranny. He popularized European dress for men, a style with military collar being named after him, but in later years he reverted to the traditional gown with a pleasure almost pathetic. China's first graduate in modern medicine, he turned when facing death to the native doctors.

He was personally gentle and forgiving as a child, yet few men have set more ruthless and bloody forces in motion. He began as a prophet of democratic political thought in China, and ended as the organizer of a new oligarchy designed to lash a sluggish people into unyearned-for reform. Yet he continued to proclaim "people's power." He was quite as frank, but not as analytic, as Mussolini.

II

Soft rain fell over a little plain knee-deep in close-standing rows of lush rice stalks. Among the paddy fields, determining the slope for their water supply, rose a hummock whiskered with cane and tufted with bamboo. Since this was in the flat delta of the Pearl River, men dignified it, calling it Hsiang Shan, or Fragrant Mountain. At its base, on the side called Blue Valley, stood a cluster of huts framed of bamboo and walled with cane, split and woven from the hummock and thatched with straw from the paddy field. Before each house was a courtyard fenced by a scrub bamboo hedge. Here would stand a straw mat shed for the buffalo, neat cocks of rice straw, a crude wooden plow and seeder, and in the center, surrounded by the pounded-earth-and-lime threshing floor, the two great stone husking disks.

One courtyard was entered by a two-leaved gate done in bright pig's-blood enamel decorated with gold and supported by brick pillars—a mark of special afflu-ence. For, as any of the straw-sandaled villagers would ask you—by way of explanation—was not its venerable master the father of a son who had "effulged foreign wealth" in the Incense Islands (Hawaii)? And in addi-tion to that signal fortune, did he not benefit to the extent of four ounces of silver per month from the Public Righteousness Concern (Church Missionary So-ciety) for distributing the Foreign Devils' holy books through the countryside? The ancient Mr. Sun (ac-tually in late middle age) was a communicant of the strange religion, although the lithographed god-protec-tors of day and night still clung—one on each leaf—to his gate.

As the genie, who, in his cave in the Ancient Hills, keeps the record of the sojourns of spirits in this earthly sphere, was turning up a clean page for a new entry, this paternal Mr. Sun sat in his brick-floored library-bedroom listening to the soft swish of the rain on the sea of standing grain and its gentle crackle on the thatch overhead.

Eventually the midwife came and knelt with her clenched fists together in congratulation. "Fortune, Ancientness," she shrilled. "A son! Thrice brilliant is the child of full years. Thus did Confucius and the other sages enter the world. Now you may look forward to decrepitude with tranquillity."

As if to satirize the thought, a wail came from the raised platform in the next room.

Mr. Sun wet his ink brush with his lips, worked it to a point on the ink slab, and drew to his hand the cloth-cased book of family genealogy. The date was November 12, 1866. The new scion was set down by number only until such time as he should receive from his schoolmaster his "designatory name"—descriptive of his budding character.

A child of so much hope, however, did seem to deserve a special personal name, and this matter the paternal ancestor took up with his quiet, determined, and task-pursuing wife as soon as she was up and about. "The birth of this boy," he harangued her, "must be assurance of heaven's returning favor. Mayhap the years of disquiet are at last at an end. The Dragon Throne is now again secure and we may hope for an era of tranquillity ahead."

The "inside person" paused at her noodle board. "Then let us call him *Yat-sen*, 'Fairy of Tranquillity,'" she harmonized. . . . The ever listening Old Man of the Mountain must have cocked an eye toward the child's future and laughed.

The storm clouds which the parents hoped had blown over hung low and real in the growing boy's mental universe. He listened pensively near the tea table while the "ancient heads" told tales of the first war between

[18]

nations of the white and yellow races (1842), in which British "lightning boats" demonstrated the destructive power of the hitherto lightly regarded barbarian, and forced trade and opium upon a haughty and unappeased officialdom. Younger adventurers, including the village schoolmaster, his uncle, recounted experiences in the fanatical campaign of Hung Hsiu-chuan, who, announcing himself the brother of the foreigners' god, Jesus Christ, and the inaugurator of the era of *Tai Ping* or Great Peace, swept from Canton to Tientsin and menaced Manchu authority from 1850 to 1862. In the midst of this the foreign devils had broken into Peking and desecrated the very seat of the Son of Heaven. Traders and soldiers passing through the hamlet told of steady French encroachments in the nearby Indo-Chinese dependencies. The serious and responsive lad's cheeks burned. His gorge rose against a Dragon Throne which was too weak and craven to protect its people from shame.

Thirty miles from Fragrant Mountain was swarming Canton, terminus of Arab sea trade since the ninth century, now metropolis of middle Pacific Asia. Down in the delta lay Macao, transformed by license of its Portuguese governors into the gambling and opium den of the Orient. Beyond the Pirate Islands off the delta towered Hongkong Peak, new Gibraltar of white supremacy in the East.

Letters came now and then from the elder brother, relating his contact with the sons of American mis-

sionaries who were supplanting the dynasty of Kame-
hameha in the Incense Islands. Missionaries visited
the hamlet and young Sun went frequently with his
father to their impressive compounds at Canton, where
English and American ladies were attracted by his
eagerness and taught him his first phrases of the foreign devils' magic language. Sun Yat-sen was to be the
first of China's immortals chiefly molded by exotic
influences.

However, he learned the native soil—too well ever to
forget it. He plowed the family paddy fields and went
to the school of the village literatus. There flared his
first rebellion—against its traditional regimen of punctilious memorization and unthinking repetition. His
puzzled father, too old and tired to guide such a fiery
disposition, debated apprenticing him to the village
coffin maker. At this crisis his prosperous elder brother
arrived on a visit to the ancestral shrine. The brother
offered to take the young misfit back with him to the
far islands. The lad cried with joy and the hamlet
breathed sighs of relief.

In Honolulu, at the age of thirteen, he entered,
thanks to his father's sectarian connection, the Bishop's
School, where he won a medal for scholarship presented
by the King of Hawaii in person—justification for
taking as "scholarly name" *Wen*—"Literary." As Sun
Wen, rather than Sun Yat-sen, his own country came
to know him. He graduated into a higher school named
after Saint Louis. Here he was baptized into the re-

ligion proffered by his kind and zealous teachers. As
with many students of Christian schools in both Christian and heathen lands, social motives rather than definite religious conviction influenced him. Yet on the
route back to China at the age of eighteen he carried
a Bible, reading it desperately.

The sudden ending of his placid Hawaiian experience
is explained in his brother's letter to the mother, now
head of the house. "Ming-day ("Brilliant Virtue"—
Sun's intimate name) is becoming too foreignized," he
reports. A family which had accepted Christianity,
and all its break with the native life—much greater a
half-century ago than now—still declined to see a member deculturized. In view of the fact that his clan at
once arranged his marriage to a woman surnamed Lu,
betrothed to him in childhood, we may suspect that
one indication of the foreignization feared was an independent love affair.

Raw from adolescent disappointment, seeking solace
in the foreigner's religion, young Sun arrived in Hongkong—to come sharp against the foreigner's arrogance.
Here and at Canton English officers of the Chinese customs service subjected him and his Chinese fellow
travelers to humiliating inspections, while "white" passengers were waved past. At an age when young Americans scarcely think of social or political questions Sun
was returning to his country with definite ideas of
material prosperity, personal liberty, and national dignity. His indignation over discrimination against his

people within their Ancestral Land gave him a cause to live for. Many a man, no doubt, has been goaded into the spirit of revolution by customs-house experiences, but this tiff between white-starched officials and pig-tailed youth was to become an event in the decline of white supremacy in the world. Sun Wen went to his village and brooded. That year the Manchu emperor gave up Annam to the French. The Manchu ruling clan at Peking could not save its people from "eating humiliation."

Photography was just becoming a fad in China. Stiff portraits of Sun, taken at this time, show him a sweet-faced, sensitive-mouthed, querulous-eyed youth in conventional Chinese costume, including skull cap and queue. His features were of the true, round-faced Chinese type—much less "Tartar" than those of the Mongolized Chinese of the North—a circumstance which permitted the baseless rumor that his was mixed blood. Open sincerity and naïve self-assurance—always his charm—are already apparent. The scraggly mustache which later hid his fine mouth was not yet in evidence, nor had the wistfulness of his countenance been obliterated by the sagging lines of suffering and egomania which record themselves so depressingly in later portraits.

After Sun had gone through the ceremonies of bowing with the Lu woman before his father's tablet, his mother, the mud cooking range, and the woven cane bed, which formally installed her in the ancestral home, he was set to clerking behind the high counter of the village pawnshop, whose sign was the "Six Stars." He did his work dutifully and won the esteem of his employers, but could not refrain from challenging country-side traditions. The docility and superstition of the peasants galled him, and he lacked either sense of humor or indifference to ignore them. Irritated to supreme protest, he climbed through the sun-shot haze of a spring morning to the tiny shrine hidden in the bamboos of Fragrant Mountain and pushed over the terrible-visaged mud Protector of the district. But instead of acclaiming the young iconoclast, the villagers intimated to his sponsors that his further presence among them would be interpreted as intentional imposition upon their tolerance.

The two village elders who owned the pawnshop summoned their disruptive apprentice to "face the chest," which is the Chinese equivalent for being "on the green carpet." "We don't believe in idols any more than you do," they advised. "But we don't concern ourselves in the matter. Our business is storing goods on commission, not correcting the beliefs of the people."

Sun eyed them determinedly. "Then continue to make that your business, Honored Grandfathers," he said. "I'll make the latter mine."

They tried once more. "Indifference is a high virtue.

But a sense of humor can, to an extent, take its place. Can't you laugh at the folk-ways, if you cannot ignore them?"

"I see nothing to laugh at," replied the young clerk.

They considered him calmly. "Probably the new age requires a man like you," they said. "You are likely to become great. Here is your fare to Hongkong, and if you are ever in need, call on us, but don't stay in our village."

The Elders took the trouble to interpret Sun's escapade in a favorable light to his overseas brother. This important person, now economic head of the house, supplied means for further schooling. He was eventually to place his entire resources at the disposal of Sun's cause. These three who were closest to him became Sun's first converts, and Chinese revolutionary scripture honors them with designations specially given by the Master: "Fathers of Racial Dignity" and "Elder Brother of the Republic."

Sun spent two years in the "Imperial Benevolence Academy" (the benevolence of Queen Victoria, not the Son of Heaven) and Hongkong Academy, then graduated at the head of his class. Medical missionaries in Canton offered him an apprenticeship and he donned the doctor's white apron. Then Dr. James Cantlie opened a medical school in connection with Alice Memorial Hospital, Hongkong, later amalgamated with Hongkong University. Sun again crossed to the precipitous island and after five years' study, in 1892, was turned out the first graduate of modern medicine in China.

Hongkong was the trysting place of idealistic students and disappointed older men. The returned student, the Oriental who had studied abroad, was just beginning to be a factor in affairs. Japan had been remade by this class into a united, if still untried, nation. Sun Yat-sen's tendencies led him into association with the returned students who naturally believed the throne should commission them to modernize China, or, failing that, should be overthrown. He and three youths who sat up nights changing the world, became known among the younger set as "The Four Rebels." The three gradually resigned themselves to money-making and the lordship of harems, but Sun was in deadly earnest and utterly blind to other interests. He was the first man of modern China to make reform a sole career.

Probably through his two old sponsors of Fragrant Mountain, Sun had received passwords to the great Chinese secret societies. These Masonic bodies of China, known as the White Lilies, the Triads and the Elder Brothers, ramified into every village, controlling guild and commune administration, and often officialdom. They were particularly strong in South China and among the millions of overseas Chinese in Malaysia, the Dutch East Indies and the Philippines, and in the communities of the Americas and Europe. Having supported the remnants of the Ming dynasty in a desperate struggle against the Manchu conquerors, the societies remained unreconciled through the following two hundred years. The throne outlawed them, but never rooted them out. They were fertile ground for the young agitator. Sun stumbled into the work which made him a power: the organizing of the secret societies for revolution.

He found it necessary to practice his profession to pay expenses. Casting about for a field where foreign influence had created confidence in Western medicine, he chose the Portuguese territory of Macao. But the Portuguese doctors there resented the threat to their monopoly, and fathered a government ordinance against native practitioners. Sun removed to Canton—still less love in his heart for the "treaty-port" white man than before. Within a year the young doctor was operating an office and four dispensaries. But while he dispensed eye droppers and salved head scabs, he saw visions of himself leading the world's most ancient nation back to its rightful position of international dignity.

Soon a plan came to him. Abandoning his practice he strode upon the stage of public affairs with a breath-taking gesture. Accompanied by a zealous young merchant he went, at his own expense, without herald or introduction, to Tientsin, sixteen hundred miles by coasting steamer, and bearded the most powerful and haughty mandarin in China, Marquis Li Hungchang, vice regent of the Empress Dowager, in his own magnificent den.

The twenty-seven-year-old physician, clothed in ill-fitting European clothes, stood before the vermilion-robed satrap who had dominated China thirty years and had been fawned upon in all the courts of Europe, to demand an immediate reform of his administration under four categories. Already Sun was a master of sententious phrases. Set forth in balanced lines of four ideographs each, his program was: Full development of men's abilities; full exploitation of earth's resources; full use of material instruments (railways, machinery, etc.); and unhampered flow of commerce.

The septuagenarian viceroy bowed ironically and asked to be excused as being too old to undertake new policies. He was not too old to be at that very moment bringing on, through his henchman Yuan Shih-kai, the war with Japan, nor later to go to that country, withstand an assassin's bullet, and negotiate a most humiliating peace.

No popular newspapers were then published in China, but the tea houses pretty adequately filled their place. Sun's action was to be the talk of the nation. China was surprised that he obtained an audience, and amazed that, having done so, he retained his head. Well for him that Confucian scripture sanctioned a subject's privilege to reprimand his ruler, and that Marquis Li, before the public, espoused Confucian humbleness and magnanimity. Henceforth the spotlight was to be always on the agitating doctor. His enemies would call him a "publicity hound." He did love to be noticed—he insisted upon it. But from the newspaperman's

[27]

viewpoint of "good copy" it must be confessed that he earned his "space."

Sun left the presence of Li Hung-chang with the conviction that the mandarin aristocracy was as hopeless as the Manchu dynasty. He would never waver in the new determination to wipe out both completely. But many bitter years were to pass before he should think through the problem of what was to take their place.

China's costly defeat at the hands of little and, until then, patronized Japan, was an unexpected revelation of her weakness to the Western Powers. They at once took advantage by demanding ports along her coast. Soon, with Port Arthur gone to Russia, Tsingtao to Germany, Weihaiwei and Kowloon to England, and Kwangchowan to France, the cup of shame was full for those who cherished the honor of the Middle Kingdom and the dignity of its race. Sun and his associates accused the degenerate dynasty of selling the country piecemeal in return for a protraction of its miserable existence. The official hierarchy of the mandarinate, whose southern members had refused to send their division of the fleet against Japan's inferior navy lest its new paint be scarred, stood convicted of the grossest lack of patriotism. Towering above all in egotistic absurdity stood "Old Buddha"—the Empress Dowager. She had used the foreign loan negotiated for naval construction to build a marble pleasure boat in her summer palace grounds.

Following his interview with Viceroy Li, Sun had crossed north China and dropped down the Yangtze Valley, making "strategic observations" and organizing revolutionary sentiment. This had been done before. But no others had prosecuted the plan he now undertook: to plant the foundation of Chinese revolution and reform in the rich and unhampered overseas community. It was his second great stroke. Without it and the first, the use of the secret societies, he could not have brought about the downfall of a two-thousand-year-old monarchy in half a lifetime.

His own overseas experience and the position of his brother pointed the way. During the Sino-Japanese War he was in Honolulu, and when he sailed for Japan, he left behind the first "local" of the *Hsing Chung Hui*, or Advance China Society. After organizing emigrants in Japan he booked passage for America. But a message from Soong Yao-ru, a revolutionary merchant of Shanghai, urging that the time had come to begin open resistance in China, took him back to Canton instead. There he organized a trading company and an agricultural association, under cover of which he prepared revolt.

Sun & Company imported a shipment of barreled ham, but the meddlesome customs authorities found six hundred pistols in them. Seventy accessories to the plot were promptly apprehended. Three nights after the head-chopping, the doctor himself was let down over Canton wall in a coolie's basket. While behind shut gates the city was being searched for him, Sun conceived a terror of being caught like a caged animal. He developed a very non-Chinese aversion to walls, and his first act, when he came into local power years later, was to have Canton city wall torn down, leveled, and its site made a boulevard. And wall-leveling has become a tenet of Nationalist creed.

The first blood had been shed in Sun's struggle with the ruling house. With a price on his head he fled to Japan, which was to be his so frequent refuge. After a time, despairing of regaining his native shores, he cut his queue, adopted Japanese customs, and took the Japanese name of Chung Shan Shao, "Mountain-Midst Woodcutter." The first two words of this alias have become the intimate name by which Sun's followers love to designate him. It is to-day borne by streets in many cities, a battle cruiser, two universities, a style of dress, pet horses, a newspaper, and innumerable baby boys.

Sun's restless activities soon betrayed his disguise. The Japanese, once more on terms with the Peking throne, had to ask him to take ship. In Honolulu he crossed paths with his Medical College mentor, Dr. James Cantlie, who was returning home after long service. The devoted missionary doctor and his warm-hearted wife asked Sun to look them up in London. They were proud that a student of theirs and a Christian should be leading a movement in China, even if a revolutionary one. They responded with almost pa-

[30]

thetic idealization to the spell of Sun's personality,
which unfailingly bewitched Westerners even more than
fellow-countrymen who came in contact with him.
True to their class and time, they unquestioningly believed in Great Britain's divine appointment to civilize
the world, feeling that any good for China must come
out of tutelage of British, as well as Christian tinge.
Sun had enjoyed that blessing.

Soong Yao-ru, the Shanghai merchant who gave his
wealth, and ultimately his children, to Sun and his
cause, financed the journey on to America. Throughout the United States Sun lectured to small groups,
gaining entry to the Chinese Tongs [1] through his secret
society connections, but succeeded in organizing only
three locals of his "Advance China Society." As yet,
he lacked a political creed capable of arousing the
apathetic merchant communities to fervor. The Empress Dowager, however, followed his activities with
increasing choler.

He went on to London, called on the Cantlies, and
then dropped out of sight. . . .

At midnight on October 17, 1896, Dr. Cantlie was
called out of bed by a woman who stated that she was
the wife of a domestic employed at the Chinese Lega-

---

[1] "Tongs" in America are projections of the clans of Canton province.
The original bond—the same surname—has been enlarged in some cases to
include men of several clans associating for mutual protection. Ignorant
of Western processes of justice and, indeed, starting in California when
these hardly existed, the American Chinese communities resorted to primitive "justice by retribution" in inter-tong disputes. The tradition continues
in the "tong wars."

tion in Portland Place. She handed him a name card
on which was scribbled the following message:

I was kidnaped into the Chinese Legation on Sunday, and
shall be smuggled out from England to China for death. Pray
rescue me quick. A ship is chartered by the C. L.[2] for the
service to take me to China, and I shall be locked up all the
way without communication to anybody. O! Woe to me!
Please take care of the messenger for me at present; he is
very poor and will lose his work by doing for me.

The aged doctor at once roused up Scotland Yard,
but got no further help than advice to go back to bed.
During the following days he anxiously besieged the
government offices in Downing Street, only to meet official indifference and clutch vain wisps of red tape.
Then he seized the last resort of every Englishman: he
wrote to *The Times*. News was slack at the moment—
space reporters on all the British papers hailed the event
of this romantic occurrence under their very noses, and
wrote columns on it. Sun Yat-sen's name became
known in the Western world as it had in the East
through the incident with Li Hung-chang. The Chinese
Legation grew alarmed at the attention focusing on it.
"Friends of liberty" wrote threatening letters backed
by a bombing attempt. Lord Salisbury was forced to
consider the case as violating British sovereignty and
her tradition of political asylum. He protested to the
Chinese Legation. The day the ship chartered to take

[2] Chinese Legation.

Sun to torture and death received sailing papers, he was pushed out the back door of the Legation.

He wrote to the Reverend F. C. Au in Hongkong:

They put bars on the windows, and set the under official to guard me. I prayed six days in great agitation but on the seventh God gave me peace. The problem was to get news of my predicament out of the building. I entrusted a message to an English servant, who handed it to the (Chinese) Minister with the result that I had my pen and paper taken away and was more closely watched. The next day an opportunity presented itself when the guards were not looking and the domestic was in the room. God helped me to persuade him, and he found a stub of pencil and I a name card. He risked his employment, or worse. . . . Much trouble—a ship, cablegrams, etc., did they go to for my hundred odd pounds of flesh. . . . The Manchu government has lost its reputation over this, and I am put in touch with the best people. . . . I feel as favored as the Prodigal Son or the Lost Sheep. Truly, this is the blessing of the Fatherly God. I hope you will write me more on religious topics. Such instruction may have a great effect upon me, and through me, upon our Chinese people.

This was probably the highest pitch of Sun's religious experience. Yet his confidence in himself and his mission, which was his real religion, is as much the real message here as in his purely rationalistic utterances later.

Upon his release, Sun went to the continent. Out of his reactions to governments and society there he constructed his first political creed. He reported that he "liked political equality, as practiced in Europe, but was disturbed at the manner in which economic inequality and class distinction grow in industrialized society."

Western champions of democracy who are shocked by the "radical" quality of reform movements in Asia should take into account that democracy and socialism burst together upon Asiatic thought. Sun Yat-sen and other "new thinkers" of China, Japan, and India discovered the writings of Rousseau, Jefferson, and Paine, Marx, Tolstoy, and Proudhon at the same time. With us the one innovation came an age ahead of the other, and democracy was already orthodox before socialism raised its evangel. But once an Oriental like Sun Yatsen had so far overcome his tradition as to cast off the authority of the Son of Heaven, he retained little feeling of an innate sanctity in the capitalistic system. Communism was no more shocking to his original mentality than republicanism.

Sun had already somewhat vaguely declared for "nationalism" and "democracy." To these, braced together under the principle of the "right to live," he now added, under the influence of socialist thought prevalent in Europe, "the right to a living," meaning government responsibility for popular welfare, and combined the three into a system named *San Min Chu I* (pronounced *jew ee*): "The Three People's Determinations." The last word is as near an equivalent as possible for "principles" in the nonabstract Chinese language. Coming later to theory of government, Sun formulated his dogma of the "Five Bases" of constitutional government—an interesting combination of American and ancient Chinese administrative science. To the familiar executive, legislative, and judicial branches, Sun added "examinative" and "inspective." By these he meant the civil service system for the selection of officials and an independent censorate to supervise all acts of administration—a direct way of accomplishing what parliamentary interrogations and senatorial investigations attempt in England and America.

The very year that Sun added the modern civil service principle to his theory of government (1905) the Manchu throne abolished the three-thousand-year-old Chinese civil board of examinations, thus unconsciously dooming the mandarinate, aristocracy of scholars and pedestal of the dynasty. The examinations had become puerile and corrupt, and foreign powers prohibited them in several provinces as punishment for Boxer outrages.

Sun published his doctrines in rhythmic captions and terse slogans which have become bywords in Chinese. He became as felicitous at coining catchwords as President Wilson, with the advantage of a language more adapted to pithy phrasing. During the thirty remaining years of Sun's career his Three Principles were to go through significant evolution. They would take the final form of the speeches of his last year under Russian Communist influence. He first planned on effecting them through a purely democratic form of government, then through Jeffersonian party rule. In the end he

[35]

would be driven to adopt the scheme of Bolshevist oligarchy to "enforce liberty" on a huge and uneducated population. Sun Yat-sen would put the dragon through the paces of a race horse. . . . And there was need for a Chinaman without patience if the Ancestral Land was to be saved from delivery into thralldom.

The first of Sun's three eastward circumnavigations of the globe was completed by way of Turkey, Palestine, and India. In Siam, Malaya, and the East Indies he was received by wealthy Chinese traders and rubber and sugar planters, and he laid the groundwork for a financial and moral support which was his unfailing asset. Women, whose traditional subordination was greatly mitigated in these exiled communities, and some of whom were business and family heads, competed in offering him allegiance, if we may trust the stories. What woman would not give heart and pocketbook to a poetic-faced, gentle-mannered hero in neat mustache and starched and ironed "whites," who had fled around the world with the largest bounty in history on his head? That Sun responded there is no question. He is quoted as having said that he possessed only two interests in life: revolution and women, but this is a treaty-port canard. Sun had not the sense of humor for such a studied banality—which is an added reason why women loved him.

In Japan, where he spent 1898, the glamor of adventure about Sun attracted students affected by the new liberalist sentiment. A number who came under his

influence at this and subsequent times were to be the
leading reformers of the Island Empire, as Dr. Sakuzo
Yoshino of the Imperial University, Toyohiko Kagawa,
Christian socialist, settlement worker, and novelist, and
Bunji Suzuki, head of the Japanese Federation of Labor.
The Japanese, so long China's docile pupils, after they
whipped her in war assumed the pompous pose of teachers. Sun, however, always commanded the tremendous
interest that Japanese have in a man of unique ideas
and their native respect for the man of self-sacrificing
courage.

But Sun's mind was taken off the agreeable task of
adding to Japanese hero worship by developments in
Peking. Two "Japan-returned" students had gained
supreme influence over the young Emperor Kuang Hsu,
for whom Old Buddha had stepped aside. They drew
up for him a drastic series of mandates, transforming
the empire into a constitutional monarchy, and ordain-
ing educational, industrial, social, and political reform
which Sun regarded as a direct steal of his fire—but
in the service of the dynasty, directed to the perpetua-
tion of the Manchu supremacy which he had sworn to
overthrow.

Sun was not delighted, as so many foreign enthusiasts
for China expected him to be. Rather, he fulminated
fiery phrases, and established in Hongkong one of
China's first modern newspapers to circulate them. To
him, Kang Yu-wei and Liang Shih-yi and their "Protect-
Emperor Constitutionalist Society" were traitors to the

cause of reform and, what perhaps rankled more, to himself as its prophet. This experience was the first step toward Sun's eventual identification of all improvements in China with himself. The second was to be disappointment in Yuan Shih-kai, which, if one may be brutally honest, came of overconfidence in his own ability to control men.

This powerful, squat Yuan of the long-drooping mustaches, who was to prove Sun's greatest adversary, comes into the panorama of the reform movement right here. He had been Viceroy Li Hung-chang's henchman in Korea, where he was severely trounced by the Japanese. After that unpleasantness Yuan was commissioned to create a "model army" with Western instructors and equipment. He was consequently hailed by the military-minded plenipotentiaries of the Western powers as China's paragon. When the reforming young Emperor sensed the rise of Old Buddha's anger over his innovations, he called on the commander of his model army to incarcerate her. Instead, Yuan, who owed much to her favor, reversed the plot by incarcerating the young Emperor, and chased his reforming advisers to Japan. The Dowager once more took control and the "Protect-Emperor Party" evaporated. In its place the "Righteous Fists," dubbed "Boxers" for short by correspondents, sprang up, were wooed from their original anti-Manchu tenet by capable "Old Buddha," and under her patronage committed the atrocities which caused eight powers to march on Peking in 1900. To

[38]

regain her throne she pledged her nation to the humiliating protocol with its crushing indemnity.

Sun, smoldering with fury, at the risk of his life, smuggled himself into China, and in the guise of an herb peddler entered the garrison of Hwayjo, north of Canton. Several revolutionary-minded young officers gave him protection. By their quiet tea table he converted the commander of the force to the idea of mutiny. Then he went to Hongkong to fetch arms he had stored there. He was frustrated by his *bête noir,* the customs service, whose inspectors recognized him and prevented his landing. The ship's purser dumped him on Formosa, now a Japanese possession. Undaunted, he at once interviewed the Japanese governor and won him to supply the necessary munitions. As these were being loaded on ship for Hwayjo, the Japanese cabinet fell, the governor was recalled, and the munitions held up. But Sun's disciples never abandoned him or even expressed impatience with him for failure. Men allied with him "for better or worse." He had the capacity of awakening a devotion blind to the absurdity of his many wild enterprises.

One young agent who was preparing in Canton to greet the expected attack from Hwayjo, made a drastic attempt to save the day by shooting at the viceroy. He missed and was tortured to death. But his example spread rather than discouraged the spirit of desperation. Students formed themselves into assassination squads, known as "Dare-to-Dies," adopting as their uniform for action the recently imported American union suit. For some years the apparition of this slick costume was as terrifying to Manchu officials as the Ku Klux Klan nightshirt to a negro.

Chinese students abroad began to organize and rally to Sun, first in Japan, then in America, and lastly in Europe. "Old China Hands," the comfortable foreigners of the treaty ports, looking on the drama with wise smiles, scoffed at the anti-Manchu agitator for so much as acknowledging the support of a few callow, meddlesome undergraduates. But their activity, spreading back into the schools of the Ancestral Land, became the "student movement" destined to upset rulers, drive out foreign imperialism with the bludgeon of the boycott, and turn down the edges of the smug smile on many a fat, treaty-port taipan. The youngsters who started it were to become the leaders of the nationalist movement and the ministers of its various administrations, and their programs were to be taken very seriously indeed behind the barbed wire fortifications of the foreign settlements. The three great enlistments which swelled Sun's forces to the point of irresistibility were the secret societies, the overseas community, and the students. And the most decisive of these was the last.

Sun traveled again in Indo-China and the Philippines, America and Europe. While the Russo-Japanese War (1904) was being fought on Chinese territory, he returned to Tokyo and summoned his first all-China revolutionary council. Representatives from seventeen provinces—all China proper save remote Kansu—attended, mostly in the persons of students in Japanese colleges. This convention of a few schoolboys and agitators meeting in exile solemnly resolved on a new name for their ancient nation: *Joong Hwa Min Gwo,* "Middle Flowery People's Country." It bears their choice to-day! They organized the *Toong Meng Hway,* "Together-Sworn Association," which absorbed the too dignified and quiet Advance China Society.

The delegates made their way home and within a year reported ten thousand converts and branch societies in every province. Under the very nose of the watchful dynasty, in the British Concession in Tientsin, Sun established a China headquarters. Revolutionary elements were to follow his example and make Tientsin for the next twenty years a foreign-protected hatching box for plots.

But while Sun's organization grew, his rebellions failed one after the other with a repetition which came to be laughed at. He was here, there, everywhere; leading invading forces from French Indo-China, inspiring a further mutiny to Hwayjo, and engineering coups in Canton. He utilized the special privileges of the foreigner which he aimed ultimately to destroy by hiring Japanese and French officers enjoying extraterritorial immunity to carry propaganda and spy out the far interior. His activities got him ordered out of first Japan and then French Indo-China, and barred from the Philippine Islands. For since the Manchu throne had been forced to give such huge pledges, the Powers wished it kept in power to redeem them. Having deprived himself of a resting place in Asia, Sun drifted around the world, leaving command on the ground to his associates Hu Han-ming and Wang Chung-hui, eventually to become the Elder Statesmen of the Kuomintang.

Sun's most onerous task was to cheer the revolutionists after each defeat by filling a new war chest. He became as skillful a money-raiser as Billy Sunday. An appealing cause and ability in its presentation are required to get money from Chinese laundrymen, but many gave their entire savings to Sun. His collections for the revolutionary cause during forty years were to total two and a half million dollars. He retained scarcely enough for his own clothing.

"Good, but a good deal of a fool," commented a worldly-wise Chinese Tuchun anent this side of Sun Yat-sen. But money-loving China was yet to defy the "fool," and spit upon the Tuchun, although the latter probably would continue to feel that it is better to be a live sybarite than a dead saint. The influence of Sun's honest "impracticality" on the student generation was to be one of his greatest works. The pursuit of personal advantage was not, perhaps, appreciably to lessen, but it was at least no longer to be commended.

At its blackest moment, Sun's movement was nearest success. On March 29, 1911, the "Together-Sworns" burst into the yamen of Viceroy Lung Chi-kuang in Canton but were overwhelmed by the guard. Lung's bloody reprisal earned him the name of "The Butcher." When he beheaded seventy-two young patriots he surmised that he was crushing the "annoyance" forever, but he was merely providing the nationalist cause with its martyrs and the Republic with its First Shrine. Chinese chambers of commerce of seventy-two world-spread cities contributed to erect a monument of seventy-two huge stones, surmounted by a statue of Liberty *à la* New York harbor on White Cloud Mountain overlooking Canton.

While the Tung Meng Society plotted an answer in the form of a coup at Hankow the next spring, Sun went to America on a collecting tour. The Throne's attempt to retrieve a railway concession granted to local merchants in far Szechuan and turn it over to an American-led financial group aroused local feeling which student agitators spurred into insurrection. An imperial army passed through Hankow to suppress it. As the troops disappeared through the Yangtze gorges a bomb exploded in a room over a butcher shop in the Russian concession. Russian police picked some documents out of the human and animal shambles and forwarded them to the viceroy across the river at Wuchang. The alarmed official seized and sentenced to death a number of young men and women who were incriminated. Students and other sympathizers stormed his yamen. The viceroy called on his troops. Their commander, Li Yuan-hung, a heavy-set Japan-returned student, blandly informed him that the officers of the garrison were revolutionists who had bought their rank from him with Sun Yat-sen's money, and offered to assist the astounded viceroy either to flee or to stand and die a hero's death. He chose the first alternative and Li escorted him in a Dare-to-Die union-suit uniform at dead of night aboard a Japanese ship.

At this crisis the scepter in Peking was wielded by a young woman, mother of the infant emperor. The Dowager Tzu-hsi, "Old Buddha," had died, after having arranged for the reforming emperor, Kuang Hsu, whom she so heartily disliked, to die a few hours in advance of herself, and after having spent what she knew was the last afternoon of her life upright in her throne dominating the choice of successor by the Imperial Clan Council. With the passing of his patroness Yuan Shih-kai had found himself in disfavor, and had retired to his estate in Honan to nurse a diplomatic "sick leg." Now he was persuaded to return to save the Throne. But instead of crushing, he nursed the turbulence which made him indispensable. He saw to it that Li Yuan-hung, who had been dragged by "Dare-to-Dies" from under his wife's bed and compelled at the point of pistols to accept command of the revolution, suffered a sufficient reverse to make him amenable to negotiation. He captured Hankow in a bloody campaign during which flames of the burning city drove several thousand inhabitants to horrible death in the river. Simultaneously, however, Yuan was permitting a down-river junta of revolutionists more directly associated with Sun Yat-sen to take possession of Shanghai and Nanking. When the Throne finally ordered Yuan to assume an uncompromising offensive, twenty of his generals presented a signed statement declining to fight. The young Empress Dowager dictated to Yuan the Dragon Throne's last mandate. "Recognizing that the will of the people, which is the will of Heaven," it read, "is for a republic, we abdicate all authority, and commission Yuan Shih-kai to establish representative forms of government."

Sun Yat-sen was in St. Louis when information of the Hankow outbreak reached him. He did not rush back—on the contrary he continued in leisurely fashion around the world, addressing chambers of commerce and public-affairs clubs, focusing on himself the attention being given to Chinese news, and collecting large sums of money. He was interviewed by traders, financiers, and ministers of foreign affairs, to whom he uniformly promised utopian conditions under the "World's Newest and Largest Republic." In the United States he painted a picture of two great sister republics shaking hands across the Pacific and assuring the liberty of mankind; in less sentimental England he held forth on the increase of trade and investment opportunities among a liberated people.

Meanwhile, in China, the Shanghai coterie of "old revolutionists" were gaining the ascendency over the upstart Li Yuan-hung and his Middle Yangtze clique. Li had been elected "Acting President" by a committee of associates, but offered to join any government the Shanghai Tung Meng junta might set up. Several figures were prominent in it, especially the witty ex-mandarin Wu Ting-fang, who had retired from imperial service as Minister to Washington when his keen political scent told him ruin was coming. Appreciating the value of foreign support and enjoying the incidental publicity, he began bombarding the foreign offices of the Powers with notes signed, "Minister of Foreign Affairs of the Republic of China." A correspondent asked him who appointed him to that office. He planted his huge sampan-shod feet, lifted his skull cap to scratch his head with the long nail of his little finger, and replied, "Why, I appointed myself!"

He had rivals for first honors—young Wang Cheng-ting (C. T. Wang) who emerged from the National Secretaryship of the Young Men's Christian Association; the veterans Hu Han-ming and Wang Chung-hui, and others. It became obvious to all that harmony could be preserved only by selecting some one aloof from the rivalry. They turned of necessity to their founder, Sun Yat-sen, lecturing abroad, whom a number had secretly planned to overlook.

Sun was sitting in the home of his old friend, Sir James Cantlie, in London, with a child in his lap, when a cablegram arrived signed "The Revolutionary Assembly of the Seventeen Provinces," asking him to accept the presidency of the Middle Flowery People's Country. He read it, passed it over to Sir James, and gravely returned his attention to the child. The delighted old Englishman jumped up to congratulate, to suggest a prayer of thanks, to envision the position Sun would occupy, to enumerate the people the new chief executive of the world's largest republic must meet at once in London.

Sun quietly listened, and patting the child, remarked, "I can count on millions of followers. They will follow me to the death, as they have always followed my teachings."

In his mind he had long been President of China.

III

At Hongkong, where this time Sun Yat-sen was welcomed and fêted, he was joined by Homer Lea, one of the several unusual Occidentals whose service to Sun's cause bears witness to his power to attract men. Years before in California this dwarf had come to Sun at the close of a lecture, diffidently taken the speaker's hand, and said: "I can help you." "What can such a one do?" the revolutionist had asked his host. "That man," he had been told, "is Homer Lea, the greatest living authority on military strategy." The hunchback had gained no less a repute than this on his native coast, through his book, *The Valor of Ignorance*. It had dealt with the popular bogie of the time and place,

the menace of Oriental invasion. Sun had accepted
Lea's plan for secretly drilling Chinese students on the
sands of Long Beach, California. Now the American
enthusiast was honored with the commission of aide-
de-camp to the first President of China. Sun's party
was further swelled at Canton by old revolutionary
comrades and hangers-on. They could give nothing,
only take, but where Sun's egoism did not dupe him his
magnanimity softened him. It was impossible for him
to refuse any one.

On Christmas Eve, 1911, Sun disembarked from a
British boat at Shanghai, and accompanied only by his
strange aide, went in a carriage to a secluded house prepared for him by his friends the Soong family. Five
days later, the self-constituted assembly at Nanking
confirmed his election as "Provisional President," voting
by provinces, sixteen out of the seventeen represented
assenting. New Year's day of 1912, with an entourage
overloading a special train, he made the seven hours'
rail journey to Nanking, the ancient "Southern Capital."
Scattering snowflakes fell on the straggling procession
as it followed the almost deserted fifteenth century
highway of the First Ming Emperor from the river
port through the monstrous city ramparts to the Viceroy's Palace within the city. The great yamen had
been literally converted into a White House by a coat
of whitewash hastily swabbed over its vermilion walls.
The motive was in part to get the greatest possible
contrast with the old official color, and in part to emu-

late the great American Republic. Revolutionists were pleased with the effect. But the populace whispered over tea cups and market baskets that white was the color for mourning and ill omen.

Students in baggy European clothes, imperially gowned mandarins, neatly uniformed military officers, and fat, silk-robed merchants stood on the wet stone flagging of the yamen courtyard and listened to the first oath of office, presidential or otherwise, ever sworn in the Ancestral Land. Men of the old era and the new were alike minus the queue, mark of submission to the Manchu, as a result of the recent intensive hair-cutting campaign.[3] Sun, with grave face and far away expression but with disarming frankness and convincing sincerity which were always his power, made a monotonic address and stepped down from the dais. Over the new Western style of handshake he was tendered the old Eastern congratulation, "joy of your work." Then the "foreign-fashion" band struck up, in varying keys: "Behold the Conquering Hero Comes" and "God Be with You till We Meet Again"—mingled.

Thereupon the official photographer, newly introduced into Chinese functionism, posed the assembly in the stiffest possible manner and took a flashlight in the

[3] The shaved forehead was imposed on conquered Chinese by the Manchus in 1640 as a mark of submission. Whereupon, following their genius for compensating themselves in another way, the Chinese grew long braids behind. The pig-tail was confused by the unhistorical young revolutionary zealots, with the real mark of servility, and peasants and tradesmen who passed through city gates were given the choice of parting with their queues or their heads. Some chose the latter.

damp, gathering gloom. The picture lies on the table beside my typewriter as I write. President Sun Yat-sen is bareheaded, dressed in the styleless military-collar type of European costume which he adopted from the missionaries, and which, designated by his name, Chung Shan, became the badge of revolutionary zeal, as did long trousers in France and the grotesque golf cap of Lenin in Russia. The figure which catches the eye in my photograph is the lone Caucasian, General Homer Lea, standing between two seated, fat mandarins, but his head just to a height with theirs.[4]

The First President's first mandate was expressive of his drastic turn of mind. As Yamagata and Ito had done in Japan, and Lenin and Stalin and Mustapha Kemal were to do in Russia and Turkey, Sun Yat-sen introduced the European calendar. To the makers of New Asia this seemed a required notification to both sluggards at home and scoffers abroad that their various societies were entering the modern world. President Sun declared the calendar changed from the lunar reckoning kept by his ancestors since 2,500 B. C. to solar, Gregorian style, and the beginning of a new chronological era with the day of his inauguration: "Republican Era Year One." Yuan Shih-kai, with his ear to the ground in Peking, announced that both old and new

---

[4].His career to be very brief. He proved too frail for Asiatic living conditions, and Sun sent him, well provided, back to San Francisco, where, as his strength ebbed, he occupied a suite in the St. Francis Hotel, and was carried in and out past whispering tourists on the back of a giant Chinese body servant in Oriental livery.

reckonings would be legitimate "for the time being." The epic political struggle of modern Chinese history was declared, orientally enough, over a *chronological* issue. But there was much behind it other than the date. Yuan, holding the north aloof from participation, declared himself "in principle" a convert to the republican idea and suggested compromise. Sun and his party, which he had renamed the Kuomintang, "Country People's Party," to signify its transformation from a revolutionary junta into a political faction, were willing to meet Yuan, providing he first admit that sanction for republican forms lay in the resolution of the self-constituted "People's Assembly" at Nanking, not in the mandate to Yuan from the abdicating imperial family. The question was far from merely academic. It involved the practical matter of whose republic China was to be.

Yuan demurred. Nanking sent an expedition against him. He suddenly professed conversion to the Nanking viewpoint, and Sun, the trustful, believed he had acquired another devoted follower. However, in return for submission to the Provisional Assembly, Yuan demanded reward in the form of prompt election to the presidency of China. He had strong talking points. Neither side could overcome the other. Quick reunion was necessary to suppress growing disorder and forestall German and Japanese encroachment. Those decisive factors, the European Powers—particularly Great Britain—having faith in Yuan who had long administered an established order, rather than in Sun who had overthrown one—indicated that they would grant neither diplomatic recognition nor loans till Yuan was made head of the new government.

Sun was not finding the office of chief executive simple. His funds had soon gone, and the swelling revolutionary army dunned him for pay. Facing danger of mutiny, in a cold sweat one night in his bare office he mortgaged the Hanyang Steel and Iron Works to Japan and then lived in daily fear lest he be accused of betraying his lifelong principles. Running a government was proving more complicated and thankless than organizing a revolution.

But it might be possible, in the interests of both the revolution and personal comfort, to let Yuan run the government while Sun's Kuomintang would "run" Yuan! The Kuomintang, being the only effective political organization at election time in the country, could easily "pack Parliament," then draft a constitution placing the President in Parliament's power. Sun's fatuousness caused him to overlook the evidences that Yuan was scheming conversely to make the Kuomintang his instrument. It was a contest peculiarly Chinese, for if there is one scheme never absent from the Celestial's thought it is to make an unwitting tool of his adversary.

Out of such hidden soil flowered Sun's world-arresting act of resigning to his rival, after four months' tenure, the presidency of the republic he had created.

He made the most of necessity, and felt repaid in glory. Few men have an opportunity of climaxing their careers, as Sun believed he was doing, with a nobler gesture. It ended in a flair of pageantry at the tomb of the First Ming on Purple Mountain overlooking Nanking. Standing with bowed head before the Emperor's fifteenth century spirit-tablet, Sun informed its inhabitant that the great Ming's achievement had been duplicated —China had once more been liberated from alien rule, and the liberator could now properly step back into private life. Sun's "face," his *amour propre,* was vindicated by this ceremony, and he withdrew in an exalted frame of mind to his ordinary citizen's compartment on the Shanghai train, while Christian missionaries divided over the question of whether or not this glorified ancestor worship was a repudiation of his Christian profession.

There followed a diverting bit of jockeying over the new President's inauguration. The Kuomintang assembly stipulated that the capital be at Nanking. Yuan Shih-kai pointed out that foreign diplomats would not abandon the costly fortified Legation Quarter in Peking, and that the Japanese menace required maintenance of the capital in the north. But at least, insisted Sun's party, Yuan must come to Nanking to be inaugurated. He assented. Just then his crack army division mutinied and looted Peking. Obviously it would now be impossible for him to leave. His presence was required every minute to restore order and reassure the fright-

ened diplomatic corps. And so Nanking sent a delegation to inaugurate him in his own headquarters. He had
won the first round.

In view of this, Sun thought it wise to have a base.
He went to Canton to build a constituency in his own
countryside. His romantic figure briefly dominated the
Canton chaos. He went to Blue Valley and fetched the
lady of the Lu clan, his wife, to preside over his "court."
He had kept in sufficient touch with her through his outlaw years to father two children. For reasons of both
sentimentality and egoism he now longed to have his
consort by his side in public appearances, even as do
the great men of the West.

She was in rotund middle age, averse to exertion,
genial-souled, and untroubled by mental effort. At his
order she withdrew her antiquated high headdress and
dowry clothes from the pawnshop where they were im-
pignorated for safekeeping, and in obedience not un-
mixed with pride waddled about after her worshiped
master. But the round of ceremonies dazed her. She
found nothing in common with the "modern" young
women who flocked adulatively around her lord. They
patronized and deprecated her, while the China of her
own generation opined that a woman's place was in
her home. She felt lonely, almost immodest, among
them. It ended with Sun's sending her back to the
village. He shortly proceeded to Peking to put matters
in order against the coming constitutional convention.

"Sun is preparing a break with Yuan Shih-kai," ran

[54]

the political gossip. To this Sun retorted on August 27, 1912: "No one thinks of a civil war in the United States simply because Mr. Taft, Mr. Wilson and Mr. Roosevelt do not agree." Was he really blind to the difference, or justifiedly disingenuous? In a personally written message to the New York *Sun*, published September 24, he stated:

"My recent visit to Peking was not made for the purpose of stirring up trouble or discord. It was, on the other hand, to assure President Yuan that many sayings attributed to me were not only untrue but without the slightest foundation of fact. I have not only confidence in his loyalty and ability and believe him worthy of the firmest support, but I repledge myself to devote my best effort to aid him in the great and noble work he has undertaken."

Sun was fully sincere in his effort to "aid" Yuan. To forestall such aid, Yuan hired assassins to shoot Mr. Sung Chao-ren, Kuomintang "party whip," entrusted with putting the constitution through Parliament. Parliament assembled in hot indignation at the murder and barred President Yuan and his secretaries from its sittings, even refusing to read his messages.

Meanwhile Sun Yat-sen had gone to Shanghai as "Director of Material Development" to outline a pretentious scheme eventually published in English under the title, "The International Development of China," for a hundred thousand miles of railway, a million miles of roadway, canal improvements, construction of three

[55]

ports, modernization of cities, and stretching of telephone lines—to be built with foreign capital. In the
making of plans without trammel of burden for their
execution he was brilliant—a poet of material and social
accomplishment. It was to become fashionable to call
him visionary, yet nothing could have been more certain
of eventual fulfillment than his very dream in all its essential details. Engineers scorned it, then went out to
confirm by sextant and statistical table what he saw
by inspiration. His scheme was the best sort of publicity for him and the Republic in the material-minded
West. But financiers made eulogistic after-dinner
speeches and watchfully waited. For President Yuan
was receiving first attention from the foreign bankers.

When it became evident that Yuan was determined
to continue resistance of party control, Sun left his
drawing table, went aboard the ships of the Chinese
navy off Shanghai, won over its officers and raised the
standard of a "Second Revolution." The convenient
admiralty flag, a large white rising sun on a blue field,
devised under Japanese influence and first used on one
of Sun's sorties from Annam, was now set against the
Republican "Five Stripes," representing Chinese, Manchus, Mongols, Tibetans, and Muhammadans, which
Sun also had designed during presidential days in Nanking. He would revise the Kuomintang ensign in his
last years by pushing the rising sun up into the corner of
a broad, red field, and it would be this "Soviet-influ-
enced" standard which would sweep victoriously over

two-thirds of China in 1926-7. But the "millions of devoted followers" failed to follow him now in 1913. His adjutants, Li Lieh-chun and Huang Hsing, held the Yangtze valley for a few months, but were dislodged, chiefly by Yuan's gold. The Peking dictator was giving the country order, business was recovering, and the merchant guilds were satisfied. Reformers winked at Yuan's assassinations in view of his drastic suppression of opium; patriots felt they had made considerable exertion and were entitled to a rest.

And so Sun found himself, a year after his triumph, a refugee in Japan, condemned as an extremist by his countrymen and as an agitator by the world, regarded as a liability by his own party, and penniless. He heard the fickle public, which had praised him as a hero of renunciation, now dismiss him as a fool whose associates had fortunately gotten him out of the seat of power before he made it ridiculous. In his heart he knew he was neither.

It is hard for those who knew Sun Yat-sen to conceive of his losing faith in himself and his mission. But he came to the edge of such collapse. The result would have been bitterness and futility. He was saved by the ministrant whom Providence provides rarely, yet incontrovertibly at times, despite this age's discredit of romance—a beautiful, devoted, and gifted woman.

As a child, Soong Ching-ling, or "Lucky Age," with her two sisters and brother had often played about the chair of the grave young physician-revolutionist who used to visit their solid but plain Shanghai home and talk so long and confidently with Father Soong. The fine old merchant bequeathed to his children all his affection for his patriotic cause and his concern for its adventurous leader. Ching-ling grew up into an English education and went to Wesleyan College of Macon, Georgia, where she became "Rosamund." Her next sister—eventually to become the wife of Chiang Kai-shek, private secretary of Dr. Sun and Generalissimo and statesman of the Nationalist cause—was to finish at Wellesley, while her brother, the budding financial genius of Nationalism, would take business administration at Harvard. An elder sister was to marry the Oberlin graduate and educationalist H. H. Kung, descendant of Confucius, in the seventy-fifth generation, and provide the connecting link between Nationalist leadership and the northern disciplinarian "Christian General" Feng Yu-hsiang, in whose entourage Kung represented the arts of peace.

Rosamund, returning from her American college, stopped in Japan. We see her in a group photograph taken in Dr. Sun's paper-walled headquarters on "The Bluff" at Yokohama, the very site of which was thrown into the sea by the earthquake of 1923. Her round face looks earnestly from under a huge "picture" hat, and her skirts drop to the ankles, but she constitutes a very modern phenomenon for Pacific Asia of 1914.

Some say she served as Dr. Sun's secretary. She

denies that, but not that she was his strength and his renewal of life. He had loved her as a child, and lo! here she was a woman, and loved him. Now, in his disgrace, the revolutionary leader possessed what he had longed for in his triumph, a consort equipped to stand by his side. In assent so complete that it did not need to be expressed, these two souls joined forces. Ching-ling went to Shanghai to fulfill the ceremony of asking her family's consent and returned promptly to Sun's side.

The problem of the wife in Fragrant Mountain Village had to be surmounted, not, fortunately, for her own sake, but for that of Ching-ling, who like all "new" Chinese women, had sworn not to be a "secondary" wife. So it was given out that Sun had divorced the lady of the Lu clan, but the "divorce" consisted of nothing more than just this declaration. There was no occasion for sending her back to her family, according to customary Chinese clan divorce. Legal divorce, although one of the reforms attached to Sun's movement, was not availed of. It would have been unnecessary cruelty to the mother of his children. Both Sun and Ching-ling later met her on the friendliest basis. Certain it is that she took his "divorce," if she ever really heard of it, as another of those newfangled ways of the West past her understanding, and continued to regard herself as his wife and the new woman as the proper and inevitable "second." Sun's children showed no resentment. His son, Ko (in Cantonese Fo), about the same age as the young wife, became her devoted friend.

One wonders what the life-scarred man of forty-nine and the vital girl of twenty-three got from their quiet partnership. Sensual enough to satisfy the warm blood of a young Chinese woman he probably was, even at this age. Yet there was no playful touch about him. He never laughed, rarely smiled. But he treated women with a frank respect—to an occasional woman of both East and West as precious as romanticism. Sun took the girl as an equal into his sorrows, plans, theories, and friendships, and leaned on her like a rock. On her part, she served him with a steady, unobtrusive devotion in which Oriental woman excel. Henceforth she was with him in every adventure, and traces of her keen mind are found in his more mature reasoning. She was able to smooth the edges of his egotism, and with her woman's suspiciousness to meliorate his ruinous trustfulness.

Her own mental development is no less interesting than her effect upon her husband's. She participated in the bewilderment of her generation over the superiority of Occidental civilization. As the spectacle of Christendom's insincerity and savagery unrolled before these Western-educated Chinese, they passed through disillusioned cynicism into a pathetic groping after any theory which promised utopia and despised conventional "democracy." Ching-ling leaned toward extremism, the linking up with Russia and adoption of radical socio-economic theory. Without this radical impetus, Sun's cause, indeed, would hardly have swept the country at last. But this fervor was to leave Sun's young widow a pathetic self-ordained exile in Moscow, denouncing her brother and sister as "traitors who have sold our Master's cause to the bourgeoisie."

In China developments were justifying Sun. Using the promise of a foreign loan, upon regularization of the government, Yuan Shih-kai procured from Parliament improvement of his status from acting to constitutional president. From this vantage point he declared the Kuomintang a traitorous organization and proscribed its members. Since without them Parliament had no quorum, he then prorogued Parliament. To this absolutism, the Chinese nation submitted, but when in 1915 Yuan essayed to take the titles of dynasty, it squirmed and called for Doctor Sun Yat-sen again.

The rejuvenated rebel was ready for the call. He issued manifestoes, gathered an entourage (or, rather, let one fasten upon him) and landed in Shanghai with éclat. Here he pompously declared a "punitive expedition" (that was always a favorite phrase) "against Emperor Yuan, traitor to the Republic, puppet of the encroaching Powers." This last was unjust to Yuan, although he had been compelled partially to give in to the Japanese Twenty-one Demands. But Sun, like all humans, was suspicious of his enemy's falling into the sin which he himself had not avoided. The campaign went forward elaborately. Just as it was reaching a serious stage, death stepped in and took Sun's prey away from him. Yuan, crushed by the defection of some of his most trusted men, had crumbled like a pillar of rotten granite. A short period of madness ended in death on June 6, 1916.

And Sun, as was invariably his experience, found himself triumphant only to be baffled. From his dramatic feud with Yuan he emerged survivor, but that sour adversary, in going down to defeat, had not given him victory. The punitive army, with nothing to punish, evaporated, and with it Sun's organized strength. He was left in the position of an ordinary politician, waiting in Shanghai for developments.

Fatuously, he sat for the laurel to descend upon him as in 1911. But Vice-President Li Yuan-hung, the squat garrison-commander of the Hankow revolution, took the presidency, and no worthy place was found for the Father of the Republic. The splinters of Yuan's broken baton were grasped by many waiting hands closer than Sun Yat-sen's.

Sun was hardened by this "let-out." Not that he entirely overcame his fatuousness. Fatuous he remained to the end. No expectation of his life was more fatuous than that which was to set him off on his last journey. But henceforth he operated in closer accord with the theory that one gets only what he takes and keeps only what he clings to.

For the next eight years China's history was to be the often farcical, sometimes gallant, usually sordid

story of military adventurers, heirs to portions of
Yuan's army, who fought one another for supreme control and were backed first by one foreign power and
then another. Japan proved the worst offender. The
military clique which ruled in Tokyo during the Great
War boldly endeavored to end China's national existence.

It was not comfortable for Sun Yat-sen in Shanghai
and he returned to Canton, the city where he began,
and which, no matter how many times it drove him
out, always again gave him a following. Here he began
all over. He took with him the decrepit Chinese Navy,
and the hardly less aging Chinese Parliament—the
original Parliament assembled at Peking to control
Yuan Shih-kai—forcibly prorogued, later reassembled
by Li Yuan-hung and then redismissed at the behest
of the military. The M. P.'s always preferred Peking,
but when the capital was untenable, never had failed
to come for bed and board to the compassionate—
and always flattered—Dr. Sun, author of their honors.

Sun and his Parliament were at once confronted with
an acute problem of statesmanship. The West, which
cannot believe in Jehovah or Ford cars or cutting throats
without forcing its cause upon the whole world, was
dragging China into the arena of its World War.

Chinese took much moral comfort out of watching
Christendom, whose self-assumed ethical superiority
they had reluctantly begun to admit, reveal itself in
the World War. Sun Yat-sen, who more than his fel-

lows respected Western culture, grew cautiously critical. Others, with less knowledge of the West, became merely supercilious. Young returned students alone were caustic. That attribute was borrowed from the intolerant, caring, Western mind.

But all Chinese who did not have ulterior motives opposed the involvement of their nation. President Woodrow Wilson had idealistically issued a pressing invitation to China, along with the other neutral nations, to join in making the world safe for democracy. When he had discovered that the traitorous "Peace and Joy Clique" [5] in Peking planned to make use of this to bring China's army under Japanese command, he had advised the Chinese to pay first attention to making China safe for democracy. Sun Yat-sen delivered a scathing rebuke to Lloyd George for desiring to involve China. Li Yuan-hung, under pressure from the foreign plenipotentiaries at Peking, had tried half measures—breaking relations without declaring war. But an intrigue of attempted Manchu restoration ousted him. That in turn collapsed, leaving the "Peace and Joy"-ites supreme to railroad the Peking government into formal war. Whereupon Sun, advised by his younger diplomats, brought Canton also into the War, lest corrupt Peking should have its way at the peace conference. When that met, Canton's delegate, young

[5] Viz.: The *Anfu* government went under this most misleading, bizarre name—taken from the names of two provinces beginning with these two folk-loved words, and applied first to the Chinese convivial organization (*à la* Tammany) out of which the political faction grew.

C. T. Wang, dominated the Chinese delegation, because he had the confidence of the Chinese people, south and north.

Old Wu Ting-fang, who had declined to follow Sun Yat-sen in 1913, now joined him in Canton, as did the gifted Tong Shao-yi, who had been Yuan's premier. Their discussions were chiefly conducted in English, in which they were all more fluent than in one another's dialects. The three became known as the "Canton Triumvirate." Wu was the wit, the fashionable eccentric, who lent his well-staffed mansions to friends, lived in simple style on a vegetable diet, and spoke epigrams after the manner of George Bernard Shaw. Nor was he a less resourceful self-advertiser. One of his last little pleasantries was a hoax on the press of the world. While editors were "burning up the cables" trying to get further reports of a monarchical restoration at Peking on which Wu had "sold" them, he was giving Lord Northcliffe an interview on the great service of the foreign press to China in making true conditions known to the world. Tong was the luxury-loving financial wizard and dignified controversialist who kept aloof in his Hsiang Shan botanical gardens from the turmoil he helped to foster. The association marked a new phase in the career of Sun Yat-sen. With his comrades setting off the fireworks, yet contenting him with full homage as their chief, he could apply himself to the indoctrinizing of the masses. Patiently he reiterated simplified lessons in political and economic theory to these beginners in the school of Nationalism. Now he was at his truly constructive—his lasting—work.

"What," he asks, writing in the language of common talk, long before Dr. Hu Shih in Peking won recognition of it for literature, "are the Three People's Determination? They are, put together, a save-the-country determination. What is determination? [We might translate the word "principle."] It is belief, hope, and force united together. Before the first of these, belief, must come investigation, or understanding. . . . When may we say China is saved? When in international intercourse, government, and communications she is equal to other nations, and assured of permanence on the earth, we may say our country is saved. If with high hope it is possible to combine great force, we can save China."

Through such kindergarten catechism did Sun start millions of infants in citizenship to thinking on the problems and fate of their nation. He created for it an entire political and economic vocabulary.

Sun's Rump Parliament elected him "Generalissimo" of a new "People's Army" to punish the northern destroyers of the Republic. The command seemed to be the important thing. The army, apparently, would come later. Sun's fatuousness and vanity were usually sublime. This one time they became ridiculous, as the stubbly-mustached, priestly-looking doctor donned an ill-fitting and incongruously designed field marshal's uniform, and posed hand on hilt before the cameras.

[66]

He realized the effect himself—it was his only effort to be "military."

Sun was shocked when the legislative checks he had invented for Parliament to put upon Yuan Shih-kai were now proposed by the unimaginative M.P.'s for himself. In the course of the resultant dispute, reactionary forces from up-country swept into Canton, and Dr. Sun withdrew, in yet another defeat, to Shanghai. Against the apparent likelihood that these experiences would continue to be repetitious, he philosophically established a "refuge cottage" in the French Concession of that city and installed his library—and Ching-ling's favorite song birds—there.

While in China this checker game was being played, at Versailles President Wilson, unwilling to entertain Japan's "racial equality" motion and bludgeoned by her threat to walk out of the Conference and League, had consented to her retention of her seizures in the Chinese province of Shantung. The Peace and Joy clique were of course party to the game, the rest of political China simply wrung its hands in indignation and despair, and the populace was in oblivion. Then "riotous youngsters" of the colleges and middle schools organized into Student Unions and marched in mass—carrying patriotic slogans and the picture of Dr. Sun Yat-sen. The demonstrations developed into the "student revolution." Youthful ebullience backed by the army and strategy of General Wu Pei-fu overthrew the Anfu clique, and organized students and chambers of commerce sobered Japanese jingoism with the boycott. The fervor of its youth, and effectiveness of passive resistance as its weapon—prime factors in Asia's fight on foreign domination—were now first demonstrated.

Dr. Sun was quick enough to claim full credit for the development. We laughed at his egoism and opportunism, as was then the fashion. Looking back now, we see clearly that without Sun Yat-sen there would have been no student revolution.

The wave of patriotic sentiment floated him back to Canton and power. A young soldier, Chen Ching-ming, of the Hakka, China's only (and strictly localized) pariah class, attracted to the aging leader because of his complete blindness to social dividing lines, stole into the South and prepared the way for a pro-Sun coup. In the chief's wake came the usual following of office and notoriety seekers, advantaging by his amiability and vanity. The Rump Parliament varied the order this time, electing him President Extraordinary in place of Generalissimo—hoping for better luck.

He was learning whom to use. Chen the Hakka, of course kept command of the army. The fact that he had possessed himself of the command before Sun gave it was perhaps not in his favor in the President's mind and foreboded trouble. Sun made his son, Ko, mayor of Canton, and Wu Ting-fang's son (both were American university graduates) head of construction and works. This "second triumvirate" made up in business-like vigor its lack of the picturesqueness and whimsy

[68]

of its elderly forerunner. Its model administration, attracting wide notice in its contrast to the satrapies of the North, brought to Dr. Sun flattering attention.

But the veteran adventurer-reformer was no patient improver of a county. He must be the reshaper of a nation—the inspirer of a continent. He was soon looking once more for an opportunity to put his hand into national affairs. It came when in 1922 General Wu Pei-fu, factotum on the middle Yangtze, moved northward to oust the ex-bandit king of Manchuria, Chang Tso-lin, from his control of Peking.

Dr. Sun was bitter against General Wu who championed the students, and in his view, otherwise stole his fire. He ordered all resources to be put into an expedition from the south against Wu, the rival reformer, and in aid of Chang, the reactionary. True to revolutionist psychology, Sun, as earlier in the case of the "Protect-Emperor" group, hated the liberal with a more bitter hatred than he did the unredeemed reactionary. He was touchy over his position, self-constituted but sanctioned by suffering, as high priest of reform. His campaign for the punishment of Wu was stopped pathetically. Army Chief Chen simply refused to undertake it.

Sun, in spite of the fact that his participation was in spirit only, demanded all attention due a combatant. After his nominal ally, Chang, had been routed, a telegram from Sun's secretary came to the American Legation reading: "What are Wu's terms?" It was unof-

ficially turned over to Wu's American adviser on foreign affairs [6] who consulted with General Wu. "Tell
Sun Yat-sen," he ordered, "that I am not aware that
we have been at war and therefore there is no question of terms. What I want is what he has always
advocated, restoration of constitutional forms, and I
trust he will join me in bringing them about." Sun
turned his fury of snubbed egotism against General
Chen, who had rehabilitated him but who had disobeyed
him and caused him to "lose face."

In haughty language he issued an edict of dismissal
against the man who was really keeping him in authority. The actual power of dismissal was the other
way around. But hadn't the army sworn allegiance
to the President? Could he then not give it to whom
he wished? General Wu got in touch with Chen and
agreed to throw out the illegal chief executive in Peking
if Chen would eliminate the turbulent Dr. Sun, thus
clearing the decks all around. The outcome had its
tragic as well as ludicrous features. Chen fulfilled his
part by literally pushing Sun into the river. The "President" boarded a cruiser of his navy; it now bears his
name and is preserved as China's "Old Ironsides." The
venerable Wu Ting-fang, unwavering in loyalty to his
old friend Sun, traveled heartbrokenly with proposals
of compromise from the cruiser to General Chen's shore
posts in lulls between their capricious artillery duels.
He took cold in the open sampan and after a few days

[6] The author.

[70]

died of pneumonia. Many felt at the time that the bigger man had given his life in service to the lesser, yet the day was to come when they would not be mentioned in the same breath.

Eventually the ship's officers, under pressure of Chen's bribes, surrounded Sun in his cabin and informed him that they would have to deliver him up. He asked permission to make a farewell speech. That they could not refuse. In his logical, positive, monotonous voice he addressed them for three hours, revealing their cupidity and treachery, rebuking them for it, forgiving them, praising their idealism and loyalty, and offering, if they really thought it best, to go ashore of his own volition. In stinging shame and tears they pled with him instead, to allow them to put him on a British ship bound for Shanghai.[7]

Wu Pei-fu restored Li Yuan-hung, the only fully legal president China ever had, to the chief executiveship, and invited the exiled "Long Parliament," now left in Canton without a host, back to Peking. Liberal advances on travel expense induced the M.P.'s to desert their old master. Soon after, in Peking, they ratified the Kuomintang constitution which had had its first reading years before under Yuan Shih-kai. In scorn, Sun now repudiated both Parliament and its constitu-

---

[7] As party to a plot peacefully to rid China of Sun's presence, the author cabled an American Chautauqua manager suggesting that he make Sun an offer. It was done, and Sun actually entered negotiations, but the manager made the mistake of mentioning his correspondents, and Sun promptly announced that he would stay in China.

tion, largely his own drafting. He was left without definite program, open to new influence.

Abraham Adolph Joffe, one of Moscow's astutest diplomats and its first plenipotentiary to the Orient, who had been making small headway against legation influence in Peking, saw the opportunity.

IV

The Soviet ambassador, bloated by a leaky heart, his close-shaven head furrowed with scars made by chains—both souvenirs of Czarist cruelty—arrives in 1922 to sit in "refuge house" and discuss imperialism and revolution with a Sun who is growing gaunt and ruthless. More and more he is coming to see force as his only means of progress. He has sent his body-guard, a heavy-weight, "two-gun," cockney-speaking Canadian Jew named Morris Cohen, donated to him as bodyguard by the Saskatchewan Chinese Chamber of Commerce, to engage military trainers in the United States and Canada, only to be frustrated by the disapproval of the American and British governments. Sun accepts from Joffe's lips the pledges of the Soviet Republic. It, too, has a cause against the imperialist Powers. Why should not Russia's Asiatic neighbors unite with her in a confraternity of the snubbed to flatten the "paper tiger" of Western superiority? Moscow will do for Sun Yat-sen what it has already done for Mustapha Kemal, for Riza Khan of Persia, for

Amanullah Shah of Afghanistan—enabling their Nationalist movements to sweep away foreign domination in those countries. Moscow will not confine her sympathy to sentimental talk, as does America. Moscow will send military trainers, propagandists who know how to reach the masses, and, by means of the recently repossessed Russian Volunteer Fleet, rifles, cartridges and hand grenades, and Siberian furs to be sold in the Canton market for the cause of Chinese Nationalism. The Soviet group has flouted the combined strength of the world's recently victorious powers and driven their armies, invading from all sides, out of its borders. Is China beset somewhat as was Russia? Would the Proletariat's experience be of any guidance or inspiration in reëstablishing China's ancient dignity and Sun Yat-sen, its champion's, prestige?

The old revolutionist's face remains bland, but within his heart there wells up all the confidence of success, all the grandiose visions of thirty years before. It is natural, he replies, that new Russia should turn to him, the true and only representative of progress in the Orient, for alliance. Thus Sun accepts. He promises to read Marx again, and Lenin. He admits they might have points worthy of inclusion in the Nationalist gospel.

The scarred, wheezing Joffe gives Sun a political adviser, young Michael Borodin, brought from Moscow after a career as tutor in Chicago and revolutionist in Europe. Joffe procures seventy Soviet officers, headed

[73]

by the veteran ex-Austrian general, Gallin, to drill Sun's army. Then, from the footing of prestige Joffe has obtained for his government at Canton, he reaches out to reattack the problem of resuming relations with Peking and Tokyo. He is successful. He returns to Europe to confuse "imperialist" diplomats at The Hague and become first Soviet Ambassador to Rome, to drift with Trotsky into the "opposition" in his own party, be cautiously pushed out of political sight, and finally to shoot himself because the government dispensary under orders of the "niggardly ruling faction" refuses to dole him sufficient narcotic to deaden his increasing pain!

But the tragi-triumph of our own hero is approaching its climax. To get the setting for this last act in the drama of Sun's life we must go back to his flight from Canton before his truculent "child," Chen the Hakka. (Only once more was Sun to get back to his own home city—only once more to leave.) As Sun was being forced aboard that cruiser at Canton, a rustic-featured young man pushed through the partly curious, partly indignant, crowd and quietly asked to be allowed to go with and serve the Master. It was one of those rescues of Sun's self-confidence and self-importance which destiny did not fail to provide when he was in desperate need.

The young man, Chiang Kai-shek, looked after the old chief's physical comfort—something Sun was never able to do for himself. As his spirits returned he began dictating letters, issuing to followers all over the world a glittering prospectus of his next government. There was a striking contrast and yet a decided similarity between Sun Yat-sen and Vladimir Lenin, who now lay paralyzed on his bed at Gorkii. Lenin, led up to the point of action by reason and resolution, drove himself forward by will: Sun, the poet, was lead on by imagination. But both had the bland faculty of ignoring defeat and setback, of pretending that every vicissitude was part of an unquestionable progress toward the goal. Lenin talked with as "hardboiled" assurance and Sun as pompously the day after defeat as the day after victory. They had the quality of living in self-created worlds and of ignoring the different light in which conditions appear to others. Such blandness puzzles realists and diplomats and yet ultimately wins them over, for they are unable to combat an uncomfortable suspicion that the possessors are touching the essence of things, and that appearances—disunity, tyranny, dirt, and poverty—are after all inconsequential.

A refugee on a cruiser, Sun wrote orders for the destruction of the "traitor Chen," and signed them "The President." Chiang Kai-shek turned amanuensis and took the letters, and, when that was over, revealed other possibilities. He was a graduate of the Imperial Military Academy of Japan, son of one of the Doctor's early enthusiasts who had decimated a fortune in support of the revolutionary cause. He was the obvious military head to take the place of the false henchman Chen.

Sun accepted this with the same smug matter-of-had-to-be-ness with which he received every rescue of fate. In the course of his long career Americans, Englishmen, Portuguese, Japanese, scores of Chinese, old and young, had been attracted by a life utterly devoted to one end, and a magnetism of personality which its exerciser did not know he possessed. "Sun was a solemnly disturbing fellow," observed Mr. Gardner Harding of the *Christian Science Monitor*. "I gave up trying to understand him long ago. But there was something lovable about him that could not be disregarded or forgotten."

Sun received all who came without surprise and incorporated them without question. He assumed that any one who came in touch with him must be on his side. Why shouldn't men join him—he was the generalissimo of reform! Once they admitted his command, what could be doubtful about them? The amazing fact was that many remained true and sacrificed fortune and health without return. It no more occurred to Sun that his henchmen must be rewarded than that they must be watched. So the less worthy ever rewarded themselves, and the false ever played Judas. . . .

Sun is safely on the British ship headed for Shanghai. Ching-Ling is sleeping—these have been trying days for her. Chiang Kai-shek, the worn chief's new strength, comes respectfully to him. "Teacher, I have made bold to keep a diary to these stormy days. I am thinking of publishing it, that your followers may know

[76]

your stalwartness. Would you graciously inscribe a foreword?"

As Sun takes it and slowly writes on the fly-leaf, the curtain of his egotism for once goes up, providing a telling glimpse of the soul within. "Only with the feeling that it is a monument to the devoted sufferings of my supporters in this dark hour, rather than to the importance of my adventures, do I consent to the publication of this little book. Because I cannot judge men, conflagration has broken out, and is not yet quenched."

The last sentence is worthy of pause, for Sun is as incapable of writing in polite self-depreciation as in flattery of others. But his defection from himself is fleeting, and thereafter he continues to the end, as positive of his mission and his fitness for it as Mussolini.

The Seventy Guilds—merchant community of Canton—who had clandestinely favored Sun's ejection, having lacked enthusiasm for the prospect of financing his punitive expedition and feared his socialistic drift, are now finding themselves out of the frying pan but in the fire, systematically looted by successive gangs of freebooters calling themselves armies of liberation. Commander Chen is robbed of initiative by the attitude of the masses, who regard his break with the Master as little short of sacrilege. So Chiang Kai-shek, the diarist, returning secretly to Canton, as Chen did before him, is able to effect a coup, recruit an army, and drive Chen into the bamboo jungles—to the keen disappointment of foreign diplomats and military attachés who have made the Hakka the focus of their favors. In 1923, Chiang uses, to bring Sun Yat-sen back, the very reactionary up-country forces which had driven Sun out in 1917, and which Chen had in turn driven out in 1920.

Enough of this off-again, on-again, gone-again melodrama! Back in Canton, Sun undertakes with a new and motion-saving surety of touch the effort which he senses will be his last. For, although even Ching-ling does not realize it, one of his kidneys is almost consumed with disease. The plump little wife-assistant seems glad of his grimness, and in the enthusiasm of vigorous womanhood is unable to credit his presentiments. To save him the strain of accommodating himself to changing clerks (Sun never kept one secretary long) she takes the strenuous writing work herself, wielding the brush pen for hours each day. She superintends all his conferences, telling visitors when they should go.

The Russian training officers arrive. Sun places young Chiang Kai-shek at their head with orders to found a military training school at Whampoa, downriver from Canton. He sees it as the breeding bed of a new Nationalist army, which is to be taught to fight for a cause, rather than out of personal loyalty to chieftains. The most demanding problem is finance. Sun needs some one whose interest will be in floating the cause, rather than his own fortune. He must have an idealist, a man who is absolutely his, and that means a young man. Ching-ling suggests her brother, Soong Tien-wei, fresh from the Harvard School of Business and two years in the American Banking Corporation. He is assigned the task. The able, experienced bankers of Canton are amazed as well as offended. But Sun is choosing men well on this, his last, opportunity. Within a year the boy financier has brought up the value of Canton's bank notes—published by the American Banknote Company in the design of the U. S. five-dollar bill with Sun's head in place of Lincoln's—from forty to one hundred cents on the dollar, and increased the provincial revenue tenfold.

Michael Borodin is set at building a department of political education for military and populace. Its scientifically conducted propaganda clears the way for the Nationalist advance which would take place in 1926-27. Announcing that he is growing old and wishes to provide a race-wide organization to carry on, Sun calls the first All-China and Overseas Convention of the Kuomintang. He causes admission of Communist groups into the party. On lines borrowed from the Russian Communists he revamps his party into a tool obedient to the hand. It is given a central executive committee of twenty-two members, with actual management in a select inner directorate. He endorses organization of the workers and peasants. Sun is more autocratic with his followers than ever before in his life, and succeeds with them better, because they sense that he is constructing a control which his hand will soon release.

Sun's old enemies, the foreign customs inspectors, are collecting the revenue of his own rich territory from under his nose and sending it to Peking. Sun does not let opportunities for "show-downs" slip because he is ill. His physical pain seems to make him the less regardful of the Chinese axiom that sleeping tigers are best left undisturbed. He brings the issue of sovereignty infringement and the "unequal treaties" into the headlines by threatening to seize the Customs House, and watches through somber eyes—although with an occasional twitching of the mouth—as frantic appeals for protection go to the Powers. America falls naïvely into the trap by answering with five cruisers— a display of force so absurdly large that her enviable reputation as a "nonmilitaristic" nation is shattered throughout China. All factions, even Sun's declared enemies at Peking, send him telegrams of sympathy. Then the British, who have "found" three cruisers to follow America's five, and to whom the customs service "belongs" anyhow, compromise with Sun on division of the revenue.

But all the organizing, all this showing up of the Powers, are incidental activities during Sun's last year. His real work—the work that is to make him a god— is his teaching and writing. For the mind of young China he gives weekly lectures at Ling Nam University —formerly Canton Christian College but renamed under the pressure of growing Nationalism. In much simpler language he addresses groups of coolies and laborers, who leave the presence of the "Great President" in an uplift of human dignity they have never felt before. "He gives everybody 'face,'" they remark to one another afterward over their long thimble-pipes.

Many hours he spends at his writing desk. The masterful yet worshiping Ching-ling sits on the other side, copying out clean drafts, in her larger and neater handwriting, or goes to the door to tell job hunters or consuls or concessionaires or newspapermen what the Doctor himself could never say: that they cannot see him now. He feels the pain of his mortal illness gnawing within him, but he looks at her, all enthusiasm and vitality, and pulls himself upright in his chair, and rubs his pen once more upon his ink-stone. Thus are completed the thirteen large books and several score pamphlets bearing his name which soon have as their only rival in circulation in the Chinese language the Western subsidized Christian Bible. Confucius runs a poor third.

Most important of the writings are the "Twenty-five Articles for the Rehabilitation of China," drawn up, states the prologue, "in consultation with Wang Ching-wei and other tried leaders of the party"—which means that they listen and nod their heads. Although Sun is easily influenced, his standard endorsement of a co-worker is: "Wang does what I say."

The reader will wish to pause in the culminating narrative for only the briefest summary of Sun Yat-senism in its final form. The Twenty-five Articles outline a procedure for gradual military conquest of China from south to north; province by province development of military rule first into civil party dictatorship and then into party representative government on the "Five-Department" system; universal assessment of land values and institution of percentage taxation (the values, strangely, to be set by owners themselves, held to honesty by the privilege of the government to buy property at value given); and gradual restoration of international dignity by abolition of the "unequal treaties"—taking over of customs collection and jurisdiction of aliens—in step with the advance of the Nationalist armies. In a way the program resembles the reconstruction schemes applied to the southern states after the American Civil War. It was, in the main, actually to be followed in the Nationalist absorption of the country between 1926 and 1928. The authorized version, bearing a colophon in the bold strokes of Chingling, added at the doctor's deathbed, would yet have a circulation of hundreds of thousands. The world asks, "How 'radical' does the Chinese Nationalist leader become? Does he 'go Bolshevik'?"

His last writings aim briefly and frankly at an idealistic communism. Yet he does not become completely Bolshevized any more than he became completely Westernized or Christianized. No Chinese, even though as great a "sport" from racial type as Sun Yat-sen, ever becomes completely "ized." He argues:

The state must contribute economic benefits directly to all its citizens. Its function is not filled in clearing a pathway for industrialists and capitalists, then leaving them responsible for the prosperity of the bulk of the population as in the capitalistic societies of the West. On the other hand, our plan is quite distinct from the Marxian method. Russia has tried the direct method of bringing equality—through enforced communism—for six years and pronounces it a failure. We must try the indirect method—through an evolution, firmly guided and kept to schedule. Immediate steps must be equalization of land holdings seriously unequal only in limited areas of our country and supervision of capital. The state must own essential public services.

This is as definite as political theorization can be, but gives obvious enough opportunity for the division over interpretation which was to come. Although later his worshipers would prefer to believe that had the "Director" lived, factionalism would not have occurred, it is obviously coming, and Sun Yat-sen gives indication of siding with the radicals, who are the fire of the movement, and condemning his conservative military head, Chiang Kei-shek, as he had Chen Ching-ming. His oldest disciple and successor as president of the party, the widely-liked Wang Chung-hui, whose fat cheeks make him look like a perpetually humorous case of mumps, sufficiently explains Chinese relations with the Soviet in the Chinese phrase, "We must ally every treat-us-equal nation. The cause of the snubbed everywhere is our cause, for their victories will contribute to ours."

It is 1924. Sun has now carried on almost two years without breaking with his support. But a crisis is brewing to end whatever monotony may exist. He feels his idealistic freedom impaired by the bourgeoisie upon whom he has had to rely for support. He is being suffocated in the bosoms of fat merchants. So to balance his dependence upon the Seventy Guilds he fosters the new "coolie" unions. Their communistic resolutions, framed for them by Russianized students, alarm the merchants and master-craftsmen, who reply to the menace by drilling their clerks into a very respectable Volunteer Corps. The Corps imports a shipload of German arms. Scenting a move against himself, Sun seizes the arms at customs and authorizes the laborers forcibly to dissolve the merchants' corps. Fighting ensues, a rich mercantile area of Canton is burned, several hundred clerks and coolies are killed. Sun wins —but it is an unstable victory.

The annual hot-weather war between the northern chieftains is just breaking out—this summer again between Wu Pei-fu of Honan and Chang Tso-lin of Manchuria. Sun again declares against Wu and orders his Punitive Expedition northward. General Wu's subordinate, the "Christian General" Feng Yu-hsiang, betrays and ruins Wu, and Sun finds himself on the winning side. The northern militarists and politicians feel

[84]

constrained to issue him a tongue-in-cheek invitation to come up and help reconstruct the nation.

Once more—the last time—Sun's egotism swings him away from the humble and hard-fought and sure road, away from his inner knowledge that these men were using him for their own ends, away from a sense of abasement at association with hypocrites. He even brings himself to believe, superficially, in their conversion to his cause and leadership. As at the time of Yuan Shih-kai, this is a bit easier when his own situation is becoming untenable anyhow. Sun's acceptance of the invitation is the last defeat of his dignity by his vanity, his experience by his optimism and trustfulness. Only death saves him from face-robbing results.

He sets about to make the best of the opportunity, although he really knows it is no opportunity at all. He issues a call for a national people's convention, to be held in the lair of his enemies and the scene of his previous defeat. This forces the hands of his doubtful allies and turns the spotlight on himself. His journey to Peking becomes a triumphal progress—the Palm Sunday preceding an obviously approaching Calvary.

Hongkong, which for thirty years has by turns scorned, detested, and feared Sun, now banquets him and listens adulatively to his rapid, low-voiced speeches. In Japan, crowds still smarting from the blow of the new American Immigration Act [8] weep in stifled anger

---

[8] July, 1924, Congress ignored the existence of the administrational "Gentlemen's Agreement" and discriminated against "Asiatics" by declining

as Sun pictures an East uniting to uphold its racial dignity so arrogantly flouted by the white man. Sun's speech in the Kobe Y.M.C.A. marks a turning point in the Japanese popular attitude toward the recently-despised neighbor. It becomes certain that the Japanese government will never again openly join with "white" exploiters of another Asiatic people.

Sun's declarations shock Americans and Europeans, many of whom have approved and abetted his activities, and who have proudly claimed him as a disciple of Western culture. Some of them are particularly pained by his attack upon the mission movement as an "agent of imperialism." The anti-missionary business community which likes this does not like his demand for the ending of their treaty-sacred prerogatives. But they, rather than Sun, are illogical. They say that he is not well, which is true, but where they imply that he is not normal they are simply deceiving themselves.

As Sun continues northward the northern chiefs manifest resentment and alarm at his obvious intention to be the whole show. Through mental constitution as well as principle, Sun must be all or nothing. The militarists and politicians extend him a conventional welcome on his arrival in Peking, December 31, 1924. Determined to beat them down, he replies with an abrupt denunciation of their insincerity. He declines their hospitality and goes to the Grand Hotel de Pekin, the

to put "aliens ineligible to citizenship" on the quota basis. The actual working of the law chiefly affected Japanese.

lavish resort of Western tourists. The Sanhedrin counsel on how to combat his obstreperousness. Would it do to imprison him—or would that have entirely the wrong effect?

While they are pondering Ching-ling takes him, desperately stricken, to the hospital of the Rockefeller Foundation. A stroke of fortune, from their viewpoint! They send cartloads of flowers to his room, and shake hands with themselves in congratulation.

The fighter is down at last! The outlaw who has been hunted over three continents lies helpless in the city of his pursuers. His son, the mayor, hurries from Canton, and his daughter from Macao; her husband now practices medicine lucratively where his famous father-in-law had been barred. Disciples and pretenders from every part of Pacific Asia vie to get to his bedside. The papers announce the arrivals. It is a matter of personal distinction to be present.

The doctors and nurses at the Peking Union Medical College complain that the old reformer is a cantankerous patient. He keeps a half dozen of them running day and night. Ching-ling is required to remain alert with a wetted ink-brush to write messages or record ideas as the whim strikes him. She remains dry-eyed—she cannot believe that this is mortal. He constantly refuses to take his medicine, except when some very pretty nurse sits on his bed and firmly feeds it to him. He can still capitulate to feminine beauty and determination.

[87]

The doctors finally pronounced his disease a neglected bladder and kidney complication past healing. A surgical attempt proves useless. They tell him he must die. Whereupon he rebels against the wielder of the scythe, leaves the hospital in a huff, goes to the home of Wellington Koo, and issues a public announcement that he will live. And he, the first practitioner of Western medical science to graduate in China, turns to the Chinese herb doctors. It is his final rebellion, that brings him around the circle to the culture from which he started.

All vain, of course. Still he clings so tenaciously to life that report after report of the end, published through China and the world, has to be retracted. Sun comes to be more of a myth than a man, suspended halfway between the living and the dead. Then, at the end of a three days' dust storm in March, as the trees are leafing out and the inhabitants are unsewing themselves in the bright sunshine from the garments of winter, the old Director summons Ching-ling, smiles, and asks for a pad and brush. First he writes to the chiefs of the Soviet at Moscow:

I charge the Kuomintang to continue the work of the revolutionary movement, so that China, reduced by the imperialists to the position of a semi-colonial country, shall become free. With this object I have instructed the party to be in constant contact with you. I firmly believe in the continuance of the support which you have hitherto accorded to my country. Taking leave of you, dear comrades, I want to express the hope that the day will soon come when the U. S. S. R. will welcome a friend and an ally in a mighty, free China, and that in the great struggle for the liberation of the oppressed peoples of the world those allies will go forward to victory, hand in hand.

Then he scrawls "My Will" on the edge of a sheet, followed by:

I have given my utmost strength to the people's revolution for full forty years. My goal is to seek liberty and equality for China. From forty years' experience I deeply know that if our desire is to attain its goal we must arouse the [common] people of the clans, also ally earth's treat-us-equal nations and struggle along with them.

The revolution is not completed! All of the same mind with me must, according to the plan of construction I have set forth through the Three People's Principles and the proclamation of the First All-Nation Representative Assembly, unite, struggle to the utmost, take advantage of every turn of affairs, open a people's parliament: right on to the abrogating of the unequal treaties. More: you must in the shortest time push these things through to manifest fruits. This is the final command.

As, during his life, his cause has been his only possession, so, facing death, he makes it his only formal legacy. All of Sun's true driving purpose, all of his idealism, all of his vision, all of his egotism, all of his weakness is in these last one hundred and forty-five ideographs of his prolific pen.

He hands them to Ching-ling with an order to read them back. "Reads all right, but hardly a model of calligraphy. Make a clear copy for me to sign," grunts the man whose bold, simple, egotistic pen-specimens regarded to a greater degree by the Chinese than by us as index of the soul, are prized throughout Pacific Asia.

Ching-ling ministers in reverential silence, bowed, now, before the inevitable, her full heart well controlled. Since death alone can ease her lord's torment, she craves it for him.

His son and several intimate disciples enter. He orders that he be interred at Nanking, where he had received the honor of Chief Executive, on the slope of Purple Mountain beside the huge tumulus of the Great Ming. This is his sublimely challenging estimate of his own greatness, flung from defeat and misery to a supercilious world. The time will come, he implies, when the blasé "Southern Capital" will boast equally of the tombs of Sun Yat-sen and Ming the Founder. Let the reader attest that he was right!

As an afterthought, he suggests a bronze and glass coffin "like Lenin's." He is dreaming of a similar preservation of his body for the inspiration of the masses, the donation of his corpse to make a shrine to patriotism. Possibly also he craves personal notice after death. He thinks of himself as a peer not only of the medieval Asiatic Ming Emperor but of the modern inspirer of Asians: Lenin. Does this seem incongruous? Not so, viewed through Asian eyes.

On March 12, 1925, he raises himself and beckons to practically the entire Kuomintang committee which has gathered at his bedside. "Struggle—Peace," he whispers, and sinks back dead. We set down these words as he wished: for the paradoxical keywords to his soul. Peace may yet come out of his struggle—peace and power for China, and then, mayhap, if the Western world have not cast away its fetishes of domination and arrogance, the greater, finally destructive, humanity-exterminating struggle.

Immediately arises the inevitable dispute: "What were the Sainted Master's real beliefs—?" The Sovietized ones in Sun's coterie maintain that he has renounced religion during his last year and should have a purely Communist ceremony. But Ching-ling, whose political radicalism is kept in a different compartment from her religion, quietly insists upon a Christian service. It is held in the Union Medical College chapel by the extremist George Chien Hsu, Nationalist Minister of Justice, who brings forth the argument from the Bible that Christianity embraces Communism and that Dr. Sun was a communist because he was a Christian. A typically Chinese compromise, and every one is flattered, including the missionaries who crowd the little hall.

"Left and right" factionalism do not remove from Ching-ling the honor of "first lady" in China. She ranks in popular adulation with Mu Lan, the patriot woman warrior of the Han Dynasty, and Chao Chun, the tragic beauty who purchased with her life surcease from Mongol attack, but she is a hundred times more conscious of her purpose than they. The difference is that which separates old and new China. If one question whether the association with Sun Yat-sen was worth the sorrows of it to Ching-ling, he may read the answer in her countenance, more beautiful now than ever in girlish freshness. The rounded face, made sweet through suffering, the full sympathetic lips, and the intelligent eyes speak eloquently—as do every woman's of some man—of Sun Yat-sen.

The religious ceremony over, there follows the "receiving of the obeisance of the nation" in which the Communists have things more their way. In the great hall of the umbrella-roofed state library of Central Park, part of the former Forbidden City from which the Son of Heaven had been ejected so largely through Sun's efforts, he lies under draperies of Red and Nationalist flags, while M. Karahan, the Armenian Ambassador for the Soviet, comes forward as chief diplomatic mourner. His nice confreres of the Legation Quarter are therefore able to be present only through floral wreaths, in which red flowers are primly avoided. But the people look at the decorations of flaunting red and over their millet gruel and their gaming sticks whisper, "Newfangled foreign-devil idea this—the color of joy at a funeral!"

The Russian Ambassador has claimed for his government the privilege of fulfilling the reformer's last wish for a "coffin like Lenin's." Pending its arrival his body is taken along sanded avenues to the Indian-architectured Hidden Cloud Temple in the Western Hills. The cortège pauses at frequent mourning stations of elaborate matting and bamboo-work, each of which shelters an altar bearing an enlarged photograph of the deceased. At each a short eulogism is read and the mourners sign in a book. The ponderous temporary wooden coffin is drawn to the highest niche of the temple by silken cords over disfiguring trestle-work erected for the purpose.

The long-awaited bronze and glass contraption from Moscow comes on a special car via the Trans-Siberian. It is too shabbily constructed and too short to be used! So in a six-inch thick sampan-shaped box such as housed his ancestors, the Father of China—the Nation—will be entrained for Purple Mountain. A magnificent memorial will stand there, overshadowing the weather-beaten, willow-covered tumulus of Ming the Founder. Young Chinese architects of the modernized, but not Westernized, school prepare impressive designs. Art lives, as well as politics, in this China.

One year after Sun Yat-sen's death I began to write this story, and my friends, the Old China Hands, said: "Who will want to read about Sun? He's forgotten and his disciples have all found other nests." Chang Tso-lin of Manchuria, having driven the heavyweight Christian General Feng (who had let Chang into China by betraying Wu) into the wastes of the Gobi Desert with a decimated army, sat secure as dictator at Peking. Wu, in turn, was rehabilitating himself at Hankow and the little militarists of that central region were gathering to his fold. Then occurred the affair of the Shanghai

British police commissioner and the students. "It's a good job Sun's dead," said the Old China Hands. "What he would have made out of this!" But the people and little militarists of the central region were indignant that Wu tried to remain friends with the foreigners, and opened Hankow to Amanuensis-Generalissimo Chiang Kai-shek, coming north from Canton through the rice marshes and over the steep bamboo-coated ridges with Sun Yat-sen's Nationalist army. General Wu ended up in a temple in the marshes of Tibet, painting pictures.

Two years after Sun's death the Old China Hands were doing patrol behind barbed wire and in the filthy canals surrounding the Shanghai Settlement, and saying to one another: "Damn Sun Yat-sen! See the mess he started!"

And then Chiang Kai-shek, the generalissimo, and T. V. Soong, the young finance wizard, and other leaders broke with their Russian assistants. Old China Hands said: "Well, that finishes this Nationalist movement. 'Twas Russian brains that made it." There were disruption and civil war in the movement. And Japan flung an army into Shantung to protect her nationals that was a wall of safety behind which Chang Tso-lin at Peking smiled in assurance. But Dictator Chang of the delicate hands and pearl-topped hat could not prevent the sale of Sun Yat-sen's photograph and "Three Determinations" in the market stalls of his own capital, and he dared not oppose the becoming of Sun's bier in the high niche of Hidden Cloud Temple a shrine of patriots.

Chiang Kai-shek and T. V. Soong and their fellows turned to the new industrial plutocracy of Shanghai for the support they must have now that they had cast off the Russians. Ching-ling, beautiful widow of the founder and inspirer of the cause, repudiated them, and retired to Moscow, saying, "I would rather see the Master's cause go down in ruin than be sold to fat Shanghai merchants." But her young brother, Soong, said, "It is the unavoidable evolution which every nation must pass through. Out of feudalism into industrial plutocracy, then gradually through democracy into socialism. It is useless to try to outrun natural laws. Great Britain, America, Japan, are all following this evolution. China cannot be an exception." There were heartbreaks enough. The author bore the message to Ching-ling in Moscow, bowing at Lenin's tomb, pale as an angel: "Your younger brother, Tzu Wen, salutes you." Her eyes were already large with the beauty of the dread white plague. "I have no brother," she replied, clear, low and sad. With her into exile went the Chinese-British-African firebrand, Eugene Chen, early secretary to Sun, who had outfaced the plenipotentiaries of the Powers with his biting diplomatic repartee.

Three years after the Master, now generally the "Sainted Master," went into the niche in Hidden Cloud, Generalissimo Chiang marched from his Nanking base once more upon Peking. Once more a Japanese army lay in his path, and nasty incidents occurred, and he was stopped. But Feng the Huge had come down out of the Gobi and built a new army, and C. T. Wang of Shanghai, no longer young, had become his liaison with Nationalism of the Shanghai bourgeois stamp. And Kung of the house of Confucius, who had married Ching-ling's sister of the house of Sun, persuaded Model Satrap Yen of Shanshi province to come out of his sixteen-year seclusion into national affairs, and Feng and Yen came down on Peking behind the Japanese lines. Chang Tso-lin had bigger and better armies but Sun Yat-senism had captured them—the soldiers would not fight. Chang fled out of Peking to bump into a charge of dynamite under the Japanese railroad trestle at the entrance to his own city of Mukden, and the movement bearing Sun Yat-sen's name was supreme.

Generalissimo Chiang and Finance Executive Soong came up to Peking to demote the proud city to a provincial capital, change its name to Peping [9] and remove the government archives to the capital chosen for the new nation—necessarily near to Shanghai money— Nanking. "The Legations will be in no hurry recognizing the new régime, or following it about the country to whatever new seat of government may for the moment be chosen," said the American Minister to me

[9] Peking, "Northern capital," properly pronounced *bay jing*, now changed to Peping, "Northern peace," pronounced *bay ping*. Nanking, "Southern capital," properly pronounced *nan jing*.

[96]

under the acacia blossoms of his beautiful garden one evening in June. The next morning at ten o'clock (a cable had come from Washington) he signed a tariff autonomy treaty with T. V. Soong which gave American recognition to the Nationalist government. A few days before New Year of 1929, Great Britain outdid America by firing twenty-one guns to Chief Executive Chiang Kai-shek, who after the example of George Washington, had laid down the sword for civil office. The saluting ships lay in the same spot in the Yangtze River from which British vessels had bombarded Nanking in 1842 and (in alternation with American) in 1926.

The great coffin may come down now from the niche in Hidden Cloud Temple; the Guards of the Corpse, who were youths of Chiang Kai-shek's cadet school when assigned this distinguished watch and are now grown men, may end their long vigil. Sun Yat-sen may have his last ride between the endless lines of worshiping admirers: through the city which he robbed of its throne and whose forbidden parks are now playgrounds of laughing children and whose golden-tiled palaces are hushed museums, then on across the sun-drenched width of a now conquered North China, through the new capital city on a sixty-foot wide avenue constructed for his passing, on to the great, simple, pagoda-like sepulcher beside the brown tumulus of Ming the Founder. And as the shadows fall over Purple Mountain, named for its sunset beauty, and over broad Lotus Lake at its foot, and the hewn-rock walls of the new-old city beyond, Sun Yat-sen's children in the faith can turn from installing the sacred remains to announce that Modern China has officially begun and that Nanking has received the seal honor as its new capital.

Nanking sends a special delegation to the proud city it now flouts to escort the corpse on its journey, and on March 9, 1929, the great wooden coffin is placed in state in the court of the one-time Viceroy's Yamen where seventeen years ago Sun Yat-sen confidently took the oath of office as first Chief Executive of China, and where his one-time amanuensis now exercises the great seal of President. Three days later, third anniversary of his death, he reaches his final resting place, and Chiang Kai-shek, Sun Fo, and the hundreds of party leaders and delegates of the Third All-China and Overseas Congress of the Nationalist Party turn from Purple Mountain to the Congress hall to struggle over which faction, conservative or radical, and what policy shall fall heir to the Sainted Master's name.

Ching-ling has come across Eurasia from Switzerland, to accompany the beloved remains from Peking and spend her last energy in the fight, and politicians are a little silent and awed when she passes.

Thus does the spirit of Sun Yat-sen go marching on. Whatever the vicissitudes of the fascist régime known as "Nationalist," it is certain that it will continue to march on until "in international intercourse, government, and communications China is equal to other nations, and assured of permanence on the earth." More: the Sun Yat-sen idea will persist until all Asia has attained recognition of political independence and social equality from the now dominant West—or until its effort to attain these has ended in the cataclysm of civilization.

Enlarged reproductions of Sun Yat-sen's formal will in Ching-ling's open characters and his own quavering signature hang over the dais in Kuomintang headquarters in every village of China and every city throughout the world. It has been memorized by more schoolboys than the preamble to the American Declaration of Independence. "The Revolution is not completed!"— tocsin of Asia's awakening!

But those of us who are more attracted by the infinite nuances of the human heart than the awakening of races will turn rather to the crumpled note found under the dead revolutionist's pillow when the embalmers picked up his body.

"I beg Ching-ling, my wife and comrade, to accept my books, my old clothes, and the house in Shanghai, not as a bequest—because my few accumulations cannot be called an estate—but as a souvenir."

YAMAGATA AND ITO

1838–1922   1841–1909

YAMAGATA

I

AMERICANS acquainted with the plan of this book while under preparation have usually taken Sun Yat-sen, Gandhi, Kemal, and Stalin for granted, but have looked blank at mention of Yamagata and Ito. Yet the nation makers of modern Japan have been no less spectacular in life and deed than those of China, India, Turkey, or Russia. It would seem that although Japan is the best apprehended Asian nation in the West, its leaders are the least known to Westerners. Perhaps Admiral Togo's name alone has become a household word in Europe and America—as if Japanese should know, in American history, only the name of Dewey.

No more thrilling story exists than that of the rise of two young pages of feudal Japan to the rank of princes in a modern world power. Ito the Astute built the Japanese political structure. Yamagata the Masterful built the Japanese military machine. There are of course other names in the group of young knights and pages who undertook to make an obscure group of Asiatic islands into a world power, succeeded in a generation, and gained for themselves reverence as "Elder Statesmen" before they were forty. Kido, Okubo, and Saigo the Greater mixed the dough. Itagaki, Inouye, Saigo the Lesser, the Gotos, Okuma, Saionji, Matsukata, and half a score others added leaven. But the personalities of Yamagata and Ito determined the shape of the loaf and the conflict between them provided the heat which baked it.

Both men sprang from the impoverished lower fringe of the samurai or warrior caste and both served at tender ages as servants of their more fortunate fellows. Yamagata was to bring about the abolition of this hereditary warrior aristocracy and build in its stead a modern military caste, while Ito, after risking his life to obtain an education abroad, enduring both dangerous and ludicrous adventures, was to establish Japan's foreign relations, and ultimately become the father of Japanese democracy.

The two were born of the same clan, went to the same school, and were always promoted in rank simultaneously. Beginning their active careers in their teens with a Joshua and Caleb mission to spy out the strength of the feudal tyranny, they fought side by side for fifty years in the cause of establishing the dignity of the Kingdom of the Rising Sun among the nations. They were the inner confidants and real advisers of the worshiped Emperor of the Restoration, Matsuhito, now glorified posthumously as the Meiji (Enlightened Administration) Emperor. Many pretty stories are told of the intercourse of this very human Sacred Person and the two men who molded his young manhood and were cherished as his friends.

The lives of Yamagata and Ito were a recurring duel.

While Yamagata was building the modern army, Ito was drafting a constitution. While Yamagata was establishing a new military oligarchy, Ito was attempting to found party government. While Yamagata sought empire on the continent, Ito sought peace abroad and progress at home. Paradoxical Japan of to-day with its strengths and its weaknesses is the result.

To the Emperor must be given credit that from the clash of these opposite temperaments came a resultant force meaning, on the whole, progress to the nation. Yet the Emperor was often used in a manner which must have been anything but pleasant for him.

Ito fought for the love of fighting, Yamagata never fought without a cause. Ito, who in youth was a healthy swashbuckler, grew into horror of military methods and became Japan's great protagonist of peaceful growth. Yamagata, as a child delicate and retiring, and a dyspeptic throughout life, established Japan's warlike reputation, and became the patron of jingoism.

Ito was reckless of his own life and money, democratic in bearing, loved society, and made innumerable acquaintances. At heart, he was something of a snob. His strength in the duel lay in the unconventionality of his friendship with the Emperor, a control of official patronage, and such loyalty as a politician can reckon on. Yamagata was painstaking, aloof, and aristocratic. His weapons were control of military promotion and the respect of the nation for his samurai austerity. He sincerely desired the welfare of the common people but did not see it coming through democracy. He kept his heart as steel because he knew his heart was tender.

Ito could handle delicate situations which Yamagata would not dare to touch. But when it was necessary for the good of the Empire as he saw it, Yamagata, the calculating, would control Ito, the intuitive, like a puppet on a string. More and more as the years of their public life continued, the two men clashed and compromised. Ito submitted, more and more hating his submission; Yamagata, while forcing Ito to do his will, despised him a little for his weakness, pitied his unhappiness, and silently loved him.

When the conclusion of Ito's last ambiguous, and this time dangerous, mission on the continent was reported in a message to Prince Yamagata—"Safe in Harbin"—the old marshal breathed a sigh of relief that his rival had come through alive. Then, a few minutes later, the Japanese Imperial Telegraphs, true to their whimsical custom, sent a second messenger with the correction of one Japanese syllable, which changed the sense to "Shot in Harbin."

Thereafter, until the last of his fourscore and five years, Marshal Prince Yamagata was supreme in the empire, but he was very lonely.

II

In the lush spring of 1850, three years before Commodore Perry sailed into Tokyo with President Fillmore's isolation-ending demand, and while knowledge of Japan in the West had not greatly advanced beyond that found in Marco Polo's secondhand reports of the "Islands of the Far Indies," a small-boned, wiry man trod a footpath through a field of knee-high rice overlooking Japan's Inland Sea, bearing a burden strangely inconsistent with his garb. For he was a samurai, who swung from his belt the two swords of the reverenced and ruling caste—the long one to cut down enemies or any yokel who might happen to obstruct his path, and the short one to cut out his own bowels in event of dishonor. But on his back, riding the seat of an *oikko,* a man-yoke for carrying firewood, was an undersized, pale, nine-year-old boy. As the man stopped and straightened up, allowing the support-stick of the *oikko* to touch ground and take the load, the lad unclasped his long, pale fingers from the "warrior's knot" on his father's head by which he steadied himself.

"Risuke, son," said the man, placing one hand on the long sword, "when you shall have to move your family you will take your son in a palanquin and your women in litters. I proved that noble blood could raise rice. But the village feud and the usurers wiped us out back in the old home. Now that our rank has been restored through the fatherliness of the noble Ito-san to whom we go—and whose grandson, remember, you now are—it will fare better with us. Don't forget the proper obeisance when our master receives you."

They turned about and waited for the little mother,

who in plain married woman's kimono but bright butterfly *obi* or bustle, pushed along her wooden *geta* with her little turned-in feet, bearing the silk floss pads of the family bed.

Juzo Hayashi, a defamilied descendant of the Emperor Korei, had ambitions for this delicate but precocious nine-year-old. He hardly saw so far as to envision Risuke achieving the title of Prince in a new world power. But he was pleased to think that the lad would now have his chance, since Buhei Ito, a samurai footman to the Daimyo (or "Great Name") of Choshu, had, after the Japanese habit, preferred the reliable Hayashi to his own offspring as son and heir. And Choshu, guarding the southwest extremity of the main island, was most powerful of all clans bordering the Inland Sea.

The custom of adoption has enabled Japanese families to retain their amazing vigor century after century and made the Imperial House the only one in history which has not "petered out." Of doubtful good is the tendency to abandon it. Surnames have been more readily shifted in Japan than given names in the West, and it was as "Ito" that the honest Juzo husbanded the estate and young Risuke grew up in the little west-coast town of Hagi, seat of their lord's castle near the Korean strait.

Memories brought by the observant lad from his birth village of Tsugari-mura were of transplanting, flooding, and gleaning the rice, and the little lore of the village school, where, aged six, and having dropped the baby name, Jukichi, he had begun the routine Chinese classical course. He had already received his earliest impressions of public policy, too, as with one hand firmly clasping his father's kimono sleeve he had listened to discussion in village councils, or had heard with vague inner disturbance his father's anxious talk to silent wife and mother of thirty per cent interest and rentals, grain levies of the feudal lord, and offerings to the temple. Now, at the Daimyo's castle town, among fighting retainers of the clan, the boy was plunged into an entirely new atmosphere of resentment and belligerency. The dissatisfaction of the common people was surpassed by that of the aristocracy. Under the firm and guileful hand of the Tokugawas in Yedo (Tokyo) who had reduced both Imperial House and remaining feudal lords to submission, peace and isolation had continued for two and a half centuries—far too long for the good of the warrior caste.

This class was thoroughly dissatisfied with the Shogunate's sponsorship of schools of Chinese philosophy, poetry, and *No* dancing, rather than tournaments at arms and wars against the northern barbarians or Korean neighbors. It was having to go to work on the land—even to go into trade—the same as any despised commoner who could be cut down on the street to test the sharpness of a sword, and it was standing by and witnessing the gradual granting of the rights of humanity, which it had always arrogated to itself alone, to these same commoners, who were becoming more and more necessary to the Shogunate as the samurai were becoming more and more alienated.

Furthermore, the government at Yedo was compromising the dignity of Nihon by dealing with the Western barbarians pressing her shores. This was unforgivable sin, justification enough to conservatives for any violence or intrigue. For His Sacred Person's sake and that of national pride, the Emperor must be liberated from domination by shoguns of the Tokugawa house, and put under guidance of real patriots—such as (it was implied in Choshu) the knights of Choshu!

The controversy was idealized, after the manner of childhood, in young Ito's mind. He would become a bold knight, he would himself murder the wicked Tokugawa who usurped the Son of Heaven's prerogatives! Getting his ambitions and history somewhat mixed, he called himself the "new conqueror Hideyoshi," and daily as the gloom of evening made it impossible for him longer to read, he drew a cartoon of "Great Monkey-face," the sixteenth century nation-unifier really responsible for the rise of the hated usurping Tokugawa system. This Hideyoshi and his successors had driven the pale or rather "pink" barbarians and their religion of the cross from Japan in the sixteenth and seventeenth centuries when Spain was the vanguard of Europe's thrust. Now that the thrust was being resumed under Anglo-Saxon leadership, a new Hideyoshi was needed. China, Japan's great tutor empire, had for the first time been humbled by a Western Power a year after young Ito was born. The repercussions of that event in anxious Japan were among the first sounds in the lad's precocious ears.

Beneath his pale skin, in spite of scrawny limbs, Risuke carried a stout heart. He had an affable, ingratiating manner, becoming at once a part of his surroundings, yet was at the same time a good deal of a bully. From childhood he made friends in hosts, but throughout life was to be liked rather than loved. In imitation of the elders, most of his games were war games, and he contrived often to be leader on the winning side. Sheer love of fight, outlet for a nervous instability, dominated his teens, and, years before he was twenty, game and contest were replaced by fierce realities of duel and ambush.

When cornered he showed a quick-witted ruthlessness. One day the opposition onslaught with bamboo spears, childish bows and arrows, and mud bombs from the slimy tide flats, forced a retreat in spite of Ito's desperate generalship. He thereupon led windward into a dry field and whipping out his flint and tinder set fire to the grass. The pursuers to leeward escaped, with severe burns, and Risuke was praised for resourcefulness by the samurai—including some fathers of the scorched children! "He will be a great man or a vagabond," they said. Either prospect satisfied their flair for the romantic.

Samurai Japan was a curious combination of ebulli-

ence and nicety—heroized "wild West" violence along-
side most refined manners and ceremonialism imported
from China. One might commit an assassination for
the honor of his lord or himself on the way to a tea-
drinking ceremony or incense-smelling party.

In the new home, Risuke attended a very good private school, which, however, "also took commoners."
His mother's uncle, the old Buddhist monk Keiun,
meanwhile tutored him in Chinese writing and versify-
ing, which became his proudest accomplishment, and
in as much of the Buddha's placid gospel as the hot-
headed lad was willing to absorb. Buddhism in Japan,
however, compromised notably with the active Japanese
nature.

One winter's day, Risuke was sent to a distant house
to return a pair of *geta* (wooden "stilt-shoes") lent his
master to wear home during a sudden snow flurry. The
road was slushy and the air as raw as southern Japan
ever knows. The shivering lad passed by his own home
and would have slipped in to hover a bit over the charcoal brazier, but his mother, discovering that he was
on an errand, refused to admit him across the veranda.
The mothers of Sparta and Japan had similar ideas of
child training. His grandmother, who witnessed the
incident, related: "He turned back to the road without
a word of complaint, but piteously. The picture will
never fade from my mind."

Between errands Risuke read the romantic pseudo-
histories of his country, and each night drew his pic-

ture of Hideyoshi. Then his father would arrive home, give him enough octagonal coppers, come by through the day, to buy another night's fuel for the lamp, and the lad would plod through the dark a mile and back to get the means of cheating the night for an hour or two. Ito, studying Confucius or tales of Hideyoshi at a smoky bean-oil wick and warming one extremity after another at a tiny charcoal brazier, may not be as picturesque as Lincoln reading his Bible and Weem's Washington before a roaring backwoods fire, but there can be no doubt he was quite as uncomfortable.

Risuke was servant to the knight Ryozo Kuruhara, and thirteen years of age, Japanese count—twelve by ours—when the entire nation was electrified by the arrival in Yedo harbor of the "black monster ships" of an unknown but evidently powerful new aggressor. For Japan could look upon Commodore Perry's squadron, which came to exact guarantees of safety for American whaling and trade, in no other light.

The Shogunate government at Yedo had been warned by the Dutch king—the only Western potentate with whom Japan had maintained relations since Hideyoshi's time—of the power and determination of America. But more, it feared an uprising of the truculent clans should it compromise the traditional policy of haughty aloofness, or, on the other hand, impair the national "face" by an unsuccessful clash with the foreigner. And so it temporized with the Commodore, asking him to come back next year, and made a pretense of common purpose with the chauvinist clans by ordering them to guard the coasts and asking the daimyos for advice, and of consideration for the Emperor in keeping his minions informed of events and assigning new levies to defend Kyoto. The net result was that Yedo authority got under suspicion and contempt all around and raised a storm of semi-open discussion that it never again could stifle.

The Choshu samurai were made responsible for a section of coastline just south of Yedo. It gave them a welcomed chance to concentrate forces near the headquarters of the dominant Tokugawa. Ito's master Kuruhara seized the opportunity to become an officer in the coastguard at Sagami. When Risuke had turned fifteen, Western reckoning, Kuruhara sent for him and inducted him into the clan army as a page. He personally took charge of the young man's training in the samurai spirit. In winter he rode past Ito's barracks before dawn, summoned him out of bed, and took him off on horseback, discussing letters as they rode along. He did not allow the lad to wear the *tabi* (cleft-footed socks) in winter—he had to swing his *geta* through the snow with bare feet.

Perry, waiting in Chinese harbors, received a letter begging him to postpone his return three years, on account of inconvenience due to death of a Shogun and selection of another, but the American admiral waited not even a full year as the government had assumed from their agreement, and returned immediately after

Chinese New Year's—technically "next year." The
Japanese negotiators had not supposed this idiom to be
used by barbarians, but the shrewd Yankee had ascertained that it was common in Japan.

He caught them entirely off guard—they had hoped
in six months to say from behind new defense works:
"Get out, or we sink your ships." But to their chagrin
he passed their uncompleted forts with a copy of the
treaty signed by President Fillmore to exchange for one
signed by "His Majesty" the Shogun himself. That
worthy had hoped in vain to keep out of the business
personally. As to the Mikado, intervention by his In-
effable Eminence was not dreamed of just then. Yet
Japan's isolation was ended, though every castle
buzzed with discussion of means for brushing away the
barbarians.

Knight Kuruhara was so pleased with his ward that
he sent him back to take lectures under his intimate
friend, the distinguished samurai Yoshida Shoin, whose
school of patriotism in the dark foothills southeast of
Hagi was the most noted of recent "mushroom" institutions adopting that name, though the master was but
twenty-seven. The typical school was simply a gathering of youths about a fiery personality on the floor of
a plain Japanese room, or a group practicing *judo* and
swordplay in a field, shifting often from place to place
for fear of government suspicion.

Yoshida had been let out of confinement to take
over a school his uncles had started, because he had

answered a pamphleteer who had dared to advocate abolition of the Shogunate. But he taught the chronicles that pictured the glory of Dai Nihon (or Great Rising-sun Land) in days when Emperors were supreme, and showed in dark colors the long lines of regents before the Tokugawa whom it was forbidden to criticize. His philosophy set the worth of men and their training strictly in ability and will to link thought with action. He fired his pupils, scions of both higher and lower nobility, with resolve to exalt the Mikado, end usurpation, restore the warlike prestige of Japan, and make her more than equal to driving off the invaders who had put heels on India and China and were now reaching the Sacred Isles. He could teach not only traditional arts, but through his scant lore of Dutch and the meager translations extant, he could and did impart an idea of Western arms, tactics, and fortifications. Yoshida had been taught by Sakuma, eminent as advocate of foreign learning since 1842 and high counselor on coast defense in the interim of Perry's visits. Yoshida's pupils knew how he had gone from port to port trying to leave the country like an animal newly caged, and how he and his great teacher had both been imprisoned on occasion of his attempt to leave with Perry.

For a few months, about the beginning of 1858, Risuke was privileged to join the students humbly kneeling about the elevated mat upon which Yoshida sat lecturing in his little twelve by twenty hall. Those

few months were to be a lifelong influence, acknowl-
edged long after by a shrine to Yoshida's memory
erected by *Prince* Ito. Squatting outside on the grill-
work veranda among the bodyservants, but listening in-
tently at the slightly slid back *shoji*, was a youth a bit
taller and older than Risuke and of most serious bearing.
It was Kiosuke Yamagata, who was to be Ito's fellow-
patriot, lifelong rival, and eventually, destroyer.

It developed that young Yamagata, like himself, was
of the sub-samurai, but even poorer. He had become
personal servant to one of the more aristocratic pupils
in return for the privilege of listening from the porch.
The young fellow's first name, *Kiosuke*—"mad," or
"wild"—attracted Risuke, although it was nothing more
than an evolution from Kosuke, "small," suggested in
turn by his birth name, *Tatsunosuke*, "snake." after the
sign of the zodiac.

In spite of the general good manners of Japanese
children, both boys came in for abuse from pupils of
higher rank. Ito replied characteristically with challenges to fight, and soon stopped the scoffing so far as
he was concerned. Yamagata in his different way
quietly promised himself revenge by demonstrating
superior ability. The two became friends and Yoshida's
most trusted pupils.

Yamagata's father, who, like Ito's, traced ancestry
back to the Imperial House—in this case through Prince
Mototsune to the fifty-sixth Emperor Seiwa—had
brought him to Matsushima village where the school

was. Though born within Choshu he had not been so fortunate as the Hyashi in finding a patron, and he and his son had to eke out the rations for five which were his as a warrior by common work. At need a samurai might do this without loss of caste. Thus the great Yoshida and his highborn students could undertake to plaster their school building. The earnest and adoring Yamagata, throwing mud to the teacher, inadvertently struck him full in the face. All the master's persuasiveness was required to keep the abashed youth from committing suicide.

Whereas Ito from heredity and popularity in youth was free with resources, Yamagata learned from infancy to hoard. Saburo Yamagata, although very poor, was a learned man, and himself taught his son reading, writing, and Japanese versification, for which he was to become as well known as was Ito for the more classical Chinese composition. A main formative influence in Kiosuke's life was his Spartan grandmother, who took charge of him when at the age of five he lost his mother. From a discouraging start he grew into a vigorous lad under her care. Stoicism, shyness, and determination which could temporarily compromise but always reached its aim, were his qualities, as affability and impulsiveness were those of his fellow Risuke.

At fifteen Yamagata was known for accomplishment with spear and in *judo*—commonly called in the West *ju jitsu*. A less impulsive fighter, he was a better soldier than Ito, for he used violence cold-bloodedly, as an instrument to attain a purpose; only victory counted. Ito, by now big-boned and broad-shouldered, with a wide head that reminded one of a hammerhead, and who scrapped as recklessly before twenty as Bismarck, was to lose the love of battle along with the romantic outlook of youth. Yamagata, frail, with a long, narrow head that reminded one of a spearhead, always personally mild-mannered, was to become a consistent militarist. One of the greatest mistakes of our modern cartoonists is in picturing war-lords foaming at the mouth!

With the single-mindedness of youth and the natural impulsiveness of his character, Ito devoted himself to two great hates: of the Tokugawa usurpers and the foreign aggressors. Meantime his fellow Yamagata was pursuing the same ends more deliberately. Rushing off to swing a sword on the beach at steel battleships sitting arrogantly in the harbor did not appear to him so necessary as feeling out for unity among opposition clans and studying the secrets of the Western barbarian's strength.

Yet it was to be the ability of these two so different minds in abandoning hate, or turning it into something else when the time for it had passed, which was to make them stand out from the many youths who enlisted in the patriotic cause with equal ardor and opportunity.

A third pupil of the school formed, with Ito and Yamagata, its trio of distinction. He was the imaginative Takasugi, scion of a more aristocratic family. He was to do amazing exploits in his twenties, and die violently at twenty-nine—spoken of, in connection with his military alliance with Yamagata, as a "meteor hitched to a fixed star." He now showed a poetic interest in Ito by suggesting that he change his name from Risuke to the more elegant form "Shinsuke." Ito, in his middle twenties, started as a statesman, and needing a "career" name, was to appeal again to Takasugi, and receive a phrase from the saying of Confucius anent the two joys of the scholar: "To study with diligent application and greet a friend from afar." Ito "Hirobumi," "greeter-from-afar," was to be Count, then Marquis, then Prince.

At twenty-two the quiet, diligent Yamagata, nicknamed "human crane" by his fellows, was to have been graduated in sword and spear—a samurai, and no longer subject to insult. But great events dispersed the little community of youth before that time. They began when young Ito's good patron, Kuruhara himself, arrived back from the "front" a prisoner. He had given a battalion some Western military drill, and been immediately attached by "hundred per cent samurai" fellow officers. It was as if an American drill master of 1918 had obliged Yankees to practice the goose step. To calm the furor, the Choshu Daimyo, Yoshichika Mori, who really liked Kuruhara, put him under arrest and sent him home. He was allowed to visit Yoshida's school and the pupils overheard fervent discussions between the two intimates.

Japan, they agreed, was now too feeble and backward (for which they blamed the Tokugawa isolation) to conclude treaties on equal footing with Western nations. But the country must never compromise its honor by allowing itself to be dealt with as an inferior. Therefore the policy of isolation must be strictly maintained and efforts at communication repulsed until the nation should be brought to a military level with foreign powers. Two things would have to be overthrown: the decadent and stultifying Tokugawa court régime and the excessive sentimentalism of the patriotic clansmen who confused foreign ways and weapons with truckling to the foreigner. These men thus early analyzed a situation yet to occur in every Asiatic nation. Mustapha Kemal has recently and drastically dealt with the same difficulty. What in their case the Japanese pioneers failed to see was that it would be as difficult to postpone intercourse with the besetting white man as it would be to deal with him as an equal before having demonstrated equal military power.

A move must be made against the Tokugawa before they should, in weakness, sell out the nation to barbarians. This was possible only by raising the cry, "Down with usurpers, reverence to imperial authority," which appealed to all Japanese like the call, "Liberate the Pope," to good Catholics. Yoshida ascertained that nobles of the Imperial Court at Kyoto would favor the movement and permit use—within limits of discretion —of the Sacred Person's name. That millennium-old but long-isolated court was composed of human units whose pride still chafed at being superseded in actual power by the staff of the "Barbarian Quelling General" (or Shogun) in Yedo. They might well suspect that some of the "reform" leaders had ulterior ends and would like merely to take the Tokugawa's place—but they saw ground for hope in the sincerity of such as Yoshida.

Yoshida did not confine himself to pedagogy. On timid assent of the clan council stipulating repudiation if discovered, he sent six students to Kyoto to do what older samurai had not the stomach to attempt. For the Tokugawa Shogunate maintained one of the most elaborate espionage systems known to history—two hundred years old, working as silently and ruthlessly as drouth. Besides unknown agents of all kinds, each ten families had a chief, compelled to send in minute reports. As on the Chinese principle of responsibility the whole group suffered with an offending individual, so each had an interest in watching the rest.

This was, besides, a time of special disquiet. Long historical research, patronized by lords of Mito, a collateral branch of the Tokugawa, had fostered a school that taught the supremacy of the Emperor. This group had conspired to have the Emperor nominate the successor to the now vacant Shogunate from among the scions of the Tokugawa clan, suggesting one Keiki, of the House of Mito. Such revival of Imperial initiative had been forestalled by quick action of the great Lord Regent Ii Naosuke nominating the child Iemochi. Four great daimyos had been confined to quarters in Yedo for intriguing to get the Emperor Komei to decree annulment of treaties that Yedo had felt forced to make, and Lord Manabe had been sent to Yedo to stop the movement.

Led by Takasugi, Ito, and Yamagata, the sixteen to nineteen-year-old pupils of Yoshida visited Imperial House officers and Kyoto representatives of the far-flung clans, under eyes of Shogun agents, sounding the possibility of a nation-wide restoration movement. The emissaries returned safely, bringing the rumor that northern adherents of the "Oust-Foreigners" party had plotted the death of the Lord Regent, at Yedo. Concerned lest he should be behind in zeal for the Emperor, Yoshida impetuously went to Kyoto to organize assassination of Yedo agents there. The chief victim was to have been Manabe, the "Controller" who was keen on the trail of all "Oust-Foreigners" men, to send them to torture and death, and used all means in favor of the Yedo treaty policy. But Yoshida's plans miscarried. Clan authorities had to confine him in Choshu and finally to hand him over to the Shogun's agents— for they were not yet disposed to rebel.

That spring, with the just-freed Kuruhara, Ito had been sent down to Nagasaki on the southern island to learn what they might of Western military methods in that open port, a Tokugawa outpost in Hizen clan territory where as of old the Dutch, and now British, French, and Russians, were making themselves at home.

[123]

When he returned and learned Yoshida's fate, Ito gathered fellows of the school about him and sealed with blood an oath to rescue their master or exact adequate revenge. The helpful Kuruhara commended the young swashbuckler to his brother-in-law and active fellow clansman, Kido, who was about to take charge of the clan's school in Yedo. But at Yoshida's Yedo prison, which was the goal of Ito's pilgrimage, Kido and Ito were turned away, and one autumn day (1859) the jailer called them to behold the teacher's beheaded body in the prison yard. He was martyr to his cause at twenty-nine. A space for malefactors in Yekoen temple grounds is now famous because there, weeping with rage, his young disciples buried him.

"Better die by mistake than live by mistake" had been his teaching. Scheming lords might covet the Shogun's place or detest his monopoly of the profitable foreign trade. They were inferior in spirit to young idealists whose slogans they adopted. The Confucian epigram: "Better a crystal, broken, than roof-tile, intact"—farewell shout to Yoshida by a fellow sufferer—expressed the exultation in their mission that inspired his pupils.

Passion for revenge plunged Ito into a period of bloody adventuring. Outwardly he carried on as assistant schoolmaster to Kido, studying also, diligently, under that accomplished scholar. Political frays and assassinations were an almost weekly occurrence these years, and Ito lent a ready hand, though he was seriously neglecting martial training. Kido's influence told from the start. Ito was to become chief advocate of that "philosopher-samurai's" unfulfilled policy of "progress by peace." At Kido's institution, in the great residency which Choshu like the other clans was obliged to maintain in the Shogun's capital, the young man was meeting all the personalities whose names were to go down as fathers of the new nation. They were anything but dignified "fathers." They varied from Alexander Hamiltons to Kit Carsons and Jesse Jameses. Many of them were *ronin*—"wave men"—free lance samurai, made by fate some cutthroats, some heroes, some both.

The bitterness of "patriots" increased as the embassies of Great Britain, Russia, France, and Holland, which had followed America in rapid succession in exacting treaties of diplomatic intercourse, arrived to establish themselves in exclusive Yedo. The lust for assassination did not spare foreigners and their retinues, and for a time, forgoing right of residence in the capital, they retired to Yokohama. Their presence and the continuing negotiations were constant irritation to the radicals. The Mito group, Spartacus fashion, planned to fortify itself in volcanic Mount Tsukuba back of Yedo, along with a Prince of the Blood, and issue a rallying call to the nation from there. Ito joined and escaped arrest merely because the Book of the Junta discovered by the police was on old copy made before he had signed on.

Lord Ii's head fell to partizans of Mito in 1860,

but a court council took up his work and a Lord Ando in charge of foreign affairs continued his policies. The proposal to obtain the Emperor's sister as a wife for the youthful Shogun was actively pressed. That would strengthen the Tokugawa at home. And the innovating tendency was stressed by the purchase of a steamer and the sending of it on the first voyage of modern Japan across the ocean—which proved a somewhat lugubrious beginning of one of the world's greatest merchant marines.

Between plots, Ito, in the spirit of his time, was engaged in convivial affairs in which he made a name for debonairly carrying respect-commanding quantities of *saké*. Also, he and his friend Inouye managed to get a slight start toward the knowledge of English which was to serve him so well.

Meanwhile Yamagata was sent south over the Inland Sea to Kiushu island, to seek liaison with the Lord of Satsuma, master of its southern region, most haughty and independent of Japan's feudal barons. Satsuma did not leap at Yamagata's proposal of alliance with its old rival across the strait, but he discovered that Satsuma was arming and drilling largely with the new modern arms and preparing a large contingent to go to Kyoto and assume paramount influence there in bringing Yedo to terms. His report aroused the Choshu patriots. They felt that if any clan deserved a lion's share in the campaign of supporting the Emperor and expelling foreigners, it was Choshu. Kido and Ito were ordered down to Kyoto to look after the Choshu interest at court and Yamagata was hurried this time north to Yedo to get the Lord of Yedo to authorize drastic action, lest Satsuma take the honor and the spoils. The Lord of Choshu was at the Shogun's capital in fulfillment of the obligation of every daimyo to spend half the time with his family, held as hostages in the clan residency at that place. Yamagata found his lord lukewarm, desirous of playing safe. Kido and Ito reaching Kyoto discovered that a high councilor of their clan was playing into the hands of the enemy by favoring the marriage alliance between the Imperial and Shogunate families. This nobleman, Nagai Uda, sincerely believed compromise to be the fairest remedy for animosity between the houses, and was unquestionably encouraged by the timid Lord of Choshu. But he drew upon himself the abhorrence of young patriots who chose to regard him a traitor to imperial interests.

Ito characteristically got up a party to assassinate him, but they were beaten off by the warned Nagai at the Fushimi gate of Kyoto. Here Yamagata stepped in, with action as different as it was equally characteristic.

Purifying himself with ceremonial washings, putting on the white kimono of the dead, and carrying only the short sword used for self-destruction, he went to Nagai's quarters and obtained audience.

"I challenge you on the honor of the samurai, either to abandon your scheme or commit *harakiri* here with me now," he quietly addressed the astonished knight, with a deep bow. The two men regarded one another with masklike faces for some moments.

"You may live," capitulated Nagai, lifting his cup of tea in sign of dismissal to the younger samurai. The affair had a pathetic aftermath—a miniature of the tragedy out of which grew the new Japan. Ito's patron, the beloved Kuruhara, who happened to be a nephew of Nagai, torn between family commitment and loyalty to the cause of his young friends and protégés, satisfied honor by the ceremonial suicide. Ito, for a second time, performed the last courtesies for a beloved dead master, cutting the warrior's knot from Kuruhara's head and carrying it to the bereft family. Feeling in the clan re-acted so strongly upon Nagai that he was imprisoned— with the consent of the opportunistic Lord who had used him—and a little later, when the patriotic party was supreme, he was "permitted" to commit *harakiri*.

Meanwhile plans went forward among one group for the marriage of the Shogun and among the other for the assassination of Ando. Choshu patriots were con-nected with the latter project through Kido and Ito, again in Yedo. Five Mito samurai in the ronin band that attacked Ando's cortège at the citadel gate were killed after only wounding him. A sixth had missed the party and came to Ito's school declaring that honor required him to die. Kido and Ito persuaded against it. He asked them to leave a moment while he wrote a letter, and when they returned, he had cut out his bowels, leaving them with a tell-tale corpse on their hands while official agents swarmed through the town. Ito ended a fruitless powwow by going to the door and boldly calling in the police. Nothing worse happened than that Choshu authorities were ordered to hold Kido and Ito under surveillance for a time.

Ando retired from public life, but to the chagrin of the radicals, the wedding was pompously celebrated that year. That year also came Lord Regent Shimadzu of Satsuma to Kyoto with a strong force, and with his support the initiative passed to the imperial court. He escorted a princely messenger to Yedo with "recommendations" that included installation of Keiki as Guardian at Yedo, and a visit of the Shogun himself to Kyoto. These measures, the latter a consideration for the Emperor unprecedented in two hundred years of Tokugawa rule, the court at Yedo was humbly fain to concede. Satsuma's projects were, however, too plainly aimed at harmony between the two courts to satisfy the continually augmenting host of free-lance ronin in their fanatical anti-foreignism and Imperial devotion. Ando and all his coadjutors were being disgraced, many assassinated, and those who had favored Keiki's nomination before were set at liberty. But when, in response to an imperial invitation that Kido had procured for him, the Lord of Choshu came down to Kyoto, he found himself in the hands of the pro-imperial party of his clan and the ultra-patriotic party rallied around him, rather than Satsuma.

Under Satsuma's pressure the Shogun's court made a fatal concession, abrogating in October, 1862, the old rule whereby the daimyos' families had always been kept at Yedo. The aristocracy, major and minor, began at once in great numbers to establish themselves at Kyoto, the Lord of Tosa among the first. So it came about that guiding spirits like Kido, Ito, Goto, Yamagata, and Saigo the younger (his older brother was now in exile for excess of zeal) were able to begin weaving the ties of the Sat-Cho-To, the union of the southernmost clans of each of the three main islands, which was to overthrow the old régime. Tosa was to be the mediator between the other two, naturally rivals. And fate decreed leadership to Ito in choosing the cause for Choshu which history was to vindicate.

Ito and Takasugi posted the ten days' journey to Yedo to bring home the body of Yoshida, whose crime and disgrace were now canceled. They buried it in Choshu, and Ito reported back to Kyoto, to be dispatched at once to investigate a rumor that the Hikone clan planned a coup to seize the Sacred Person and proclaim direct imperial rule. A tactful diplomat the young *samurai* proved (for in reward of patriotic zeal both he and Yamagata had just been promoted to full knighthood, authorizing use of surnames). He dissuaded Hikone from the rash project and lined up the clan with the general Restoration movement.

Returning to the clan house at Yedo, he joined some fellows in putting out of the way a confidant who was believed to be a government spy. His next exploit was participation in the murder of Jiro Hanawa, a learned scholar of the day, whose historical studies were giving comfort to the Tokugawa, and, most disgusting to patriots, supporting *lèse majesté* by throwing doubt on the continuity of the imperial line. Speaking of this exploit long after Ito said, "It was rather a miracle that I survived. I was quite in danger, for the clothes were blood spotted in which I had to pass government detectives. Had they noticed, I would have been questioned and condemned." "To do great deeds one must often be ready to risk his life," he was to counsel his son, shortly before finally going to death.

In spite of the imperial pressure to expel foreigners, the government was rapidly completing their legation quarters in Yedo. By the way of protest at the "impiety," Ito, Takasugi, and Inouye,[1] fellow clansmen all and pupils of Yoshida, organized an arson gang and burned down the British buildings. The American Legation met the same fate shortly, when Ito had gone.

The Britisher, Richardson, had fallen to Satsuma swords because he did not cringe at the roadside as their cohorts passed—which was to cost bankrupt Yedo and proud Satsuma very dear—but the final settlement was still future. Altogether the ronin chauvinists had

---

[1] Inouye was to hold almost as many offices of government as Ito and Yamagata, but usually as a faithful henchman of Ito rather than an independent mind. He started as "Inouye," became "Shido," and just before his foreign adventure with Ito was again adopted back into his own family. Their friendship was sealed long after by Ito adopting Inouye's son as heir in place of his own.

made Yedo of early 1863 intolerable to foreigners and they were retiring to Yokohama. Kido next entrusted Ito with getting the most radical "patriotic" clansmen of Mito out of Tokugawa territory to Kyoto, anticipating a possible appeal to arms. The time was drawing near when the Shogun must fulfill his commitment to confer with the Emperor, and his officers were establishing themselves in Kyoto. At last, accompanied by 3,000 instead of the 300,000 retainers which a former Shogun had led to Kyoto, seventeen-year-old Iemochi bowed before "the dragon face" April 21, 1863. He would have answered the "call of urgent affairs" and returned to his capital at once, but nothing would do at the Kyoto court but that a date should first be set for "purging barbarians from the Sacred Isles." He tried to leave with the issue pending but threat of assassination by Ito's patriotic gangfellows deterred him. The Emperor set the date as June 25, 1863. In vain Iemochi's chief officers went back to start arrangements, in vain he himself sought excuses to leave until just before that date—when an army and navy expedition from Yedo was on its way to bring him back by force.

Meanwhile Yamagata, "the Crane," was efficiently carrying out missions, though he lacked the sensational touches his younger friend Ito seemed so capable of supplying. His charge had to do with fortification of the coast of Choshu, at Shimonoseki strait especially, against the fateful 25th of June. Coming and going he had passed the door of the higher-bred, gay-kimonoed Tomoko, made her acquaintance despite the semi-seclusion of Japanese young ladies, and developed a very determined love affair. Through the usual middle-man he asked her hand. Her family objected because of his low rank, his "mad" name, Kiosuke, and the disconcerting "gang" he ran around with. He told them there was no hurry, but he would be back to get her, and went about his missions.

Yedo authority had long prohibited all subjects from going abroad—but of late had secretly sent its own men to learn the strength of the West. The patriots felt they must gain as much knowledge as their rivals. The necessity was most obvious when, having bought a steamer from Jardine, Matheson & Company in 1862, the Choshu clan had to hire "barbarians" to engineer and navigate.

Inouye got secret permission from the clan council for a group to go abroad, with the usual reservation that if caught, the clan would have to repudiate it. Ito, sent from Kyoto to Yedo in the spring of '63 with an order on the clan strong-box there for ten thousand gold pieces, illicitly to buy arms from the newly estab-lished British firms at Yokohama, met Inouye bound for Europe and was promptly enlisted in the party. The other lads were Yamao, afterward Viscount Endo, and Nomura.

They went to an official of the British Legation for suggestions. Their conferences were suspended a while

—pending a plot to attack this very legation again. It came to nothing and they went back to the unsuspecting Weigal who referred them to his brother, in Jardine, Matheson & Company employ at Yokohama. He advised that a round trip to London and a year's stay would require a thousand gold pieces each. They had from the clan treasury six hundred, for the four!

The impulsive Ito met strong temptation to abscond with the ten thousand in his charge. After all, he was going for the good of the clan, and the information he and his fellow young samurai would gain would be of immensely more value than a few guns. Perhaps fear of clan discipline rather than conscience kept him from yielding to the pressure of his eager fellows. But he worked out a good and characteristic compromise. He gave the order for munitions to a Yokohama merchant and then, with tacit aid of a sympathetic elder at the clan house, "held him up" for a five thousand *ryo* loan.

It was remitted direct to the Jardine-Matheson agent who put it in the form of an eight-thousand-dollar draft payable in London—leaving the party pretty short of ready cash. Their long swords had been left at a fellow clansman's tea house, where they donned a ridiculously fitted outfit of foreign garb—sailor togs obtained in Yokohama secondhand stores—and repaired in the dusk to the merchant's home where the captain was eating dinner. While awaiting his pleasure they got their samurai topknots cut off, and felt their bridges burned. But at first the captain sent word he would not run the risk of getting afoul of the customs officials by taking them. They firmly told the merchant that the alternative for them would be *harakiri* on the spot, as they could not escape capture now. Not liking to fancy his parlor used for that purpose he remonstrated with the captain to such effect that the old salt changed his mind. Then the runaways composed a lengthy letter to the clan authority, explaining their ideals, preparations, plans, and assuring their loyalty and gratitude. In the dark small hours of May 12, 1863, jabbering something which customs sentries on post were expected to take for a foreign language, the five followed the captain aboard a dirty steamer and hid while it got under way for Shanghai.

Their letter must have had scant attention among other matters claiming attention from the clan council. The Shogun was still at Kyoto, and hottest argument and darkest diplomacy were resorted to in the struggle between supporters and foes of the Tokugawa—to advantage largely of the foes, led by Choshu. The Lord Regent of Satsuma would have strengthened the other side more had he not felt obliged to keep his forces at home to meet impending British vengeance for the death of Richardson. Secret anti-foreign fulminations from extremists pretending to speak for the Emperor supplemented the proclamation through the regular channel of the Shogun after an audience on June 5, which set the 25th as date for sweeping away the barbarians. Transmitting this to foreigners in his territory

the Shogun's officials had added that no action would
be taken on it. But in Choshu, Takasugi and Yamagata had bent intense effort toward "up-to-date" fortification of the straits, following their meager Dutch
authorities. Not only had batteries been placed along
their own shore, but judging the Kokura clan territory
on the other side to be inadequately guarded they attacked and seized a point for fortification there. Had
there been a telegraph to carry recent news to Yokohama, Ito and his young bloods would have rushed to
join the scrimmage and would have been diverted from
the experience that was to prepare them to be saviors
of their clan and nation.[2]

The lads were "getting broken" to the outside world
in a manner to satisfy the sturdiest believer in rough
discipline. They stayed hid in the coal bunkers until
beyond Japanese territorial waters. Then came the
nasty Yellow Seas and *mal de mer*—endured for a week
till their vessel reached the Yangtze and crept up to
fetid Shanghai, just growing out of tide-flats to be
Pacific Asia's new trading capital. Their Yokohama
friend had a brother in the same employ at Shanghai
who, instructed by a letter brought by the captain, fer-
reted them out and demanded in his blunt British way
what sort of experience they were hunting. Inouye,

[2] Various Japanese historians and biographers have the firing on the
U. S. merchantman *Pembroke* taking place on May 10, while the boys
were waiting to steal out of Yokohama. It is probable that their reckoning is in old Chinese calendar which would bring the dates a month and
some days earlier than the modern calendar.

the proud Japanese, drew from his slight English the one word "navigation." He understood that meant "navy," which it was his chief intention to learn about abroad. "Keswick nodded to himself and put Inouye and me aboard a schooner, understanding we wanted to become sailors," recorded Ito in his journal.

We may suspect the merchant Keswick was indulging in a heavy and possibly remunerative practical joke in signing those two young knights as common sailors. Their three companions he placed aboard a larger and faster sailing vessel as passengers. Ito's naïve narrative runs thus:

Supposing we were guests, we were surprised at being commanded to work very hard as the sailors, handling sails and rigging. We were fed salt beef and biscuits and had to drink from a discarded tin. We appealed to the honorable captain, bowing low, but he would face us fiercely and say "Well, what's the matter? You'll have to talk to me in English!" Neither of us knew a word, and when we tried to speak to him in signs he would turn his back, until the quarter-master drove us again to work. The other sailors, who were dirtier than any men we had ever seen, used to treat us ill and call us "Janey," which we understood was their manner of speaking contemptuously of our people. They never took a bath! There was no privy for sailors but a plank projecting from the edge of the deck. We did not understand and were beaten for starting to use the officers'. I had bowel trouble and was obliged to sit on the plank quite often. Inouye, anxious lest I grow too weak to hold onto the railing, especially during the tossing of storms, used to tie my body with a rope, fastening the other end to a little post so I would not fall into the sea. The sailors would shout wickedly and make as if to cut the rope, and were pleased when Inouye would fight them off like mad.

These young noblemen of the most scrupulously cleanly and courteous nation on earth were subjected to four months and ten days of this before their ship, sailing around Africa with never a port of call, nosed finally into the Thames. They hailed sight of the land of their imagination as the end of contumely, hardship, and homesickness, and were willing to write off the experience as a valuable lesson in the school of life. Still they had to suffer a climactic indignity. The ship docked before breakfast, and all hands scattered, except the two Japanese, left to sit on deck, without food, and all hatches locked. They were left entirely in suspense until at mid-afternoon a clerk from Jardine & Matheson came with a cab and escorted them to a hotel on American Square where they found the three comrades so abruptly separated from them in Shanghai.

That such an introduction to the white man's world did not utterly embitter these young men, but that they soon became the sincerest friends of Westerners and champions of their civilization, and were able in after life to relate their humiliation with the greatest good humor, is testimony to the sportsmanship, as well as comprehension, of the Japanese nature.

Five Japanese boys in the strange world of London, forerunning the appearance not only of a new nation but a new continent in world affairs—one to become a

prince and the formulator of his country's relationships
with the world, two others to become marquises—are
disdainfully led to a tailor shop, a barber shop, and a
bathing house, and when their new clothing arrives, see
a British "slavey" contemptuously pick up their
discarded "heathen clothes"—filthy enough indeed—between thumb and a forefinger and stuff them into the
grate.

They called upon Mr. Matheson, the stolid Scotch
missionary turned founder of a trading company which
was to become one of the greatest agents of British
empire in Asia. He referred them to a Dr. Williamson,
university professor, who took Ito, Nomura, and Endo
into his own home and found places for the others.
According to their words, they "studied English very
hard." Occasionally university students introduced to
them by Dr. Williamson took them about the city. Of
all its sights the military drills on the parade grounds
most fascinated them. Witnessing modern tactics and
equipment, they all, but especially Ito, the swashbuckler, experienced a profound change of heart regarding "immediate expulsion of the barbarian from
the Sacred Land."

Shortly after they landed, reports had reached England by mail and cable from Ceylon of the use to which
Yamagata and his colleagues were putting the new batteries. On the appointed 25th of June (1863) the
Choshu "navy" had fired on the American merchantman *Pembroke,* which slipped its moorings and got

away with slight injury.[3]   Then a little later the Dutch *Medusa* had fought through the straits with loss of life and serious damage.   Other vessels shortly suffered, and there followed reports of vengeance taken by the American warship *Wyoming,* and by the French.

This had not, however, opened the straits.   The astounding progress of the boys in English was practically demonstrated when at the end of four months they were able to discover from the stilted English of *The Times'* dispatches pointed out to them by Dr. Williamson the exceedingly serious situation which confronted their clan.   It was the first news they had received from Japan and it was to the effect that Satsuma's capital, Kagoshima, had been bombarded off the map by British gunboats, and negotiations were going on between Great Britain, America, France, and Holland for a united reprisal upon Choshu, failing its drastic punishment by the Yedo government.

Ito and Inouye conceived it their duty to return home forthwith and convince their lord and his councilors of the necessity of making friends with foreigners before the clan should bring annihilation upon itself.   They courteously explained their purpose to Dr. Williamson and Mr. Matheson, but these men were unable to com-

---

[3] A writer in the "Britannica" says that the *Pembroke* was not hit. The Japanese official history states that the *"Pembroke* was taken unaware by sudden firing from two Choshu warcraft, the *Koshin Maru* and the *Kigai Maru,* and spontaneously from the forts, and she was obliged to escape in such a flurry that she did not have time to weigh anchor but left it breaking the chain.   Choshu discharged twelve shots in all, three out of which hit the ship, and one tore the rigging off the mast."

prehend their motive. The trading company head commented gruffly that boys of their age should not bother their heads about political affairs! The pair quietly insisted and finally Matheson, remarking, "It's a thin excuse to get away from studies," got them passage on a primitive steamer. They found themselves again stowed in the forecastle, but this time rebelled and transferred to a clipper which after a three months' sail with incidental desperate peril off Madagascar, put them off at Yokohama on the 10th of June, 1864.

The other three had wished to return also, but had been dissuaded by Ito and Inouye. However, the five had sworn in blood that if Ito and Inouye were killed by resentful clansmen, the others would follow and take up the cause.

The two young samurai had endured eight months of hardship in travel to get but five months of study; they had gone away militant anti-foreignists and now came back advocates of international intercourse and westernization. In them was presage and personification of the energy and adaptiveness of the Japanese mind that was to save Japan and amaze the modern world. They entered a situation most unfavorable to their propaganda. To have questioned their countrymen might have brought summary death, so they went direct to their friend Weigal, who greeted them with the information that they were now under double disability, as illicit foreign travelers and as members of a clan recently declared outlaw by both Shogun and Emperor! The previous autumn all Choshu men had been expelled from the guard in Kyoto for fear they were planning to take the Mikado into their own custody. Since then their Shimonoseki batteries had sunk without distinction a steamer belonging to the Shogun and another to Satsuma with much loss of life. Their fortifications were stronger than ever, and the contumacious clansmen had avowed that no foreign-built ship should pass. The Shogun had just come back from Kyoto with a decree giving him a free hand to punish both the rebels and the seven court nobles who, being involved in the alleged plot, had gone south in their protection. And if the ability of the Shogun to punish were in doubt, the result of Choshu was not, because the British representative, Sir Rutherford Alcock, was head of the accord among the Powers which promised effective action in any case.

While fearfully awaiting an opening to be of service, the returned exiles had to bear the effect of racial arrogance—from the reverse side—for disguised as Portuguese they put up at a hotel for foreign seamen, where Ito was called "Deponar." The two young samurai, licensed to slash at any commoner who might obstruct their way, had to listen while hotel boys made speeches to them for one another's benefit in supposedly non-understood Japanese: "You look like real Japanese and intelligent people, but, poor fish, you are nothing but the lowest kind of barbarians!" They asked by signs for a mosquito net to protect them from the onslaught of the tiny, vicious Japanese man-eaters, and heard: "A mosquito net for dogs of red-heads! [—the comprehensive term for whites.] Rather extravagant of them, eh? Give them one with a hole in it."

The twenty-day ultimatum of June 30 on opening the straits was about to expire, when Ito and Inouye, with authority from neither side but the divine presumption of youth, plunged in to mediate. They promised the Legation official that they would be able to procure reparation and a change of policy from the Lord of Choshu if he could hold back the attack until they could get to him. Weigal took them to Ernest Satow, gifted young student-interpreter of the Legation. Ito's eager, desperate bluff touched him. From that moment Ito and the West's first sympathetic, profound student of Japan were friends—which was to mean much for the new nation in its moment of travail.

Sir Rutherford Alcock was persuaded to see them, and they left their lodgings for the Legation in the night to avoid the Shogun's spies. The British dignitary, already "sick to death of Oriental trickery, futility, and dissimulation," and convinced that "one gunboat is worth ten treaties," as he had written his Foreign Office, received them cynically: "So you wish to hold up the naval action of four Powers while you go to persuade your lord, who has refused to listen to us and to his own government, to repent! And what will you do if he is unimpressed?"

Ito looked him in the eye. "Your Excellency, our

lord has not had the right conception of your nation, and it is not entirely his fault. We believe he will listen to us. If he does not, we will ask to be placed in the front rank of our lord's army, to fight you until we are killed."

The Minister stroked his mustache. "Hm! Spirited! —How long will it take you to get to Choshu?"

"We must go the far inland route through the mountains to avoid capture by Tokugawa spies. We ask you to hold up the attack thirty days."

"Too long," grunted Sir Rutherford. "We'll send you around in a warship."

There accompanied the suddenly bloomed young diplomats their new friend, the interpreter Satow, a French naval officer and a Dutch, and they bore a letter in Japanese direct from Sir Rutherford to the Lord of Choshu:

The hostile attitude of your lordship is intolerable. Firing on the flags of treaty countries is altogether against international law, and compels the allied Powers to deal with your lordship as an enemy. If your lordship upon more accurate information regarding the wealth, power and policies of the Powers should open his ports for trade he will bring good out of evil. We learn your lordship has sent several capable and promising young subjects abroad to study foreign civilization and two of them have returned. In compliance with their wishes to reach Choshu in shortest possible time, we have given them transport on one of Her Majesty's warships. Let this be proof that Her Majesty the Queen of England has no inimical feelings against your lordship and only desires peaceful relations. Through these two men who have been in

England and are your lordship's most faithful subjects, we warn your lordship before disaster comes through ignorance and misinformation.

The letter was hardly a help to Ito and Inouye, leaving as it did large opportunity for the accusation from rivals and conservatives whose suspicions they had already incurred by visiting Europe, that they had been bought or sentimentally influenced by the barbarians. The fact that the naval officials, true to tradition in making use of everything that came their way, took advantage to reconnoiter along the way in the straits, increased their danger and diminished the chance of success.

Ito persuaded the captain at least not to compromise them by landing them direct on Choshu soil, so they were put off on an island near the opposite shore. They were to meet the ship in twelve days at another island with satisfactory apologies and pledges from their lord —failing which the Allied fleet would come into action.

The two negotiators disembarked in foreign clothes, but the islanders mistrusted they were foreigners and they had to return to the ship and search out some nondescript kimonos and try again. By dint of high argument they got a dubious fishing-sampan master to take them again, and the sun was still young when their friends on the war vessel saw their open boat heading northward. Chances were six or seven in ten, remarked Satow's Japanese tutor, that their heads would fall. The beach was being patrolled by a mob in high excitement, for the foreign ships had been reported. But they managed to reach the local magistrate. They saw even children and women armed, the latter in special dress and carrying formidable bamboo lances to attack barbarians. They won the magistrate after some difficulty and got from him samurai skirts and swords for their journey. They hoped if any one noted the abscence of their warrior topknots, to be taken for physicians, but got through without being stopped, and found their lord had come inland to the stronghold of Yamaguchi. Also they found that a large expedition of his army had left or was about to leave under leadership of the clan councilors to "remonstrate" with the forces in control at Kyoto, since "tearful prayers" had not availed to get Choshu back into favor. Nothing is said of their meeting Yamagata at this time, and doubtless he was at "the front."

They announced their return to their lord, placed themselves under his protection, and asked for an audience to report "conditions in the barbarian countries with which we are in conflict." Their appearance was a sensation. All the leading samurai who could come were there the appointed day, about the last of July, 1864, when these two youths from their few months' experience gave first a lecture on geography illustrated with a gourd globe and a pen-drawn map, then a talk on Western contemporary culture, and a third on international relations and law, and a fourth on the contemporary crisis in Japan, with an impassioned peroration recommending friendly relations with the West and concentration of energy on the restoration of the Imperial House to direct rule over a united nation. It was the true founding speech of new Japan—an expression of the spirit of Yoshida Shoin, enlightened with a cosmopolitanism that his straitened horizon denied him opportunity to acquire.

The lord was impressed. He summoned them back several times. True to form he vacillated between their wisdom and the foolishness of his "wise men." The boys were right, he confessed, but the clansmen were too aroused against the foreigner by now to be restrained. The truth was, he was more willing to have his subjects of Bakan blown to pieces than to risk deposition by his conservative retainers. It was a nuisance having these young men around to stir his qualms. Their lives were under constant threat and he did not want to be bothered with responsibility for protecting them. So he sent word commending them for loyalty in coming all the way from the barbarian's land to report, and offering to send them immediately back to continue their investigations. Their reply deserves a place in the heroölogy of the new nation.

Our forefathers have been subjects of the Mori daimyo for generations. Samurai do not take into account their lives. We comprehend that the decision of his lordship and his councillors is to fight the foreigners even at a cost of destruction of the clan. This is greater bravery than we had comprehended and we can only humbly beg for a share in it. We

[147]

can hardly study while our clan perishes. When we considered returning home, we expected to be threatened with mobbing or assassination. If killing us will free the spirits of our clansmen, then do away with us. If, however, his lordship sees reason in our suggestion for saving the clan, we suggest he dismiss those officials who oppose it.

Their bravery was put to the test. A bully named Nakaoka called at the house where they stopped and asked for the two "vile foreigners." Their host said only Japanese were in the house. "Ito and Inouye—they are no Japanese!" he exclaimed, and pushed up the stairs, finding them quietly squatting on the mats drinking rice-wine with some friends.

"Do you fellows know what '*Yamato damashii*' [4] is?" he demanded.

Inouye's tendency to sarcasm overcame him, even in face of this insane rage. Punning the words, he replied, "*Yamato damashii*—a fruit, I believe—or is it a vegetable?"

"Know nothing of it, eh? Here it is—can you see?" and the bully, red-eyed, thrust a dagger in Inouye's face.

"Ha, ha! that's your *Yamato damashii?*" was the cool reply. "I have a bigger one," pulling out his sword. "Let's compare them outside—the inside of a room is no place!" The other men intervened and the affair ended by Nakaoka drinking saké quietly and departing.

The clan council was in a terrible quandary. The

4 Yamato (old Japan) "second to none."—The "Japanese spirit."

"ins," that is, the group having the lord's confidence at the time, were the radical loyalists. The "outs" were the "conservatives" willing for matters to jog along under the Shogun's leadership. Now came Ito and Inouye, disciples of Kido who was then in Kyoto, and known as convinced loyalists—and yet unlike the rest they were advocating conciliation toward foreigners. They were juniors, yet spoke with conviction, and many, including their lord and Sanjo, one of the loyalists of the Kyoto peerage who had fled to Choshu the year before, were more than half convinced they were right. But they belonged to no party yet—were neither "fish, flesh, nor fowl," and the idea that they should take over the clan government was too preposterous. However, they might serve as "good red herring" to distract the attention of their "friends" the foreigners, and as such the party in power determined to make use of them.

Accordingly more troops were shipped to Osaka for the demonstration before Kyoto, and leading counselors went along, commissioned to restrain the ardor of those already there. If these could succeed in combination with the strong radical party still in Kyoto, then Choshu would soon be leading all Japan against the world and in the Emperor's name. In the meanwhile, Ito and Inouye were charged with a message to their foreign friends explaining that the closing of the straits and the firing on foreign ships had been in obedience to many imperial mandates, and that therefore His

Majesty would need to be consulted regarding the proposed settlement. "Would the Allies allow three months for laying the matter before the August Presence?"

The more blunt Inouye objected to carrying such a message on ground that it was childish and would certainly fail to convince the commanders. But Ito persuaded him that it was the best they could do within the time limit toward saving the clan from destruction, and that they ought therefore not to refuse.

Rushing to the coast under escort, they made the battleship on the eve of the last day of grace. Aboard, all was activity, as she was about to weigh anchor and head for Yokohama on the assumption that the two young negotiators had lost their nerve, or been killed. Satow, returning from a reconnoitering trip in another boat, against which the first shot of the war had been fired as a warning down near the narrows, hailed his friends gladly and treated them to dinner and champagne. Then came time for formal report on the success of their efforts, and they repeated what they had been told to say. Thereupon they were asked for the official letter from their lord. Ito volunteered to go back for one, but the British commander dismissed them with: "I am sorry but we will have to bid you good-by and meet you again with cannon." However, Satow informally advised them to have an official letter covering their representations, together with copies of the mentioned mandates from Kyoto and Yedo regarding expulsion of foreigners, conveyed direct to the legations in Yokohama. He and other shrewd Britishers were trying to get to the bottom of the three-cornered struggle between Emperor, Shogun, and clans, in which the puzzled foreigners were made scapegoats.

The young men, feeling they had failed in the mission they came from England to perform, and with a dread of great disaster to their clan and country in their hearts, returned and reported to their lord. They found him more exercised over growing tenseness at Kyoto than at the danger from the coast. Against their pleading he sent his heir to court with the message "Choshu will protect the Emperor from the foreign barbarian." At the same time Lord Mori suggested that if the Allied fleet actually did appear, Ito and Inouye meet it and endeavor to stave off attack. The young men knew "barbarian" psychology too well to agree to do this. It was then suggested that they go direct to Yokohama and try to delay things through the Ministers there. Inouye was "fed up" by this time and insisted that he would stay home, fight the foreigners, and die; but Ito would let no possibility of saving the situation, however slight and face-losing, escape. When they parted, Inouye, as the last thing he could do for his beloved comrade, wrote to a wealthy friend in Yedo to supply Ito with plenty of money in jail, for his apprehension by the Tokugawa seemed certain.

Ito started by way of Kyoto to see Kido and do

what he could to insure caution in precipitating trouble there. A radical change had come over him since he had hid in the coal bunkers going out of Yedo bay. No more the swashbuckler, he was possessed by an undiscourageable sense of responsibility which was to save his nation untold difficulties and make him the most indispensable personality of the transition period. He was still the adventurer, of course. Who but a youth of that breed would have the self-confidence, the presumption, and the will to set himself up as plenipotentiary for his nation and proceed to act, although outlawed by his government, discountenanced by his clan, and suspected or smiled at by his clients, the foreigners?

Halfway to Kyoto he met a Choshu force returning, defeated. The Shogun's party had won in Kyoto, and Choshu's conciliatory blandishments to the Emperor had been met with threat of punishment for attempting to intimidate the court. Then the southern samurai had appealed to arms—to be defeated after a frightful affray that raged around the palace and in which the streets of the city were strewn with corpses and a large part of it burned.

It was impossible now for Ito to reach Yedo, and he returned to Yamaguchi to find Inouye shamelessly preaching jingoism. When Ito got his old comrade by himself and asked for an explanation, Inouye answered sardonically that since the pigs insisted on going to slaughter, there might as well be some éclat about it.

Ito reprovingly convinced him that this was no way to carry out the spirit of their London agreement.

Rumors of the approach of eighteen "lightning ships" threw the populace into panic. The warriors on coast duty under Yamagata and other officers remained steady enough, but the jingoes in the lord's castle began to weaken in their knees. They saw themselves now far indeed from being leaders of Japan. Inouye and Ito convened a "scrub" council which belatedly decided on peace. Young Ito undertook the wild enterprise of intercepting the fleet. He hired a fishing boat and with a comrade pushed out into the Inland Sea. The gunboats steamed past his tiny craft without notice. Inouye had better luck. He got aboard the flagship with a petty official, just before the fleet assumed its battle formation, but was told the time for negotiations had passed. Back on shore Ito had come upon his old fellow-filibusterer, Takasugi, now commander of a force that he had modeled on foreign lines—specially hired commoners, not samurai—and trained with rifles, which no samurai would carry. They took sedan chairs for Bakan, toward which the fleet was steaming, presently meeting Inouye who was hurrying back to Yamaguchi to urge the Daimyo to come personally and inspirit the defense. The three "pals" joined in the mission.

Halfway on their hasty journey they heard the opening of the cannonade between two hundred and seventy-odd guns on the allied side (just one American) and the seventy or so of inferior range that Choshu had been able to mount.⁵ Yamagata's little fort on the south side was the first to be wrecked (September 5, 1864) and he took to a boat. The next day a shot went through his knapsack, grazing his arm as he was lifting it to drink. He soon saw the hopelessness of the enterprise and declared the necessity of a different policy toward foreigners. Two days of fighting them wrought the same drastic mental shift in him as a few months of observation in London had in Ito.

Ito, Inouye, and Takasugi had found their lord preferred to remain where he was. He did, by way of endorsement, give them his personal firearms to use, and they hastened back. When they appeared, the officers in command on the coast, decidedly awed by the allied shellfire, had decided to take matters into their own hands and sue for peace, ignoring the Daimyo and his council. The three young samurai were at once commissioned to negotiate: Takasugi, because of his higher rank, as "envoy," and Ito and Inouye as "interpreters." (Total period of English study, five months each!) As they were seeking means of getting out to the at-

⁵ The Japanese Official History states that the bombardment was started from a fort built by Choshu on a little island. Satow publishes a chart of the scene showing no island, and says the fleet opened the bombardment. Satow probably overlooked the little island of Hikojima, outside Shimonoseki Strait, facing the Japan Sea between the Kokura and Choshu promontories. The two forts of Deshimachi and Yamatoko on this island stood to the last against the Allied fleet and only when they were subdued did the Choshu force assent to armistice. As to who fired first, we may gallantly allow that "distinction" to the Japanese, since they received the worst of the action. As in the controversy over whether the *Pembroke* was hit or not, Japanese *amour propre* may have something to do with the records.

tacking fleet, one of the clan councilors intercepted
them and engaged Takasugi in hot dispute over his
authority to act. Ito, disgusted, left them arguing and
climbed a hill to observe activities. Landing parties
were ashore, wrecking what was left of the batteries,
and compelling the defending troops to retire by
superior mastery of rifle fire. A few houses at one end
of the town had been burned, and Ito remembered how
the inflammable wood and paper houses of Satsuma's
capital had been destroyed by incendiary missiles from
the British the autumn before, and the suspense became too much for him. He would proceed alone! All
night he searched for a means.

By next morning (September 8) he had succeeded,
through combined bribery and intimidation, in getting
a fisherman to sail him out to the largest gunboat of
the fleet. The amused gunners let him approach. He
asked for the flagship and was directed to the British
Euryalus. His friend Satow, coming back from an ex-
cursion to see the dismantling of some forts, found him
there at noon.

"Oh, Mr. Ito, are you tired of the battle?" was his
greeting.

"Yes, that is why I am here—to negotiate peace,"
the self-ordained diplomat replied.

So he was taken before the captain, at the moment
having a bullet wound dressed. "See what you devils
have done," was his not very cordial welcome. But
Ito persuaded the captain to signal the arrival of an

envoy of truce, and the British *Kupfer* and the French *Jaures* were soon on their way, as also a boat to bring off shore the accredited ministers whom Ito had announced.

Boarding the ship, the British Admiral looked skeptically at Ito and asked if he were to consider one lone young soldier a peace delegation. Evidently Takasugi had lost his argument, for the returning ship's boat brought three hereditary councilors of the clan. All their written messages dated from before the battle, so the Admirals laid down terms and gave them forty-eight hours to secure acceptance. Ito had no rank or gorgeous raiment, but Satow remarked how the dignitaries had learned from events to give great weight to his counsel. It was only the ordinary Japanese way in those times for "great names" to take the honors while lesser functionaries from the Shogun down planned and executed what had to be done. Ito also turned over certified copies of the orders which had gotten Choshu into trouble.

The guns were stilled on the coast, but serious trouble was not far away at Yamaguchi, where the "Oust-Foreigners" men were desperately struggling to survive the discredit of their policy. When Ito and Takasugi got up there, friends told them some older clansmen had sworn to kill them if they tried to see the Daimyo. They were forced to hide in a farmhouse, while their enemies undertook to negotiate—but soon proved unable to propose anything practicable. Finally, Yamagata, distinguished in the fighting, and who, though of the younger group, was beyond accusation of being barbarophile, went in his quiet, determined way before the lord and convinced him. Then he went to his schoolmates' hiding place and escorted them to the Daimyo's presence. A fully accredited delegation in which Ito had a part was made up on the spot, and went forth to accept the peace terms offered.

Peace was sealed by the exchange of presents. The British Admiral sent a silver vase to the Daimyo and gave a pistol to Ito in recognition of his services as "interpreter." Some of the negotiators, with Ito still in this capacity, were taken up for a visit to the foreign authorities in the shelter of their settlement at Yokohama, which was a surprisingly pleasant occasion for the recently "Oust-Foreigner" enthusiasts. The peace terms had included stipulation of "ransom" for the town of Bakan because some shots had reached the allied forces from there as well as from the forts. Ito began feeling out Sir Rutherford's idea on the amount, as his instructions had been primarily to minimize any penalty upon his lord's treasure chest. Imagine his surprise when Sir Rutherford waved this aside, saying, "The Shogun has attended to that for you." The Yedo government, in a last effort to preserve "face" before the Powers, and also, doubtless, desirous of avoiding the opening of a rival port to Nagasaki which was the alternative offered, with its possibility of enriching a rebellious region and giving foreigners territorial foothold in Japan, had taken over responsibility for the three million dollars. Maybe it hoped to collect them from Choshu—but before the ten years granted for payment were up, it had passed out of existence.

The delegation went back safely in a British warship. Ten pieces of silver was Ito's recognition from Lord Mori for saving the clan!

Hearing that his friend Inouye had been wounded by an assassin, Ito hastened to Yamaguchi to see him. This deed brought on the appeal to arms between the two parties in the clan. The conservatives got their men in as councilors, and arrested those who had ordered the expedition to Kyoto. Takasugi escaped and his band scattered. Then Saigo of Satsuma came down to suggest terms that could be made before the Shogun's approaching army should arrive. The terms were hard, including *harakiri* for the arrested councilors, but were accepted to save the clan, and the oncoming army was disbanded on January 30, 1865.

Against this capitulation, the hitherto deliberate Yamagata declared himself in an indignant memorial to the Daimyo. There was no reply. The feudal lord had allowed himself to be shut away in a temple by his councilors. While heads of his former colleagues were falling in the blood pit, Yamagata, disguised as a tonsured priest, attempted to see his lord. He reached the apartment, only to be told that his lordship was "busy" and his heir "in bed." This decided him, and he began rallying men who had fought under him at the straits of Bakan.

Conscious of their weakness in loyal support, the councilors called on another clan, to help restrain their own men. This "traitorous" action cost them such respect as was theirs. Yamagata nevertheless had a rough winter of it. The common people, frightened by their clan officials, refused his men shelter and supplies. They were compelled to quarter in temples and live on temple offerings and saké, and on many nights to pillow their heads on the images. The force was finally reduced to three hundred and seventy-five veterans, whom Yamagata clothed in coat and trousers and drilled and armed as near as he could in European style. It was the most effective of early attempts at modern military organization in Japan, from which was to grow one of the world's greatest armies. Like Takasugi, Yamagata confidently recruited common people. These peasants, fishermen, and merchants were to whip in battle the samurai who scorned them. Loving his country more than his caste, and driven by necessity, Yamagata was sounding the death knell of his caste. It would yet be counted great honor to have been of the now sneered at *kihetai* or "Strange Troops" as these forces were called. They were the first of a new military aristocracy.

Ito had gone down to the port of Bakan (now Shiminoseki, just inside the straits) to recruit a little force, and Takasugi only a few miles away was in touch with his veterans. Ito, who always took more interest in scheming than in actual soldiering, and wanted to be free for any opportunity, merged his force in Takasugi's.

Yet another kind of romance involved him about this time. He was hiding in an inn from pursuing assassins, and a maid of about fifteen named Umeko Kida managed to conceal him beneath the floor of her chamber. Armed searchers came in, questioned and coquetted with her, but she sat with innocent face over his head. She not only saved a future prince of Japan, but became a future princess when next year (1866) during a lull in the turmoil, she became his wife, to be the faithful companion of all his succeeding years.

Yamagata's Kihetai were getting the worst of it in the latter part of January, 1865. The ill-informed commander for the Shogun, regarding opposition as doomed, was disbanding his army when Takasugi took the field. The tide turned. Hagi fell to the rebels and presently the council had to sue for peace.

Yamagata's victory determined death or hiding for the conservative faction and the clan embarked on a new policy, dictated by younger men, of whom Kido was counted first, with Yamagata, Ito, Takasugi, and Inouye. Their program was to fight it out with the Tokugawa, and prepare by building and purchase of warships, collecting munitions, and creation of Western-style militia and police. The clan income, equivalent to around five million dollars a year, was no mean

backing for the project, nor were the forces Yamagata succeeded in recruiting, numbering about forty
thousand. On the other hand, the nearly bankrupt
court of Yedo was straining every nerve to overmatch
these preparations and keep the sympathy of other
clans.

Realizing that his unique position in the clan depended upon knowledge of the West, and having accomplished, as he felt, what he had come home for,
Ito planned to return to London, taking Takasugi with
him. Inouye—most able in the money-raising line—
secured the appropriation. They went to Nagasaki to
get help from Ito's British merchant friend, who had
removed to the southern port from Yokohama. This
man advised that they await the arrival of the new
British Minister and endeavor to win him to sympathy
with the Restoration.

Sir Rutherford had been recalled from an unpleasant
post to explain his initiative in the Choshu expedition
and be promoted. In July, 1865, came energetic Sir
Harry Parkes. As an orphan lad he had joined rela-
tives in Macao, had started in the consular service at
fifteen, made a name in the capture of Canton and as
ruler during its foreign occupation, and later as climax
of adventures had been tortured at Peking while the
Anglo-French forces approached. Now at thirty-seven
he was transferred to Japan as Minister. The young
men returned to Bakan to propose to their party the
opening of that port to trade, as a bid for the new

British Minister's favor. Their counsels leaked out, and again they were pursued from clan territory by assailants. The ever-influential Kido arrived from Kyoto to take control of the situation, and they returned under his guaranty of protection.

In Sir Harry's first months in Japan he got the Shogun's treaties accepted by the Mikado, and began collection of the Bakan ransom from the sorely worried court of Yedo. These diversions allowed time for new developments in the South. Certain leaders like Saigo of Satsuma and Kido of Choshu had long secretly harbored the project of allying the two clans, but each had been afraid to make first offer, anticipating rebuff from the rival clan. Now men of Tosa, a clan sea-protected yet near the capitals, intervened in the cause of imperial loyalty and got them together. The scholarly swordsman Ryuma Sakamoto formulated the secret agreement early in 1866 whereby both clans were to coöperate for the common end: Satsuma to endeavor to get Choshu restored to favor, and Choshu to buy British arms through Satsuma—for the Shogun controlled open ports strictly and outlawed Choshu could not buy direct.

In accord with this understanding Ito and Inouye went down to Nagasaki to get seven thousand rifles and a small steamer at rather outrageous prices. Having completed this mission, the two went on to Kagoshima in hope of interviewing Sir Harry, who was expected on a visit that summer. Finding they had

[162]

a month to spare they utilized it for reporting back to headquarters.

When Ito and Sir Harry finally met, both young, both adventurers, they became friends at once. An alliance to continue many a year was formed—one that enhanced the reputation of Englishman and Japanese equally. The former is credited with "discovery" of the Emperor of Japan, and the latter's intimacy with Parkes was to make him a name in the first Secretariat for Foreign Affairs of the Empire. Through association with the young leader of the Restoration, Parkes was able to complete that training of Japanese officialdom in world outlook and diplomatic procedure which the patient, studious, and dignified American diplomat, Townsend Harris, had begun in the fifties. Britain and the southern clans had been foes but shortly before, but war once over, the spirit of chivalry came in to insure to Sir Harry a good welcome in Kagoshima, and he cultivated the favor of the Restoration party the more whole-heartedly because the French Minister was backing the Shogun.

All this intriguing aroused the Tokugawa to action. Ito's visit with Parkes was cut short by news that four government forces were converging upon Choshu. On way to battle he was thrown from his mount and injured. When he recovered he was kept busy with liaison and supply work. Never again was he to engage in actual combat. Fate had turned the career of the swashbuckler into peaceful channels. The calm

Yamagata's life was as definitely set the other way.

Yamagata, Takasugi, and Inouye were in the field. Their eighteen months' preparation more than enabled Choshu to hold its own. The government's most telling work against the rebel clan was in raids upon Choshu harbors and fishing fleets by four gunboats operating from a base in Kokura territory on the Kiushu side of the Inland Sea. Choshu had no ships large enough to engage them, but made a landing across the straits. Yamagata showed his resourcefulness, commanding an army of Kihetai that embarked in fishing boats by night and led a successful storming of the enemy's naval base. The Tokugawas' Kokura allies proposed peace and Commander Ogasawara withdrew the Shogunate forces to the main island, virtually ending operations. Meanwhile high events had occurred which were soon formally to end the campaign. The Shogun died. The decks were further cleared when he was followed to the "Yellow Springs" by the anti-foreign Emperor Komei early in 1867. Keiki, the loyalists' former candidate, succeeded as Shogun, and was glad to stop the war in the South under pretext of the mourning ceremonies, disbanding his armies to show sincerity. The Imperial Throne meanwhile was taken by a child of great promise, Mustuhito, who came under direction of nobles whom Kido had to some extent educated in national and world viewpoints.

The time seemed ripe for a definite stroke for the Restoration. Shogun Keiki was begging the Throne to withdraw opposition to the opening of the new port near Osaka and not far from the Emperor's capital, Kyoto, which he had agreed to in his treaties. Okuro of Satsuma and the other loyalists plotted that if the port were to be opened, the Shogun should not do it. They maneuvered to get other clans besides the "Sat-Cho-To" combination into sympathy with their objects, and the occasion of the coronation made it the easier to get clan heads into counsel at Kyoto. The measure adopted was to persuade the Daimyo of Tosa, very friendly to the Tokugawa by tradition, to suggest resignation to Keiki as a way either of proving his strength, or at the worst, making an honorable exit from his difficulties. Choshu, officially in disfavor, was unrepresented at Kyoto. But Ito was there, quietly observing, by order of his lord, and Yamagata obtained audience with the Satsuma Regent through an ac-quaintance of his early visits to Kiushu, Saigo the Lesser, brother of the older Saigo, and equally a loyalist. After hearing Yamagata's views, the Regent of Sat-suma, a very different type from Mori of Choshu, cryp-tically told the young soldier to return, organize his clan, and await a message through Saigo.

Yamagata found time to get his girl, Komuko, before events were precipitated. His memorial had convinced her parents he could *write* as well as fight—which brought their assent. Ito went down to Nagasaki again, arranging for British steamers to transport troops in the projected war against the Tokugawa. After helping assemble a large force from three clans at Hiogo, near Osaka, he tried to take an officer's command, but Kido told him he was needed for the more important commissions of peace. He returned to Choshu bringing an American, whom he installed as first foreign teacher and adviser in the clan. He had gone a long way in the five years since his attempts to burn out and assassinate all "barbarians." Foreign *sensei*, from Chamberlain to Hearn, were to play a large part in bringing Japan into equality in the world's race— a part in many cases eventuating tragically, for their work was to make themselves unnecessary.

Keiki's leading minister was assassinated, and the letter which Yodo of Tosa had innocently written recommending resignation got past the outer chancelleries into his hands, in the autumn of 1867. He went one better on the idea and called representatives of about forty clans to sign in token of approval a petition asking relief for him and his house from all responsibility for national administration, suggesting that function be "taken back" to the Emperor's immediate care, with coöperation of *all* clans—a slap at the self-assumption of the southern group. Satsuma, Tosa, and Aki headed the list of signers with rude but significant promptness. The day after receipt, November 10th, the petition was imperially granted. A few days later, Keiki, seeing that he had lost, sent in his resignation as Shogun. He was forestalled by an edict taking back all administration into the imperial court.

His friend, the Lord of Tosa, had not intended this, and still less that more would be required. But the southern conspirators feared that as long as the Tokugawa were first in land and wealth they would be first in power, so after a council at Yamaguchi their forces moved north. The younger bloods were forcing their lord's hands; the "samurai spirit" was too highly excited to stop before it could wave a bloody sword over its prostrate foe.

The third of January, 1868, saw another coup at Kyoto. All unexpectedly Keiki's Aidzu guardsmen found substitutes at their posts ahead of them, and fortified by an imperial decree. To avoid bloodshed if possible, Keiki retired to Osaka and told representatives of the Powers he would rely on moral suasion against the hard terms being dictated from Kyoto. Then news came down from Yedo that Satsumas had started trouble there and his followers had taken up arms and burned the Satsuma residences in retaliation. Reluctantly he was persuaded by retainers that war had come, and that they could easily overpower the forces guarding Kyoto (which they far outnumbered) and remove the Emperor's "evil counselors."

They were too sanguine, for Yamagata and other officers of the Sat-Cho forces had their contingents set to advantage along the narrow roads, and chose emplacements for their field artillery in a way to more than make up for smaller numbers. Prince Ninnaji's name was used as commander, and prominent in the staff was Iwakura, a court noble who had led in the loyalist coup.

A little shrine, the "Four Saints Hall" was long after to be raised by Ito to Iwakura (the others being Kido of Choshu, Okubo of Satsuma, and another court noble, Sanjo), in appreciation of their part. No soldier, Iwakura, but not the type to be expected among nobles of a court that had been kept century after century in poetry-writing, incense-smelling desuetude. His doughty spirit showed when he silenced dogged protestation of the Daimyo of Toso against harshness to the Tokugawa by apprising him that "next time" he would invite him to "step outside" and they'd settle it with swords.

Through Iwakura, Yamagata got approval of the policy of using the Imperial Chrysanthemum on the battle standards. It gave unity to his side and a touch of mystic fervor. Fighting against the "Sacred Person's" emblem was too much against the grain for some of Keiki's army, and one flank gave way, surrendering secretly at night, bringing defeat to the rest.

Sending a circular to the foreign ministers to say he could no longer protect them, the Shogun quickly made off to Yedo in one of his warships, while all his officials around Osaka scattered. Some of the imperialist troops converged on Osaka while the main campaign swept northward, not to end until more than a year later, upon capture of the last Tokugawa adherents in the north island. Yamagata, chief of staff under the elder Saigo, field commander, distinguished himself for careful actions, not only victories, but definite strokes toward end of the conflict. In a few cases there was inexcusable barbarity, as the slaughter almost to a man of the faithful Aidzu samurai and the prompt self-immolation of their Spartan mothers and wives, who in many cases killed the children first.

The closing tragedy of the Shogunate was to provide Ito a chance for the bold strokes that "made" him. The situation was doubly dangerous because of the position of the foreigners. The group now in power was declaredly anti-foreign, restrained only by a few young men with their eyes open, such as Ito.

Apparently unaware of the change in administration and oblivious of danger due both to the fighting and their unprotected status, the entire diplomatic corps and a large number of foreign merchants and missionaries came from Tokyo to Osaka by sea to celebrate the opening of the first port of the Inland Sea to foreign trade, which function had been previously set by the Shogun for January 1, 1868. The foreigners had just arrived when the Tokugawa, crushed at the battle of Fushimi, fled toward Osaka with the imperial army in hot pursuit.

The mob and assorted factions of soldiery held Osaka. The Shogun's great palace in the citadel was burned. A party of French killed a few in a crowd that set upon them. Their legation and the Dutch were burned. Although Satsuma and Shoshu leaders might incline to

friendliness, with the soldiers and rabble the end of
Tokugawa rule meant withdrawal of protection from
the barbarian. Diplomats and accompanying friends
took small boats or waded through the sticky rice fields
eighteen miles eastward to Hiogo, in hope of finding
protection in this fishing village designated as the new
open port. The magistrates there had fled. Two attendants of the French Minister almost precipitated
tragedy by dodging through a marching line of con-
temptuous Bizen clansmen, drawing pistols when
roughly reprimanded, and fleeing under fire. The
offended samurai shot at every house in which foreigners were putting up. The soldiers and civilians, led
by American marines, promptly launched in pursuit and
chased the surprised Japanese out of sight. The
Westerners stopped traffic on the great highway, sent
word they were ready to make this a case against all
Japan, in default of proper amends, and then raised bar-
ricades, set cannon, and seized the native shipping in
the harbor. The enraged samurai and populace went
out to stir up the entire imperial army and the nation
to make a complete sweep of barbarians. There was
the possibility of the imperial régime being ushered in
with an incident that would have set the whole world
to destroy it.

It was, of course, Ito's quick wit and audacity that
saved the situation. Through Endo, his friend of the
London adventure now studying under Mr. Satow, he
learned that it was the expected thing for the heads of

new régimes to apprise diplomatic corps formally of the change and renew assurances of protection and treaty-faith, and that this must come in the name of the Mikado himself, if his government were to be regarded as friendly. Two young partisans brought a most indignant account from the British Minister. Sir Harry wanted to know if the Emperor, after British good will had helped so in establishing him, was going to repudiate the duty of protecting foreigners, and seemed especially put out that his nationals should suffer for the actions of the French. Ito relayed the news with some educational remarks of his own to Prince Komatsu. The mills of authority ground rapidly for once, and presently Ito was aboard a little steamer on embassy to Hiogo as aide to the court noble Higashi-Kuze, to whom had fallen the new-made office of Imperial Foreign Minister. Four days after the outbreak (February 8), he presented to the assembled diplomats in Hiogo a letter with the Mikado's own signature—but face-savingly dated the day before the trouble—in which the Throne assumed full responsibility for the government and all the treaties made by the Shogun. As Throne envoy, Ito promised the required amend for Bizen hostility, and the diplomats agreed to withdrawal of troops and release of shipping.

Two days more, and the diplomats were apprised that young Ito had been appointed customs inspector and governor of Hiogo and of their little settlement named "God's Door" (Kobe). Hiogo town was to be swallowed up by its growth into a great cosmopolitan port. What Ito lacked in rank he made up in fitness for the post. His leadership constituted the men he influenced into a kind of party devoted to progress and enlightenment and made Hiogo for a time an eye for the Empire. Thus haply a poor sub-samurai of a rebel clan became leading expert in foreign affairs for a nation, launched on the career of official honor at the instant the new government he had helped to found was born. It is hardly possible to believe, but he was only twenty-six. The eventful years seemed long, stretching back to when he used to dream of becoming a second Hideyoshi. The dream had merged into extraordinary fulfillment. Ito had turned, and after him the nation was to turn, from the romance of the past to the lure of a world of new nations, new ways of living, new codes of thinking. Forty years of increasingly responsible public life, and a dramatic death, were ahead for him.

Ito put a last thorough touch to his handling of the Hiogo affair, early in March, 1868, when he presided at the *harakiri* of the Bizen officer who had ordered the volley that swept Kobe. Ito had suggested clemency, which the majority of foreign plenipotentiaries voted would be bad policy. So Ito made a diplomatic social affair out of it and invited them to be present. One and all found themselves to be previously engaged and sent their secretaries. Satow sat opposite Ito.

The samurai did not resign themselves without incident to the inferred new policy of deference to foreigners. Tosa clansmen killed eleven French sailors in a man o'war's boat near Osaka. Yet more serious was the attempt by two intransigeant souls to assassinate Sir Harry Parkes, en route to Japan's first imperial audience to the diplomatic corps.

Ito was furious at these efforts to undermine the newly established relations. Imperial apology, the *hara-kiri* of eleven Tosa men, and indemnity for their victims' families was his way of clearing up the first incident. But the defiant death poems of the self-immolated circulated through the land and made them popular heroes. Rushing to Kyoto over the outrage to his friend, the not safely affronted Parkes, Ito concurred in having the assailant degraded and beheaded as a commoner. Swashbucklers finally had convincing evidence that the good old days were past.

Many years later, Ito, Prime Minister, was to visit the ashes of his old comrades in Kyoto, come suddenly upon a stone erected to Parkes' would-be assassin, and angrily protest its presence in such an honorable place. "But," he was to be reminded by some one present, "did not many of the men whose graves Your Excellency honors commit violence against foreigners?"

"When such action brought trouble upon the Sacred Person's enemies, it was not culpable," was to be Ito's reply, doubtless made with a mind to his own adventures. "But when it endangered the Sacred Person it was villainy." In Japan, as elsewhere, the hero and the dastard have often been distinguished by a slight matter of success—with the added embellishment that the successful one has gone down in history as a supporter of the Son of Heaven. Ito was more right than his explanation. In times of political development there is no sin like consistency.

Ito's bold stepping into the breach at Hiogo put him considerably ahead of the older Yamagata in fame and claim on court favor. His lead was increased by one rash day in the life of that usually careful soldier. The imperial court, well advised by Okubo, Kido, and other elder statesmen, removed from its ancient seat at Kyoto to Yedo. This strategy effected several psychological results. In harmony with ancient tradition, it marked the beginning of a new era in imperial policy. Again it served as notice to several ambitious clans that the Shogun's prestige would not pass from the fallen Tokugawa to one of them, but would in fact thenceforth be absorbed by the court. The name Yedo was now dropped for *Tokyo,* Eastern Capital.

As the imperial procession made its stately progress from Kyoto to Tokyo along the famous Eastern Sea Road, it came upon Yamagata who had been in a "mopping up" campaign where beautiful Suruga bay laps the foot of the sacred White Mother, Fujiyama. Kido invited the young commander to share the honor of joining the Emperor's retinue. The triumphant march into the Shogun's capital was too much for Yamagata, who was impelled to relieve his feelings by hieing with some fellows to a saké house and drinking

[174]

beyond discretion. On coming out, the party encountered a group of Tokugawa samurai whose mien Yamagata thought much too haughty for recently defeated, although amnestied, rebels. An argument ensued. Yamagata fired his pistol, but when he saw men closing in from all sides he dodged through into another street, clambered into a waiting sedan chair and prevailed upon the surprised bearers to start off with him—anywhere. Then he promptly fell into a contented sleep. The uninstructed coolies assumed—as they would to-day— that there was one destination which could not be wrong, and they took him to Yoshiwara. In this notorious mart of an ancient trade he was bundled out and handed over to the Butterflies, who stowed him away. But his enemies soon came upon him. He would have been overpowered and dragged to their camp if an imperial patrol had not just then happened along and taken an interest in the hubbub. The roistering hero was reproved and sent back to Osaka, with a grant of a life annuity of six hundred *koku*—around $2,400. He humbly petitioned to go abroad and in the second year of the new Emperor, whose era was to be known as *Meiji* ("Enlightened Rule") he and Saigo the Lesser of Satsuma were dispatched for a year of observation. The thin, dyspeptic soldier was thus to overcome his "setback," and from now on he would increase steadily until he held the Empire in his hand.

Upon the establishment of the régime at Tokyo, Kido and other advisers of the young Emperor thought it wise to announce a general constitutional basis on which government would hereafter be conducted. Since no one, in theory, could exact a pledge from the omnipotent Emperor, it was arranged that he should pledge himself, in the form of an oath. This was a brief document, published in June, 1868, and as Kido wanted it "modern" it was phrased to sound liberal, progressive, and even democratic. It called for centralization of power and modernization—*i.e.*, imitation of the West. beginning with the arresting article:

The practice of discussion and debate shall be universally adopted, and all measures shall be decided by public argument.

High and low shall be of one mind, and social order shall thereby be perfectly maintained. It is necessary that the civil and military powers be concentrated in a single whole, the rights of all classes be assured, and the national mind be completely satisfied.

The uncivilized customs of former times shall be broken through, and the impartiality and justice displayed in the working of nature shall be adopted as a basis of action. Intellect and learning shall be sought for throughout the world, in order to establish the foundations of the Empire.

On one of Kido's visits to Kobe he informed young Governor Ito that the Satsuma clan was going to offer from its fief territory to be directly ruled and administered by the imperial government sufficient to provide one hundred thousand koku of rice (around four times the number of dollars) yearly. Kido proposed that Choshu ought to go one better by proffering a one hundred and fifty thousand koku estate. Ito, citing what he had learned of development from feudalism into naationalism in Europe, stated his opinion that the clans should not put the Emperor in the position of being patronized by receiving grants from his vassals, but that they should turn over the fiefs in entirety as well as the clan military forces, enabling establishment of truly centralized national power.

Kido went to work on the suggestion and its accomplishment was to become the monument of his life. His power was great due to his being a *yoin* or business manager of his clan government. He made contact with his contemporaries in other clans and through them convinced the Daimyo that they would be better off, as well as patriotic, if they turned over their fiefs in lieu of pensions, with no expenses of government and no risk of weather or popular revolt. The *yoin* would of course be more important than ever—in charge of finance and business for the Emperor direct without the necessity of pleasing a feudal head. By March 5, 1871, through a combination, as the British Legation Secretary McLaren describes it, of appeal to principles, sentiments, cupidity, and fear, "Kido was able to unite the lords of Satsuma, Choshu, Hizen and Tosa in a proposal to restore their fiefs and hand over their registers of land and subjects to the Emperor." The document, a well-drawn historical and legal argument, was to become second in fame only to the imperial oath. It was accepted at once. The three hundred lesser lords of the archipelago could but follow the example. In July the throne was strong enough to announce that those who had neglected to do so would be compelled to hand over their registers. A mandate abolished the ancient distinction between court and feudal nobility, making all who furthered imperial policies members of a new "democratic nobility" of one rank only, called "Flowery Families." The next year Kido and his Satsuma friend Okubo, with the aid of the blue-blooded Iwakura, visited the great clans with the result that the daimyos of Satsuma, Choshu, and Tosa permanently left their ancient seats to reside in Tokyo, leaving the bulk of their forces to be merged into an imperial army. Yamagata, returning from his trip around the world, impressed with the equipment and regimentation of the French army and the conscription system of von Moltke, proceeded to whip the new army into shape. By August 29, 1871, the young oligarchs about the throne felt strong enough to issue the drastic Rescript on Abolition of Clans, transforming their territories into imperial departments. Feudalism had been fallen, in half a generation!

Its human product, the knighthood, remained to be dealt with before the old era could be said to have passed. Young men, born on the fringe of this aristocracy, who had struggled their way into it, now unblushingly inspired denunciation of its recently sacrosanct status in the newly born press (which was to continue as vituperative as it began). The samurai were dubbed "parasites on the people." The daimyos who signed over their fiefs had been granted perpetual pensions from the imperial treasury of one-half their average rice-collections—this was an advantage for them as they escaped levies, responsibility for public works, upkeep of clan armies, and philanthropy toward the unlanded samurai. The central government now offered a less liberal scheme of income to continue for "one or two lives" to the landed knighthood, whose serfs were to consider themselves as belonging only to the Emperor and were henceforth to pay taxes instead of croppage.

Ito had left his governorship to establish the new department of trade and commerce, had negotiated with the British for the beginning of railway construction, and had made a trip to America regarding the renewal of the Townsend Harris treaty. He was encouraged to believe that he might negotiate changes in the treaty limitations on import tariffs which would give Japan revenue at this needy time, and he went back within six months along with Iwakura, Kido, and Okubo. This formidable and earnest three-year mission failed completely in America and Europe, bringing home to Japanese that the treaty advantages gained over them by the Western nations would only be won back through a long hard climb to modern juridical standards, machine industry, and military power. The effect was to straighten the backs and stiffen the lips of the nation at large, but it was hard on Inouye. When that impulsive patriot, whose ability to raise money for the patriot group had caused him to be entrusted with finance in the first imperial government, reckoned up and discovered that he was expected to support three hundred daimyo and four hundred thousand samurai households—no less than two million persons out of a population then numbering forty million—he quit in disgust, taking with him his councilor, Shibusawa, a budding financial genius who was to become one of Japan's first industrial plutocrats, and live ninety years into the age of post-war power, great fortunes, and social unrest.

Okuma, a young Emperor supporter whose opportunity was not so large as his talent because he sprang from the lesser clans of Hizen, was then given charge of finance. England, glad to build up a foil to Russia in the Orient, offered loans. With these and the decimation of the pension obligation, Okuma pulled his government through the critical years of 1871-81. The enforced liquidation of pension claims by government bonds appeared to the samurai, however, as breach of faith on the part of the new government.

Samurai resentment manifested itself in ronin filibustering in Tosa and Choshu, an attempt on the life of the noble Iwakura, somewhat inconsistent appeals for representative government based on the imperial oath and a revival of Yoshida Shoin's jingoism. Saigo the Greater was head of military affairs, with cool, hard-working Yamagata under him working to build such an army as he had conceived out of his on-ground studies of the American Civil and Franco-Prussian Wars. When Kido and Ito, returning from their fruitless mission, memorialized the throne against imperialist ventures, advising concentration on peaceful constitutional development as a necessary requisite to equality among the nations, Saigo the Greater, always a chauvinist at heart and a sympathizer with the restless samurai, withdrew from the government and returned to Satsuma. That clan virtually left the coalition, becoming estranged from its sole member in high councils, Okubo, who thereupon requested Ito temporarily to take the ministry of the navy normally considered a perquisite of the seafaring Satsumas. It was Ito's first membership in a formal cabinet.

The Emperor of Korea, better supplied with traditions than power or cabinet ability, haughtily refused to recognize the new Japanese régime. The ronin flocked to Saigo, who founded patriotic schools after the manner of Yoshida Shoin. They demanded a war on Korea at once, to be followed up by the conquest of China. To let off steam the government authorized an expedition, with the acquiescence of China, against the Formosan head-hunters; whom the Chinese authorities were unable to prevent from cooking and eating Japanese who adventured among them. The younger Saigo led three thousand malcontents in a brief campaign. Its success was limited, it cost five and a half million yen, and Kido resigned in protest. He never came back to the government but was to die of tuberculosis during the soon-to-arrive civil war which his protests failed to prevent, depriving the nation of the philosopher of the Restoration.

Saigo's withdrawal left Yamagata free to go the whole way in building up an all-business "commoner" army. The conflict with old samurai ideas was at once intensified until Yamatata as a final, ruthless stroke, after four months' insistence obtained an edict abolishing the caste by making the wearing of the swords a criminal offense. He had to fight to enforce it.

The samurai about Saigo, thirty thousand strong, committed Saigo to a campaign to "rescue the Sacred Person from the hands of craven oligarchs." The Emperor was visiting at the old capital Kyoto when the news came by Ito's new telegraphs that Satsuma was in revolt. A panic took the city. Ito and a friend, Hayashi, took the just-completed railway to Osaka to inform Okubo, head of the government. He amazed them by his silence as they sped back through the twilight. In the last analysis he was a Satsuma man himself, they said in undertone to one another. He dismissed them at the gate to the palace.

The next morning they stepped out of their inns to find the old capital placarded with an imperial edict outlawing Saigo and ordering a punitive expedition under a royal prince with Yamagata in field command. Okubo, by his drastic action, had forestalled talk of compromise, and had set Saigo's old disciples and friends free to fight him in the Emperor's name.

Yamagata moved his Kihetai south, reënforced them by conscription, and led a vigorous offensive into Kiushu. He sent a message to Saigo: "It is unwillingly that I come against a master and friend. But loyalty to the Son of Heaven requires. I believe it is your students who have forced your hand. You will understand me."

The "last of knights" replied: "I understand you and approve of you. Let us fight!" Modern military tactics and equipment were soon supreme over samurai bravery and picturesque coats of mail. To prevent the exhibition of his head by the victors, Saigo entrusted one of his followers to cut it off and hide it in a straw stack (September, 1877). Yamagata did not cease pursuit until he had discovered the trophy and sent it back to his superiors. Head-taking ceased to be a requisite part of victory in Japan with this war.

Yamagata was generous in victory to the living, feeding and clothing prisoners as his own men. He had proved his men and methods—established a new military caste and destroyed the old one. It cost the life of Okubo, who was assassinated by irreconcilables, even as Lincoln, after he had granted amnesty.

Kido, Saigo, and Okubo, whose authority and rank had enabled them to put into effect the radical changes suggested in the reports of younger men, had now all gone tragically from the stage. Japan was left in the hands of the second generation of her moderns. The issues, henceforth to be constitutionalism versus military oligarchy, were to be personified in Ito and Yamagata.

III

Ito and other young Japanese upon first observation of Western countries gathered that national unity and strength sprang from expressed constitutional forms of government. The ambition of the patriots for their country was nationalism—that new and not yet questioned invention of Europe which was yet to be goal for young Indian, Chinese, Turk, Persian, and Egyptian patriots after Japan had led the way in Asia. The young patriots used the unapprehended but vaguely qualm-stirring call, "constitutionalism," to prevent older *Sat-Cho* clansmen from brazenly substituting their domination in place of the Tokugawa's. However, it was a weapon equally good against the existent thinly disguised oligarchy, and was promptly made the cry —sincere, or disingenuous—of every opposition. Always it was based on the famous imperial oath, worded as it was partly to provide opportunity for Ito's Occidental ideas and partly to placate the samurai with hope of sharing in "representative government."

The death of Kido, who was bold and yet sane, left Ito with the conscious loss of a balance-wheel. This loss, the appropriation of his democratic platform by political rivals—Itagaki, of Tosa, and Okuma—the responsibility and pride of high office and the necessity

of the ruling group to retain power—first law of political life and probably justified in such dangerous times
—combined to turn Ito temporarily conservative.
When, in full years, he was to revert to his early convictions and openly declare for party democracy at
home and nonaggression abroad he would find that he
had played hopelessly into the hands of the always
consistently autocratic Yamagata. Since he would
never be cowardly nor resigned in temperament he
would go forward inevitably to tragedy.

Yamagata, whose work, up to the Restoration, had
been at home in building military power, had formed
no early opinions regarding Western politics. When
he made his first rapid world survey from 1869 to 1871,
however, he cast a shrewd eye upon its political as well
as military systems. Particularly in Germany did this
"tall, slender, military Oriental," quite a new type to
Europeans, ask pertinent questions. "Did Bismarck's
system leave the monarch absolute, the military un-
trammeled?" If so, it seemed good. In the midst of
the Disraeli-Gladstone struggle, British party government appeared fraught with unnecessary disturbance,
and America presented to Yamagata's appraising view
the most undignified era of its political history—the
South a chaos from demagoguery and the federal government passing from the petty contentions of John-
son's administration into the scandals of Grant's. "For
the good of his country, Lincoln should have made himself the dictator," this Asian noted in his diary. An-

other entry diverts us: "Americans have no bridge to cross the Mississippi, their largest river!" Of course width of water had been no argument for bridging it in Japan, but the Asiatic expected of us consistency in modernity.

Yamagata came back convinced, in harmony with his character, that any representative or party system to be introduced in Japan must be thoroughly tamed to obey wise masters of the state. Sir Harry Parkes, as a true Englishman, advised this young von Moltkian in their first conversation that the basis of a modern nation must be civil, not military, and commended to his support the democratic tendencies of Ito and Okuma. Parkes was unaware of what was happening to Ito's principles at the time.

Yamagata sent for his lady, Komuko, and settled in Tokyo in a lattice- and paper-walled home with a miniature private park. He was promptly summoned to audience with the Emperor. His diary entry was, "How very young is the August Personage but how able to comprehend matters of state and information of interest to him. It is my duty to expend every ounce of strength in his service " Yamagata had the Bismarckian sense of responsibility and reverence for the crown as an institution and in addition a personal liking and fatherly concern for its wearer. He would have sacrificed his life and many another to save one hair of Mutsuhito's head. The young Emperor reciprocated his friendship, but in a shrewd way. Conscious that

he had opportunity to be the first of his long line outside the realm of myth to exercise decisive influence in
the state, he trusted Yamagata's honor implicitly, but
kept their relations always formal. Far differently did
he react to the almost sacrilegiously informal Ito.
"Marshal Yamagata is my soldier, Marquis Ito is my
drinking companion," he was to remark.

Yamagata, occupying in succession the offices of vice-
minister and minister of war, chief of staff and commandant of the imperial bodyguard—his creation—dictated Japan's military development. He stuck to the
simpler French system, in spite of much criticism after
France's defeat by Prussia—for which the French
government, in a typical gesture of *amour propre*, bestowed on him a medal. In two years he had won the
civil war which put the new régime beyond challenge,
abolished the clan armies by imperial rescript, located
the country's garrisons and defense works, established
the Imperial Military Academy, and installed universal
military training—in this adopting the German system.
Of course it was to be decades before funds, organization, and equipment were sufficient to call up all young
men. Establishment of the morale which must under-
lie all these things was Yamagata's easiest task. The
privilege of being soldiers, for centuries reserved to the
haughty samurai, was eagerly grasped by the plebeian
class to whom it meant social elevation. And then there
was the universal burning desire of a spirited and
Spartan people to prove itself second to none in the

world family to which it had been so abruptly annexed. The most primitive criterion of national standing is of course military prowess.

To the popular mind the prime motive behind the suddenly introduced universal education could only be enhancement of the glory of Nihon. Hence it was easy enough for Yamagata and his coterie to make public schools the ground step of their military system—preparatory institutions for military training, greenhouses of jingoism. With such material and incentive Yamagata was within twenty years to compel the respect of that world which knows force as its convincing argument. Because Japan had a Yamagata and Yamagata had a Japan, his nation was able to save itself the indignities and interferences suffered by its Asian sisters, China and India. Mustapha Kemal and his Turks were also to begin with military demonstration. But in saving his nation, Yamagata was to steer it close to the reef of imperialism.

Two conditions Yamagata required which remain only dreams for most military builders: absolute freedom from interference by politicians and unstinted financial provision. His fight to assure these took him into political life and his duel with Ito.

Jealousy of a Choshu man's supremacy in the army and navy naturally grew in the other great military clan of the Restoration, Satsuma. Just then a wealthy contractor for the army, Wasuke, a veteran of Yamagata's Kihetai, committed suicide. His was one of the early spectacular fortunes of the new Japan, founded upon a loan of five hundred gold pieces from Kido, and made by speculation in dollars and then purveying to the government. He had recently been to France and fallen in love with a French girl. On return he discovered a clerk had lost him 800,000 yen ($400,000).

That Wasuke might get his business in shape to carry out arrangements for marriage to his French sweetheart, who was to arrive shortly, Yamagata advanced him that sum from army funds against the next year's supplies. A minor clerk informed the Satsuma chiefs, who demanded an immediate audit. Yamagata had to require the money back. Wasuke pled with him to juggle the books but Yamagata refused. He tried to satisfy the audit with a note but his Satsuma enemies demanded to see all the money in cold cash. One midnight Wasuke's trusted assistant, later the wealthy Baron Fujita, called on Yamagata to plead for a last effort for his master, but Yamagata could do nothing more. At daybreak Wasuke committed *harakiri*.

Many of the Choshu condemned Yamagata for abandoning an old retainer. The Satsuma on the other hand accused him of complicity in corruption. The French girl arrived—to become a desolate figure weeping at Wasuke's grave in a temple yard—and Yamagata became the object of indignation of the sentimental Japanese public. Between these fires, he resigned. The army went badly. This was before Satsuma rebelled, and it was Saigo the Greater who went to the

Emperor and had him summoned back. But the navy was separated from the army and henceforth remained under Satsuma administration. Both branches fared better, although the navy, lacking a Yamagata, lagged far behind the army up to the twentieth century. At the outbreak of the war with China (1894), it was to consist of only twenty-eight ships, totaling 58,000 tons. The great seafaring clan was satisfied, and Yamagata was relieved of its jealousy.

Ito, in the political field, was not so fortunate. His return in 1873 from the fruitless treaty-revision missions abroad definitely marked his entrance into the psychological rather than physical state called middle age. Until this was past he was to remain cautious and take the easier way. Then with the coming of what in ordinary men would be called old age, the veteran was again to become the bold and, if necessary, lone innovator that the young knight had been.

Ito found Yamagata established as military autocrat, exerting immense influence in the government. Immediately made Councilor of State by the young Emperor, he first bent himself to forced cultivation of industry by government patronage, holding the post of Minister of Industry. Then when Okubo left to negotiate the Formosan dispute with China he received the mantle of home ministry. Failure promptly to initiate the representative institutions he once advocated gave opportunity for frenzied agitation by men of foreign experience whom misfortune in not being born in either dominant clan, Satsuma or Choshu, had barred from power. Ito replied through imperial rescript, "The people are wanting in culture and intelligence sufficient for popular government," as proved by the failure of the clan assembly. Itagaki, Goto, and their fellows came back in a heated memorial, designating this as "shocking self-conceit and arrogant contempt of the people." A refrain from the American Declaration was heard: "The people, whose duty it is to pay taxes, possess the right of sharing in government affairs, and of approving or condemning. . . . No representation, no taxation. . . . It is necessary to establish a council chamber chosen by the people," they continued. "The present government is neither by the throne nor by the people. An infant knows that it cannot go on."

The controversy continued fifteen years. Japan's first great newspaper, *Nichi Nichi Shimbun,* or "Day by Day News," was "made" by wisely taking the conservative side where power and money lay. Neither side knew nor cared to be pinned down as to just what it meant by "the people." At the time of the imperial oath that term of course meant the samurai, commoners not even being thought of in connection with political rights. But now the samurai prestige was fading fast, and Yamagata was taking plebeians into the new military caste. This ambiguity, exploited by politicians, was to bring "citizenship," still uncraved and undemanded, to the masses of Japan.

In 1874, the bold and conscientious attitude of Kido,

who had left the government over the Formosa expedition, compelled Ito to arrange a conference at Osaka at which Okubo and he represented the "government." The young statesman had the burden of outlining as basis of agreement between the two leaders a scheme for reorganizing the administration. They accepted, but it was a hybrid, designed to keep liberals innocuous by stealing their fire—and yet to go no further than exigency required. Henceforth Ito's was the pathetic rôle of time-serving "official sponsor of democracy" on behalf of a group of oligarchs.

The Satsuma rebellion distracted attention for several years. Upon Okubo's assassination in 1878, Ito took the controlling posts of President of the Cabinet, and Minister of Home Affairs, with Inouye as his faithful lieutenant. Okuma, doing amazing things with government finance, but feeling that the Satsuma-Choshu dominance restricted his career, resorted to the political weapon of scandal, the effect of which he had doubtless observed in Western bodies-politic. Using "inside information" gained as treasury chief, he revealed the tremendous dishonesty that had marked the development of Hokkaido, the "frontier" northern island, and the scheme to sell the government investment of ten million yen for a few hundred thousand to an intimate of the oligarchy named Kuroda. Mobs stormed the government offices in Tokyo. Okuma was the hero of the populace. In 1881, to confirm himself as their champion and test his power, he made a demand for the establishment of a parliament in 1883.

Ito, backed by the Heavenly Ruler's prestige, replied by conventional fire-stealing. "We hereby declare," read the edict published within twenty-four hours, "that We shall, in the twenty-third year of Meiji (1890) establish a parliament, in order to carry into full effect the determination We have announced, and We charge Our faithful servants bearing Our commissions to make . . . in the meantime, all necessary preparations to that end. We perceive that the tendency of Our people is to advance too rapidly, and without that thought and consideration which alone can make progress enduring, and We warn Our subjects high and low to be mindful of Our will, and that those who may advocate sudden and violent changes, thus disturbing the peace of Our realm, will fall under Our displeasure."

Okuma had to get out of the cabinet. Ito had won a victory in person but not in principle. Rather he had been forced into a place where he stood for nothing. Itagaki and other opponents attacked his government so unrelentingly that he was driven to resort to police repression which forced five hundred outstanding liberals from Tokyo and compelled the papers to engage "jail editors" to work out recurring sentences.

In February, 1882, he went to Europe officially to study constitutional forms. He had conversations with

Bismarck. The German combination of divine right dogma with practical politics seemed to him to fit Japan's case. He went on to St. Petersburg to attend the coronation of Alexander III. The first evidence of the deep influence Germany had upon him was the abolition, shortly after his return in August, of the "Flowery Families" and the establishment of a Prussian-type nobility of five ranks, in which he and Yamagata ranked as counts, two steps below the princedom, then reserved to royal blood, and one below the "old statesmen" of the Restoration. There had to be a live nobility, explained Ito, so that Parliament could have a House of Peers. He was thinking of forms, more than of democracy.

He found it necessary to take Yamagata, and Kuroda the scandal-tainted, into collaboration in the 1882 memorial to the Emperor which outlined his proposed constitution. He was at once made Minister of the Imperial Household that he might draft the basic law of the land in the Emperor's bedchamber, so to speak, safe from political interference or liberal suggestion. The newspapers were warned that neither criticisms nor surmises would be tolerated while the work went on. His fellows on the drafting committee were Inouye, Ito Myozi, and Kaneko, a Yamagata henchman.

The young Emperor frequently dropped in to the drafting room where work on the constitution went forward. His intelligent interest was interpreted to the worshipful public in pious bulletins which gave the impression that the document issued from the lips of the Sacred Person himself. In all these things Ito allowed himself to be pushed forward by his own fear of placing machinery of government in the hands of irresponsible elements, and by the cool determination of Yamagata. The idealist in him was forgotten for a time—by himself and those with whom he dealt—under stress of making the government "go." It was to revive, in a manner annoying to his fellow oligarchs and tragic to himself. Japan's father of the constitution compares illy at this time with America's—or with old Stein of Germany, whom Ito, in such a different spirit, claimed to follow.

Ito was, however, following Kido's old objectives, peace and concentration on problems at home. He was beginning to see, too, how foreign embroilment would put Yamagata and the military in complete dominance. He left the sacred enclosure within the moat in Tokyo to spend February to April, 1885, in Tientsin conciliating the spoiled Li Hung-chang over a clash of interests in Korea. Yamagata accepted the resultant treaty and calmly told his followers to get ready for war. On Ito's return he prepared to put the constitution into effect by replacing the council of state with a German-style cabinet of which he took the presidency, issuing ordinances defining the duties of ministers of government.

Another exposure of official corruption followed by demands of the liberals for "Cabinet responsibility to

Parliament" forced Ito to push forward one year the date for promulgation of the constitution.

Although the document itself was thoroughly reactionary, its true effect would come more from its interpretation than its text, and the first government under the constitution would set the precedent for that. With a caution characteristic but, it would seem, hardly necessary in view of Ito's drift, Yamagata planned that Ito should not head the government. The soldier, who had been again briefly to Europe to "check up" on forms adapted to Ito's constitution, mistrusted Ito's conservatism—possibly feared that his complacency in drawing such a reactionary instrument might have been mixed with a sly intention to counterbalance it by a liberal application. Therefore Yamagata suggested to the Emperor that Ito's great work must be rewarded by nothing less than the greatest honor of the kingdom— that of president of the Emperor's privy council provided for in the new document. Delighted to honor his friend and bring him into closer intimacy, Mutsuhito acceded and Ito found himself withdrawn, in a cloud of glory, from the arena which he had set.

It was a strategy yet to become commonplace. Ito doubtless felt relieved although he could not but resent the way he had been manipulated. He, champion of democracy, did not care to face the storm which would break from liberals on seeing the instrument he had drawn up. He had a bit of sardonic revenge on Yamagata. There remained no one else strong enough to face the inevitable, and the soldier had to do what must have galled him—turn politician and take the prime ministership of the first government under the constitution. Yamagata had once said, "One who cannot read a red [that is, English] telegram should not head the ministry." However, he kept up to date on world affairs through the aid of private translators. Viscount Kaneko was to draw a lively picture of the fifty-one-year-old general impatiently awaiting his henchman's arrival from London, and receiving him with a wry smile and peremptory demand for instruction on parliamentary procedure while he held under his arm Ito's new published *Commentaries on the Constitution*.

The long-awaited document was endorsed by the privy council and ratified by the "Throne, source of all change," and promulgated with elaborate ritual on February 11, 1889, before high officials only and members of the diplomatic corps in full regalia—a poor birth ceremony for democracy! All radical papers had been suspended in advance and others warned. The date was mandated a national holiday, *Kigensetsu.*

The day of the publication of his handiwork was one of anticlimax for Ito. A chronological error in the young Emperor's speech, misdating by two days his promise of 1881, provided, Japanese-fashion, opportunity for those who wished to humiliate the father of the constitution. Restrained from commenting on any-

[197]

thing of importance, the newspapers devoted pages to the "shocking incident." As head councilor, responsible for the Emperor's utterances, and the loss of prestige involved in the Infallible One's inexactness, Ito had to resign. But Mutsuhito, bigger than tradition, good-naturedly bid him think less of trifles and carry on, and the furor was automatically hushed.

The Heavenly Ruler having spoken, the constitution could not be opposed, but Itagaki, and Okuma (who had for some time been playing in with Ito and was fully aware of the document's content) headed an indignant opposition against the government. Elections in December filled the first House of Representatives with unorganized protesters expressing resentment by disorder and opposition. Ito took the presidency of the upper house and organized that as a support of the oligarchy. By military intimidation and bribery Yamagata got his budget through the first Parliament, but weakened by temporizing in his Cabinet, he had the Emperor dissolve the second Parliament and resigned in disgust. A Satsuma man, Matsukata, then undertook the premiership. The lower house demanded that Premier and Cabinet be responsible to it, British fashion. The constitution was ambiguous on this point but Ito, its drafter, for the sake of efficiency and the power of his clan oligarchy was compelled to interpret it as making the government entirely independent of Parliament and responsible solely to the Emperor— meaning the oligarchs of the privy council, whose inner group, still only middle aged, came to be called, somewhat satirically, *Genro,* or "Elder Statesmen."

Okuma, maintaining his activity as a "corruption sleuth," accused Inouye, who, of course, was in the Cabinet, of venality in connection with the great trading and shipping house of Mitsui. The charge was easily enough made, most of the oligarchs and their retainers as well as the imperial household having accumulated fortunes through connection with the government-sponsored firms of either Mitsui or Mitsubushi. But it was hardly gracious of Okuma, who had multiplied his wealth through connection with the government, to make cause of the custom of the time. The oligarchs and their opposition were at this time known by the significant names of *Koshin* and *Soshi,* that is, the "Distinguished Persons" and the "Enterprising Persons"—a sly Oriental circumlocution for the "ins" and the "outs."

The attack on his faithful Inouye drove Ito unreservedly into the reactionary camp. Where loyalty to fellow and clan conflicted with idealism the latter had to go, and that is the characteristic of Pacific Asians. The choice was final determinant of the tragedy of Ito.

Asking the Emperor to put Yamagata in his place in the privy council, Ito himself took the ministry in 1892, determined to down Okuma and the more admirable but not less irritating Itagaki, even though such accomplishment should stunt for decades the growth of the tender plant, democracy. The lower house of

Parliament, filled with Itagaki and Okuma men, stiffened in responsive anger. When Inouye, stating that Ito was ill, got up to read the Prime Minister's opening address for him, the House refused to receive it, and forced Inouye from the rostrum by hubbub, showing that it was an apt imitator of some older legislative bodies. Yamagata put in a heavy military budget, enjoying the situation of Ito's having to support it. The House threw the bill aside, drew up an impeachment address to the Emperor, and adjourned for eighteen days. Ito went to Mutsuhito. In three days the Emperor's legislators were summoned back like naughty school boys, read an imperial rescript commanding the Cabinet to proceed with its policy without fear of annoyance, endorsing the budget with the Chinese proverb that "a single day's neglect may bring a century's regret," and setting a good example by donating three hundred thousand yen yearly for six years to the army and navy from the Emperor's privy purse. The climax was an imperial order that the holy example be followed by all military and civil officials to the extent of donation of one tenth of their meager salaries to the treasury. Members of Parliament drawing about fifty cents a day, and put to election expenses greater than their total salaries, paid with the rest. Ito's sense of humor did not make him popular with the housewives of officials at pay-check time!

Scandals centering about Hoshi, Mark Hanna of Japan until he fell by an assassin's dagger, gave the next opportunity for attack on Ito's oligarchy. Itagaki, Goto, and Okuma, who had begun to organize political parties, combined forces in the next Parliament and impeached the Cabinet to the Throne. Ito calmly finished off what democratic pretension might cling to the constitution in the imperial reply: "The appointment and removal of ministers of state is absolutely at the will of the sovereign and no interference will be allowed in this matter. The Minister President and his Cabinet are bidden to retain their posts." But democracy in Japan was tenacious if not virile. Party chiefs bowed before this dictum but did not accept it, and Ito was yet to be on their side.

Ito was negotiating with Great Britain for the abolition of the treaty restrictions on sovereignty over aliens and customs tariffs—considered by all Japanese as indignities "slipped over on them" by the wily Western Powers in the Tokugawa days of ignorance of international comity. Inouye, as Foreign Minister, had in his *opéra bouffe* way, encouraged Tokyoites in the winter of 1866-7 to believe that if they imitated the British sufficiently the unequal treaties would be abolished. There had followed an orgy of dressing in coats and trousers, Japanese-foreign social mixing—even taking up of Western dancing and the suggestion that English be substituted for the national tongue. When the British government remained unmoved about the treaties, the reaction brought about anti-foreign riots, earnest return to native customs, a police ban on dancing, to be frequently revived, and one of Inouye's disgusted resignations. Ito had wrecked later negotiations by Okuma—this was too bright a feather for a politician's cap to be allowed to go to a rival. Now Parliament tried to embarrass Ito's negotiations by demanding retaliatory measures against the Powers. Ito suspended Parliament by imperial rescript.

Elections again. Great harshness and repression of speech failed to prevent the selection of a thoroughly hostile House. Its first act was another impeachment to the Throne. When the memorial went to the Emperor through the usual channels it was refused. The president of the House then personally took it to the household department. He was summoned next day and told: "We shall not adopt the views contained in the address. A written communication will not be made to it." He was then handed a rescript in a single sentence dissolving Parliament. A newspaper came out with a black border of mourning and was promptly suppressed.

Mutsuhito had stood by his friend. Ito, using the Heavenly Ruler's prestige, was triumphant over his enemies. But how badly he had defeated his own soul! He had made a constitution, its chief innovation a Parliament which for three successive sessions he himself was compelled to dissolve.

Ito had unusual ideas about domestic as well as imperial government. When his son Bunkichi was five, he sent the child to a private school near his own old haunts of Hagi and Yamaguchi, to be raised in ignorance of his parentage until middle school age. Each one has his particular genius, he was to tell the lad; some have genius for but a humble lot, and life in accord therewith is a success and not to be deplored, if it include loyalty to the Emperor. There was a younger son, Shiuichi, and two daughters, the first and last born. But he made the son of Inouye the heir of his name and title—the greatest tribute a man can offer his friend. Ito was always gallant and a little supercilious toward women, never (in consequence?) compelled to be lonely for them, and never giving them a major place in his interest. Of his faithful Umeko he was always proud, like a true Japanese gentleman of the old school, in an impersonal sort of a way. If Ito made, himself, no pretense to what the West calls fidelity, he did not offend the prejudices of that day and society, and found happiness in his family.

Yamagata was flourishing. Having used Ito to get his army equipped, he was ready for war. A marked change had come in his household. Always fond of the scintillating geisha dancers, a very good performer of the classic *No* dance himself, Yamagata had some years earlier taken into his home an intelligent and artistic geisha named Sadako, a Tokyo girl, daughter of one Yoshida. Thus Yamagata, who could be so cool at affairs, pandered the streak of romanticism in him. With assent, or at least acquiescence, of Kokumo, he enjoyed Sadako as his concubine. He was one of the last of the great men of Japan to appropriate the privilege of concubinage, about this time officially abolished. In 1893 his quiet Kokumo, with whom his relations had been very sweet, although lacking intellectual and playful companionship, died. To the surprise of his "set" he married the geisha as his "full" wife. But in his loves as in his political life, Yamagata paused little before outside opposition. Sadako was to prove very devoted and satisfying to him. After the tradition of women of her nation, she was to put up serenely with his humors, although she was to write wistfully in her diary: "Prince is very quick-tempered—at least so at home. Especially when he is running a war!" For Sadako herself, marriage was to be a slow process toward social recognition, in which she was to pioneer the way for many girls of her class yet to marry into Japan's new aristocracy.

Ito had opposed the spirit of challenge to China over Korea, and between 1888 and 1903 had found time in his busy, variable career to cross the straits of Tsushima ten times in endeavors to preserve the balance between Japan and China in Korea in harmony with his 1885 convention with Li Hung-chang. Now Yamagata, acting as Minister of Justice in Ito's cabinet for the purpose of lending it strength against the politicians, resigned, announcing "fundamental differences with the Minister President." Ito reciprocated the honor Yamagata brought upon him some years before by having his military peer made president of the privy council.

But this failed to quiet the gaunt soldier. Ito, threatened with attack from "behind the curtain" in addition to an increased storm from below, accepted the war policy. It was his final betrayal of his principles. But as a rescue from immediate troubles it had electrical effect.

Gray leaders, then young clerks and retainers, now tell a pretty anecdote of this time. When the Chinese were driven from Port Arthur, Ito was in Tokyo. The dispatch reached him and Yamagata at the same hour —at night. Yamagata carefully dressed himself in court uniform and decorations and proceeded to the sacred enclosure within the gray walls and moat, ceremoniously to inform the August Person. Ito simply put on a greatcoat over his night-kimono and dashed off to share the jubilation with his imperial friend Mutsuhito. At the gate he was stopped. "No one enters here in a night dress," the guard politely but firmly informed him. "—But I am Ito, the councilor." "We cannot make an exception. You may wait here while we send in for instructions."

Word went to the Sacred Person that Marquis Ito was at the palace gate in night dress. "Bring him to the audience hall," was the command. "And bring me a night dress just like the one he is wearing." Soon he was receiving Ito in a garb which set both at ease. The goods news demanded celebration. While they were drinking saké, the page announced General Yamagata, on an official call. "He will have to wait," commanded the Emperor. "To receive him I must don ceremonial dress."

The government removed to Hiroshima, on the continental side of Japan, and here a suddenly docile Parliament, exulting in the nation's opportunity to demonstrate its new-born power, gave Ito everything which Yamagata, through him, demanded, to prosecute the war. Factionalism and democratic agitation alike disappeared under the magic touch of Mars.

The inevitable reaction came upon Ito's head. Yamagata, the soldier, and his generals had won victories everywhere and received only plaudits. But Ito, the government, received the mob's unthinking anger for stopping the triumphal progress before China was "rolled up like a curtain," suffered its resentment against increased taxes now required by the same Yamagata to maintain the enlarged war machine (for one victory requires another, and Russia was in the offing), and its hysterical curses when prudence compelled return of half the fruits of victory in the face of sudden interference by Germany, France, and Russia. Men who made attempts on Ito's life were heroized by the public. He was embarrassed by a "patriot's" stabbing of the ancient Li Hung-chang, arriving under sanctity of truce to negotiate the treaty. He had to repress his people ruthlessly, which in turn they called his reward of them for sacrificing too unstintingly through the war! The Emperor was unfailingly steadfast and sympathetic. He elevated Ito and Yamagata to rank of Marquis, and bestowed the highest Order of the Chrysanthemum. But the only true appreciation of the lonely man's state of mind came from the Minister of Foreign Affairs of Belgium, whose friendship with Ito, made on his European travels, showed a strain of true affection: "You have sacrificed your name and career to save your country. The extent of your countrymen's misinterpretation of you is the extent of your honor."

Out the Tokaido line on the "Outside Sea" (Pacific Ocean) was the old-fashioned fishing village of Oiso. Ito, seeking a retreat, built there his "Villa of Blue Waves." It really included two main buildings, one foreign, one Japanese, looking altogether, says his secretary, "like a country post office," although convenient and sumptuous within. He scorned the "retinue like a clan lord's" indulged in by many officials of the time, keeping only two pages for the gate and some housemaids. He almost lived in an upper room at a long table bearing Japanese and English books—poetry, Napoleonana, and a miscellaneous armload on current events representing his latest visit to the Maruzen book store, the London *Times, Contemporary Review, North American Review,* and *Graphic*—piles of letters official and personal, stationery, Chinese writing brushes and American fountain pens, his latest acquisitions in swords, several cigar boxes, the slender, vaselike porcelain saké bottle with thimble-size drinking bowls, and, three times a day, a tray of food. Every one had

to see him here, except princes of the blood and foreigners, whom he did the special courtesy of taking to
the reception room. He gave interviews from early
morning until late in the afternoon, usually on a Japanese pickled plum and a cup of tea, but occasionally
with a British breakfast of ham and eggs. For his
afternoon and evening meals, he customarily ate "Japanese," the delicious-appearing but palate-disappoint-
ing bowls of raw fish cubes, sea weed, and bean curd.
His one gastronomic indulgence was *s'kiyaki* of wild
boar (cooked on the table over braziers) which he
pretended "gave courage." In drinking he had mod-
erated the custom of his younger days, but still occasionally showed a capacity that astonished his juniors.
More than a decade later a young general (of forty
or so) was to tell how after a night of it Ito set off on
foot at such a pace he had to hire a rickshaw to keep up.

When friends remarked on the unnecessary diligence
with which he investigated everything to which his sanction was asked, he replied: "It is because the Emperor
relies so trustfully on my opinion. I shall be fully
responsible for the imperial assent no matter how
trifling the matter."

In a room near his den was a bed and a couch. He
used to say that he rested better "hard," but had so
frequently to go abroad that he installed the bed to
keep in practice. As a matter of fact he compromised
between the clean "hard" *tatami* of his ancestors and

[208]

Western springs and mattress by sleeping usually on the couch. Lady Ito fluttered in and out like a butterfly and occasionally ventured to remonstrate when he indulged too hotly in argument with his secretaries—an intervention which invariably caused him to plunge in the harder. He was gentlemanly to her, and, on the whole, ignored her.

Officials and plutocrats flocked to Oiso in Ito's train and it became a fashionable watering place. But the man who made it could often be seen in sockless feet shod in geta, and old kimono, loitering about its little shops, or swapping yarns with fishermen among their boats down by the beach.

Within view was Yamagata's less pretentious, more artistic, purely Japanese villa. He lived in a household ordered according to military regimen, and enjoyed companionship of both passion and intellect with Sadako. "As the war with China loomed," Sadako relates, "the princes were tens of times a day going and coming to one another's studies. Every train from Tokyo brought a score of officials to interview them both. Frequently they conferred all night, and I would see their figures through the *shoji* (opaque paper panels) sitting upright like statues of *bushi* (the old stoic warriors) against the light. Even when they had saké brought in the good manners were surprisingly noticeable!" she remembers with wifely commendation.

Yamagata worked long hours too, but more systematically than Ito. He always arose at seven, washed in cold water regardless of temperature, and drank several cups of tea. Later he would breakfast on bread and milk. Vegetables and fish, Japanese style, were his lunch, but except when attacks of dyspepsia and rheumatism were acute, he allowed himself European food for dinner. Since his youth he had partaken sparingly of saké, but he drank two cups of vermouth before retiring. He was very fond of sweets. Somewhile a cigar fiend, he took later to cigarettes, using two packages of the vile Japanese government-monopoly product a day. He was a great reader, taking joy out of thorough reading whereas Ito nibbled for brilliant excerpts ōr passages affecting his work. He never mastered English as did Ito but with the help of translators kept up with leading English and German publications.

Utterly lacking Ito's joviality, and seldom smiling, Yamagata, however, exercised consideration and a paternal responsibility with his sternness. His avocations were writing the miniature Japanese poems on nature, fate, love, or martial courage—many of which became nationally popular—brush painting, the classic gesture-dancing for which natural lightness and grace of movement fitted him, and singing of the dramatic librettos—*yokioku*. Whereas Ito collected swords of all countries, Yamagata characteristically specialized in Japanese weapons—the samurai weapons which he had abolished!

Occasionally the two rivals played chess. Yamagata was always good, Ito always bad—but eager to accept another challenge.

Yamagata preferred to work in the army as in politics—from behind the curtain—and pushed Oyama forward to the rank of Marshal. However, in view of the political insecurity at home, he considered initial success in the war with China so important that he personally led the first division against the Chinese in Korea. When he reached Antung on the great Yalu river, border of Manchuria, he fell ill of his chronic bowel trouble but remained, commanding from his cot. The Emperor, worried, sent a general to see him, with the advice to take a little wine each day. Yamagata replied that there were many sick and wounded soldiers who could not have wine, so he would do without. The army surgeons said that for him to remain at the front was to imperil his life. He insisted that he would stay and take the risk like any common soldier. But the return of Mutsuhito's emissary was followed by an imperial mandate to turn over field command and return at once, which he had to obey. At the port of Ujina he was welcomed by soldiers and populace with wild demonstrations. People, remarked a politician, began to say "the Japanese army of Yamagata" more often than "Yamagata of the Japanese army."

Ito's pro-Russian tendencies caused the sending of Yamagata to represent the Emperor at the coronation of Czar Nicholas, but he proved greatly inferior to Ito as a negotiator. His convention over Korea and Man-churia was all Russia's way. Possibly Yamagata cared little, in any case. He was planning to settle that issue by direct action. His self-confidence and determina-tion were amazing in view of his physical health. On the ship home, his catarrh of the stomach aggravated by seasickness, he was told that he would die. "If I do," he commanded, "bury me at sea."

By a rescript amending the constitution, issued dur-ing the war excitement, Yamagata had freed the mili-tary entirely from parliamentary interference and put himself in a position to wreck any cabinet that would not meet his wishes. The ministers of war and navy must henceforth be high ranking officers. Yamagata had both control over rank and the fealty of the men who bore it. He could prevent any prime minister from filling these posts and filling a cabinet. He had now gained the end he had quietly set himself twenty-five years before. There was a slight struggle with Ito over whether Japan's empire—it had begun with the acqui-sition of Formosa in this war—was to be controlled by the civil or military branch of the government. Yamagata won, of course. Territorial governors would be part of the military oligarchy.

Yamagata had made Japan into a duarchy, a two-faced monster whose formal government could pledge one thing and whose military could do the exact op-posite, as China and the Western Powers were to dis-cover during the World War. His sincere aim was to make Japan respected. But he was to make her mistrusted and stigmatized.

Ito had let himself be pushed out of his convictions. For what seemed the good of his country he had turned upon and crushed his own causes. But he had only got the contumely of his people and been degraded into the tool of his rival. The soul of him was ready to revolt.

The first election after the war filled the House of Representatives with another vituperative mob, encouraged to attack him the more freely because of his universal unpopularity. He could rely on the Emperor, but a too frequent use of such arbitrary power would undermine the prestige of even the Son of Heaven, and Ito was too loyal for that. Anyhow, he had decided to promote instead of longer thwart party government. So he suddenly allied with the Jiyuto ("Liberal Party") of Itagaki, whom he had secretly admired for unswerving constancy to the democratic ideal although it had brought no office. Ito openly proclaimed that he would base the government upon political party support.

The oligarchs were affronted and the House of Peers, formerly Ito's strength, turned obstructive, blocking all legislation. Yamagata, shocked and hostile, actually denounced Ito to the Emperor. Ito resigned, sardonically recommending Yamagata to Mutsuhito as his successor.

It was 1896. For four years and a month, including

the period of the nation's first foreign war, Ito had headed the government—the longest administration since the establishment of the constitution. He had negotiated the abolition of the early treaties infringing on Japan's sovereignty, steered the nation through the grave crisis of the Russo-German-French ultimatum, started it toward recognition as a world Power and negotiated its first acquisition of empire. Ito's record appeared a triumph, but before his own soul he had failed. He had let himself be carried into divergent paths. And so he was torn asunder.

The ex-Minister President and the prince of the blood, Arisugawa, who had ranked as commander against the Satsuma rebellion, went as emissaries to attend Queen Victoria's jubilee. Ito sailed up the Thames, uniformed and bedecked, surrounded by attendants, greeted by the Queen's noblemen, a military parade and a band. But his hosts found him a bit absent-minded—thinking of two shanghaied, starved sailor lads who had come up that river and not been allowed to land (for no country is so cold to the unknown and so cordial to the celebrated as England). But Ito, squatting on the deck of a sailing boat, caked in filth, red from the blows of the bosun's mate, high with hopes and idealism, had been at peace with himself—happy. . . .

IV

Yamagata passed the honor of the premiership on to Matsukata, who, to assure passage of his budget— the one thing which the oligarchy ever needed from Parliament—had to take Okuma as finance minister. The oligarchs were forced to admit dependence upon his political faction. The press, which had become important and was largely conservative, attacked the government with charges of bribery in the elections, a spoils system in connection with party support, and appalling military brutality and corruption in Formosa. Okuma, after his habit of executing coups, resigned. The cabinet dissolved the diet and quit. The Emperor, alarmed, personally thrust his trusted Ito again into the breach (January, 1900). How honors that men will struggle for may become a burden to them! Okuma and Itagaki united parties to fight him in Parliament. They attacked the "Satsuma-Choshu clan government" as "no better than the Tokugawa." Ito asked the Emperor for a rescript limiting the session to twenty days. Then he went before the Genro in meeting and proposed the definite necessity of Cabinet alliance with the majority party of the lower house.

Yamagata bent forward among the offended oligarchs, like a lean gray hawk. "You propose political party government?" he asked.

All eyes were fixed on Ito, the Emperor's in puzzled questioning. "It has become obvious that political

[215]

parties must have a place in modern government," the Minister President replied. Yamagata's long figure drew to full height. He saluted and bowed deeply to the Emperor. "When you framed the constitution," he said to Ito in his low, staccato voice, "you placed ultimate sanction in the Throne, not in demagogues and mobs. I remain loyal to the Throne. I shall not permit you to violate your constitution."

Ito answered with an astonishing coup. Bearing his seal of office to the Emperor, he asked Mutsuhito in the name of their sacred friendship to appoint his deadly rivals, Okuma and Itagaki, to head the government. At last the long-suppressed romantic spirit in him had asserted itself.

These demagogues were taken utterly unawares. Their combination was but five days old and their forces were still unorganized. But they couldn't appear before the country as having clamored for party government for years, and then declined when asked to head it. So in June the first "party administration" in Japanese history was inaugurated. Ito, uncompromised now by connection with the militarists at home, sailed for China to renew his efforts for peace on the continent.

Yamagata watched his opportunity to destroy this— to him—bastard thing which Ito had brought into power. Ozaki Yukio, a slight, earnest man combining the qualities of student, demagogue, and journalist who was given the ministry of justice, walked right into the trap. Speaking, with characteristic contortions of his tiny face, against wealth in high places, he said: "Even in America where the plutocracy is all powerful, the people do not elect a millionaire to the presidency, whereas, if Japan were a republic, the people would be sure to place the richest man in office." Immediately the military organization vociferously accused Ozaki and the entire cabinet of desire to overthrow the Heavenly Ruler and make Japan a republic. *Lèse majesté!* Treason! Sacrilege!

Amid popular furor, Okuma's cabinet fell, and Yamagata had himself and a cabinet of military men gazetted in eight days—before Ito, rushing back from China, could arrive to advise Mutsuhito. Then Yamagata, who always applied "practical" methods to politics, bought Okuma's party away from its chief and made it his own by offering its leaders, through the unscrupulous Hoshi, "amnesty" and jobs. Okuma could no longer provide spoils. Certainly it was wise to go over to the winning side!

By reckless bribery, involving the Tokyo tramways in scandal, Yamagata's party whip, Hoshi, contrived to get his enormous budgets—in preparation for the Russian war—through the House. Ito set forth to make a speaking tour of Japan in favor of party government. It was the first important appeal to the only possible weapon against the military oligarchy: public opinion. Yet when the Chinese Boxer outbreak involved Japan, Ito threw all his support to Yamagata through the crisis, sitting once more with him in council through many nights at Oiso.

This over, Hoshi, the double-crosser, came to Ito complaining that his party was sick of being the tool of the military and would turn against the government if Ito would lead it. Thus far he had not affiliated with any one party. Now he went this last step on condition that the party would unquestioningly follow his direction. Even yet his aristocratic soul shrank from the possibility of being jockeyed into too radical a leadership. Even Okuma and Itagaki pledged allegiance. It seemed that the man worthy to lead the crusade to democracy, and a party (to be called the Seiyukai) sufficient to carry it through, had at last been brought together.

Ito's speech inaugurating the party still evidenced, however, a privy-councilor mentality. Cabinets, he said, must be responsible to the Emperor and parties must not be obstructive. Ito had to be loyal to his Emperor and his Satsuma-Choshu fellow clansmen. In action he was willing to go much further than word. His party council of twelve was dubbed by the press "The Twelve Apostles." All of its members were destined to attain fame or notoriety.

Yamagata, his budgets passed, resigned in the face of Seiyukai opposition. Ito was hesitant about taking the premiership. No one else dared to, with Ito controlling the lower house. Mutsuhito talked with Yamagata, who promised not to obstruct Ito, and the administration that was to be Ito's last adventure as the head of government began.

Ito owed his place to the corrupt Hoshi. Like President Harding, he made the mistake of being grateful to rascals who supported him. He put Hoshi in his cabinet. There was a popular outcry against the unblushing crook. Ito transferred him to the position of Parliament whip. It did not greatly help. The House of Peers, offended at Ito's party affiliations, refused to pass his budget.

Yamagata had promised not to obstruct Ito. He went further than that. He helped him get his budget through by having the Emperor issue a rescript simply commanding the peers to pass it. They were furious at the indignity which of course they attributed to Ito. Meeting in angry silence they voted in blanket all the bills that had been or might be sent them. This was to stand as the most ruthless, underhanded coup of Yamagata's career—unless he really can be charged with arranging Ito's death.

Ito could not throw a shadow over the face of his friend the Emperor Mutsuhito, by denial or retaliation. Self-restrained and tragic, he petitioned the Emperor to strip him of all his titles. Mutsuhito of course refused. But the rest of his life Ito spoke of himself as plain Hirobumi—"the stranger from afar."

Playing the old game of "turn-about," Ito asked Mutsuhito to appoint Yamagata Premier. The old soldier side-stepped and had the post offered again to Ito and Inouye to humiliate both his friend and the office, and then put it on a little known lieutenant Katsura, who turned out to be surprisingly capable. Ito once more went abroad—to be honored with the degree of LL.D. at the Yale centennial celebration.

From America he crossed to England, where Premier Salisbury gave a reception for him on his estate in Hatfield. After the event Prince Ito remarked to an aide: "I think Lord Salisbury will soon resign." This was a live subject in British politics and Ito was besieged as to what the Prime Minister had told of his plans.

"Not a word," replied Ito. "But his daughter, guiding me to a painting of Prince Bismarck, commented that the German statesman's last years were pathetic because he did not resign his post when the Emperor whose confidence he enjoyed passed away. She told me this story unintentionally, but Queen Victoria, whose confidence her father particularly enjoyed, has recently passed away. Lord Salisbury will retire." The observant Japanese was correct. Salisbury soon stepped aside and was succeeded by Balfour.

Yamagata favored a military alliance with Great Britain, the value of which to both nations had become evident in their anxiety of the steady spread of Russian influence in China. British aid toward the uplifting of Japan had indeed, from the very beginning, been dictated by the desire of creating a check to her fundamental rival, Russia, in the Orient. Always looking at European politics through German eyes, Ito favored Russia, and he didn't want war which would fasten the octopus of militarism more firmly on his people. "On his own" he rushed to St. Petersburg in a vain endeavor to get Russia to offer as attractive terms as the British. "Yamagata's Cabinet" disavowed official status to his visit. Only Mutsuhito remained loyal, and on imperial insistence Katsura had to dispatch the final amendments to the Anglo-Japanese treaty by special messenger to St. Petersburg, for Ito's perusal.

The die was cast. With Ito it was always "my country right or wrong," once the issue came to that. He returned to compel his party to support the military budget. Okuma furiously accused him of having taken the chieftaincy of liberalism only to betray it. Ito had furthermore offended other rough and ready party bosses by openly disapproving their methods in the recent election campaign, in the course of which Hoshi had been murdered. Ozaki led a revolt in Ito's party. Yamagata saw that the time was ripe: he had Ito again elevated into the privy council. Thus Ito's political party connection ended. The headship of the Seiyukai was passed on to Saionji—a scion of the Imperial House who had captured the popular imagination by returning soon after the Restoration from school in France to start a paper advocating a republic—quickly closed at imperial suggestion. The Saionji family furthermore was thought romantic because for generations it had observed its founder's vow of celibacy (barring wives, but not concubines).

As in her China conflict, Japan attacked, and after the surprised Russians had been taken at disadvantage, came the formal declaration of war (February 10, 1904). Again Yamagata was made chief of the general staff and commissariat. He remained in Tokyo, directing from the Emperor's side. A prime requirement of his strategy was the extension of military control over the Korean government, accomplished through the venal Korean Prime Minister Li. Yamagata made capital of Ito's reputation as an anti-imperialist by dispatching Ito to reassure the aroused Koreans. At the close of the war Ito was made the first resident-general, and he took the post hoping to be able to prevent complete annexation, while Yamagata wished to use him as a stepping stone to that very accomplishment. He was ironically compelled to advise the Koreans to submit quietly to the military administration lest worse things befall them. They could not understand his attitude. To them he was the agent-in-chief of conquest. They stoned his railway car, crashing the glass of his window, which severely cut his head.

Yamagata understood Ito well. He had never regarded Ito as a competitor. Jealousy was not in his nature. He had admired Ito's talents, personally liked him, been pleased to see him advance. He held Ito to be good at argument but weak of will and dangerously visionary. Unrelentingly he compelled the application of Ito's talents to further the nation on what he saw to be its path to greatness.

Ito did not grasp Yamagata's sincerity. He took Yamagata's interference to be inspired by personal rivalry. In such a contest Ito felt that he possessed every advantage: intimacy with the Emperor, ability as a public speaker, a personality which appealed to the public imagination, intimacy with Western civilization, and wider acquaintanceship at home. Yet Yamagata, popularly regarded as unapproachable, unable to speak five minutes in public or make his voice heard the length of the Parliament chamber, won every bout. Ito alternated between active resentment and discouraged acceptance.

Yamagata hid behind his soldier's uniform, made samurai sternness and aloofness bases of public confidence, and through unfailing constancy to his "boys" built up a select personal following that he could rely upon. Obedient loyalty of men like Katsura, Kodama, Tanaka, Kiura, Hirata, Oura, Matsuoka, and other soldiers, industrialists, and scholars was the secret of his strength. Only one was to flout him, Katsura, and that one would be punished, surely and terribly.

Yamagata was not sullen and inconsiderate as many thought. His henchman Kaneko relates his sudden departure on alleged business from American Ambassador Mutsu's summer home in Watergap, West Virginia, when he discovered that Mutsu was overtaxing his frail body in hospitality. But he was exclusive and hard to reach. The newspapermen got few appointments with him and were careful to "sew on all their buttons" before going. When he did see them he was disarmingly gracious and wholesome and to the point. So he carried more weight in the press than the informal, voluble, somewhat cynical Ito. Yamagata was a good listener, and men said they left his presence "like a squeezed lemon." He had a way of making young men "his" for life. Ito dispatched young Kaneko to Hokkaido to report on administration in the northern island. He was invited to show his report to Yamagata. "A fine report," the soldier commended. "No one could have made such an analysis but you!" Forty years later Kaneko would quote this with pride.

At his most venerable and powerful period the army chief was to dress in full uniform and "practice up" an interpreter for an hour in preparation for a brief interview with an American newspaperman. The young liberal leader Tsurumi brought from the South Seas a box of rare and prized mangoes for notables of the capital, and remarked that the great Yamagata was the only recipient to acknowledge the gift. He was as punctilious in courtesy as he was thorough in work.

When President Roosevelt's proposal for a peace conference came direct to the Emperor, Yamagata, sitting in council, determined acceptance. He went personally to Mukden to discuss the terms with his field marshal, Oyama. The Emperor loved Ito, and it was with some regret that he was compelled to work rather with the man who was motivating the nation in the path of its destiny. After plenipotentiary Komura had literally tricked Count Witte into signing peace in Roosevelt's summer retreat at little Portsmouth, New Hampshire (for the Czar's instructions were not to end the war but to gain time), Mutsuhito gave a dinner for the statesmen and commanders who had contributed to victory. With smooth chin and military mustaches Yamagata flanked the imperial seat; Ito, in a shaggy goatee, faced it across the table. Suddenly, in excess of feeling, the sixty-five-year-old author of the constitution, rising, proposed a toast and three *banzai* ("ten thousand longevities") to the Emperor, carrying the guests with him, but leaving them quite aghast at his breach of ceremony. Doubtless it was the highest spot of the function for the Sacred Person. Soon after the Emperor's banquet, Yamagata and Ito were elevated to the highest rank open to nonroyal blood, with the titles of "Prince."

Ito proceeded to the shrine of the Virgin of Ise, where the ancestors of the Emperor back to Amaterasu (Daughter of the Sun) are enshrined, and offered thanks for his country's victory. His religion was the patriotic pantheism into which he and his peers had transformed the old animistic Shinto. It required the stoicism and loyalty of the *bushi* combined with "divine right" doctrine glorified by evangelical ardor. It was a religion of "good example" on the part of Ito, Yamagata, and the elders of the nation. Ito's inner religion was really the Confucian universalism. He was thus able to regard both Buddhism and Christianity with sympathetic approval.

There was a popular storm against the peace. Why had not Russia been made to pay for the war, instead of Japanese taxpayers who had already given their sons? Why had Japan not annexed all of Manchuria, and Siberia as far as Lake Baikal? A mob, locked out of the Hibya Park, Tokyo's central plaza, crashed the iron fence, burned police boxes throughout the city, and pillaged the homes of cabinet ministers. Peace delegate Komura had to return from his triumph by way of a tiny outport, to dodge assassins. Yamagata was strong enough to take the responsibility. He put Tokyo and other cities under martial law and controlled them with his troops. The Emperor issued a rescript saying that everything had been done according to the pleasure of the Sacred Will.

However, the military government stepped out and allowed Saionji's Seiyukai party to take over, but any illusion that democracy had at last won was soon to be dispelled. At elections the Seiyukai triumph set a record, which was merely signal for Yamagata skillfully to wreck their cabinet. As first move, his son, included as Seiyukai Minister of Communications, demanded an excessive sum for railways. The Minister of Finance, fearing the Yamagatan name, offered a compromise. Ito's old friend Inouye, also in the cabinet, whose impulsiveness was planned on by Yamagata, fiercely condemned the compromise, and Saionji's government was so torn he gladly accepted Yamagata's offer of promotion to the privy council. Then all the ministers' resignations were accepted excepting those of Yamagata, Junior, and the treasury chief, the railway matter was promptly postponed, and Yamagata's militarist disciple Katsura took the government.

The public were told that Saionji had given up headship of the government because of ill health. Ito, over on the continent endeavoring to reconcile the Koreans to the loss of their sovereignty, issued a manifesto revealing the truth of the intrigue. The military were perturbed. He would go to such lengths! He was growing less docile and discreet with age. Even though he were Japan's senior statesman, it might be necessary to put him out of the way. . . .

Yamagata and Katsura were ready to annex Korea. Ito came forward with a system of division of authority between Japanese and Koreans. It was decried by the military. Ito, they decided, must be eased out of responsibility in Korea.

During July, 1907, the alarmed Korean Emperor sent an emissary to plead his case at The Hague. In treaties with America, European powers, and Japan, the integrity of Korea had been guaranteed. Japan had made sacred declarations upon entering her wars with both China and Russia that her aim was to preserve the sovereignty of Korea. Now the military received assurances from President Roosevelt and governments of the other Powers that these treaties would be ignored. But airing of the matter at The Hague might prove unfortunate. It was understood that Western governments frequently repudiated little private understandings under the pressure of publicity. So, by bribery and threats, an internal crisis was brought about in Seoul, and the king was forced to abdicate to a protectorate headed by the traitor-prime-minister, Li. When the king's emissary reached The Hague, he was representing no one.

Korean feeling ran high and was directed particularly against Ito, the official representative of the aggressor nation—who was personally innocent and helpless. An abdication ceremony was arranged particularly to impress the foreign plenipotentiaries. Ito's staff strongly opposed his attendance in person. A dozen desperate plots existed to take his life on that day. He sat in the resident-general's office greatly troubled. A telephone message arrived from the throne room announcing that everything was ready. Ito asked himself if he, who so many times had risked his life, was cringing? True, it was easy to die fighting for one's own cause. This situation required the greater courage: to step out and take the counterblow for an attack he had not inspired, to be cursed for crimes he would have prevented, to be made a hero-martyr in a cause he detested, to take upon himself the retribution for the sins of his nation. Bushido, the spirit of the samurai, resurged with him. He arose and wiped the

[228]

perspiration from his broad, furrowed face. "I will go under any consideration!" he announced to his aides. Miraculously he escaped that day, but henceforth he accounted himself dead. His struggle was over. He knew his fate, and he awaited it stoically.

In June, 1909, Ito was removed from Korea by the old expedient of making him president of the privy council. A Yamagata man, Sone, succeeded. The annexation scheme was put before the diet, convened in strict secrecy. For a huge consideration to himself and possible objectors—including a refuge in Japan which he expected to need—the prime minister of Korea was ready to present a formal request to the Japanese Emperor to take over the government of his country. There remained the question of Mutsuhito's sanction and that, they knew, would be withheld if Ito so requested. Then, of course, some overt act of provocation was needed to precipitate the coup.

Ito was doing what he could to obviate hostility between the two peoples. He had toured with the new Korean king through Korea, making conciliatory speeches to the people, and now he took the Korean Prince Li about Japan, making thirty lectures in twenty-four days. Yamagata applauded the work. He encouraged a similar good-will tour of Manchuria.

Ito, knowing well that he was being sent out of the way, planned the tour. Then he went for a few days' visit to his villa in Oiso. His secretary overheard an after-dinner discourse to his son, Bunkichi, later to be

Baron: "My boy, you are now a graduate of the university and a man. At this instant I would like to impress upon your mind the word 'loyalty' and nothing else. I like to believe that the summary of my more than fifty years of official life is 'loyalty to the Emperor.' Our country cannot expect to flourish unless it is governed by this spirit, binding its people in complete union. Should any member of the house of Ito lack in this loyal spirit, let him not be considered my descendant. I should be willing to see my sons suffer and be penniless, but I cannot sanction any departure from the spirit of loyalty in the family of Ito forever."

Then he called in the village fishermen whom in former days he had frequently invited to his gardens, and filled them up once more with noodles and saké. Some years before, he had started each school child in the village on the way to fortune with a bank account of ten sen. He now gave the children a fête and inquired as to the state of their deposits, adding to those accounts which showed thrift. He formally thanked the scrupulous little Lady Ito for her care of himself and his household and told her that this journey, his thirtieth across the channel, would not be protracted. En route to Shiminoseki port, his train passed the school children of Yanaitsu village, marshaled in military formation to salute him. He handed their head master a hundred yen bill with which to start postal savings accounts for the children. Ito's secretary, Furuya, on visiting the village four years later, was to find that the

[230]

five hundred children had built up accounts aggregating 3,200 yen. The prince's gift they were keeping in a separate account, which totaled 127 yen.

Sixty-nine years old, with the vigor of a man of forty, squat and a bit stout, wearing his bushy goatee, white hairs alternating with black topping the kindliest face in the world, Ito stepped on to the continent of Asia with a "Life" of Peter the Great under his arm. At the Sino-Russian city of Harbin he detrained to review some Russian troops at nine-thirty o'clock on the morning of October 24, 1909. A wild-looking Korean dashed unhindered to his side and fired a pistol into his abdomen. *"Baka!"*—Fool—exclaimed Ito in a low voice, and sank to the ground. The assassin turned and wounded his secretary Mori, the consul-general Kawakami, and the director of the South Manchurian Railway, Tanaka, eventually to be known as "Yamagata's last disciple."

Ito was carried aboard the train. Thirty minutes later, repeating a poem of Oda Nobunaga, forerunner of the Hideyoshi he had as a child emulated, he died.

Life is short; the world is a mere dream to the idle.
Only the fool fears death, for what is there of life that does not die once, sooner or later?
Man has to die once only;
He should make his death glorious.

"He should make his death glorious." Sent out of the way by a rival—shot down by a mad assassin!

One madman's bullet provided removal of the obstruction to a final move against Korea, and the provocation to take it.

There were those who said, softly in their inner chambers, that the Japanese military party had hired Anjukon, the assassin. Yamagata had been finding Ito increasingly difficult to manage. Yet it is hard to accuse him of going to such an extreme against his schoolmate of Yoshida Shoin's academy. One prefers to believe that he just let matters take their course. The charge that Prince Ito was insufficiently guarded was never satisfactorily answered. If, when Yamagata saw Ito off for Korea, he expected not to meet him again, his steely old heart had softened into remorseful apprehension, for he anxiously awaited the end of Ito's journey, and was shocked and broken when the corrected message apprised him of its dénouement.

Ito's body was brought home on a cruiser and he was given state funeral on November 4. Field Marshal Prince Yamagata, seventy-two years of age, tall and straight with sparse white hair, face long, emaciated and of a dyspeptic pallor, was, after Emperor Mutsuhito himself, chief mourner. Newspapermen, who were very hostile, looked for some betrayal of exultation on his part. The old soldier's only remark was: "I am alone now. Prince Ito was the only man with whom I could discuss state matters as an equal."

Ito's estate proved small. He had not very well exercised the thrift he sedulously taught children. Neither had he, after the fashion of the time, built him a fortune from political prestige. During the crisis precipitated with Korea by Ito's death, Yamagata held a special troop review at Utsonomiya. It was attended by the Emperor and all the high officials and commanded by the veteran Marshal himself. The Emperor had, as vantage point, a little tent on a hillock which proved utterly inadequate to protect the Sacred Person from a drenching in the violent storm which arose. Inasmuch as the troops were not equipped with greatcoats, the Emperor declined to put one on, saying that, on such occasions, he was one of his men. Just as the listening reporters were drafting telegrams about this on their soaked writing pads, Marshal Yamagata strolled up the hillock in a greatcoat, comfortable and dry. There was triumphant excitement among the newspapermen who had been watching keenly to "get something on" the old autocrat. Here were a selfishness and discourtesy bordering on *lèse majesté*. The people of Japan would conclude that Yamagata was making himself greater than the Emperor. The tide of indignation would sweep him from power! They bent themselves to write stories which would stir a nation and upset a dictator.

They dispatched their runners with their articles. Then one reporter ventured to approach the chamberlain in attendance. "Is it not time you called this to the attention of the Son of Heaven?"—pointing out Yamagata's garment. The chamberlain, evidently concerned, said he would mention it. A bit later he returned to the reporters' stand. "The Heavenly Person deigns to explain that Marshal Yamagata is wearing the greatcoat against the Marshal's protest but at the express command of the Emperor, who desires that he should have this special protection as a mark of Imperial affection for his venerable body, and as a special honor before the army in recognition of his great work in creating it. The Emperor [who was then fifty-eight, and was not long for this world] chooses to regard Marshal Prince Yamagata as his father."

The flabbergasted reporters raced for their offices to instruct their editors to change the attacks into encomiums. Elaborations of Mutsuhito's signal honor to Yamagata with résumés of the old soldier's fifty years of public life covered pages.

The Korean matter was soon accomplished. Resident General Sone gave way to Terauchi, Yamagata's most ruthless disciple, who had been Minister of War since 1902. In August, 1910, the annexation was announced. The young Koreans struggled desperately for several years, and the sympathetic American missionaries were accused by Japanese military of inciting them. But Terauchi crushed opposition with terrorism and spying.

Yamagata had completed his broad foundation for Japanese empire. He had captained Japan to the acquisition of Formosa, Liaotung (Port Arthur) peninsula, Korea, and the Russian built South-Manchurian Railway. The great entry avenue to Japan's continental empire, leading from the best equipped port in Asia to the circular heart of the great city of Dairen, properly received the name: Yamagata-dori. Dairen, third in port tonnage in continental Pacific Asia, becomes the type of a new, capitalized, industrialized, skyscraper-proud, machine-powerful Japan.

Yamagata had a typically Asian idea of "democracy." He favored elective assemblies as a means whereby people might keep in touch with governors—that the latter might better provide for their needs and direct their growth. Represented majorities, controlling and unmaking administrations, were beyond his conception. His government was that modification of Eastern tradition by Western importation so absurdly called "republican" in Turkey, China, and elsewhere. Political party rule was to him positively immoral. To prevent it he encouraged a multitude of little parties, which he could coalesce for passing budgets and promptly disperse again. He inspired the restriction on public gatherings, organization, speech, and press, finally developed into blanket suppression of anything disliked by the police under the charge of "dangerous thoughts."

With Ito gone and Yamagata's ideas to combat, the Seiyukai became first an opportunistic group serving any government, then for a time a purely obstructive mob opposing every government. But as surely as Yamagata, however indestructible he seemed, had yet to release the helm, so surely the party leaders would

[235]

have their day. Demos would then suffer at the betraying hands of politicians instead of under the repressive heel of autocracy.

In 1913 Mutsuhito died. He had been the Emperor of the Restoration of Japan to world dignity as well as of the Throne to supremacy. His nearly half-century reign had seen the complete reshaping of his nation's life and the setting of an example soon to be followed by the rest of Asia. His people deified him not only because he symbolized such accomplishment but because he had been wise and lovable. His son, taking the throne as Taisho, was not a strong character. Yamagata was left more than ever the chancellor of the realm.

Sadako, no longer the girlish geisha, but alert of body and mind as ever, made a record of a sensational incident connected with the Emperor's passing.

General Nogi called on Prince Yamagata. We were living at Shinzan Mansion, Tokyo. The Prince was wearing a loose bath kimono when he learned the General was at the gate, and sent at once for a *hakama* [ceremonial skirt] without which he deemed it a discourtesy to receive any one, even his most intimate friends. But before he could complete tying this on, the General came impetuously into the room.

"You do not look well," exclaimed the Prince, startled by his drawn face. General Nogi passed it off, but reached out from where he squatted on the guest mat and drew a box of paper, brush, and ink-slab to his side. "I have been composing a poem," he said, and wrote out a *hokku* [seventeen syllable miniature stanza].

When he went out he dropped it on the ink-box. The Prince picked it up and read it, and murmured: "To read between the lines of this, I think he must die." He handed it to me with the comment: "Here, Nogi composed such a queer poem. Keep this carefully." It read: "Yearning for our Great Emperor who passed away from this empty world, I have prepared to him a special prayer."

It was not signed, so I asked Prince to note something on it whereby we could identify it. He wrote "Nogi's Poem" on an envelope in which it has since been kept. All through supper the Prince was very troubled over General Nogi. [Nogi had been one of his most faithful and brilliant commanders. He and Admiral Togo were the popular heros of the Russian war.]

A week later, on the night of the Imperial funeral procession (September 13, 1912), the Prince returned home quite late, and came to me in agitation saying: "Nogi is done." Stupidly I asked, "Who killed him?" "No," replied the Prince, slowly, "he committed *harakiri* at the first gun of the cortège starting. When he was writing the poem I nearly said to him: 'I see death on you.' It is better that I did not speak." That night he retired very broken and disheartened.

The old autocrat was not, however, too broken to take advantage of the succession to conduct what he regarded as a desirable bit of strategy. Katsura, under Yamagata's protection, had waxed powerful and too rich and too independent. He had shown his ambitions by having himself, when Prime Minister, given the title of Prince. He was on a pleasure trip in Europe when Mutsuhito died, and rushed back with political ambitions, to find himself recipient of an appointment, dated on the very day of his arrival, to an office Yamagata had invented for the occasion: Court Chamberlain and Keeper of the Privy Seal. Katsura had to accept and announce that he had stepped out of politics to devote his life to the young Emperor. Yamagata then asked the Cabinet, again heeded by Saionji, for two more army divisions for Korea. Saionji and his party balked, whereupon Yamagata forced the fall of the administration by withdrawing his henchman who was Minister of War and prohibiting any other general from taking the post.

There was a storm of popular indignation which Katsura thought to capitalize. Boldly making use of his position as Keeper of the Privy Seal, he issued in the imperial name a rescript relieving himself from household service because of the "great necessity" for his services as premier, and imperially summoning a general to serve as war minister. Yamagata had not reckoned on such daring. To protect the imperial authority he told his uncomfortable officer to serve, and sat back to watch Katsura make a cabinet and win control in the lower house.

Katsura, too long Yamagata's fellow-Choshu militarist, had no sympathy from the democratic elements. The only weapon he possessed against the prestige of the genro and military was money. He set out to do a complete job. Determined not to be checked by an obstreperous Parliament, he founded a party of his own to control it, and openly offered two thousand yen for each "ordinary" M.P. of the other parties who would swing over to his—fifteen thousand yen for those known as orators. The established parties were infuriated.

Katsura got his majority but an exasperated populace mobbed and dispersed it. Yamagata, controlling the army and police, would give no protection. Broken politically, financially, and physically, Katsura stepped out, and within a year he was dead, while the seventy-six-year-old autocrat, without a smile, set Japan's political house in order again. It was evident that Yamagata would not, like Bismarck, pass from the stage with the monarch he had helped to establish. Somewhat disgraced by this internecine fight, however, Choshu yielded for a time to Satsuma, and General Yamamoto of that clan took the premiership. The navy benefited in consequence, enjoying its greatest period of expansion.

Yamagata and Sadako moved out to a secluded villa at Odawara. But it was the old Prince, when the World War came on, who dictated Japan's entry through the opening in the much-modified Anglo-Japanese treaty. It was he who placed in power Okuma, who did not see liberalism and chauvinism as incompatible, on the compromise that the policies of the military would be supported. Yamagata authorized the reduction of German Tsingtao, the invasion of Chinese Shantung. Odawara came to be called "the hidden capital" of Japan. Here he worshiped the Meiji Emperor, on each imperial anniversary, in a specially built pavilion. The winter Prince Yamagata was eighty-two was especially severe, but he went out in three inches of snow and performed the ceremonial ablutions. The result was pneumonia, and

Emperor Taisho's sending his personal physician to bring the aged marshal through. There came a mysterious "Imperial House matter" on which the newspapers, not daring to publish details, attacked Yamagata as "traitor to the Imperial House." It seems that he denounced a royal marriage into his old rival clan, the Satsuma. Yamagata told his fellow genro, Matsukata and Saionji, that he would remain of the same opinion forever, but would resign all honors. Against their protests he did so, but the Emperor returned his resignation with the advice that the offense was overlooked because of his sincere heart.

Not until the Twenty-one Demands on China, and their face-losing dénouement for Japan, does it appear that the grasp of the old samurai was weakening and his jingo disciples were running away with the bit. The unskilled bluntness of this attack on China's sovereignty and the unblushing diplomatic deceit used to cover it, in exasperating the disunited Chinese, irritating Western Powers, and strengthening liberalism at home, are not in keeping with Yamagata's accomplishments. Or was it because he did not have Ito to velvet-glove the mailed fist for him?

This mistake gave party government its first real chance in Japan. The journalist Hara reorganized the Seiyukai, and made himself the first plebeian party-chief premier of the country. He headed a Cabinet backed by the new industrial plutocracy, which was disappointed with the poor returns from the military ventures in China and Siberia. Yamagata could not lord it over Hara. Yet the plebeian premier conferred most respectfully with the scholarly, eighty-year-old oligarch on the cool mats and under the perfumed pines of Odawara. In 1921 Hara was assassinated by a young "parlor chauvinist," gone fanatic, who thought he would duplicate for his party and Emperor the benefits of the elimination of Ito. Yamagata saw no advantage this time. Tools of such sharpness must rarely be used, and according to a master plan. The news excited him to the point of fever but he insisted upon going to Tokyo at once. When assurance came that the younger men were keeping their heads and carrying on, he consented to go to bed instead.

He did not rise again. But at eighty-four, dyspeptic and rheumatic, he could still hold death at bay with his tremendous will. He was concerned over the evidences that a creeping disease was incapacitating the Emperor mentally. The intelligent Empress was acting as imperial mind. Yamagata sent for the tutors of the heir apparent, then approaching manhood, and questioned them carefully. They convinced him of the Prince's soundness and ability. "It is well," he said, and stopped fighting.

As with Sun Yat-sen, he was ill so long that he became a myth. "Is the Ancient Marshal still alive, or dead?" people would ask one another in the market-place. All visitors were denied him. "But one morning," says Sadako, "he heard that Prince Matsukata had come. Matsukata was one of his few living ties with his generation. 'I want to see him!' demanded the Prince. Approaching the bedside, Prince Matsukata, who was by now deaf and spoke in the loud voice so frequently adopted by the hard of hearing, shouted: 'How are you? Be courageous and feel strong,' to which Prince Yamagata replied with a smile: 'You are always healthy and it's good for you!' Matsukata said: 'As soon as you get through with this, let's do our best again in state affairs,' and the two octogenarians nodded at one another."

After Matsukata left, the old prince called in his family. "*Yoroshiku*"—"best regards"—was his military farewell. "Thank you for your many kindnesses." Then he stretched out his arm and took Sadako's hand, and ceased to breathe. It was February 1, 1922, and the old soldier was eighty-five. His death was kept secret and the corpse conveyed to Tokyo before the announcement was made. A national funeral was given him which cost eighty thousand yen. Radicals in the diet fulminated against the expense.

He left a simple family. Kokumo had been childless—which to the most puritanical Japanese would have justified his taking a concubine, but was not likely the motive thereof. He had adopted his sister's son as heir. Then Sadako bore him two sons and two daughters. As was so often done in Japan, Yamagata made his own son heir of another house. In late life, he changed his own heir, choosing his favorite grandson,

son of his surviving daughter and Baron Hunakoshi of the plutocratic Mitsui family, who was to bear the title of Baron Yamagata. One of the Prince's grandsons, connected with a Japanese bank in New York, a kindly, broad six-footer, inherited at least some of his famous ancestor's traits, for he was gracious enough and reticent enough silently to listen through a young American's lecture on the life of his grandfather before the Japan Society there.

Upon Ito's assassination Yamagata had taken the Presidency of the Privy Council and he retained it until death. This oligarchy was hardly to survive him. In a month Okuma, who had come into the group from his compromise cabinet of 1915, followed his old rival, and Matsukata lived only two years more. Saionji, at heart the liberal and Ito-ite, petitioned the Emperor to let the institution of the genro die with him.

At the time this is being written prime ministers are chosen for the Emperor no longer by the president of the Privy Council, but by the very Lord High Chamberlain whose office seemed a joke when Yamagata created it. The important thing is that invariably the leader of the majority party is being selected. Party government is accepted. Universal manhood suffrage has come. Japan is evolving toward a British parliamentary system and the national conception of the Throne is changing under a new young Emperor who has been abroad and played golf with the Prince of Wales. It is a democratically tending new Japan, and yet it is as surely the continuance of Yamagata's Japan as republican Germany is of Bismarck's Prussia.

Yamagata the silent plowed a straight furrow to a definite objective. He achieved in his tremendous span of activity a personal success, without setback or defeat at the end, unrivaled, I believe, by nation-builders. From the standpoint of "hardboiled," practical, Machiavellian statesmanship, his was one of the greatest careers ever lived. But to him it was not "Success." It was just a job accomplished. There was no streak of vanity in him.

"He was brought up in a stern tradition. He never smiled, except among his closest intimates. He was sensitive to influence and yet never allowed himself to be swerved from his aim. Loyalty to Emperor, army, and nation was his makeup. He was not conceited but he felt perfectly sufficient in himself. He was a man taught to talk with actions, and to spend no time explaining himself.—In Japan we *had* this type!" concluded a grizzled ex-samurai with a tone of assurance and also regret to his American listener who seemed a bit unable to grasp *Bushido* over the tea-cups.

> Soldiers are for fighting—
> Good wine is to drink.

Yamagata had written on the last photograph which he signed.

Present Japan hates him and idealizes Ito. When I first made known my intention in that country of writing the military Prince's life I was besieged by editors, civil officials, liberals, students, and even some army men to give to the Western world Ito instead. Then I found I must write on both, for either is an enigma alone, and Japan, without comprehension of their half-century duel, is not understandable.

Nothing could stand against Yamagata except the strong new force of the social movement—the gradually accumulated force of self-conscious public opinion. And so Yamagata, in fullness of years and power and honor, died with the hatred of a new liberal age concentrated upon him, while Ito, the defeated, lives on as its inspiration and hero.

MUSTAPHA KEMAL

1879–

MUSTAPHA KEMAL

I

WHEN after the twenty-two-day battle of the Sakharia the Turks of the present generation gave their savior, Mustapha Kemal, the solemn and tradition-hung title of *Ghazi*, "The Conqueror," they exhibited the change that has come over Asia. Imagine a secular-minded, yellow-haired, sharp-chinned, Parisian-tailored, French- and German-speaking Muhammad or Emperor Osman!

Europe required three centuries to come out of medievalism into modernism, but Asia, in self-preservation, with the way pioneered by the West, accomplishes the tremendous change in half a generation. The Turks, counted but yesterday the most hide-bound of all Asian peoples, have indeed done it in ten years, while Europe and America have been convincing themselves that the War is over. In Turkey as elsewhere the transformation was preceded by the painful rise of a generation of earnest, indiscreet, fanatical, patriotic new thinkers, but the amazing speed of the change itself, robbing Japan of the "record" in nation-remodeling to date, is due to the mental vitality and physical energy of one personality still in his mid-career: Mustapha Kemal, the Ghazi.

In another way, Turkey is an interesting comparison with Japan. It now excels the Pacific Power in giving

[249]

us the most simple and straightforward as well as rapid example of the modernization of an Asiatic country. It enters the list with Japan and Siam as the most "enlightened," in our narrow Western sense, of Asian nations. A comity of interest, cemented by diplomatic and commercial missions, has sprung up between these three so different Asian countries of near, middle, and far Asia.

The life of the man Kemal is as straightforward as his country's recent history which he has dominated. He conceived his purpose in boyhood—he seems to have been born with it. By early youth he had perfected his technique. It was: unquestioning yet not entirely conceited faith in himself, a deep though demanding trust in his associates, an unrelenting pursuit of information pertinent to his cause, an unsurpassed ability to bide his time, and a heroic courage to contravene or ignore tradition and convention. With the ability to flout the established order possessed by Sun Yat-sen he combined the balance and sense of responsibility of Ito. With the vision of Sun he combined the determination of Lenin and Stalin. With the diplomatic qualities of Ito he combined the military and organizing gifts of Yamagata. He excelled all in genius of generalship. In originality he did not compare with Lenin or Gandhi. He never undertook to establish an original ideology in the mind of man, but merely to take from what was around him.

Since he is not the founder of a new religion or interpretation of life but simply of a modern nation, since he is a careerist and not a seer, his work is much more easily understood by us of the West. At the same time he and his nation remain fundamentally Asiatic. The Caliph and the fez are gone, but not the psychology which made the Koran, the Turkish odes of love and leisure, or the mosque of Brussa.

One involuntarily wants to compare Kemal and Mussolini. The Italian followed a devious path to power, varying from radical agitation to Fascism (after all, the two are very alike when successful) and from activity as a spy in the employ of a foreign government to that of a super-patriot. Kemal followed a straight road from the beginning. Both show great knowledge of the minds of men of their own and alien races with whom they have to deal. Both have courage and amazing energy. Kemal is not so good an advertiser as Mussolini. He equally insists upon being everything, but, having unquestioned authority, he seems better able to endure the risk of this not being in the forefront of his people's consciousness. As to the comparative greatness of their work: Il Duce controls sixty million people, the Ghazi thirteen million. But Kemal has remade a nation in a sense not approached by Mussolini. In any case, I make bold to hazard that a renewed Italy is not so important to world history now as a revived Asian nation.

Kemal has profited as much as any of our figures by the ideas and work of forerunners and contemporaries—many of whom he has dropped or slain. Yet for clean-cut conception and execution of a seemingly impossible task Kemal deserves recognition as the world's greatest living statesman. On all counts he probably remains the most important artist in nation remodeling since Lenin's death.

He is the outstanding present example of that category of Asiatic leaders who flourish by challenging the accepted Asian order. Yet he works on the safe basis of race pride, appealing to, rather than contravening, the basic traits of Turkish character. He is determined to make Turks as self-confident, materially powerful, and mentally alive as Europeans, and he is oblivious of spiritual values involved.

But his greatest significance to a watching West is the demonstration in his personality and accomplishment that Asia, sterile as she may seem, carries within herself the seeds of her own salvation, and that these, at times when the world least expects, receive unexpected fecundation from the violating West, to be brought to birth in the travail of the East's indignation.

II

An army of small, dark, Turkish lads dashed through the stalls of the market place which in 1889 served as playground for the primary school of Saloniki, in pursuit of an imaginary enemy, led by a ten-year-old boy whose corn-yellow hair gleamed in the sunlight and whose steel-blue eyes narrowed deliberately as he gave his commands. Then, as the turbaned priest-teacher called shrilly, he led his "soldiers" back to sit on the ground and be prodded into careless repetition of the Koran by the master's long stick. The boy Mustapha had but lately returned to school in his native city, after a year or two of running wild among the fields and woods at the uncle's home whither his strong and adored mother had taken him after the death of his father. That one-time sitter at the seat of custom had left his small family no legacy, so Mustapha's ambitious mother impressed upon her son the necessity of his winning his own education.

Graduation day came, to see Mustapha proudly bearing home a scholarship to the secondary school in the near-by city of Monastir. He went with high hopes. The modern buildings, the desks, and the books promised a new and exhilarating life. A quick, brilliant student, he started, under this inspiration, to carry double work. Particularly was he taken by the new courses in history and science introduced from Europe. And then his enthusiasm turned to dust and ashes when he ran afoul of a punctilious and tyrannical old-fashioned Arabic teacher. It was the first time the spirited youth had been forced to undergo what was to him indignity. And there arose within him the beginnings of that revolt against misrule at home and aggression from abroad which were to make him the rejuvenator of a dying people.

[253]

In spite of his mother's bitter opposition to a soldier's profession and the fact that he was below regulation age, he ran away from Monastir and registered in the Staff School. There he found teachers, friends, followers, and audiences. His mathematics master, whose given name was also Mustapha, bestowed upon him the popular "career" name of Kemal, "Perfection," honored by the nation's greatest literary figure, Nanick Kemal.

Already the youth was guided by a sense of boundless vitality, inner strength, and superiority. He awakened the admiration and retained the loyalty of his school friends, many of whom were to become his companions-at-arms. He took naturally to military regimen. He was lovable, with a sense of whimsy rare among the Turks (which, like his fair coloring, can doubtless be traced to his Roumelian descent), but he had a steel-strong will and a naïve faith in his own destiny which, although it did not make him mutinous, rendered him impervious to influence and made the imprint of other personalities negligible.

The military school was rife with gossip of the cruelties of the ruling Sultan, Abdul Hamid, whose fear of assassination was so great that he took the precaution of destroying or banishing any one whom his many spies led him to mistrust. No Turkish life was safe. While other boys slept, Mustapha read about the French Revolution and its benignant effect upon the people. He visualized his own people freed from the galling tyranny of a ruler who was both weak and cruel and who combined in his person the absolute political and religious power. After his all-night reading orgies he made speeches to his gaping young schoolmates.

This grew into the establishment of a little paper, edited by Kemal with unfailing regularity, devoted to protests against superstition and misgovernment— an activity by no means unknown to the countless spies of Abdul Hamid. They seized Kemal upon the very day of his graduation and took him to the Yildiz Palace, where he was subjected to weeks of questioning. He fortunately got off with a temporary banishment to Damascus.

Here in the world's most ancient city where peach and almond blossoms filled the air with fragrance, the young exile had an opportunity to study at first hand the military and civil disintegration of territorial Turkey. He went from the villas of the officials to coffee houses on narrow, winding streets—from the colorful bazaars to hovels of the poor. The fact that he was a student of advanced thought and of art in all its manifestations did not cloud his intuitive understanding of the humble merchant and vine-tender. Slender, graceful, about six feet in height, there was an indefinable air of elegance about him, and he wore faultless European clothes in a manner that would have done credit to a Mayfair drawing-room. Yet he frequently went among the peasants, living quite sufficiently in their flat-roofed mud huts, divested of all luxuries.

He gradually gathered about him a group of young men whom he organized into a secret political society which he named *Vatan*—"Fatherland." When news of his activities reached Constantinople, his further banishment to Jaffa was ordered. To be confined in the seaport of the Jews was considered a special disgrace in the Turkish army, and Kemal particularly, who was stigmatized as being a Saloniki Jew by his enemies, had no relish for the place. He won the favor of the local commandant who shut his eyes while Kemal's friends spirited him back to his own Saloniki, by way of Alexandria and the Piræus. For eight months Kemal remained in hiding in his cypress-studded city by the gleaming sea, and took advantage of his situation to introduce his revolutionary society into the European provinces. This branch of the *Vatan* was to be absorbed by Enver Pasha's Union and Progress Society, usually known as the "Young Turks."

On second thought, the Sultan concluded that mere banishment was not sufficient for so potentially dangerous an enemy as Mustapha Kemal and sent an order for his arrest to both Damascus and Jaffa. The helpful commandant at Jaffa reported that the young officer had been sent into service against Egypt, then in revolt. Abdul Hamid forgot him, and he remained quietly in Saloniki until his friends could bring about his reinstatement in rank and a "transfer" to the General Staff in Saloniki—where he had been secretly living the entire time!

In 1908 the general Mahmoud Chevet, needing a man familiar with European military tactics, took Kemal as chief of staff. The young officer studied his soldiers as carefully as he had studied accounts of the French Revolution, and set to work to infuse a new spirit and more efficient organization into the army, from its very foundations up. He was careful to appear submissive and not to awaken the jealousy of his superiors until the propitious moment for showing his strength should arrive. Hence he was entrusted with more and more authority.

The Union and Progress party came into power, but Kemal was soon running afoul of his former political allies. Enver, the outwardly suave little leader of the Young Turks, whose vanity and jealousy soon marked Kemal as a rival, began a campaign against his potential enemy which was to react to his own downfall.

Mustapha Kemal disapproved of the manner in which politicians were interfering with military discipline, and he decided to give up politics for the time and to turn the full force of his energy toward rehabilitating the army. His efforts in this direction won approval, and in 1910 he was sent to study the French army maneuvers in Picardy. Returning, he spent several months in Paris, a formative experience in his development. The contrasts of Oriental and Occidental culture thrust themselves upon his attention. He was particularly impressed by the strength to their nation of the socially free women of France, in contrast with the immured women of his own country. He made mental notes of the changes in civil and commercial life that would have to be introduced into his Oriental society. He decided in his own mind that his people, who were supposed to be hopelessly "Oriental" and backward, illiterate and poor, could be inspired to compete with the nations of Europe, and he quietly pledged to himself that he would perform this task. He improved his already excellent French to fluency at this time and developed the flair for things French which was instantly to endear him with French men and women who would come in contact with him.

He held the rank of colonel when Italy made a sudden onslaught on Tripoli in 1911. He and Enver and Fethi Bey were the outstanding heroes of the campaign. He remained at Tripoli until news of the outbreak of war in the Balkans reached him in 1912. He mustered his forces and hastened to repulse this greater threat— only to learn, when he had advanced as far as Egypt, that his country had been defeated and his native Saloniki had fallen.

Hard upon the heels of this conflict a third war broke out—again in the Balkans. Kemal was appointed chief of staff at Gallipoli Peninsula. He made an intensive study of the Dardanelles, and his knowledge was soon to be a decisive factor in world history.

Peace came between Turkey and Bulgaria, and Kemal remained at Sofia. The enmity between him and Enver, then Minister of War, was growing more bitter. Suddenly the war which was to be called "world" overwhelmed Europe. Kemal rushed to Constantinople to oppose Enver's desire for participation. His strongly voiced prediction that Turkey's entrance was premature and that Germany was doomed to eventual defeat gave rivals the opportunity to rule him from active participation. However, his ability to get the best from soldiers was soon needed in the desperate resistance at Gallipoli. He remained in the background, with an under-officer's commission, but every day more obviously becoming the one man the soldiers trusted. More and more the German command leaned upon him.

It is August, 1915. Liman Pasha (General Liman von Sanders) is at the end of his rope. He summons Kemal to staff headquarters. "We are in a vise. I can do no more with your damned Turks," he says.

The young Turkish officer springs up, his blue eyes flashing, his usually masklike face setting in determination.

"Let me act here. I can do much more with them. Give me the command!"

Von Sanders and his fellow Germans shrugged their shoulders. They know the men have ears only for Kemal's voice. Without gazette, Kemal takes the fate of his country and the lives of 160,000 soldiers into his decisive hands.

His fellow officers are at first doubtful about his authority. But when, leading in person at Adana, he is struck down by a fragment of shell, rises again and calmly draws a shattered watch from over his heart, he is acclaimed as the chosen of Allah to lead the faithful. The Turks fear to follow one whose luck is evil, but they will go anywhere behind the Allah-protected.

Kemal slowly forces back the last and "decisive" British attack, and decimates the reëmbarking Australians. He shatters the Allied hope of a speedy victory through the Eastern front. The exchange in Liman Pasha's tent proves to have been one of the "decisive conversations" of history.

When Gallipoli had been evacuated by the British, Kemal proceeded to the Caucasus front, where he was able to reclaim Bitlis Mush from the clutch of the Russians. His reward was the rank of Pasha.

But the German commanders as well as the Turkish rulers began to fear the weapon they had used lest it be turned against themselves. So they sent Kemal to Asia as "Inspector of Troops." To the Hejaz in far Arabia he went, in full realization of the reason for his journey but intent upon using it to advantage. He promptly advised the recall of the forces in the Hejaz in order to strengthen the position at the Syrian front.

The growing animosity of Enver and of von Falkenhyn, who succeeded Liman von Sanders as German Chief of Staff, led to the disregard of his sound advice, and when his urgent plea against the disastrous attack upon Bagdad was ignored, he resigned. With unfailing prescience and exactitude, his report, dated in September, 1917, traced the causes of the Allied victory which was to result. It is interesting to think that Kemal and Colonel Lawrence—so alike in resourcefulness and self-confidence—were on opposite sides near Bagdad. Kemal was vainly advising a withdrawal which would have robbed Lawrence of the opportunity for his exploits.

In 1918 Vahydu'd-Din Efendi became Sultan. In compliance with his desire, Mustapha Kemal assumed the leadership of the Seventh Army in Palestine. It was then too late to avert the disaster he had foreseen but he managed to keep the remnants of his army together and to conduct the retreat after General Allenby's victory in a masterly manner. He was later Commander-in-Chief of the Yilderim group in their thundering assault upon Bagdad. The pro-German Enver Pasha fled into Soviet Russia to engage in spectacular adventures which were to lead to his death.

Kemal had opposed the German intrusion into Turkish national affairs. Now, when Turkey made armistice, he advised equally against complete surrender to Allied influence. Due to the stiffening which he provided, Turkey procured terms less severe than those soon to be imposed on other belligerents. Under the Armistice of October 30, 1918, the Allies were to control the railways and to hold Batum and Baku. They occupied Constantinople and reserved the right to occupy Thrace, the six Armenian villeyets of Asia Minor, and any strategic point necessary to protect the security of the Allies. The internal affairs of Turkey in Asia would not be subject to their interference beyond a line running from Aleppo to the Persian frontier along the Taurus range.

If the Allies had followed up their advantage and forced their terms at that time, the Turks would have submitted. The English were regarded with hopeful respect in Turkey and their penetration raised no protest. The Peace Conference presented so many problems that seemed more immediate than that of Turkey, however, that she was left uncertain as to the requirements of the victorious Allies for nearly two years. Doubtless she was considered defenseless and beaten—done for, waiting to be divided up as spoils when the larger issue could be laid aside—so she was not even disarmed.

In the meantime, groups of local Robin Hoods began to band together in the remote parts of Asia Minor. They were joined by Russian Bolsheviks in the Caucasus and the Tartars in Baku and the Azerbaijan. When Kemal was to form a national army some of these ruffians were to prove difficult to discipline and were to become enemies, but they now provided a beginning of resistance.

Kemal's influence at headquarters was not regarded as helpful by the British High Commissioner, and the supine Sultan agreed. "Get this man away—anywhere —quickly! He is dangerous," was the order which sent Kemal to Anatolia to demobilize the regiments there.

He went to the weary, defeated, depleted troops and began heartening them for whatever fate lay in store for them, individually or as an army. They could not be demobilized until they were first organized, he said. He was far from resigned to the death of his nation. The Allied Commander-in-Chief, General Milne, authorized a skeleton force around Erzeroum. Mustapha Kemal spent hours revising his commission so as to leave him a free hand. Damad Ferid signed, and Kemal appeared as representative of both the Allies and the Ottoman government. He was waiting for fate to give him his cue. Events soon played into his hands.

On April 4, 1919, the Italians, piqued over President Wilson's refusal to grant them Fiume, walked out of the Peace Conference at Versailles.[1] They had a further grievance: as far back as 1917 their allies had promised them Smyrna as their share of Turkey. It was a deal similar to the one which promised Japan the province of Shantung, and by reaction started nationalism in China—although more honorable, as it is more honorable to carve up an opponent than an ally. The Italians, now relying more on action than on table talk, began to occupy Turkey's ports from Adana (April 29, 1919) north in the direction of Smyrna. They met with little resistance from the disheartened Turks. But the "Big Three"—Lloyd George,

---

[1] In two weeks they were back.

Clémenceau, and Wilson—were not willing to have Italy thus prosper while flouting them. They decided that Smyrna was a "strategic point necessary for the security of the Allies" and planned to throw troops into the Ægean port before Italy could. But what troops to use? British opinion would support no further expedition, and French troops had virtually threatened mutiny at the suggestion of more service in the near East. Venizelos of Greece, looking for territorial acquisition to save himself with his chauvinistic people, came forward with offer of the Greek army. And the insouciant Lloyd George let loose primitive hates which might have given pause to the King of Darkness, an action which was to mark the beginning of the decline of the British—history's greatest—empire. Venizelos' proposal was accepted.

On May 14, 1919, an Allied fleet under the British Admiral Calthorpe sailed into Smyrna and requested the Turkish garrison to disarm and turn over the port in accordance with the "on demand" terms of the Armistice. They did so, but inquired anxiously about the rumor that the coming occupational forces were Greeks. They were told that said forces would be "Allied."

The next day a Greek army disembarked in a parade of triumph for the "Greater Greece" idea cherished since the siege of Troy. Turkish indignation at the "betrayal" and mutual hatred between the ancient enemies at once flared up. Some one fired on the

[264]

parade. The Greeks retaliated with a massacre under the eyes of the British navy. Desperate fighting broke out between the Greeks and the straggling Turkish forces in the surrounding area.

World attention made expedient an Allied commission of investigation and conciliation. American High Commissioner Admiral Mark Bristol headed it and compiled a report which the British government declined to publish.

Bristol was able to bring about temporary cessation of the fighting, but all Turkey was aroused. The occupation of their greatest Ægean port by the Allies would have been accepted as part of the fortunes of war, but to have it turned over to the pillage of their old enemies the Greeks was another matter. This was pushing victory too far. Defiance spread like wildfire among the soldiers, filling them with new vigor and spirit. The waiting Kemal organized feeling into a force. On July 27, 1919, he called a congress of a handful of patriots at Erzerum, followed by a resolving body at Sivas on September 13. It went to pains not to appear insurgent against the Sultan, seeking means to "safeguard the Sultanate and the supreme Caliphate and integrity of the country while the Turkish government was under foreign compulsion."

The first act of the Erzerum provisional committee, of which Kemal had by general assent become president, was to send an appeal to the Turkish Parliament in Constantinople, asking that the Caliph request the

Powers to terminate the Greek occupation of Smyrna, and that he divest the notoriously pro-allied Damad Ferid of authority enabling him to make in the name of Turkey such terms with Europe as his recently negotiated Treaty of Sèvres. In its telegram the committee stated that it would wait a certain number of hours in the telegraph office for the Caliph's reply before acting. Hour after hour passed. No reply. The Nationalists left the telegraph station free to follow out their own plans for the protection of the new Turkey and also in open rebellion against the government at Constantinople.

At first the British who dominated the Constantinople government did not attach any importance to the new "Nationalist movement." What harm could a few patriotic fanatics do to their secure position? The Sultan was under their control. He had accepted Lloyd George's personal support—oblivious as to how this was to lead to his overthrow in the offices of both Sultan and Caliph.

Aubrey Herbert, a scion of the English nobility, whose understanding of the Near East gained as diplomat and as adventurer made him an authority, has tersely summed up the situation: "Mustapha Kemal, who was engaged in disarming the Turkish forces, became Turkish Commander-in-Chief, and owed his title as directly to Mr. Lloyd George as any British multimillionaire who had contributed to party funds."

But Kemal could not long be ignored. He equipped his army with the weapons left in Turkey by the German evacuation. He reorganized the old Union and Progress Party and added it to his forces. He incorporated and armed the ruffian bands of Asia Minor. The vehicle was being assembled with which he hoped to restore the lost dignity of his country in the eyes of all the nations of the earth.

When Constantinople learned of Kemal's activities, his immediate return was commanded. His response to this was to stay on, resigning his position and rank under the government of Damad Ferid. The Sultan tried to obviate open repudiation of Kemal, who was then his honorary aide-de-camp, but the British insisted upon his public dismissal. Damad Ferid, ignoring Kemal's resignation, outlawed and degraded the "rebel."

Turkey now had two governments—each claiming to be the only lawful one. Nationalist sentiment spread and many open Nationalists were elected to the old Parliament in Constantinople. The election of Kemal himself was even suggested. He refused to consider going, on the grounds that under existing conditions in Constantinople no legislative body there could express the "will of the people." Already in his mind the break with Constantinople was clear, but there remained much loyalty among patriots and much fanaticism among the populace and he had to move cautiously. Also, when he envisioned the force making new Turkey he saw himself heading it.

Kemal moved his own governmental headquarters from Sivas to the ancient, classical, expanse-protected seat of Angora, and his influence and power grew rapidly throughout Turkey. His forces came into conflict with the French in Cilicia. When the French were driven out of the Marash district the remaining Armenian and Greek population was massacred with some of the cruelty that the Greeks in Smyrna had wreaked upon the Turks. The Italian forces were not molested, their differences with the Greeks over Albania and the Dodecanese making their presence desirable as a balance to the Greek occupation of Smyrna. Also, the Italians were, according to reports, furnishing arms to the Turkish Nationalists. They performed a similar service to various factions in China, although officially they subscribed to the arms embargo. Kemal sent the semi-bandit irregular forces to harass the Anglo-Greek invaders. Their successes were constantly counterbalanced by British reënforcements of the Greeks. A thrilling story of the saving of the rock-bound port of Samsun by Refet Bey is told by Madame Berthe Georges-Gaulis, a Frenchwoman whose semi-official presence in Turkey was designed to promote good feeling between her countrymen and the Turks. The British colonel debarked at Samsun in advance of his men to investigate the size of the protecting force. Taking soldiers marching in the distance to be the vanguard of a large army, he discreetly retired. The "army" was composed of a hundred or so of Refet Bey's de-

voted followers who had passed and repassed within
view of the officer.

There were rumors of an impending British coup
in Constantinople. Life became more and more wretched
for the Muslem patriots. The Armenian and other
Christian elements long accustomed to insult were having their turn at arrogance. Halide Edib, the dainty
and intense Turkish woman novelist, relates the offen-
siveness of Christian to Turkish women in the railroad trains and the barring of Turkish women from
street cars by Armenian conductors. "We will report
to the British" was the threat under which they conducted their petty tyranny. Various leaders slipped
away from Constantinople to Angora, and when the
British occupied the city and dissolved Parliament on
March 16, 1920, making further departures impossible,
there was a nucleus of very interesting characters
around Kemal, each remarkable in his own way.

We are indebted to Halide Edib for a deathless picture of these men during the year of almost unbeliev-
able stress which she has called the "Turkish Ordeal."
She presents them as they appear to her sensitive nature, with unquestionable coloring one way or the other,
and yet of equally unquestionable honesty. Kemal she
paints in red and death-gray, and doubtless these colors
are prominent in the many-sided leader. We see him,
a man of sharply cut lines, a slim elegant figure, thin
lips cynically curved over tightly closed mouth, eyebrows bristling over flashing steel blue eyes, with a

narrow, slender, sensitive hand ready to spring like a tiger's claw. His mind she describes as "two-sided like a lighthouse lantern," alternating between clear flashes of intuitive intelligence and inconsistent sophistry. He dominated the headquarters table, where they all ate, with a brilliant but cruel irony which spared no one, while on the other hand he was always personally courteous to those about him. Suffering from internal trouble and fever, he would sit all night examining in the light of a yellow flickering lamp the dispatches from his harassed Anatolian followers who were gradually being pinched between the foreign aggressor and the fanatical supporters of the old régime.

As the night advanced and the yellow light went pale because of the coming dawn, every one looked weary and haggard—Mustapha Kemal Pasha the most of all. . . . There were moments when his eyes and his whole mien seemed like a powerful tiger's caught in a trap. . . . It was always morning when we went down to get a few hours sleep but we did not know the moment when the Caliphate soldiers might come and tear us from our beds and kill us in one of the many horrible ways they had found of killing every Nationalist they could lay hands on. It was during the days when they dragged our wounded officers from the hospital of Bolou and smashed their heads in with stones.[2]

Apparently difference of race is not required to inspire atrocity in Turkey.

Of Kemal's staff, Ismet Bey was to work best with

[2] The quotations from Halide Edib in this chapter are taken from her *Memoirs* with the permission of The Century Company, publishers.

the difficult temperament of the leader, becoming Pasha and Chief-of-Staff of the new Turkish armies. He was an older man than the others with "a little dark and wistful face, wondering child-like eyes," punctilious old Turkish manners, and an unfailingly kind heart. He was slightly deaf which gave him a sort of clown-like air; a witty talker, but never bitter. The man to attain second prominence in military accomplishment was Colonel Refet, a handsome, fastidious dresser with steel muscles and nerves who once dealt with brewing insurrection in Konia by inviting the notables there onto his train for a conference, suddenly starting the engine, and bringing them all, thus kidnaped, to his chief, Kemal, at Angora. There was Colonel Nazim, who treated his soldiers like a father and was equally beloved by them—the Nazim who used to declaim: "There is only one way to improve the world, first incite the soldiers to kill all their officers, and then kill all the soldiers." Tewfik, early chief of Kemal's military cabinet, was a jovial spirit who announced the crucial victory of the army at Kars to his staff with the declaration: "The Department of the East shall have sweet dishes to-day, but the Department of the West shall have only leeks boiled in water." The commander of this first successful expedition of the Nationalist junta which opened the way to Persia and the Caucasus, the only friendly territory about Turkey, Kiazim Kara Bekir, loved his violin. Murreddin Pasha, who the rarely eulogistic Kemal said "gave us all our ideals of liberty," was an idealist who soon dropped out of prominence in the hectic days.

The self-effacing Dr. Adnan acted as Minister of Public Health and in any other portfolio where differences with Kemal had created a vacancy, and tended the women and children who flocked from the villages on the rolling plain. And one must not overlook Madam Edib herself, wife of Dr. Adnan, whose hungry black eyes watched everything from a birdlike face surmounting an exquisitely fragile, tubular body which bent in a chair like a green bamboo. A woman of obstinate opinion, sensitive perception, supreme intelligence, and great courage, she always reminded one, with her wide-eyed harmlessness and resignation which covered like a coat of feathers the taut, quivering spirit inside, of a captive bird. She is as outstanding in her new nation and society as Sarojini Naidu in hers, and it is a sign of the time that New Asia should produce probably the two most gifted littérateuse-stateswomen of the age.

The dissolving of the Constantinople Parliament gave the Angora group the opportunity to appeal to all devotees of representative government as the champions of Turkish democracy. They set about framing a constitution, but this had to be announced as temporary due to the still surviving loyalty of the people to the Sultan. Kemal took a stiff stand against most of his associates in opposing the traditional tri-departmental republican form. It was, he said, both too new—it would scare the Asiatic population—and too old—it was already discredited in Europe. The new experiment in Russia was doubtless affecting Kemal, but more likely it was the innate prescience of the born dictator which caused him, like Lenin and Mussolini, to seek some new, loose form. And Kemal's conception of democracy is one of the things which prove him an Asiatic. Kemal was to prove the ideal Asiatic administrator, providing the type of rule under which Orientals are most prosperous and content. He was the informal but none the less all-powerful dictator, always willing to listen to the people and at propitious moments explaining his intentions. In a speech delivered in December, 1921, he took them into his confidence regarding the program he had mapped out for the National Assembly. Kemal proved as effective an orator as he was a soldier. Tall and blond, his face in masklike serenity beneath his tall kalpak, he commanded his audience. With a musical voice, rich vocabulary, and gracious gestures, he expressed his nuances of feeling. The speech lasted five hours. He made it clear that he saw no light in the administrative specialization which Anglo-Saxons have as the basis of Western democracy and which Americans hailed so enthusiastically as the sesame to perfect government. The Oriental genius runs to consultation, deliberation, headed by one-man responsibility and authority. Neither rulers nor ruled had understood the imported constitution which had resulted from the Young Turk revolution of

1908, and in consequence the people were exploited for personal aggrandizement.

The Asiatic "Republic" is a natural evolution from Oriental benevolent despotism. The "Republics" of Turkey, China, or Persia apply our terms and organization to the old Oriental principle of the despot embodying all authority, administrative, legislative, and judicial, without specialization. This is, however, done in harmony with the traditions and feelings of the people, now expressed more articulately than before through a representative assembly, copied so far as make-up is concerned from Western constitutions, but having nothing in common with them in function.

He contrasted laws of the past which had brought the country to ruin to new laws with which Turkey was being rebuilt, justifying the latter by rules of utility and reason. When he was asked to what the new government could be compared he said: "Our government is neither democratic nor socialist. It does not resemble any other, and represents the national will and national sovereignty. If one must say what it is from a social point of view, we will say, 'It is a government of the people' "—that is, a Western student would qualify, in harmony with the people's instincts and directed toward their survival on a competitive basis in the modern world. Kemal, says Madam Edib, often argued all night for his scheme. He worked, talked, and gesticulated with frenzied energy to get control of the dispersed forces which were not his at all. The result was a convention form of organization with ministers of departments called commissaries who formed no responsible cabinet but were severally responsible to the Grand National Assembly (called for short Mejliss) of which Kemal was President. It made the dignitaries of Anatolia, who composed the Assembly, feel that they were receiving the power, and although it meant much annoyance for Kemal within the first few months, it provided inevitably the excuse for a dictator. The Assembly proclaimed that the Sultan-Caliph had become a prisoner in enemy hands, and since he was no longer a free agent, Kemal was taking over the temporary rule of his people. It is curious to note that enough loyalty to the Sultan survived to compel the use of the word "temporary."

A struggle took place between the advocates of "Westernization" and those of the "Eastern Ideal" in the new régime. The latter held that Turkey was throwing off the tyranny of the West and would do poorly to identify herself culturally with her oppressors. Some were convinced of Gandhi's teaching that the West was doomed to destruction and asked why Turkey should follow a light that was going out. They felt that affiliation with Russia, and introduction of Soviet organization, would go hand in hand with a distinct Asianism in manners, dress, and life. This was true in a sense, but not the sense in which they hoped. The "Westernizers" maintained that the tendency of the Turk since his departure from Asia had been westward and her true genius dictated fulfillment of the trend. Mustapha Kemal negatively encouraged the formation of a Communist Party—with an eye to Russia's place in Turkey's freedom and to frighten the Powers from drastic policy. When he had cleared his country of foreign troops he was to continue Russian diplomatic friendship gladly but place the death penalty upon Communist agitators.

The Sultan's government did not take all the developments inspired from Angora supinely. The self-confident young premier, Damad Ferid, tool of the British, issued death warrants against all the Angora leaders, including the woman Halide Edib, and procured their religious confirmation by a *fetwa* or "holy court." This made them enemies of Islam and their assassination a sacred act. When the news reached Angora the condemned sat around with thoughtful faces. "I feel very much upset myself—I hate to be condemned to death. How do you feel about it?" asked Dr. Adnan of the Pasha. "I mind it very much," said Mustapha Kemal. Their answer was typically Oriental. The Assembly solemnly condemned Damad Ferid and his associates to death, and summoned in a *fetwa* of countryside muzzeins to sanctify their action.

Plots against Kemal's life were formed—and in time unveiled. The attempt of Greek agents to assassinate him in 1920 was followed by reports that he was dead, or that he had been bought with English gold.

The depth of the intrigue was revealed to the most

cynical during the trial and confession of an English
agent in May, 1921, who had assumed the name of
Mustapha Saghir (or Saguir).

He had gone about his work in a Kiplingesque manner and was captured in stock detective story fashion.
The English, before sending him to Angora, had pretended to imprison him in the dreaded dungeons of
Agopian-khan. He pretended to escape to Ineboli.
He posed as a deputy from the Indian Caliphate Conference and volunteered for the additional duty of
carrying news from Angora to its intelligence office in
Constantinople. The Nationalists pretended that they
did not know these things and received him as a fellow
sufferer from British imperialism. He spun a network
of investigation, little dreaming that his coachmen were
gendarmes and his every movement was recorded.
When he had gone far enough he was arrested. A gentleman of breeding and education in his early thirties,
he stood calmly and free from self-justification before
his judges, revealing names and dates and vast sums
of money that made the high kalpaks of his listeners
stir in amazement. The people of Angora sat breath-
less as he punctuated his words now and then with a
frank, poignant smile. He was a young Mussulman
from Benares who had been taken to England as a
child. In return for his education, he said, he had been
required to swear, upon the Koran, fealty to the English king and the Viceroy of India. When he graduated
from Oxford he was sent to Cairo to spy on the Egyp-

tian Nationalist movement. Soon his field of activity included Persia, Turkey, Afghanistan, and India.

He told the amount of money the Sultan received from England each month. Mustapha Kemal, he said, could have seven million dollars if he would take instructions from the British. The Ghazi smiled, remarking that he had not before realized how large was his "commercial value." He revealed the plot to assassinate Kemal which was sponsored by the Sultan, members of the Damad Ferid government, and English military men in Constantinople. He had been chosen to carry out the actual murder in Anatolia.

"Why were you chosen for this?" he was asked.

"Because of my success in an even more dangerous errand in Afghanistan," he replied, "when I assassinated the Emir." In return for complete confession, he asked only that he might go to death without revelation of his real name—for the honor of an ancient Muslim family.[3]

More serious was the desultory war which Caliphate troops conducted against the Nationalists, gradually occupying most of the Anatolian railway. Kemal's

[3] Emir Habibullah Khan was murdered in his sleep by a suborned aide February 20, 1919. He had been regarded favorably by the British, but was the rallying center for a Central-Asian Islamic confederation which they might have feared. The official *India Yearbook* (1927) lays his death upon reactionary religious elements who feared his progressiveness—the same elements which were later to upset Amanullah. Following the assassination this young prince, head of the arsenal, treasury, and army and supported by Russia, was—to use the British report—"practically forced to fight the British by the factions in the kingdom" and invaded the Punjab. An armistice was reached May 14. A Russian economic penetration followed, interrupted by Amanullah's overthrow in early 1929.

agents were preaching further sacrifices for the saving of the nation in all the towns and cities of Anatolia and in reaction fanatic religionists were mobbing and killing the "infidels who shaved and wore collars." Yielding to the war weariness and anti-militarism of his Assembly men, Kemal had almost completely disbanded the regular troops who had fallen to his command, and now he had to call upon roving bands of irregulars to protect the Nationalist movement. Merely glorified bandits, they often practiced extortion and license upon the populists which threw the whole movement into disfavor. Only the fact that when they leaped out of the frying pan they found themselves in the fire held much of the countryside submissive.

As the Greeks undertook an offensive, Izzet Pasha arrived from Tewfik Pasha who succeeded to the headship of the Sultan's cabinet to offer compromise and union. Fearful of the weak-kneed allegiance of his people, Kemal adopted the bold stroke of placing Izzet and his embassy under honorable detention and publishing that they had come to strengthen the Angora régime. Edhem, the arrogant dandified Robin Hood who enlisted even women in his, the largest, irregular army and conducted a newspaper against "a regular army and militarism," made cause of this to demand compromise with the Sultan and attack Kemal's few regulars. Seizing the advantage, the Greeks moved inland —past Brussa—to within twenty-five miles of Angora, but the invaders spoiled the triumph within sight by pushing their advantage too far. When they made alliance with Edhem they thought everything was done, but even his bandit soldiers were too good Turks to countenance his borrowing Greek rifles to shoot Turks and they turned upon their commander. In cold January, 1921, Ismet stopped the Greeks at Inn-Eunu and old Izzet was quick to go to headquarters and join in the rejoicing! It is of these dark days that Halide Edib wrote:

This was worse than civil war. There was the Sultan's government preying on the people; there were the French occupying Cilicia and sending Armenian legions to persecute the people too; there were the Greeks around Smyrna massacreing, burning, ravaging, and violating every human law; there were the Allies in Istamboul oppressing the Turks at their pleasure—there was the whole Western world with its everlasting "Down with the Turks!" There were Western statesmen insisting that the big stick should always be used with Orientals, with the unspeakable Turks; and, amid it all, there were we, the Nationalists, fighting to free our people from all their alien oppressors. I realized then as I had never realized before the ordeal of the Turkish people, walled in by the world's hatred, divided against themselves by internal strife.

The identity of Turkish cause with that of all revolt in Asia is expressed in Madam Edib's record of Mustapha Kemal's choler against the British speech on how to handle Eastern peoples.

I realized then that we were no longer a nation of empire-builders who were unconscious of their own superiority complex; instead we had now become one of the peoples who suffer from the superiority complexes of other great empire-builders.

MUSTAPHA KEMAL

When Mustapha Kemal Pasha came into my bureau I laid the translation of the speech before him without comment. He flew into one of the most violent rages I have ever seen him in.

"They shall know that we are as good as they are!" he shouted. "They shall treat us as their equal! Never will we bow our heads to them! To our last man we will stand against them till we break their civilization on their heads!" It was as if the whole East were crying out in his voice.

I felt at that time that even the massacres by the Greek army, and the Allies' high-handed occupation of Istamboul, were insignificant compared with this insufferable assumption of superiority by the West. I had come to know through long and painful experience that there is no outrage which is committed by human beings on each other which cannot be forgotten in time by some common interest and sympathy arising—except one: the assumption of superiority; the one who assumes it and the one who has to submit to it are irrevocably divided. And I would say that if the much-talked-of clash between East and West should ever become a reality, and all the latent hatred become expressed, then the fundamental cause will be this assumption of superiority by the West and the resulting two codes of justice, and not all the economic and political difficulties we so often speak about. As long as the world lasts, herd feeling will culminate in such ghastly and ugly deeds as recent history records, whenever it is stimulated and used by leading politicians to satisfy their greed and lust for power. But nothing they effect can be lasting; only the struggle to level all nations and classes and men will never cease till man stands with man on a basis of equal dignity and justice.

There is a trail of blood from Erzerum to Smyrna, shed by the unknown and the unrenowned, each one dying to save his country from the ignominy of slavery and to create a free and independent Turkey which should be an inspiration to all other suffering and enslaved peoples.

Out of the heat of Turkey's ordeal and the mouths of a soldier and a woman novelist, comes the most definite and arresting statement of the resentment of New Asia that I have found from Tokyo to Cairo.

We have glimpses of Mustapha Kemal in Angora standing among his men as a mast among sails and rigging, working ruthlessly to make a movement out of his dispersed forces and sympathizers. He now had a legislative body as well as traders and foreign aggressors to struggle with. He cajoled, persuaded, and bullied, became irritable and again forced himself to appear cool. He was by turns, says the critical Madam Edib, cynical, suspicious, unscrupulous, and satanically shrewd, but in every mood he displayed superhuman vitality.

There are men around him who are greatly his superior in intellect and moral backbone, and far above him in culture and education, but not one of them could cope with his vitality. It was perhaps just because he was a colossal personification of one part of every day human nature that he had a better chance of controlling the masses than might a man who possessed subtler and more balanced qualities or more profound wisdom. I can still see him standing in the middle of the room talking everyone to exhaustion while he remains as fresh as the moment he began, and I can remember saying to myself, "What an astounding man! Is he just some elemental force in a human form? And how can this cyclone ever come to rest when the nation has reached its goal?"

When there was no stress of work, he loved to try out his powers in argument, reminding the Hanum of Sultan

Murad IV who took exercise between fights by cutting donkeys in two with a sword slash. To prepare himself for the unavoidable struggle with the priesthood, he studied the Moslem religious traditions and early history. "While among us," says the jealously watchful lady, "he was as strictly pure as a sincere Catholic priest, but some evenings he disappeared," to make merry with the clergy—and then attack their hypocrisy. He showed no personal religious inclination, giving his time entirely to pragmatic affairs, but Madam Edib accuses him of a superstitious trait in regard to mystic inscriptions and dreams. His underlings were always having propitious dreams for his benefit, she says. She accuses him of paling and hesitating when shooting broke out around the hut which was headquarters. His bravery in battle was not open to question, but Madam Halide concluded that he "lacked the courage to face a mob and which can survive without a gallery." She gives an incident with strange undertones to illustrate his severity. Two of his best officers had been treacherously captured and tortured almost to death by Sultanate forces. They were saved by two officers who asked in return personal safety should they fall into Nationalist hands. They fell into the hands of Edhem before that irregular chief's defection, were condemned to death, and the death warrants were sent to Kemal. He wanted to sign them, stating that "war was no place for mercy, pity, and sentimental morality." Ismet and the others spent an entire night of hot arguing dis-

suading him and in the morning procured an angry
note asking reprieves, but it was soon discovered that
meanwhile Edhem had executed the men. In politics
he was opportunistic and ruthless. The Assembly, very
suspicious of its President Kemal's power, attacked
the loyal Minister of Interior Jami Bey for favoring
Kemal's policies. Kemal refrained from backing Jami
—which, the Assembly seeing, turned about face and
gave Jami a vote of confidence. Feeling that this would
bring embarrassment upon Kemal, the Minister insisted on resigning, but it is always true men fear those
whom they have wronged and Kemal insidiously pushed
Jami Bey out of public life. Usually suave in his en-
mities, Kemal forgot himself and called Himdullah
Soubhi Bey a liar. He tactfully withdrew this, and
Himdullah Soubhi became his Minister of Education,
but Kemal eventually undermined and got rid of him
also.

Kemal required unquestioning obedience but he
found one assistant, a lady, who was to flout him. The
beginning of this memorable feud is recorded in Halide
Edib's memoirs in a brief conversation:

"I don't want any considerations, criticisms, or advice. I
will have only my own way. All shall do as I command."

"Me too, Pasham?"

"You too."

"I will obey you and do as you wish as long as I believe
you are serving the cause."

"You shall obey me and do as I wish."

"That night," she records, "I determined to write my memoirs and to write them in English."—"Is that a threat, Pasham?" she had asked him. "I am sorry," he had said. "I would not threaten you." But when the author saw Madam Edib in Madison, Wisconsin, in the winter of 1928-29, she was very sure that "Kemal Pasha desired her death more fervently than that of any other living creature," and possibly with good reason.

Edhem's insurrection drove the Assembly to support Kemal's regular army and a cool, reliable military machine was rapidly built out of the patriotic peasantry of Anatolia. The opportunity to lead the nation after having been dragged at the tail of Constantinople for centuries appealed to these primitive Turks and enabled Kemal to carry out changes there which even the great metropolis would have considered impossible innovations. And Constantinople was accustomed to foreign occupations whereas the upstanding Anatolians would not accommodate themselves to the idea. From nowhere else in Turkey could salvation have come, and Kemal knew what he was doing when he "buried himself among the primitives" while the "civilized" laughed. Kemal saw too, in the alkali wastes and green expanses of Anatolia an ally as undefeatable as "King Winter" in Russia. When the Greeks had penetrated the farthest in January and March, 1921, at Inn-Eunu, and Kemal's associates were on the verge of demoralization, he seemed the most confident, saying, "The expanses of our Motherland will swallow them up." This of course was negative assistance. The positive assistance which brought triumph was the loyalty and toil of the Turkish women who raised the crops, sent half of them to the army, and turned themselves into its transport carrying on their scantily clothed backs, or in their farm carts, supplies, arms, and ammunition.

Some outside support was coming to Kemal. The Soviet Power, beginning its policy of supporting Asian nationalism to break down the British Empire, made a military convention with him giving him what money and few arms it could spare—for it was very hard pressed. Formal treaty came in March, 1921, treaties with Afghanistan and Azerbaijan the following October, and sympathetic dealings spurred by Soviet agents were entered into with Persia, India, and Egypt. Indian Muslems were stirred, but bewildered by the Caliph's denunciation (purchased by Lloyd George) of the Nationalists as rebels and traitors to Islam. It became clear to Kemal that the people of Turkey would have to outlaw such a purchasable viceroy of God, and he began quietly preparing the minds of his people for this coup which the world would not have believed any one could dare.

The Greek army, backed by British influence, gold, and ammunition, had thought to legalize its position in Smyrna through the Treaty of Sèvres. But the treaty was destined never to be ratified. Only in allowing the Sultan to retain Constantinople was it less devastating to the Turkish Empire than the one handed to Tewfik Pasha the preceding summer. To that Kemal had sworn resistance to the end, and he now threatened the Sultan with deposition and outlawry if he dared the break-up of the Ottoman Empire by signing this betrayal. It would have given the part of Thrace that remained in Turkey's possession after the Balkan wars to Greece, who had not fought the Turkish Empire until after the Armistice. It provided for an independent Armenia, an autonomous Kurdish state; it placed the Greeks in a position to attain the Hellenic Empire that has been the ambition of the peninsular people since the days of Pericles. It required the internationalization of the Straits both in peace and in war. The Turkish army was to be reduced to 50,000 men, with distribution of war materials in the hands of the Allies. Fortifications were to be destroyed. Turkey was to have no air force and no navy. She was to be divested of her Arab provinces, to admit the independence of the Hejaz, the British annexation of Cyprus, French rights in Tunis and Morocco, Italian rights in Tripoli, and the Italian and Greek possession of her islands in the Ægean and Mediterranean Seas.

If this treaty had been presented to the Turkey of 1918, it might have been accepted. In the interim of nearly two years, the Greek occupation had aroused the people, and the National Party under Kemal's leadership had sprung up to protect them.

Fate, which had played into Kemal's hands when the

ambition of Venizelos flared, now again played into his hands with that statesman's repudiation by his own people. His downfall, the death of the Greek King Alexander, and the recall of King Constantine, reduced the Greeks to a state of utter confusion. Italy resented the occupation of Smyrna; France withdrew her support when Constantine returned, as she held him responsible for the shooting of her soldiers in Athens in 1916. Even the support of England became less enthusiastic, although Lloyd George upheld the Greeks with orations. Hope of ratification of the Sèvres treaty was abandoned. France seized the opportunity to pique England by signing a separate treaty with the Turks and promising her influence toward better terms with the other Allies. With this disunion in their favor the separate delegations from the Angora Nationalist capital and the Sultanate in Constantinople went to a peace conference with the Greeks in London in February. Kemal was not only strong enough to compel recognition of his faction but to completely dominate, through his friend Bekir Sami, both delegations. They joined in a demand for radical changes in the Sèvres draft. These were not granted. Kemal now determined to risk everything on the high adventure of a great offensive against the invaders.

Bekir Sami, the diplomat, did not feel so bold as Kemal, the soldier, and he made a proposal to Lloyd George which, as Halide Edib reveals, had melodramatic repercussions. He offered to make Turkey a buffer state against Bolshevism if Great Britain would end foreign occupation. Lloyd George, riding high, laughed at any idea about the Near East emanating from Near Easterners. Strangely enough a copy of the conversation fell into the hands of Chicherin in Moscow, inspiring an angry message to Kemal, who was receiving Soviet support. Bekir Sami resigned, and Kemal prepared to attack the Greeks.

They anticipated him, confident in their hundred thousand men and best British supplies against his twenty-five thousand and female human transport. The Turks were pushed steadily back to within a day's horseback ride of Angora. Then the panic-stricken Assembly granted Kemal what he had been waiting for: a supreme dictatorship over army and government. The new *Bash-Commandan* rode out on April 5, 1921, to take field command, only to be thrown from his horse and break a rib. He was carried back to Angora, but returned to the front within twenty-four hours. Through this decisive campaign he changed his headquarters continually with the advancing army, and worked day and night, although he could not move at his desk without pain. He snatched his sleep sitting bolt upright in his chair, and when he thought it necessary crawled in the trenches or surveyed the country on horseback. Even Halide Edib was swept away and wired the Commander-in-Chief personally an offer of enlistment. He accepted as gallantly, by return wire, and once again she was clerical aide at staff head-

[289]

quarters—this time as a regular private. By the end of the struggle she had been promoted to sergeant, but she bore the responsibilities of a general. The make-up and officering of the army, with their intricate changes from day to day, Kemal kept in his mind, showing perhaps the greatest gift of the modern general, that for detail. Like all possessors of abounding vitality and optimism, he had his rages of despair—fumed and swore and paced; and when every one else had given up he was cool and certain and deft. Hovering over him and looking, says Madam Edib, like his double, was his schoolboy friend, Colonel Arif, who knew the lay of the land to the last molehill. Like every true soldier, he had stomach for the game of war, and spoke ruefully, with a mind on his twenty-five thousand men, of the time when, at the Dardanelles, he could afford to sacrifice eleven thousand men in one fight. Yet, in spite of huge losses, he had forty thousand men behind him when the war was over—so completely was Anatolia behind him and so thorough was his recruiting organization.

"General Anatolian wastes" had already sapped the vigor of the Greek offensive when Kemal took supreme command. It was really expert soldiering which allowed them to stretch themselves to the utmost. The complete change in personnel of the Greek command, due to frenzied politics in Athens, had made vulnerable the morale of their army. Yet they overflowed into the broken valley of the River Sakharia in spite of

Kemal, and for twenty-two relentless days and nights in September, 1921, he fought to hold them there. He was personally on the field—his horse was shot down under him. His losses—including three division generals the first day—began to indicate the end for such a small force. On the last evening arrived news that the Greeks had broken over Mount Tchal, indicating the failure of Turk resistance. And at two in the morning as Kemal stormed and paced came a telephone call that the Greeks were giving along their line. The victory had been too great a strain for them.

The story of Kemal's conduct at this battle did for him—and much more immediately—what that of Washington's crossing the Delaware did for the Colonial leader. It made him a hero—a demigod to his people, credited with superhuman coolness and endurance. The Assembly was quick to promote him to Field Marshal and proclaim him *Ghazi*—"The Conqueror." In the minds of patriotic Turks he was ranked with Muhammad, Ali, and Othman.

When Kemal heard that the enemy was shipping home everything transportable and burning even the Christian villages, he chuckled, saying, "They are going and don't expect to come back." The retreat became a rout, with burned villages, slain children, tortured old men, and unspeakable violations of women in its wake. As the victors advanced, horrible revenge was taken on isolated and wounded Greek stragglers. Latife Hanum, appointed to investigate atrocities, shuddered at a report of the lynching of a Greek soldier by wronged women. The gentlemanly old Ismet, who was her mainstay during these months, brought her this rebuke from her chief: "Pasha deplores your weak heart, which cannot bear violence." We are told that the American word "lynch" was popularly adopted into the Turkish language at this time, and Kemal chuckled again.

He had gone for a respite to his Angora home—a spacious country landlord's villa set aside as official residence—to allow his rib to heal, to fight an opposition which organized simultaneously with his popularity, and receive at his capital his revered mother. She was, describes Madam Edib, seventy, built on a majestic scale, her big, round face with its milk-white complexion hardly lined. In spotless headkerchief and white gown she was a "typical Macedonian woman of the people and pretended to nothing else. Her son was the same Mustapha of school days, his position did not matter, she loved him and scolded him and spoke of him as she had always done." She was ill, and sat all day upon a pallet on the floor. "She did not bother much about the struggle in Anatolia, her native city was Saloniki, and she would have no new dress made until her son Mustapha should deliver it from captivity."

She showed a traditional mother's scorn of her son's housekeeper, a frail, wistful cousin of Kemal named Fikrie, who had been brought to take charge of a home and a man, both, according to the worried Dr. Adnan's advice, in need of a woman's care. Fikrie, "delicate and devoted, but not shrewd enough to make her great man marry her," half-fearfully believing that if she remained patient and hopeful her consuming love must be rewarded with his, bowed in silence at the old lady's scathing comments on the younger generation, meant for her.

Rested and confident, Kemal went back to lead the final march on Smyrna. "Soldiers, your goal is the Mediterranean," he concluded in ringing voice a speech to his army, and the drive was on. Four and one-half Greek divisions were trapped and left in heaps in one narrow valley. Kemal "purred like a royal tiger." The two highest Greek commanders, Tricopis and Dionis, were captured and brought to his office where he gave them an egotistic but sportsmanlike reception. He engaged them in length in discussion of their mistakes in the game of war and how these might have been avoided or rectified, but when they fell to quarreling between themselves as to the blame for the collapse, he felt disgusted and cheated at having been matched against such material.

The Allied consuls sent a proposal to give over Smyrna, accompanied by patronizing cautions about the treatment of the people. Kemal pounded his table. "Whose city are they giving to whom?" he asked. On September 9, 1922, his troops entered the city, and the last of the Greek army took ship, leaving huddled on the wharfs thousands of miserable, terrified Greek and Armenian civilians. Five days later holocaust climaxed the horrors of years. The fire broke out in the Armenian quarter, crowding the population toward the quay. General Ismet's headquarters claimed the fire hose in the city was found cut to pieces. Dynamite and munitions hoarded under churches and in private homes exploded. In three days beautiful Smyrna was a black and crimson ruin.

"After the Greeks we will fight one another," said Kemal sardonically, referring to the rising fear of his power and growing political opposition. "When the struggle ends it will be dull—we must find excitement somewhere!"

On August 4, Lloyd George, rendering no other help to his tools the Greeks, rewarded them with a fiery speech of endorsement. Poincaré replied bluffly by announcing on September 19 that France refused to join in operations against the Turkish Nationalists and advised withdrawing the Allied establishment from Chanak, which Kemal planned to attack next. The British Parliament at last dismissed Lloyd George; Bonar Law succeeded. The Allied Powers suddenly found no reason not to deal with the "outlawed" government at Angora. On September 29 at the Moudania Armistice, France, England, and Italy agreed to withdraw troops from Constantinople, retire the Greek forces, and vote Turkey into the League of Nations. Protection of minorities was all that was left of the

British plan to create an independent Armenian state.
Kemal in turn engaged himself not to send troops to the
European side. But Refet Pasha went into East Thrace
to prepare the culminating *coup d'etat*. The British
sent naval reënforcements to hold Chanak at all
odds.

Diplomatic legalization of what had come to pass
would eventually follow.

There remained no Power or combination of Powers
likely to attempt Europe's aim of extirpating Turkey.
Almost all Great Britain had fought for in the East
was abandoned. Kemal had saved his country to his
people. There now remained the task of building a
nation to retain, and prosper, in it.

III

Kemal's next, even more heroic task was to be his
country's transformation from a medieval ecclesiocracy
into a modern national society. Kemal's venture
amazed the whole world. Particularly to the cock-
sure West, the truth comes as a surprise when the
Orient, thought slaughtered and merely waiting to be
butchered, suddenly demonstrates in men like Kemal
that it carries within itself the spark of its own vivifi-
cation.

After the victory of Sakharia, Mustapha Kemal addressed the Assembly on the aims of the new Turkey:
"We demand nothing more than to live in complete

independence within the limits of the national frontiers, we demand only that Europe make no attempt against our natural rights: that she admit for us what she admits for every other people." Seizing the prestige and ardor of the moment of victory, he began the supreme task of "winning the peace."

Kemal at first received personally and freely all who came to interview him, explaining earnestly his motives and his hopes for the future. His words were distorted, his messages garbled, and his personality misrepresented. Ultimately he realized that he had no chance against the chauvinist press of England, the rhetorical press of France, and the jealous press of Constantinople. Correspondents came with one intent—of injuring him. They branded the movement "Kemalist," as if he were some rebel upstart. He resented the term as he did not want to establish "Kemalism" but a new Turkey, nor did he wish to incite the resentment of the Nationalists. He believed Napoleon's failure was due to his ambition for personal glory rather than for a cause. (It is interesting here to note how differently the Russians felt about the term "Leninist," which was accepted with alacrity.) In Kemal's reasoned but determined way, he excluded unofficial interviewers altogether. Years later, when newspapermen wished only to eulogize him, he was to excoriate their fickleness and to adhere rigidly to his rule. Therefore he receives surprisingly little publicity compared to the other dictators of the world.

When Kemal had become convinced of the superciliousness, unfairness, and deep-seated hostility of the
West, he became a part of the general Asiatic protest
and sense of affront against the West, and accepted
support from Russia and encouragement from Japan,
China, and India. In 1920 Tokyo and Constantinople
had for the first time exchanged ambassadors. The
Japanese diplomat had been one of the first to see that
the real power would come out of Angora.

His revived Turkey was promptly claimed by religionists as the hope of Islam, but Kemal soon made it
clear that he did not sympathize with pan-Islamism or
militant religionism. His gorge rose at the conception
that the Turkish nation existed only for the glory of
Islam. To his mind, the ideology which had destroyed
the empire was the subjugation of the political entity
to religion. The continual warring against the infidel,
the sacrifice of Turkish power and progress for the
traditions, superstitions, and propagation of Islam was,
to his thought, a betrayal of the nation—the use of the
nation for purposes outside and beyond the nation.
Not that Kemal was not a willing believer in Allah and
his prophet, and an ardent, uncompromising upholder of
Muhammadanism as the basis and unifying factor of
Turkish culture. But as France had repudiated Ca-
tholicism as an enforced or national religion, so the
national life of Turkey was to be separated from and
to become independent of the religious life. Briefly,
Kemal was a modernist emerging from a medieval so-

ciety and destined to make the same change in its
thought in one generation. He did not, of course,
stand alone in this view. Before him, as before Sun-
Yat-sen, Gandhi, or Lenin, currents of thought cleared
the way and created a new intelligentsia—the well-
spring of the revolt in all Asia's nations. But Kemal
was the one in his land who gave voice to the group,
organized it, and led it to supremacy.

When Mustapha Kemal entered Smyrna in triumph
he did not imagine that he was going to meet a power
by which he was to be conquered. From youth he
had been too busy and cynical to fall in love. "You
may spend your affection on women, but I have my
horses," he had remarked to a companion at cards.
"They give better return and satisfaction." Like all
Orientals, his affection for woman had gone primarily
to his mother. Now, however, when he had less time
than ever for affairs of the heart, romance awaited him.
It came not, as with Sun Yat-sen, in the valley of
failure, but on the very peak of victory and achievement.

In the early days of the Turkish offensive, Latife
Hanum, the lovely young daughter of Mouameron
Chaki Bey, a rich and influential merchant with connections on the New York Stock Exchange, had returned
to her home in Smyrna from a visit to France to find
her parents were away from home and the city in a
terrifying state of disorder.

She had openly spoken her patriotic feelings, and the angered Greek authorities had accused her of secretly supplying Mustapha Kemal with information. They put guards around her house, allowed no visitors, and constantly threatened her arrest. She was well aware of her danger in remaining, and of the fate of many of her friends of like beauty and youth, but she declined every opportunity to escape and lived in the great mansion at the top of a thousand steps, alone except for a few servants.

Latife, no doubt, owed some of her modernistic opinions to Halide Hanum, the novelist, whose pupil and unknown devotee she had been. As early as the revolution of 1908, when she was a young girl, she had proclaimed that the Young Turk movement was "a false thing unless it not only released the male population from political serfdom, but also the women from social slavery." She had lived in Paris and Biarritz, spoke French, German, and English fluently, and was a fine scholar of the Turkish language—a rare thing in the women of her country. She was, at this time, taking up the study of law.

The handsome deliverer of their country appealed to the imagination of all Turkish women, and half the women of Europe, so it was natural that Latife should let her thoughts dwell upon him as she wandered through the vast, empty rooms of her house and waited for his victorious entry into her besieged city. He was putting into execution the things she desired and dreamed of for her people. Even the cause of social freedom for women was near to his heart, as it was to hers. It was because of her undisguised championship of him that she found herself virtually a prisoner in her own house. She pledged to herself that he should have it as his headquarters when he should come.

Mustapha Kemal rode behind his vanguard into the city and entered the improvised staff headquarters tired and dusty from travel and battles. He was somewhat disconcerted to find, waiting for him there, a beautiful young Oriental woman dressed in a Parisian gown, her veil worn around her hair, not covering her face. She asked him, in the French of a Parisienne, if he and his staff would make her father's home their headquarters during their stay in Smyrna. Surprised, perhaps a little resentful of her suggestion, which might have savored of effrontery, he at first refused, but when she explained her reasons for inviting him, he assented and moved with his staff to the luxurious quarters of the merchant's home.

The first evening of his visit, the Ghazi found himself talking to his hostess of his hopes and plans and problems as he had never talked to a woman before. She was a sympathetic listener—a brilliant conversationalist. She seemed to him an embodiment of all the qualities with which he dreamed that Turkish womanhood, through freedom and education, should be endowed. She had knowledge of the manners and customs of the West, with the basis of Muslim beliefs which kept her a true daughter of Islam. Before they said good night she had offered to assist him in secretarial duties during his stay, as she was particularly adapted to the task of translating foreign communications. For four days they worked together over the ticklish foreign issues created by the victory. Each night they had long talks during which the topic gradually shifted from impersonal themes to the inevitable subject of "thee and me." Kemal found her beauty and charm increasingly disturbing. Halide represents him as strutting over a new "kill." "She wears my picture in her locket," he boasted. "Half the women of Turkey have your picture in their locket—it means only their gratitude to the deliverer of their country," she would have deflated him. But no man could take it that way. And it is impossible to acquit Halide Hanum of a certain interested slant.

On September 16 she writes: Mustapha Kemal Pasha is Latife Hanum's guest now. Her house was the most sheltered and remote from the fire. He talked of her most pleasantly in the car. . . . It all sounded like the beginning of home building for the hardy soldier at last. . . . He was not in need of her wealth.

We passed through a pleasant old Turkish garden which overlooked the blue waters of the bay. The steps leading up to the veranda and the veranda itself were muffled with ivy, wistaria, jasmin, and roses in charming profusion and disorder. A very little lady in black stood at the top steps and received us. Although she was said to be only twenty-four at the time, she had the quiet manners and the maturer ways

[301]

of a much older person. Her graceful salaam had both dignity and Old World charm. She wore a black veil over her hair and her face was very pleasing in its somber frame. The face was round and plump, so was the little body. Although the tight and thin lips indicated an unusual force and will power, not very feminine, her eyes were most beautiful, grave and lustrous and dominated by intelligence. I can think of their color now, a fascinating brown and gray mixed, scintillating with a curious light.

Mustapha Kemal Pasha disappeared for a little time and came back dressed in white. His colorless fair hair brushed back, his colorless fair eyebrows bristling as they always do, his pale blue eyes gleaming with internal satisfaction, he stood by a table covered with drinks. She sat on the sofa by me and looked at him all the time. She was dazzled by him and he was frankly in love. So the strong current of human attraction between the two enlivened the evening. He said:

"We are celebrating Smyrna—you must drink with us."

As he raised his tiny decanter of raki he pointed at me and said: "This is the first time I have drunk raki in the presence of this Hanum Effendi: we were always a bit uneasy in her presence."

We passed the evening simply, listening to Mustapha Kemal Pasha's talk. He was enjoying this favorite hobby of his to the full.

"You still have the sign of corporal on your sleeve: how is that? We must change it at once," he said. Then he gave orders right and left, got three signs of sergeant-major, and Latife Hanum sewed one of them on my sleeve

When I took leave finally, he said: "Have you a coat in the car? It is cold." I had not.

"Wait a moment: I am going to give you my cape" he said, and disappeared. He came back with a long old gray cape. I remembered it very well. He used to wear it in the days when we were outlawed and condemned to death, and working with infinite patience and passion for the cause. How often he had sat wrapped in its ample folds by the fire the whole night, giving orders and making plans when we were expecting to be attacked and killed at any instant! When he put it on my shoulders I had a vision of the great man in Turkish history—a vision even the figure of the present dictator cannot entirely efface. I looked back as I went down the steps, the cloak trailing on the marble. He and Latife Hanum were leaning over the rails and nodding.

On the fifth day of their association the first conflict of wills between the two strong, vital personalities came about, when Latife repulsed his passionate advances. That she loved him she admitted, but only with the sanction of a marriage ceremony would she be his. To him, this was no time for consideration of marriage, so he did the only possible thing under the circumstances —he abruptly left.

Four months passed, and the Ghazi maintained a complete silence. Latife, thinking the conflict over, sighed little sighs, and then, as becomes a young lady of the modern school, turned to the next thing and prepared to go back to Paris and her study of law. Suddenly, without warning of any kind, the Ghazi returned to the merchant's house ready to yield his "principles" against marriage to her principles requiring it.

"We will be married, if it be at once!" he said. So Latife conquered the conqueror and imposed her own terms. She was to learn how ineffectual such terms could be—how short such a victory.

Events in the lives of the great soon take on the color of myth. Already there are a number of versions of the story of the wedding which took place so hurriedly. According to one account the couple went out the next day and stopped the first *imam* (priest) they met. "I have decided to marry Latife Hanum," the Ghazi announced to the astonished holy man, who at first could not understand what he was expected to do about it. In vain Kemal repeated his many names and titles. At last he assumed an air of command. The *imam* was convinced—the Ghazi's air of command would convince the most skeptical. The necessary words were spoken and Latife replied in the affirmative to the question: "Do you accept as husband Mustapha Kemal Pasha in return for a gift from him of ten drams of silver and on condition of a nuptial indemnity agreed upon by you in the event of separation?"

The possibility of the end of marriage was reckoned with at its beginning, it seems. Nothing about "till death do us part" in that ceremony! The Turkish husband, until lately, had the right to divorce his wife by saying three times that she was divorced, or some equally simple recognized form. That is changed now, and with the modernization of Turkey the divorce laws are not unlike those of America. The Ghazi was to be invested with the power of granting divorces—in time to grant his own.

Another version of the wedding tells that a party in honor of the recapture of Smyrna was being held at the home of the merchant when Mustapha Kemal suddenly and unexpectedly appeared. He asked for Latife, who was in the kitchen supervising the feast, and persuaded her and her parents (who had come home in the interim) to make the celebration a wedding party. Among the fifty guests who were assembled there was a *mufti,* an official who corresponds to an English registrar, and he performed the ceremony. The ring was purchased later by the representatives to the Lausanne Conference and brought to the couple by Ismet Pasha, who was as excited as a child over his romantic errand.

This was the first Turkish marriage ceremony to be performed with both parties present. Always the groom had been represented by proxy. Other ancient Turkish traditions were on their way toward oblivion through this union. While on the honeymoon, a banquet was tendered Kemal at Konieh to which he requested that women should be invited. For the first time, Turkish women were present at an official function, and for the first time they were allowed to venture forth after the sunset call to prayer.

Before he went for his bride Kemal had ordered his adulative housekeeper, the wistful young Fikrie, to a sanatorium in Munich for the tuberculosis she had contracted. "She continued crying all the time," said Halide Hanum, who chanced by when Kemal was seeing her off and pressed her hand in the darkness. "I will stay a few days in Paris and get myself some beautiful dresses," she told Halide, trying to convince herself as well that she would return attractively clothed and restored to love. "She was in Smyrna," Halide sets down Fikrie's thoughts: "Perhaps she thinks it only a passing fancy. He might marry me when I come back. He wouldn't marry me before my consumption is cured." The rest of the story is given as follows:

This was the last I saw of Fikrie Hanum. A woman who had been with her in the sanatorium at Munich told me of her utter collapse, her tears, the sorry love story which she repeated over and over again deliriously, when she was informed of Kemal's marriages. The little Turkish world in Munich which had received her in state on her arrival deserted her when they knew that she had no future any longer. She had left Munich uncured in body, sick in heart, with only one merciful and pitiful woman to see her off. I heard the last of her from an official communiqué from Angora in 1923. A woman called Fikrie Hanum, a distant relative of Mustapha Kemal Pasha, after trying in vain to gain admittance to Pasha, had shot herself not far from his house. It is best to wish her peace in her grave.

The lovely Latife accompanied her warrior husband to review his troops, sitting beside him as his aide, mounted on the Arabian horse which was one of his wedding gifts to her, dressed in a smart riding habit, her shining black hair held in place by a scarlet ribbon. The Ghazi looked more severe, tall, slender, and blond than ever, in contrast to the dark, plump, merry little wife beside him.

A friend who visited him shortly after their marriage tells of the changes wrought in the Ghazi's study by a feminine hand—how flowers were interspersed among the rich gifts of his admirers, his books, and *objets d'art* in the long room where the culture of East and West met and blended as in the personality of its owner. She interviewed the bride in her suite in the tower, where she sat like a little princess among her wedding gifts, and told of the great bond of similar interests which encircled her and her husband. With perhaps too great fervor she threw herself into the affairs of state which now consumed the Ghazi's every moment. She sponsored the proposed law of compulsory marriage which, however, was not passed. The law which abolished polygamy, combined with the postwar financial difficulties of the men of Turkey, had made the increasing number of bachelors and the rapidly increasing number of unmarried women alarming in a country where "old maids" had been unknown, and Latife apparently wanted all other country women to enjoy the same blissful state as herself. She allied herself with many new movements and reforms and received surprising recognition from the Nationalist Party.

In the interim between his courtship and his wedding, Mustapha Kemal had had full revenge against the wavering Sultan. With his customary ability to wait he had been watching for the moment to act. It came with the Allied invitation following the taking of Smyrna to a peace conference at Lausanne, extended to the Sultan and the Nationalist government, to Greece, Jugo-Slavia, Rumania, Japan, the United States, and in part to Russia and Bulgaria. Kemal intended to have Turkey no longer represented in conferences by two delegations, and he and his assemblymen were angered by the "brazen proposal" of Tewfik, the Sultan's premier, to share in the negotiations over Angora's victory, which he had in every way hindered. On October 1, the Ghazi turned over his president's chair to Dr. Adnan and made the fiery speech which brought forth the historic proclamation headed: "Down with the Ottoman Empire, Long Live Turkey!" declared a new sovereignty in Turkey, abolished the Sultanate and the Ottoman Empire, voided all official acts of the constitutional government since March 16, 1920, and provided that the Caliph instead of being the Sultan should henceforth be a purely religious dignitary elected from the house of Osman. Kemal celebrated with his associates that night at his home, Tchan-Kaya, until four in the morning, and as all became mellow with wine they made bold to reprove him for using "desperadoes" in his political schemes. "They are only the tongs with which to handle dirt," he assured. "I will never allow them to come between me and my real brothers." Yet he was soon to be estranged from most of them. On the fourth, Refet Pasha, getting into Constantinople from Thrace, conducted a *coup d'etat* under the very noses of the Allied garrison and forced the Sultan's government to resign. He then demanded its evacuation from the High Commissioners. On the 17th the Sultan-Caliph and a portion of his harem went on board the British battleship *Malaya* to refuge in Malta. Abdul Mejid Effendi accepted the Caliphate—for what proved to be a very brief term.

The "Sublime Porte" had gone out of existence. President Kemal headed a unified nation. Three days later Ismet Pasha entered the first conference at Lausanne to require from the Powers of the world an utterly new attitude toward a renewed people.

On the eve of the conference where Kemal, through his able representative Ismet Pasha, was to defy the world and assert the existence of the new Turkey, a colorful gathering of the young makers of the nation had been held on the heights above the Sea of Marmora. The vivid picture and the striking conversation are preserved for us by the enterprising Madame Berthe Georges-Gaulis. Kemal seated Madame Gaulis at one end of the table and occupied the other end himself, filling the places between them with the principal members of his staff. He alternately called upon his favorite poet-friend Yahya Kemal, with whom he frequently collaborates, to recite, and stopped him to describe to Madame Gaulis the heroes she had about her.

Yahya was reading his poem called "The Voice." "The Turkish bard comes back to the Bosphorus, he feels recovered from death and rests in the light of the Turkish sun, setting in the Bosphorus."

"The Turkish sun doesn't set!" imperiously interrupted the Pasha. "Red rose, death, love, the Bosphorus! Ah! these poets! they are incorrigible."

Then he, who is noted for never praising his friends,

began to tell, in smooth-flowing, musical French prose, of the many virtues of his colleagues—particularly of Ismet, to whom he referred as

the best, the nearest to perfection among us all. Not only do the Turks of Turkey and of the whole world know exactly what his Nationalism signifies, but the Muslem peoples admire him as the defender of honor, of virtue, and of probity. The National Assembly has full confidence in him.

Turkey has generals of great courage and worth; all are strongly united. The highest virtue of Ismet Pasha is to be for all of them the best of comrades. His greatest friend is Kiazim Karabekir Pasha. I myself knew at the first hours of the struggle, well before they got to Erzerum where they were going to join me—I knew that those two strengths assured happiness to the Turkish people and the Turkish country. Knowing that I had confidence, my energy was doubled. The day that the National Government was constituted, while many were still hesitating Kiazim Karabekir, without waiting for instructions so slow to come, fixed our eastern frontier himself by force of arms, surmounting all the incidental difficulties by his intelligence, his hardihood, and his military capacity.

His politics, his sense of organization, enabled him to create an army with which he marched eastward. He thus gave us our victory of Kars; he took from the enemy more cannons than Ismet Pasha could count after our recent victory. He sent us the good news that stable conditions had been reëstablished in that corner of the country. That news was the first sign of strength in the National Government.

Every one then understood, in Anatolia that the Turkish nation still had all its strength and vitality, and none more than Ismet appreciated the immense services rendered the country by his friend Kiazim Karabekir. No one knew better how to make them appreciated by the National Assembly.

We also owe that, as many other things, to Ismet Pasha. He at once saw the moral scope of the successes of his comrade, which were to decide hesitating souls to turn to us. I shared that sentiment, but I did not let it be seen, for I like each of us to have full responsibility for his acts.

Mustapha Kemal then turned to intellectuals surrounding him, bringing them in to his talk, one by one:

Thou, Moueddine Bohali, O deputy of Brussa, thou who chantest the charms of thy city; thou, Hamdoullah Soubhi, celebrated national orator, all you who were entirely attached to our cause, you never rose to speak, when the National Assembly attacked Kiazim Karabekir. It is I that had to mount the platform and impose silence on those foolhardy ones! I told them practically this: "Gentlemen, you are not of sufficient strength to understand a man like Kiazim Karabekir Pasha. You'd do better not to weary yourselves further in the enterprise; excuse me for saying it, it would be an impertinence. Let that man, whom the nation loves with all its heart, fix the frontiers that he has reconquered." They shut up, and found nothing to answer.

As Ismet Pasha sat, absorbed in thoughts of the task which lay before him, and the listeners grouped around the Ghazi occasionally interpolated a word or joined in a discussion, Kemal reminisced about his early struggles and hard-won victories, gradually coming back to Ismet Pasha and the work at hand.

"All we are worth to-day," he said, "all that we maintain, we are committing to Ismet Pasha. He is our representative before Europe. The fashion in which she may treat him is the touchstone of its sentiments

[311]

toward us. Certainly we want peace, we desire it ardently, with all our heart, with all our soul. But if they force us to it, we'll manage to carry on warfare to the end. Am I wrong in calling for a halt before Chanak? The Lausanne conference will tell."

As he concluded his talk, his voice grew crisp and metallic, and his steel-blue eyes narrowed. "I have said before you all to Ismet Pasha what I expect of him, what Kiazim Karabekir expects of him. If, by misfortune, Ismet should not respond to the hopes of the nation, he would have us all against him. But he has assured us that supported by the friendship of France," and here he eyed the French woman diplomat shrewdly, "he will get us a firm peace, the peace that we await to reconstruct our home and give back our men to their fields. He has told me: 'My dear Commander-in-Chief, stay where you are and give me freedom to accomplish this task without the use of my army, which is capable of crushing the English force.' And I responded to Ismet: 'Go to Paris, go to London; get them to understand us, make peace. I will accept the conditions that you will accept. But if you come back empty handed, we will all do our duty. The essential for our nation is to act together—without the absolute accord we would not exist.' "

None of the Turks broke the grave silence which his words spread. Finally the Frenchwoman eased the tenseness by asking the Ghazi to describe his recent victory. "In rapid, close-knit words," she says, "he showed us the slow preparation, the tragic arguments with himself, the risks that always subsist at the time when the final considerations of the problem in hand were being weighed. According to his invariable method he had long meditated on his plan, and the solutions were logically linked together without any gap. 'The rest was nothing; the execution was easy. But the most difficult thing remains to be done, to utilize the victory.' "

Still Ismet sat in silence. How difficult a thing it was to follow the Ghazi's instructions—to make Europe understand the demands of the revivified nation, and accept them, was soon to be found. With this task at hand, it is not strange that Ismet should seem preoccupied during the "threatening" praise of the demanding Ghazi and the discussion that followed.

With Oriental wile, Mustapha Kemal Pasha used this indirect means to forestall a rift between his two most important men, Ismet and Karabekir, and as well to warn them both as to who was, and intended to remain, their master.

Almost a year after the battle of Sakharia, the Greeks were finally cleared from Turkish soil, and Kemal was besieged with requests from his enthusiastic army to allow them to break through the Allied lines and put the foreign forces out of Constantinople. He told them to await the outcome of the Lausanne conference. Ismet Bey found a series of difficulties and misunderstandings awaiting him at Lausanne in spite of the Franklin-Bouillon and other treaties.

The possibility of a war with England, which would have necessitated a military alliance with Russia, worried the people of Turkestan and other Muslim peoples who were represented at the conference and who dreaded being in the power of Russia. These things had to be considered, and Ismet Bey, who had been in daily touch with Kemal, returned from the first conference with no decisive result—other than Latife's wedding ring. Both he and Kemal were reproached bitterly for this and there were murmurings of dissatisfaction because the orders to march on Constantinople were withheld.

In the unsettled conditions which followed the armistice, all patriots had been welded together by martial necessity. Now factionalism appeared, and men expressed criticism of Kemal the political leader that they had not felt concerning Kemal the military hero. Was he planning to assume dictatorship over the country he had saved? What program would the National Assembly undertake? What laws would be enforced, what reforms instituted? These questions the Turkish people asked themselves. The Old Turks resented the prospect of enforced westernization. It was an auspicious moment for Kemal's enemies among old Moslems, "Friends of England" societies, and English, Greek, and Indian agents generally to sow seeds of revolt among the people—and for suspicion of some of his most sacrificing comrades to grow in his mind. The old Union and Progress Society raised its head in opposition to President Kemal. Opposition was insurgency, to the Ghazi. And association of his friends with it to him was treachery.

The President went on a speaking tour to content the grumblers in the eastern villayets and Turko-Syria. Nothing could show more clearly the adoration of the people for their savior than a description of his address at conservative Brussa, original capital of Osman the Great, in the large cinema hall, where he solemnly received the delegation from Stamboul. The war orphans, proudly wearing their uniform, were massed about. Men and women teachers predominated in the audience—the women three times as numerous as the men, their faces uncovered, uniformly dressed in the black *charchaf*. The eyes of the excited, eager crowd were fastened upon the platform, where the chiefs of the new Turkey sat, all in colorful uniform except Mustapha Kemal Pasha, who was in European dress. A huge Turkish flag at the back of the stage formed a striking background for his fine head, as he rose to speak. The women wept, some of them sobbing unrestrainedly. The eyes of the men also filled with tears, and frantic applause followed his periods.

"We have gained a great battle," he told them, "very great, very complete. Nevertheless that is nothing, if you do not come to help us. Gain for us the battle of education, and you will do more for your country than

we have been able to do. It is you to whom I appeal."
He urged the necessity of women sharing the social life
of the nation, of attaining full development through
modifying outworn customs. "And all that will still be
nothing," he continued, "if you refuse to enter reso-
lutely into the modern life, if you repel the obligations
which it imposes. You will be lepers, pariahs, alone in
your obstinacy, your customs of another age. Remain
yourselves, but learn to take from the West that which
is indispensable to the life of a developed people. Let
science and new ideas come in freely. If you don't,
they will devour you."

His emotional people were stirred by the words of
the Ghazi, by his authority, his radiance, to such an
extent that they stretched out their hands to him, and
as he left the hall tried to touch him, to kiss his hands,
his coat. Their one thought was to express somehow
their gratitude, their adoration, of this great man who
had saved them and who promised them still greater
victories.

The Mosul controversy grew so hot that war was
threatened between Turkey and England over it. Both
held Mosul by conquest. Turkey claimed it as of
supreme importance to her, while England needed it
to "secure Mesopotamia and Suez"—and for the oil.
The Union and Progress Society, even while organizing
opposition to the ruling government and showing great
anxiety to step into power, gave full support to the
government when threatened by external crises.

The first few months of his married life, following his triumph over the Sultan at the time of the second Lausanne conference, were not easy ones for Kemal. He was faced at the same time with preparations for the coming election, political jealousy and internal discord, growing financial difficulties, and threat of foreign war. The Sultanate had been abolished and the Assembly given the right to elect the Caliph. The residents of Angora, who had won their place with great sacrifice and effort, showed resentment at the continual arrival of political recruits from Constantinople. The second conference at Lausanne seemed to drag on interminably without any satisfactory conclusions. Turkey began to treat with England toward a separate peace and to look toward America for financial reenforcement. Yet Kemal, beset with dangers, dreamed of reuniting the Turkish peoples of Asia—of the time when Turko-Mongols and Caucasian Tartars could be united with Turkey. He won by playing the feared Russian menace against Great Britain.

The British made a peace which preceded the final signing of the treaty in July, 1923. They evacuated Charnak, then Constantinople itself. Kemal would shortly have been compelled by the growing indignation and assurance of his people to attack them. From their viewpoint this saved Turkey from Soviet penetration, repressed the efforts of Communism to gain a foothold in Anatolia, lessened French influence in Turkey, and aggravated the dissonance between Turkey and

Egypt and the Muslems of India over the modernistic trend in Turkey.

Having upset the hereditary nature and secular power of the Caliphate, Mustapha Kemal soon found himself driven by the hostility of the "fundamentalist" Mussulmans to go the whole way and abolish the hier-archical institution altogether. They were taking ad-vantage to make it the center for plots against Kemal. So in April, 1924, his obedient Assembly expelled the new Caliph and declared the Caliphate unnecessary to orthodox Muhammadanism. Sir Valentine Chirol, noted authority on Turkish affairs, says of this: "The pro-Turkish agitation among Indian Muslems shortly after the war had as its only justification the fact that a defeated Turkish political power would jeopardize the Sultan's discharge of the exalted functions of Caliph throughout the Islamic world. Kemal exploited the agitation until it successfully defeated Great Britain's Near East policy; then when he won the peace at Lausanne he waged war against a caliphate for which he had no further use. Furthermore, it was he who subdued the agitation by abolishing the caliphate."

To fanatical telegrams of protest from the Muslem communities of Egypt and India, Kemal answered:

The dream of the centuries cherished by Muslems, that the caliphate should be an Islamic government including them all, has never proved realizable. It has become rather a cause of dissensions, of anarchy, of the war between the believers. Better apprehended, the interest of all has made clear this truth: that the duty of the Muslems is to arrange distinct governments for themselves. The true spiritual bond between them is the conviction that "all believers are brethren."

The final adjustment of July 24, 1923, at Lausanne astonished the world which had regarded Turkey for a half century as the "sick man of the East" with its abolition of the "capitulations" and recognition of Turkey's full sovereignty. Mustapha Kemal had thrown off in two years these shackles of Western imperialism which Yamagata and Ito struggled forty years to rid Japan of and that Sun Yat-sen fulminated against so bitterly. But the same causes brought the effect in each case—possession of the "argument of cannon," and jealousy among the Powers.

At the time Kemal won this great battle for his nation he was most beset by difficulties. His most ardent adherents, wishing to capitalize his achievements, overstepped themselves with the proposal that absolute legislative veto and power of dissolution of Parliament be given the President. It gave ground for increasingly jealous fellow-workers and politicians to cry: "absolute dictatorship!" Kemal discreetly postponed the measures, but Rauf Bey, who had been a valuable official in the nationalist government, had broken off to head a political opposition, and the hero Kiazim Karabekir, who had adopted two thousand orphans, turned his military headquarters into an *academie* teaching them music, hygiene, poems to machinery, and chivalry to women, to the discomfiture of his caricatured officers, launched the shafts of the idealist against him. The half-savage Kurds rose in a fanatical rebellion for the reëstablishment of the caliphate. There was the problem of helping five hundred thousand Muslim repatriates, brought from Greece and other countries under the exchange of nationalities agreement, to reëstablish themselves. The Christian repatriates going the other way had help from the great American fund, but Near East Relief did not apply to Turks. Bands of patriots who crossed over into Mosul were driven back by British airplanes. Friction with the Soviet arose over Nationalist Party championship of the Turk-Mongol and Turk-Tartar groups on the Russian border.

Kemal's years of work, with never more than five hours' sleep daily, and often for weeks no sleep at all, now told on him. Burdened with these and many other problems, he broke under the strain. For weeks he was sick unto death. To climax this crisis of his career he fell out of sympathy with his young wife. Young and sensational members of the Nationalist Party, conjecturing too freely regarding the president-dictator's death for that person's pleasure, suggested that Latife should succeed her husband, since party politics made both Ismet Bey and Rauf Bey unavailable.

Exercising his steel will to the utmost, keeping unflurried, the Ghazi showed himself "the Conqueror," once again, gradually surmounting his difficulties. The Kurds were quelled, and Sheik Said, who would have made himself Caliph, was hung with twenty accomplices. Kemal passed the crisis of his sickness and recuperated rapidly. The League of Nations awarded Mosul to Iraq—a less harsh way of giving it to Britain. Kemal advised against resistance but did not accept the award. Then he vigorously attacked his domestic problem.

Latife left Angora suddenly, on a visit to her parents. All the Nationalist ministers and party heads except Kemal were present with flowers to see her off. The stern mind of the Ghazi and the brilliant, willful mind of Latife must have come into conflict sooner or later. Still admiring one another's genius, they formally separated. The power to grant divorces had just been invested in Turkey's president, so he was able to save any unpleasant court revelations by simply granting his own. Latife was then twenty-two years old.

The effort of the world to pry into the significance of the divorce was unavailing. The agents of the Ghazi proclaimed it a purely personal affair. Latife, in an interview, said that she loved her husband and had done her utmost to help him realize his ambitions for himself and his country. Their union stood in the way, she said, of his further progress, and as in the case of Napoleon and Josephine, when it came to a choice between his future and his mate, the woman was sacrificed. She hinted at a serpent who had poisoned the happiness of their Garden of Eden, but steadfastly refused to divulge who or what this serpent was.

According to the judgment of many onlookers,

Latife's masterfulness and her tendency to mix in political matters were to blame for the divorce. A Parisian weekly, at the time, quoted a conversation of Latife with the Italian ambassador which made Kemal more resigned than ever to life without her. She asked the representative of Mussolini how feminism was progressing in his country. "Feminism," he replied with a smile, "has made little progress in my country. The women of Italy have their own way of interpreting feminism. To them it means making homes and presenting their husbands with fine healthy children." "Oh, how behind the times all that is," exclaimed Latife.

The desire for offspring is deeply implanted in Oriental men. Barrenness is cause for divorce among all Orientals, as with the Jews. This marriage was childless. It may be that even Mustapha Kemal is not proof against all the traditions of his race. And yet he had not, to 1929, remarried, and his adopted orphan children are all girls. At any rate, he has not changed in his ceaseless effort to bring about the freedom of Turkish women since the failure of his first marital venture.

The government refused Latife a passport when she wished to accept lecture contracts from Europe and America, as it was feared that she would openly criticize her former husband. She was allowed to travel privately in Europe and live very quietly in Constantinople. Kemal made a settlement of five thousand pounds on her. The facts are unadorned by explanation, either on the part of the Ghazi or his former wife. The marriage which had seemed to promise so richly was a failure, after all.

Private and official troubles operating together had been unable to crush Mustapha Kemal Pasha. Sure of himself and his cause, he was as superior to defeat as Lenin or Sun Yat-sen. In place of their quality of blandly ignoring adversity he possessed a supreme confidence in his ability to overcome it which unnerved his enemies. He gave them the feeling always that he had resources which they had overlooked and upon which he would call at the strategic moment. This characteristic fitted well with his "poker face" and aloofness.

Kemal's final trial was disaffection in his own political household. Disclosures were made at Smyrna, just before his visit there in July, 1926, that members of Kemal's parliament and other leaders who had worked with him in the Nationalist cause, had planned his assassination. The trial the following September resulted in fifteen people, including his schoolmate aide, Colonel Arif, being condemned to death and the sentence of ten more to many years' imprisonment. Dr. Adnan was accused but acquitted—he has been out of politics and under suspicion since. What Halide calls a "reign of terror" ensued, but it left Kemal as supreme as Mussolini.

When these schemes failed, the British government gave up hoping for Kemal's elimination and characteristically changed its policy to one of flattery and suggestion of coöperation.

This caused Soviet Russia to offer a defensive and trade alliance and voluntarily accept Kemal's uncompromising position against Communism in Turkey. Risking Russian disfavor he had caused capital punishment to be meted to Bolshevik agents. Through the age-old rivalry between Great Britain and Russia, Turkey was assured of existence, as in the days of the sultans. But the new and upstanding manner in which she began to take advantage of that rivalry, rapidly making herself independent of it, represented all the difference between the new Ghazi and a sultan. Mussolini sought relations with his fellow great man of the Mediterranean, culminating in good will tours of Turkish and Italian students in one another's countries.

Throughout the crisis in his personal career, Kemal found time to further his plans for his nation. His aims are appreciatively set forth by C. K. Streit, who says: "The crescent of Mustapha Kemal is no more the crescent of yesterday than our cross is the cross of the crusades. That 'far away look' in his eyes dwells on a Turkey that I did not see, that no man has seen. It was not in the cause of victory that he fought, this victorious general who, clad in civilian clothes, entered Smyrna in an automobile. Nor was it simply to defend the hovels of sun-baked mud that the Anatolian peasant calls home. It was to bring these peasants farm implements, railways, hospitals, to rescue them from ignorance, to wipe the hovels from the rich soil of Anatolia." How like the aim of Lenin, and even Gandhi! Kemal, like these leaders, made practical experimentation in the economic improvement of his people almost his first interest. His heart and concern were first with the simple Anatolian peasants who had been the backbone of his strength. Near Angora he established a modern farm, and marked increases in crops have convinced most ignorant peasants that machines have an advantage over their primitive methods.

In a manner revealing the mind of the new Asia, Kemal set forth his hopes and methods in an address at Casamundi in 1925.

All absurd superstitions and prejudices must be rooted out of our minds and customs [he said], only thus can the light of truth shine upon the people. . . . I can never tolerate the existence in the bosom of civilized Turkish society of those primitive-minded men who seek material and moral well-being under the guidance of a sheik, possibly blind and hostile to the clear light of modern science and art.

Comrades, gentlemen, fellow countrymen! You well know that the Republic of Turkey can never be a country of dervishes, sheiks, and their disciples. The only true congregation is that of the great international confraternity of civilization; to be a real man it is necessary to do what civilization demands. The leaders of the *tekkes* [Muslem cloisters or monasteries] will comprehend this truth, which will lead them voluntarily to close these institutions, as they have fulfilled their destiny. It is my duty to my conscience and to history to set forth openly what I have seen and felt. The government of the Republic possesses a bureau of religious affairs.

This department includes a numerous staff of imams, muftis, and scribes. These functionaries are required to have a certain standard of knowledge, training, and morality. But I know that there are persons who, without being intrusted with such functions, continue to wear priestly garb. I have met many among them who are not learned, or are even illiterate. They try to prevent direct contact between the government and the people. I should like to know from them, from what and from whom they received the qualities and attributes which they arrogate to themselves.

Kemal combated these slippery religious opponents in a unique manner. His decree against the fez struck the funny-bone of the West, where it was regarded as either a frivolous or ridiculous excess of modernism in the East. Kemal felt that some outward symbol of intellectual liberation was needed for the men equivalent to abolition of the veil for women, and it was natural he should light on the over-played "headdress of the faithful" which traditionalists had already made a mark of opposition to the heresy of modernization. How often a symbol of dress plays a dominant part in intellectual movements! There have been the breeches in France, the "golf-caps" in Russia, the queue-cutting in China, the European coat and trousers in Japan, Gandhi's homespun in India, the shortened skirts of the "suffragettes"—evidence of how simply childlike still is the mind of adult man.

In all changes Kemal tended to be liberal with the church and traditionalists until forced to drastic measures. It was so with the caliphate. At first he allowed priests the use of the fez and turban. But Kurdish spies and other plotters soon utilized this to exercise special influence. Whereupon Kemal countered with a police regulation of an ultra-modern type—each wearer of the old headgear must possess a special license, bearing the name of the mosque where he serves, his name and photograph, which he must wear within his "topper," and show on demand. Dervish monasteries were closed and dervishes and sheiks deprived of their titles and privileges.

Turkish women were not required by law to unveil, although they were threatened with arrest if they publicly criticized the dress reforms. While cosmopolitan Constantinople and progressive Angora seldom see the veil any more, the women in outlying districts of Anatolia have not all been courageous enough to discard it as yet. Often the Ghazi's appearance in a small town marks the first appearance of the women unveiled. They lift timorous, trustful faces, white as those of convalescents, to the savior of their country, and try to understand the new customs he preaches to them.

The naming of all the candidates for the Assembly at the fall election in 1927 by Kemal made him absolute ruler of his party and undisguised dictator of Turkey. This power was bestowed upon him by the People's Republican Party, of which he is honorary president. Candidates had been previously selected by a committee of ten, but when every prominent Nationalist wanted to be a member of the committee and yet none was willing to be judged or passed on by it, a general request arose for the Ghazi to solve the matter by choosing his parliament himself. Naturally this enables him to quell any opposition element that might exist.

Dr. Tewfik Rushdi Bey states that it will be necessary for Kemal to exert supreme power for five, perhaps ten years before the people will be able to avail themselves of the new privileges he has won for them, and use their freedom wisely. The development of the country's resources, the building up of an adequate army, the education and freedom from religious traditions that stand in the way of progress are the goals which he must attain.

IV

Eight years had passed since the young staff officer, Mustapha Kemal, had been sent from Constantinople by his jealous sovereign to rot in backward Anatoria. He had had his revenge on conceited Constantinople. He had made the Anatolia where his enemies reckoned he would be utterly ineffectual the bulwark of the nation and the nursing ground of all Turkish progress.

At first the proud Mistress of the Bosphorus had shrugged her shoulders in depreciation. Then, since he could no longer be ignored, Constantinople had resigned herself to receive him. He did not come. Eventually she swallowed her pride and complained of neglect. Kemal had awaited his own inclination. Now, in midsummer of 1927, he signified that he would come. He sailed into the Golden Horn on the yacht which had once belonged to the Sultan, and made his headquarters at Dolma Bagtehe Palace which was once the home of the Caliph. Warships boomed salutes in honor of his arrival and sheep were killed in sacrifice to Allah on the pier of the palace, in the traditional reception to a Defender of the Faith. There were elaborate parades. The Ghazi marched past fifty miles of cheering people. Fifty thousand electric lights gleamed from the minarets in place of the wicks floating in oil which had lighted the triumphal processions of former conquerors.

Perhaps those who know the Spartan simplicity of Angora, where the young Republic is earnestly striving toward development, will wonder that the austere President would care to wear, even for a moment, the luxurious splendor of old Turkey. However, in his speech at the palace, during the reception given him on the night of his arrival, he made it clear that he sought no personal triumph, but only the welfare and enlightenment of his people. "Turkey's advance along the path of social and political development," he said, "will be guided by the light of science and civilization. I proclaim this sacred purpose from the palace which formerly belonged to the 'Shadow of God on earth,' but it is now the property of the Turkish nation, which is not a shadow, but a solid fact."

In his *Book of Mustapha Kemal*, published in Constantinople in 1926, Abel Adam thus describes the change of feeling toward the caliphate:

We used to be taught that we belonged to the King, the Shadow of God on earth. This implied that there could be nothing to oppose the power of the Calif of Almighty God on earth; that there could be no society higher than ours. Whereas the facts were telling us that in all parts of the country there was plenty of misery and hunger; every year some section of the country was snatched away from us; we had a state weaker than the very least of the European Powers; going down in bribery, confusion, and immorality, begging the West for everything. Yet we had a Shadow of God on earth with forty wives and forty boy-concubines, busy with making the nation swallow the idle fantasy of paradise as taught through the *medressehs*. We were deteriorating from within. It was only by coming in contact with the European knowledge and accepting the superiority of European mentality and examining the miseries in the land of the Shadow of God on earth that we could understand the truth. We discovered that the Shadow of God on earth was nothing else but an idol as powerless and as soulless as one of the Buddhist idols of India. As Muhammed broke the idols in Mekka and Medina we also broke down these idols of Calif, *medressehs*, *tekkes*, and *tuebehs*. This is the meaning of our Revolution and its benefit will be great to the people.

The separation of Church and State, begun when the caliphate was abolished and secular education enforced, was made absolute in 1928 when a bill was passed at Angora eliminating all reference to religion from the constitution. Deputies who were once required to swear before Allah in taking the oath of office now swear upon their honor instead. For the first time in history an Asiatic Muslem nation, the traditional defender of the faith, has dared to set out upon the perilous but commendable path of religious freedom. Mustapha Kemal has the coöperation of the mass of the people in an amazing way, although he must take precautions against both the overradical young generation and the embittered conservative old one.

If the law against teaching Christianity in the schools is enforced by small fines, it should be remembered by Western supporters of mission enterprise that the mosque schools where the religion of Islam was taught by turbaned priests for six centuries have been replaced by secular government schools. How would it appear to deposed dervishes if foreign schools were allowed to teach Christianity or Judaism when they are prohibited from teaching the young the hereditary religion. At one time, if a Turk changed his religion, he was automatically deprived of citizenship. The law which guarantees religious liberty to all the citizens of Turkey is perhaps the most radical of any of Kemal's reforms. The clause in the constitution proclaiming Islam as the religion of the Turkish State has been removed. In eight years Mustapha Kemal has put Turkey on the way to be as free from religious restraint as the United States. While the change is in process it is felt that proselyting in the schools must be banned. If the change indicated an anti-religious attitude it would be ominous, but it can be put down as another step in the Westernization process through which Turkey is passing. Kemal recognizes the fact that Europe produces no literate or illiterate "prophets" by whose revelations superstitious followers conduct their lives, promising untold joys of the next world if the present world be ignored and disregarded. These prophets and revelations have been so powerful in Asia that they have dulled critical thought. As Abel Adam expresses it: "The mentality of Europe is the mentality of this world; while we live in this world we shall act by it. The mentality of Asia is the mentality of the next world; in the next world we shall act by it."

Kemal has built as a monument to himself not only a nation, but a city. Angora should, and doubtless will, as surely bear his name as Constantinople the name of the warrior emperor of Rome. When Paul the Apostle was adventuring in Asia Minor, Angora was a Roman colonial city of high business and culture. One of the finest surviving examples of Roman architecture stands on the dusty hill top, but for many centuries it looked out on flocks of goats climbing over the surrounding ruins. Now a metropolis has again sprung up to replace the collection of flat-roofed mud huts. In six years the population of Angora increased from 5,000 to 80,000. The city swarms with workmen of all nationalities, for Kemal did not hesitate to import artisans in the trades which Turks had ignored. The new city crests a high rock which rises abruptly from a plain. Kemal has connected it with the sea by rail—

beginning of his projected network of communication between the Black and Mediterranean Seas. Through the centuries the land surrounding the city's eminence had been allowed to become swampy. Mustapha Kemal Pasha was the first Turk who warred against the mosquito, which he drove out as vigorously as he did the Greek. It has been one of his great hopes that he might water his capital from a mountain lake sixty kilometers distant, and with that in view, he has built fountains and mains. The improvements in sanitation, hospitals and medical practice, roads, police protection, and legal procedure are all the difference between medieval and modern conditions. Statues, banned by the Koran and formerly prohibited by law in Turkey because savoring of idolatry, adorn the parks and city squares. There are three statues in Turkish cities of Kemal himself, in one of which the sculptor has made the "mistake" of representing him in the kalpak, a headgear he wore only for a short time after the fez was abandoned and before the hat had been proclaimed Turkey's official headgear.

In 1928 Kemal caused to be issued a statement of Turkey's financial status. It is conclusive proof that the "sick man" is no longer sick. Excepting the United States, Turkey was the only ex-belligerent country in the post-war world which refused to borrow. This was, however, made possible by a wholesale debt repudiation by the new republic. The statement claimed a surplus of three million dollars above the anticipated sum for

1927-8. A State bank was to be opened, with the $500,000 government gold reserve and the sum realized from the sale of the State jewels. The old Ottoman paper currency was to be taken from circulation after June, 1928. The Angora currency was first issued December, 1927.

The percentage of the total revenue spent by the Angora Republic for railroads and material improvements is twenty-five per cent., as against three and one-half per cent. spent by the old Ottoman government over a much larger area. The Ottoman régime used only two per cent. of its revenue toward education. Angora spends at least twelve and one-half per cent. in this manner. These things prove in "cold figures" that Mustapha Kemal has indeed made the new Turkey "a solid fact."

Because of continued attempts upon the Ghazi's life it has been necessary to guard his every step. When he returned to Angora from Constantinople the secret police unearthed an elaborate plan to dynamite his train, just in time to prevent its accomplishment.

He lives in a simple ten-room house set in a large garden. He has adopted six daughters, war orphans, who resemble American "flappers" as they stroll, unveiled, through the gardens. Recently he was caught by a camera dancing with one of the young ladies at the celebration of her marriage to one of his young diplomats. His chief interest is in the well-stocked stables of his farm, where he goes each day to inspect

the Arabian and English horses and gallops over the
farm on his newest acquisition—a magnificent mount
presented to him by President Doumergue of France.
He enjoys playing poker and is often heard driving
back furiously late at night from his club, which fact
his enemies have distorted into weird tales of debauch-
ery. His adherents reply that a fifty-year-old man could
not live such a life and accomplish the colossal amount
of work that he does—an obvious fact.

He is indifferent to luxury, requiring only plenty of
fresh air, books, and music. He alternates between
great music of the West and the haunting melodies of
ancient Anatolia, and always listens to music during
his meals, which consist alternately of European and
Turkish dishes. He goes in for dancing, no doubt to
emphasize the new personal liberty of the Turks, and
is fond of jazz but condemns the radical Black Bottom
and Charleston. He lives by no regular schedule—rising late as a rule, but when a piece of work is in hand
he plows through it rough-shod until it is completed.

In the fall of 1927, just before the presidential election, he prepared a 400,000 word speech for the benefit
of peasant Anatolia (the facts being fairly well known
in Constantinople and Angora). It was a complete
résumé of the building of the new Turkey. He worked
on it forty-eight hours at a stretch, exhausting one secretary after another, while his own superb energy kept
him alight with vital force as it had during the Battle
of Sakharia and upon many another occasion.

When he began his address, the great Assembly Hall at Angora was crowded with eager listeners, and there were radio connections with all parts of Turkey and the outside world. At the end of the second day the radio connections broke, owing to stormy conditions, but the speech went on for six days, and the listeners remained eager. Even those who thought themselves familiar with the new Turkey's history were amazed by some of the revelations his address contained. Chief among these were the news that Turkey had seriously considered an American protectorate in 1919—the Wilsonian principles seeming the only gleam of justice for the defeated—and the announcement that high Muslem dignitaries had offered the caliphate to Kemal, who not only refused the traditional honor, but destroyed the caliphate itself as an outworn symbol.

In the formal dress of a European diplomat, the Ghazi stood before his people and logically and clearly, but with intrinsic dramatic force, unfolded the history of those events which had "pulled Turkey out of the trough of war," revivified her, changed her from a monarchy to a republic, from a caliphate to an undenominational state, abolished polygamy, the fez, the veil, and all obsolete symbols of medievalism; adopted the civil code of Switzerland, the criminal code of France, and the commercial code of Germany; adopted the Gregorian calendar, the twenty-four-hour clock, and many modern European methods.

He looked a little older than when he first had

addressed them from that platform, his fair hair thinner over the temples, his profile sharpened, but the same air of majesty and kindliness held his audience spellbound.

Sir Valentine Chirol, a famous authority upon Turkish history, believed five years ago that "democracy" in Turkey would only mean a new form of medieval despotism and questioned what use the nation would make of her new strength in the light of her past history. He now looks with amazement upon the changes Kemal's leadership of the past few years has wrought. He praises the "world's record" six-day speech as an "unparalleled achievement" and says that the "circumstances under which the six-day speech was given were also unparalleled." He comments on the recurrence of the word "England" in the speech, as though upon England alone and not the Allies in general rested the blame for Constantinople's occupancy. He sees Kemal's sincerity of purpose demonstrated by his refusal to become caliph, and in the abolition of the caliphate he sees that "we in dealing with Islamic countries are inclined to overrate the potency of a religious factor which has so quickly crumbled away in the one country where it could be regarded as a formidable spearhead for the revolt of Asia against the Western world."

As fervently as Gandhi turns away from modern progress as the path to destruction, Kemal turns to it as the means of grace. The Turkish peasant who once toiled, half-starved, in ignorance—his darkness

[337]

lightened only by the "ecstasies" of some dervish or *imam* as to the paradise awaiting him in the world to come—now sends his children to school and is able to feed them properly. Instead of a degenerate Sultan, whose jewels were a fabulous fairy tale, living in idle luxury as the Shadow of God on earth, he is governed by a president whose greatest concern is the welfare and advancement of his people. As to their spiritual welfare, it has been given into their own hands. Perhaps the removal of such a symbol as the "Shadow of God on earth" would induce the people to look for the kingdom of God within themselves, demonstrable in this world as well as any other.

JOSEF STALIN
JOSEF VISSERIONOVITCH DJUGASCHWILLY

1879–

JOSEF STALIN

I

IN Josef Stalin's cool, determined face with its casually appraising eyes, flaunting beard, and confident chin one may read the ruthless pragmatism of the modernized Asiatic element now dominating Russia. Vladimir Illich Lenin's face, on the other hand, was—and remains, since it is preserved to view—a symbol of the combination which is his nation. His Tartar ears, head, eyes, and cheekbones, his poetic, Gallic mouth and his nose "half of each" represent the amalgamation between East and West which, in soul and mind as well as in blood, is the vast merging-land of the world's two great civilizations. For Stalin is an Asiatic from across the Caucasus, whereas Lenin was born on the Volga, where six hundred years ago conquering horsemen of the horde of Jengiz took the native "Scythian" women as prey and fathered that midway race which is now the enigma of the world—the determining factor in the clash between Western dominance and Eastern resentment, Euro-American energy and Asiatic resilience.

Gradually Byzantine culture filtered north and made that race a nation. Then Peter the Great discovered modern Occidental civilization and began the long effort to make the nation Western. His was exactly the vision and effort of Mustapha Kemal in Turkey two

[341]

centuries later. But Kemal's people, down to the most primitive Anatolian peasant, are swept along by their awakened sense of danger and the enthusiasm of his personality. Czar Peter's people, on the other hand, felt no need for the drastic change of mental habit suggested to them. So the mass remained apathetic, while the Czar's apish courtiers alone adopted European culture—and made of it a mark of caste and a tool of arrogance.

Then came Lenin, of the nobility which had profited, bitter against the superiority of his own caste, determined to give the benefits of machine and school—foundations of the West's luxury, strength, and pride—to the millions. A revelation of driving motive is his famous order, issued while his government was in its greatest crisis and Moscow was ringed by armies: "The peasants of Gorkii and Ziianova are immediately to be supplied with electric light." His worshipers become as sentimental over the incident as Lincolnophiles over pardons of deserting soldier boys. The Americanizing of Russia was as urgently important to Lenin as the repulse of the White armies. For the same reason he regarded the Institute for Standardizing Human Motions in Industry as important as the Third Internationale, and assiduously studied Henry Ford. "Bolshevism is communalism plus electricity," was his definition of the program of the new régime.

But by Westernization Lenin meant something very different from the imitative Europeanism pursued until

[342]

now by the obliterated aristocracy. His plan was rather to use Western science, technique, and application to duty, to bring to fruition a truly Asiatic idealism —a Russian secretary's idea of the millennium on earth —communalism substituted for competition, the individual submerged in the society. He was opposed to such social concomitants of science and machinery in the West as plutocracy, competition, preying, sweating, manipulation of government by big business, and class pride, and believed that he was starting a violent revolution against these things which would shortly spread throughout that West, consummating the work begun by Peter the Great of bringing Europe and Russia together—but in a far different spirit: the spirit of Asiatic Russia and not of Europe.

Lenin professed Marxism. But in fact, he was actuated by the spirit of Asia, not that of the old German professor. In 1903 he furiously set upon the true Marxists in the Social-Democratic Party, breaking it into the Bolsheviks who followed him and the Mensheviks whom he henceforth hated more than Czarists. The Mensheviks accepted the Marxian eschatology of social development from feudalism through specialized capitalism into socialism. But Lenin based his new system not on developed industrial society but upon the primitive communal life of the Asiatic peasantry.

The worker in Russia is not a separate, city-bred product as in Europe. In Russia as in China, India, and Japan, he is a projection of the peasantry; at the

[343]

most a generation or two removed from the soil, maintaining his connection with it and often going back to it. If the mill hand in Osaka, Canton, or Moscow be asked "Where are you from?" he will not state the ward of the city which contains his hovel, but the country district where his father or grandfather was born and where his clan is permanently attached to the land. When his livelihood fails in the city, he turns to his country seat for succor. Herein lies the strength of the Asiatic proletariat, as British shipping interests in Pacific Asia discovered when they attempted a seamen's lockout.

Lenin called his work "the proletarianizing of the peasant." It was rather the peasantizing of the factory worker—a developing of the principle of Asiatic peasant organization in the proletariat. The immediate system of national government by soviet grew out of the calling of the Workers Council of St. Petersburg in the revolt of 1905—a spontaneous expression of the native governmental genius of Asia. In modern Russia, Japan, China, Siam, or Turkey, this genius takes concrete form in administration by a self-made dictator mellowed by adviser-assistants supported by a ruling group.

The failure of organized labor in Western Europe and America to understand and respond to the idealism of Bolshevism drove it in its more natural direction: Asiaward. This tendency became clear during Lenin's last two years, during which time he kept his movement on the opportunistically winding path his political sense decreed by means of sharp notes to his lieutenants from his sickbed.

It fell to the man dubbed "Steel," a pure Asiatic of Russia's south country, to carry Russia forward in its tendency. Under him the idealism of the Bolshevik group was to become definitely secondary to pragmatism, its poetic theorism to Asiatic practicality, and its world program to repairing the national dignity. Russia was to become one of the Asiatic peoples engrossed in building power to compel respect from a West whose superciliousness has awakened the inferiority complex.

In Moscow, begging for biographical material, I was told that men's lives were important only in so far as they related to the "movement" and affected the "mass." For example, a leader's domestic and family relationships were worth recording only where they brought factors into the cause. Since Krupskaia became Lenin's chief aide it was related that he had a wife; of Stalin, although he lives quietly in the Kremlin with wife and child, it was not recorded in the new Communist Biographical Dictionary whether his status was multiple, plural, or single. A man's romantic loves received as little biographical notice as the number of times he breathed per minute. This self-effacement is honest and lived up to. Stalin himself proved as barren a source on himself as the newly compiled Communist Biographical Dictionary. Only in the case of the sainted Lenin was there the beginning of an exception

[345]

to this attitude. This one exception almost shows that it is not worth while. Lenin's life when fully revealed, proves to be have consisted so completely of his work that the peasantry must spin myths to give him flesh and blood. It is much the same with Stalin and other revolutionaries—save Trotsky.

The truly Asiatic spirit of submergence of personality is here. And the consequent paradox also. In Russia, where pretense of ignoring individual personality is official and orthodox, personality molds the new world. The personality of Lenin dominated the Russian revolutionary party, his striking mental make-up shaped its philosophy, and his growth was its evolution.

The personality of Stalin is its stabilizer in power.

II

The Georgians bear the reputation in Asia of being one of that continent's "fighting races." Older than the Mongol incursion, they are of related stock to the Pathans, Turks, and Armenians: reserved of speech, unconceited, easy to approach, and ruthless. The imagination of the true Slav which so often sentimentalizes his courage and muddles his purposeness is absent in these Russians; in compensation they lack the Slav's poetic sympathy and idealism.

Tucked in behind the main ranges of the Caucasus, their little country of sun-scorched deserts and mist-drenched valleys largely escaped the invasion of Greek culture from the decaying Byzantine Empire. Nor has it been greatly disturbed by outside influences since the Moguls of Tamerlane swept hastily over it en route to the plunder of Persia and Mesopotamia. Even the conquering czars discreetly controlled the independent and semi-savage people of Georgia with gloved hands. Many of them are Muslems, the rest have become nominal communicants of the Russian Orthodox Church. Underlying both these religions is their true faith— a fabric of homely superstitions indicating means of taking practical advantage of the gods, easily giving way before modern education to atheism.

Josef, son of Visserionoff, came to increase the immediate burdens and inspire the ultimate hopes of the Djugaschwilly family in 1879. They were moderately well-to-do peasants, which meant that they lived in a flat-roofed mud house instead of a cane shelter and had a chair and a cellar stocked with roots and cheeses. Their town was Gori, their metropolis flat-roofed Tiflis of the steep hill-slopes.

A cropper's share from the landlord's estate, obtained by the labor of the men, women, and children of the family provided food, and to obtain luxuries purchasable with money Visserionoff made a last and began pegging at his neighbors' shoes during light spells. He showed craftsmanship and business ability and gradually developed into a small-scale shoe manufacturer in the near-by village of Didi-lilo. Josef, growing to comprehension of his surroundings during this social evolution of the family, was well equipped to understand the relationship between the peasantry and industrial worker in Russia. Meanwhile he was learning to hold his own in contest of coarse wit or fist and heel fight by knocking about with the fraternity of street hawkers.

In the normal course of things he was to have succeeded his father in the shoemaking business. He was swerved from this course by Alexander III's decree subsidizing clerical education—issued because, Stalin's Bolshevik biography put it: "The government at that time wished to educate priests, needing the help of the church to fight revolutionary thought." The lad's mother, a pious member of the Greek Orthodox Church, warmed to the opportunity of her son's being a priest and Visserionoff thought that a little education, since Josef had this chance to get it for nothing, would not go badly even with shoe manufacturing, and entered his burly lad, in early teens, as a novice in a clerical seminary.

Josef was to fail to prove a help in fighting revolutionary thought, but he made good use of his intellectual opportunities. In him, as in the case of Mustapha Kemal, the old régime was preparing a leadership for its own overthrow. Large, unimaginative, but with a flair for theory of government, gift for organization, and ambition for leadership, the lad became engrossed with "bootlegged" translations of Marx's writings as soon as he had mastered the Russian language. Reading this same technical German economist had inspired Alexander Lenin, the son of a school superintendent on the Volga, to concoct a plot which brought him execution. His younger brother Vladimir vowed a vengeance on the established order which was to reach across the Caucasus and involve the young rebel now painstakingly spelling out leaves of Marx concealed in a litany-book. It is middle age, not youth, that requires its reading sugar-coated.

Visserionovitch began, in his quiet, almost sullen way, to interest his fellows in his find. Some of them were more interested in a peaceful promotion into clerical life. They reported to the priests, and Josef received an opportunity to argue Marx before them. He succeeded in convincing them that he ought to leave their school at once. He was just nineteen.

He went back to the shoe-last. In the evening he deserted the shop to mingle with students of the various schools about Tiflis. He organized several small Marxist circles among them. Like Carey, his business was saving souls—although in a rather different creed; he cobbled shoes to pay expenses. At seventeen he had been regarded by the radical fraternity as a full-fledged revolutionist, and during his first year out of school, upon assisting in the illegal organization of railway workers in Tiflis, Baku, and Batoum, he was recognized by election to membership in the Social-Democratic Party.

With demand for no more by way of physical necessities than a crust of bread and a plank bed, with his sturdy physique, fearlessness, and taciturnity, he became a most valuable worker for the party. The police hardly suspected such a man. Their eyes were on anemic university students. Visserionovitch had none of the ear-marks of the intellectual fanatic to attract their attention.

So he continued until 1902, when he was seized in a demonstration in Batoum, on the Black Sea. There was evidence that he had been one of its organizers. As a result he spent his first year of legal manhood in prison. His sentence was then commuted to exile in Eastern Siberia. He began an acquaintanceship with the Czar's "corners of oblivion" which was to become unusually wide.

In 1903 was held the little conclave of party leaders in which the new young leader Vladimir Ilyich Lenin split the Social-Democratic Party and founded "Bolshevism." The news was not long in reaching, through their own "underground" system, the exiles in far Siberia, and the controversy raged hot among little groups there. Visserionovitch whole-heartedly took the Lenin side. In fact, it might almost be said that Lenin had taken the Visserionovitch side. The sense of fundamental unity between workers and peasants based upon their common Asiatic traditions, and confidence in ability to go direct to the goal without the guidance of the intelligentsia and without passing through an era of industrial capitalism, were natural to young "Stalin."

For because of his coolness, strength, and ruthlessness his fellows had dubbed him "Steel." His peasant roughness made it easy to fraternize with the guards. He escaped from Siberia and returned directly to his home district to assume membership in the Caucasus Union Committee. Running a great risk of identification, he assisted in bringing out various revolutionary periodicals, and since then has not ceased to write in a direct, unimaginative, but clear and vigorous style. He did not look like an editor, and so he was able to conduct hidden publications called *Fight of the Proletariat* and *Baku Workman*. He was one of the first proletariat leaders to come out of the proletariat itself. Already he was the unconscious rival of a brilliant Trotsky. Stalin first traveled across European Russia as Caucasus delegate to the Bolshevik conference of Tannerfjord. Here he came into direct touch with Lenin, Zinoviev, Kameniev, Lunacharsky, and many other agitators with whom he was destined to associate in the government of the United Soviet Socialist Republic. Later he attended a congress in Lenin's garret in London and is said to have visited Gorky in Italy.

Back in St. Petersburg, he assisted in planning the outbreak of 1905. The Czar's conscienceless councilors had planned a "small successful war" to check the growing unrest; the revolutionists welcomed the war as an opportunity to strike. Stalin, like Lenin, however, kept in the background, his associates fearing that direct activity on his part would bring him to the notice of the authorities. They could be taken for first offenses and still live, but the arrest of men who had before been convicted and had escaped from exile would mean summary death.

The uprising—practically confined to a coup in the capital—failed. The intellectual element, finding the bloody reality of revolution too much for their stomachs and being mollified by royal pledges of representative government through the Duma, deserted the cause. Nicholas relied upon a campaign of terrorism to crush the irreconcilables.

The little group of the faithful definitely turned to the proletariat. It was the only thing left on which to pin hope.

They desperately needed money to propagandize the worker. Lapse of interest of sentimental bourgeois friends stopped contributed funds. Stalin, after trying bank-note forgery, went out in this ruthless, pragmatical way to get the money by "expropriation"—the start of a method and theory to be legalized after Bloody October. It consisted of "recovering" the "people's money" by bold "political" banditry often involving many deaths. The Tiflis robbery, carried out by a secret gang known as the "Trans-Caucasus Fighters" said by M. Aldanov to have been led by Stalin, was perhaps the most spectacular "expro." Lenin sent bombs from his retreat in Finland. The cashier of the Tiflis State Bank and his bookkeeper were conveying money under heavy guard, mounted and foot, from the post office to the bank, when from the roof of a prince's house a bomb fell with terrific explosion, scattering the escort carriage containing the money. The horses ran, dragging the wrecked carriage amid the scene of indiscriminate firing, and bomb throwing followed in which fifty people were killed or injured. A man in a droshky headed off the horses, dashed them, bleeding, to the ground with a bomb, seized his loot and drove away. It was revealed after the Revolution that part of the money had been hidden in the upholstery of the unsuspecting, pompous manager of the imperial Caucasian Observatory.

The police never found a clew to this bold exploit, but one year later (1908) Stalin, with the entire revolutionary committee of Baku, was arrested on a charge of sedition, obviously on information from the inside. He was imprisoned and then exiled to Vologodsky, in frozen White Russia. In 1909 he escaped and went directly back to Baku, under the name of Koba. Almost at once "Koba" was arrested and exiled for six years to Solovitchigodsk—a place just a degree more northerly and God-forsaken than Vologodsky. His tremendous physique enabled him to walk away through the snows when neither guards nor other prisoners dared be outside. He made his way painfully and cautiously back to the very capital of the government which condemned him—this time as Evanovitch. Several months in revolutionary journalism there, arrest again, prison, exile again to Vologodsky where he now had to take special precautions to avoid those who had known the exile "Stalin"; reëscape in December,

1911, rearrest in April, exile this time to Narim, escape to St. Petersburg again in September—such was his life from 1909 to 1913. In the intervals between his escapes and rearrests he was able to settle before the editorial desks of *Izvestia* ("Star") and *Pravda* ("Truth"), and of less regular publications entitled *Worker and Soldier, Workers' Way* and *Worker*. Lenin himself had founded revolutionary journalism, but he was now compelled to publish in western European countries and rely for results upon the few copies that could be smuggled in the false bottoms of trunks. Stalin carried revolutionary journalism into the citadel of the enemy. His prestige among partisans of a later time was to rest not a little upon this early connection with the two evangels of Bolshevism destined to become the official organs of a new tyranny.

In St. Petersburg, as David Nijeradze, Stalin organized the little Bolshevik group in the first Duma and acted as its chief. Attention was soon drawn to him and in March of 1913 he was again arrested and exiled —to a place that held him this time: Turukan inside the Arctic Circle. Each of the five times that he was rearrested it was only chance that saved him from identification as a second offender. Had he been recognized, the Communist Party would have lost its future dictator.

Stalin was compelled to remain inside the Arctic Circle, helpless to take advantage for his cause of the great opportunity of the World War. No member of the present Bolshevik oligarchy received more "stripes" for the faith than he, took more risks, and suffered more imprisonments. Others fled abroad and worked in safety from behind foreign boundary lines. Stalin the imperturbable scorned such precaution. Invariably, he returned to the very scene of his arrest to carry on his labor. The prison tortures, the deprivation, the forced labor and isolation he was compelled to suffer would have broken a more sensitive mind or delicate body. As with Lenin, Stalin's entire life was his cause: he had no interests outside it. Like Lenin, he survived by a combined will to power and natural asceticism. The more highly strung Lenin saved himself as long as he did by a gift of relaxation and play. In his Asiatic insusceptibility and capacity to wait, Stalin had an advantage over even Lenin.

Myths grew about him among the sympathetic peasantry and proletariat. He was the ogre, who, each time he was killed, reappeared in another shape. He was the tiger, they whispered, which had ten lives, the bad dream which the Czar could not prevent from recurring. He was the man of steel.

His guards nevertheless held him at Turukan until the Kerensky Revolution of February, 1917, and its political amnesty. Then he returned to Petrograd and set to work organizing soviets among the workmen, soldiers, and peasants. Lenin found small groups prepared for swift action when he returned through Germany in his famous sealed coach. Stalin brought about the publication of Lenin's program in *Pravda*, April 7. In May his associates elected him member of their *Politburo*, and he began the painstaking organizational work which was to lead him to dictatorship of the party. In July, Kerensky, forced to recognize that the Bolshevists were working for his downfall, ordered the arrest of Lenin, Zinoviev, Trotsky, Kameniev, Dzerjinsky, Lunacharsky, and others. Some went to jail and others into hiding—Lenin and Zinoviev, with 200,000 rubles "reward" on their heads, in a hayrick. The less spectacular Stalin was able to continue working with soldiers and laborers until the situation had ripened. Trotsky, clever enough to procure release, assisted. Lenin and Zinoviev escaped to Finland, but returned in disguise in October when Kerensky was falling to pieces. On the famous twenty-fourth these returned exiles united with the zealots who had braved it through at home to form the impromptu Central Executive Committee of the new Soviet government.

Stalin assumed by general consent the place of organizing secretary. He was not interested in making fiery speeches like Trotsky or writing hot proclamations like Bukharin. His interest was in the practical essence of the movement, not its showy surface. Trotsky at once recognized in him a rival, but took the line of superciliously patronizing him. Stalin, on his part, was highly impressed by Trotsky. In an article on the first anniversary of the revolution he paid him this tribute:

JOSEF STALIN

All work of practical organization of the October uprising was done under the immediate direction of Leon Trotsky, president of the Petrograd Soviet. It can be stated with positiveness that the party owes everything to Trotsky for insuring the rapid passage of the garrison to the Soviet side and the clever organization of the working revolutionary committee.

The question of the attitude of the many minor peoples—mostly Asiatic—in Russia to the new régime and *vice versa* was a pressing problem. To Stalin, the Georgian, who understood their aspirations and necessities, his comrades entrusted the responsibility of securing their loyalty. He became the first People's Commissar of Nationalities and framed the policy of autonomy for racial groups and preservation of local languages and cultures which is such a puzzling feature of Bolshevism to those who know its emphasis on centralization and standardization. But Russia is a paradox—a combination of Western economic theorism and Asiatic practicalness. Stalin, thoroughbred Asian, recognized that modern Asia demands opportunity for self-expression and development of its own genius. His policy toward the Asiatic nationalities in Russia inspired outer Asia's first confidence and interest in the new Soviet Power.

As counter-revolutionaries equipped by the "capitalist" Powers pressed in upon the Bolshevik state, Stalin's coolness and strength were needed on the Revolutionary Military Council. He had worked in 1918 with Voroshilov, rebuilding a shattered army at Tzaritzin.

[357]

From 1920 to 1923 he gave himself to military matters, personally taking part in the resistance to Udinitch's drive on Petrograd, the war in Poland against Denekin, and the crushing of Wrangel's temporary power in the Ukraine. For his success the name of Tzaritzin on the lower Volga was changed to Stalingrad. He was awarded the Order of the Red Standard by his associates. In a somewhat bored fashion, he accepted it.

He was concerned in studying Trotsky, chief of the armies. Either the brilliant Jew or the steely Georgian, it was evident, would succeed to the power of the wearing-out Lenin. It was fireworks against firmness, eloquence against reserve, Jewish idealism against Asian practicality, the power of a hand that could win other men with a clasp against a hand that held the leading strings of organization. In an Asian society, just emerging from disruption, the advantages would be with the latter type more than they would in personality-loving America. Outsiders discussed as to which of the rivals had Lenin's confidence.

Probably no man ever had from Lenin what could be called full confidence. The father of Bolshevism was too utilitarian for that. He had confidence in people, *en masse*, provided they were properly directed, but the confidence he gave his lieutenants was that which one gives an automobile or air-plane motor— that under certain conditions they will do certain work —rather than the trust one human being ordinarily gives another. Some founders have achieved success

[358]

by reposing in their disciples a confidence which inspires great deeds. Lenin achieved by an opposite method. He carefully refrained from putting himself in the hands of any human, and never made any man indispensable to his cause. He used men as cogs rather than apostles. Stalin worked such a scheme much better than Trotsky. The brilliant Jew relied upon hero worship. In his *History of the Revolution* of about this date Stalin's name was not mentioned! In exile in Constantinople in 1929, Trotsky was to say: "What is Stalin? The shortest answer is that he is the most prominent average man in our party!"

Stalin had come to be General Secretary of the Politbureau, the Executive of the Communist Party, in spite of his protest—affecting to the "low-brows"—that his manners were too rude for such a high position. Stalin's Asiatic gift for intrigue was most useful in capturing local party "nests" during Lenin's illness. It is hardly accurate to lay his activities to personal ambition, as one would more readily do in the case of Trotsky. The struggle was parallel to that between Yamagata and Ito. Stalin was ruthless to his contemporary more in the spirit of taciturn conviction of the latter's unreliability than of personal rivalry.

Lenin died. At the great funeral ceremonies Trotsky stood on a high platform in Red Square, the wall and turrets of the Kremlin behind him, and glorious in uniform and medals of the Commander-in-Chief of the Red Armies, made an impassioned oration. Stalin

[359]

mingled among the workmen at his feet in workman's blouse and boots. But Trotsky failed to assume command. Not personality but organizational ability was henceforth to dominate. On his "unofficial" throne Stalin could sit silently and solidly, hid from the public, from officials of his own making, from foreign diplomats, and from journalists, and work eighteen hours a day tightening the reins of party control on his great Asian-minded populace. It was his task to make the necessary adaptations to the mentality of the masses, direct and maintain discipline, ruthlessly suppress extraneous ideas and eliminate disruptive personalities, and in general keep vigorous and responsive the single-minded, singly directed "aristocracy" of one million people—the formal membership of the Communist Party—which is the machine through which the world's vastest nation is governed. (Yet the popular cheap journalistic representation of Bolshevism in the West has been that of a régime entirely without discipline.)

Mussolini, of Italy, controls his governing machine largely by force of his overwhelming personality. Stalin uses quiet, business-like organization. Both movements are built on attractive doctrines of the salvation and glorification of their societies. But in keeping the movement bigger than the man, in submerging the ephemeral and variable factor of personality, Bolshevism has attained the greater promise of permanence. By the same development it has lost in romantic glamour and in spirituality.

III

Stalin's victory over Trotsky establishes Russia in its Asiatic traditions. Trotsky is a Jew, but the modern Jew does not belong to Asia. His theoretical-mindedness, his vision, his lack of balance, and his effect upon history and culture connect him to European civilization. Judea sent as many sons eastward as westward but they have left hardly a trace in Persia and India, and in China have been completely swallowed up. In Western life under the most hostile conditions Jews find places where their fitness is unchallengeable. They do not flourish in Asia as surely as they come to the top in the West. So Trotsky could not adapt himself to an Asian-spirited Bolshevism.

The revolutionary movement in Russia liberated the Jews, and guaranteed to them, as to all other racials, equal treatment and standing in the proletarian commonwealth. That feature of Bolshevism, lost sight of abroad, is as great a work in the emancipation of mankind as the freeing of the blacks in America. Reacting from long repression, it was natural that the Jews should play a large part in the Bolshevik régime, although never so large as was represented by the Jew-hating refugee aristocracy.

Trotsky, Zinoviev, and their fellow Jews were the most European-minded element in the Communist Party. Trotsky's mind constantly ran westward. To him the Russian Revolution was not for Russia's sake but merely a lighting wick for a western-spreading conflagration. Highly industrialized Germany, England, and the United States—particularly England—were, rather than Russia, the ideal soil for Utopian schemes. Trotsky was internationally minded. With the lack of attachment peculiar to the Jew he was free of the awakening national pride and consciousness which is the dominant note through Asia to-day from its Pacific shore to the Polish boundary. Again, he was more readily convinced by theorizing than by observation and experience. In his unwillingness to compromise with conditions he was European rather than Asian spirited.

Clashes of the two temperaments in the Russian revolutionary cause began in 1903 between Trotsky and Lenin, and were to be carried to an ultimate "showdown" between Trotsky and Stalin. In September of the previous year Trotsky arrived in London, a refugee from Samara, where he had passed through his apprenticeship as a revolutionist. He came to Lenin's dreary flat with a contribution for the paper Lenin was publishing and illicitly circulating in Russia. Lenin liked the young man's fiery zeal and forceful style. But Plekanov, grouchy old founder of the Russian Marxian school, who assumed a sort of editorial censorship, wrote Lenin: "I do not like your new friend's pen." Lenin, who was soon to break with Plekanov, replied: "Perhaps you do not like his style, but every man can live and learn, and I think this man could be very

[362]

useful to our movement." In a few months came the famous party congress in which Lenin demanded unquestioned leadership of the party on a program of ruthless and pragmatic action. Trotsky failed to follow into his Bolshevik wing. "This man with all his native energy and talent played the part of a destroyer of the party," Trotsky accused in biting style. "Comrade Lenin mentally reviewed the membership of the party and came to the conclusion that he, and he alone, was the iron hand . . . he himself would take over the part of Robespierre the Incorruptible." Lenin retorted in characteristic brevity that Trotsky was "an empty *poseur*." Not until the summer of 1917, when both were working for the downfall of the Kerensky régime, did Trotsky, returning precariously from America, submit himself to Lenin's command in Moscow and gain admission to the Bolshevik party. Even after the beginning of their famous coöperation in the Smolny Cloister, when the outside world believed that they were in equal power and authority, Lenin exhibited his contempt for Trotsky's love of logic and words in a satirical article called "The Cult of the Revolutionary Phrase."

In this work of a light moment Lenin made clear the fundamental difference in their mentality. Trotsky lived in words, Lenin in action. The difference between the theorist and the statesman was evidenced again in the Brest-Litovsk negotiations in which Trotsky, representing Russia, refused the arrogant peace terms of the

Germans, maintaining that the German proletariat would hold their rulers responsible for the continuance of war and that this upshot would incite the social revolution in Germany and possibly spread it to yet other countries. Lenin, the pragmatic, who knew he could not make the Russians fight or the Germans stop fighting, laconically ordered "peace at any price."

Lenin saved Trotsky's talent for the cause and avoided clash of temperament for a time by throwing Trotsky into the hectic activity of "organizing victory." As Commissar of War he spent three years flying from one front to another, inspiriting the troops with his eloquence, imparting to war-jaded men his own spirit of energy, and rallying the nation to their support. Military experting was done by Voroshilov, Stalin's friend. Trotsky's great aversion was the British, who had detained him en route from New York, and his use of this scare to arouse the people contributed much toward the Anglophobe Soviet policy which had such repercussion through all Asia. Trotsky now gave allegiance wholly to the leader he had once accused of "arrogant pettiness," and his Jewish ardor was evident in the distressed statement after the first attack on Lenin's life: "When we think that he may die, our whole life seems useless and we cease to want to live."

But as the crisis passed, and revolution became régime, and outlawed theory orthodox, Trotsky's fretful spirit pulled him into controversy again. His success in building army morale led him to believe that industry could be conducted in the same fashion as war. He proposed to perpetuate and strengthen "military communism" by transforming his regiments into a "workers' army" under military discipline, and forcibly recruiting the trades unions. Lenin's common sense not only overruled plans which took human nature so little into account, but dictated the abandonment of true communism entirely, in the establishment of the New Economic Policy of 1921. Competitive labor and a graduated wage scale were recognized. The military forces were discharged or put on a peace-time basis under Voroshilov. The time for Jewish theorism was past; utilitarianism, the trait of the Asiatic element, was needed. War-Lord Trotsky's importance waned and that of Organizer Stalin increased.

As Lenin sank through the long months into the frozen form which is preserved for the worshipful to view, the outside world expected Trotsky to succeed to dictatorial power. There was not the remotest possibility of that being accomplished through the regular party machine. Stalin and other leaders of the "Old Guard" looked askance at him for many reasons. He was a Jew—and that came into account in spite of the Bolshevik doctrine of racial equality. While they had suffered imprisonment, hard labor, and exile, Trotsky had lived safely in Europe and America. He had returned and joined the Bolshevik party just in time to share in the glory of victory. They could not but feel resentment over his having occupied a position practically as *duumvir* with Lenin during the war years—although Lenin granted him this only for the utilitarian reason that during war the Minister of War is the most important member of the cabinet. They were naturally jealous of his versatility in every activity from art criticism to field strategy, his unquestionable excellence over them as a writer, and his ability to capture the public eye. There was only one way in which Trotsky could have made himself supreme in the face of this feeling: a sudden military coup before the army was pried too much out of his grasp.

It may be more to Trotsky's credit than otherwise that he did not raise the standard of rebellion for the sake of personal ambition. Kerensky has called him weak—lacking in audacity—but that charge would bear more weight from a man with less reputation for weakness himself. In spite of a temporary career as warlord, Trotsky was a man of diction rather than action. Also, only to be scientific, we must remember his Jewish heritage. Napoleonic coups are not in the Jewish nature.

So he resorted to his own weapon, writing history and open letters which embarrassed his peers and attracted the younger generation. We pause with interest to note that his most bitter opponent at this time was his fellow Jew, Zinoviev. In retaliation the party chiefs put under way, through the organization, a thorough campaign to discredit Trotsky. He resigned as War Commissar in 1925 and lived until summer in retirement in the Caucasus. During this interval Zinoviev and Kameniev came to loggerheads with Stalin, Premier Rykov, and Bukharin, Stalin's successor in the *Pravda* office, and were condemned by the party machine. Trotsky returned to ally with these old enemies, and, under the slogan "Back to Lenin," to accuse the party of losing its revolutionary character as a fosterer both of world revolution and radical communism at home. Specifically, he pointed to growing alliances with capitalistic nations, and the accumulation of small wealth by the larger peasants and private traders. The *Christian Science Monitor* correspondent remarked that the program received more attention from the Party "intelligentsia," in large proportion Jewish, and from university students, than from the poorer workers and peasants for whom it plead.

Trotsky asserted the right to remain in the party and yet take issue with the policy of its directors. More and more he was veering toward the political institutions of the Anglo-Saxons whom he hated. It was his normal development. In an advantage when the fight was with words, he wished freedom to play upon public opinion and would have introduced the "government by palaver" of Western democracies. Again it was the genius of Europe against that of Asia.

Stalin and his machine moved too coolly and slowly to give Trotsky and Zinoviev a desired opportunity to appear as martyrs. Stalin gradually took all responsible offices away from the "oppositionists" but re-

frained from expelling them from the party or its committees merely on grounds of differences of opinion.
But when they resorted to unauthorized or forbidden
means to propagate their discontent, the case was no
longer a matter of heterodoxy but one of undermining
the régime. The Trotskyites were discovered to be
operating printing plants with assistance of out-and-out
opponents of Bolshevism. The White colonies in Paris
and other cities, whose irreconcilability is mated with
their undying hope of counter-revolution, began to
prick up their ears.

The Central and Control Committees ejected ninety-
eight "little fellows" in Trotsky's following from the
party as a warning. But the challenged Lucifer only
grew more defiant. Carl Radek, chief publicity man
of the Third Internationale, which Walter Duranty describes as "The Foreign Missionary Society of the Bolshevik Church," associated himself with the "opposition." The party chiefs were annoyed at the threat
that supporters of communism abroad would be led to
oppose them personally. The success of Russian agents
in China in 1926 in embarrassing Great Britain and the
other imperialist Powers gave Trotsky's group opportunity to demand increased emphasis on the world
revolution. When the Russian influence in Chinese nationalism collapsed, Trotsky scathingly charged the administration with giving it insufficient support. Stalin's
quiet suggestion that the failure was perhaps due to
ebullient indiscretion in dealing with Asiatics without

care for their sensibilities was little noticed. There may have been double-crossing among Bolshevik heads on this China campaign, but Borodin was temperamentally a Trotskyist. Karakhan, of Armenian extraction, who resembles his fellow Georgian, Stalin, in build and mentality, seemed neither surprised nor greatly disappointed at the outcome in the land where he was ambassador. He is more interested in political results than dogmas and air castles.

Trotsky appeared before a party committee meeting in late October and threw it into a turmoil of anger with his barbed eloquence. Stalin refrained from final action until the tenth-year jubilee celebration of the U.S.S.R. should be completed. On November 7, while a million persons paraded in the Red Square in honor of Bolshevist accomplishment, Trotsky dashed about the city in an open car making street speeches and a few university students marched with placards: "Long live Trotsky and Zinoviev, the chiefs of the World Revolution." Clashes occurred in which rotten vegetables and fruit were thrown.

When the shouting was over and the many Russian and foreign visitors to Moscow who might sympathize with Trotsky had departed, Stalin called a joint meeting of the Central and Control Committees of the party. Trotsky was summoned to account for his actions. He immediately assumed the rôle of accuser rather than defendant. He charged Stalin and Bukharin with tyrannical use of the *Gay-Pay-Oo* (secret political police),

[369]

reiterated that the opposition would disobey any orders designed to prevent the publication of its platform to the party membership, and accused the party leadership of shifting to the right, building a new bourgeoisie, and abandoning the worker for the politician in Asia. He denounced "policy" and eulogized stark frankness. While angry cries drowned portions of his sentences he insinuated that the government was receiving bribes from the rich peasants and proceeded to quote from Lenin's posthumous letter in which the founder castigated "for the good of the movement" all of his followers: "Stalin is too rough. Remove Stalin, who can bring the party to break-up and destruction." In the momentary silence Trotsky declaimed: "The roughness and lack of loyalty about which Lenin wrote are not simply personal qualities, they have become the qualities of the ruling faction and its policy."

The outsider is amused to think of Lenin stigmatizing Stalin as "too rough,"—Lenin who had told Gorky his own chief duty was to split skulls ruthlessly, and who had become angry at a suggestion that, in appeal to peasants, a death threat to any who aided enemies be omitted. And he may well laugh at the picture of an erstwhile commander of Red armies quoting this before an expostulating audience.

Cries of "Old Slander," "Shame," forced Trotsky off the platform, but he had delivered himself. The Man of Steel presently replied in an unperturbed voice. The Founder had called him "rough." But in the same letter he had called Trotsky "not a Bolshevik" and implied that he regarded Trotsky's reunion with the party in 1917 as purely opportunistic. Trotsky's collaborators in opposition, Zinoviev and Kameniev, were virtually accused in the letter of "making mistakes" at the time of the Bolshevik seizure of power that were "not accidental." Stalin reiterated his willingness to resign secretaryship of the party if committeemen felt Lenin's accusation required it. At least he had not been accused of making willful mistakes and he was not conducting what amounted to counter-revolution. "You have heard," he concluded with a dour sneer, "how strenuously the opposition has abused Stalin. This may be explained because Stalin knows possibly better than anybody else, all the knavery of the opposition." He was cheered, and four days later Trotsky and Zinoviev, refusing to pledge different behavior in the future, were expelled from the Communist Party. His followers, including Zinoviev, later recanted in greater or less degree. Trotsky remained defiant and the Bolsheviks sent him, as the Czar had done them, into a "corner of oblivion" in central Asia.

So the only element which would have carried the original radical program into full execution was eliminated. Stalin goes forward in Lenin's example of accommodating theory to conditions, although very careful to sicken his people on orthodoxy before exhibiting any tendency toward heterodoxy. "Theory is not a sacred thing but merely a working tool," is the dictum, found in a letter of Lenin to Gorky, which is bringing Russia back into relationship with the rest of the world and compromising with human instincts of competition and acquisitiveness at home. Trotsky, after the manner of a Western reformer, would have his theory in the face of all dubitation until he had either ruined the opposing world or had ruined Russia. Stalin, the Asiatic opportunist, is seeking to restore Russia to power and dignity in the world, with preservation of as much of the dogma as is necessary to preserve the confidence of his fellows.

Self-possessed, young-looking save for the sinister crow's-feet leading back from his eyes, with jet-black hair oiled and brushed back in a pompadour, prominent Oriental nose emitting now and then a punctuating snort into bushy mustaches (the "Lenin" goatee sedulously aped by the Jewish comrades is disdained), his huge hand now and then going up to a hairy chest revealed by carelessly open khaki jacket or giving a tug at his high top boots, Stalin sits behind his worktable, under Lenin's picture, listening to members from the carefully cultivated party "nests" or communists and workers from abroad. He listens patiently and is chary of words in reply. With the same poise, backed by his immense physical vigor, does he sit in the "College of Cardinals" of the Bolshevik world in January, 1929, and demand the exile of Trotsky. It is granted to him by a majority of one—because one discreetly, albeit sullenly, declines to vote, and Steel is warned that humans, volatile as ether, may yet escape his grasp.

The more formal and important the caller, the less likely is he to get to Stalin. No foreign ambassador has spoken with the power behind Tchicherin and Litvinoff, and since Stalin does not receive newspapermen they consider him their most valuable prey, while passing by the open doors of the High Commissars and publicists.

He lives with his wife and child in a small flat in the Kremlin and never goes to a public place save occasionally to some workman's club. Now and then he may be seen at a meeting—never on the stage except on the rare occasions when he speaks—but in the background, conversing in a low tone with his neighbors in his Caucasian brogue with its Orientalisms. He writes without profundity, precisely, simply, and dully, in the official party organs. He is known for utter lack of interest in women or social functions, but for good fellowship in his own crowd. He makes no bid for popularity: his portrait appears seldom among those of the proletarian heroes which adorn posters, walls, books, and papers everywhere in Russia.

He is accused of inciting others to action and then awaiting the result before involving himself. It is not a bad gift for a politician. His crude, opportunistic phrases reach the point. "Enough of that idiotic slogan, the World Revolution," he exclaims. He cuts down the budget of the Comintern—the foreign mission society of Bolshevism. He says it is necessary to build up the peasant in order to build up agriculture. He broadly invites foreign capital to invest in Russia. At the same time he adopts the most extreme portion of Trotsky's program popular with proletarian devotees and inaugurates a new campaign of state control of industry and trade and oppression of the *kulak*, or better-off peasant. His slogan is party solidarity, with himself sitting solid on the party. No doubt his greatest asset in politics, like that of Kemal and Mussolini, is his tigerlike physical vitality. Governing is after all more a physical than a mental job.

"Stalin is a more dangerous and subtle help to Indian revolt than Trotsky," says an Englishman (India comes next on the program of Asian self-assertion). This is doubtless true. Yet Mr. C. F. Andrews tells of the visit of a young Hindu to the Bolshevik chief. "He was fascinated with Russia, but utterly repulsed by Stalin." Human beings can hardly be further apart than the crude, direct, physical Georgian and the sensitive, super-cultured Hindu. Yet a common resentment sets them to making history together.

IV

From Peter the Great to the Bolshevik revolution Russians were ruled by a dynasty and aristocracy European in outlook and largely European in blood (the Romanoffs recruited their queens from Germany).

The government tried with crude, violent methods to Europeanize its subjects and saw Russia's destiny in an imitation of European industry, shipping, militarism, and imperialism.

This régime is gone, and the responsible head of the one hundred and forty-seven million Russians is not a Germanized Czar, but an Asiatic from Georgia. Russia, separated in theory from Asia for several centuries, has openly gone back to affiliation with Asia. The boundary between the continents can no longer be described as the long overemphasized Ural mountains. Poland, breaking away from Russia, has eagerly turned westward for cultural and political affiliation and has renewed her devotion to the Roman Church, while Russia, Asia-like, develops her own religion of utopianism. The boundary line between Europe and Asia to-day is the red and white "barber's pole" standing halfway between the double lines of barbed wire demarcating the Polish frontier.

But modern Asia, of which Russia becomes a part, is not the Asia of the seventeenth century, and the spirit of Asia which dominates Russia to-day is a notable evolution from that which Czar Peter combated. In such distinguishing psychological fundamentals as their attitude toward time, toward material comforts, toward sex, in their fatalism and ceremonialism, Asia, and Russia, remain Asiatic. But they are aroused to race consciousness; they are possessed of an inferiority complex which only attainment of equal mechanical and military status with the Western Powers and the recognition of equal dignity in the world will appease. Russians are moved by the same deep feeling of resentment against the economically superior and ofttimes arrogant nations of the West as stirs Chinese, Indians, Turks, Persians, Annamese, Filipinos, Javanese, and even the advanced Japanese. They are full-fledged members of the "confraternity of the snubbed."

Bolshevik Russia encourages and champions the weaker and more backward members of this fraternity and makes it impossible for the ruling nations of the West to crush them outright. Bolshevik Russia schemes diligently the break-up of the British Empire, the bulwark of the West's supremacy in the world. Occasionally the Soviet makes mistakes in dealing with its Asiatic neighbors. These are quickly righted, as in the cases of Turkey and Persia. Able men: Karakhan, Asiatic Armenian; Pashtuhov, Slavic "White Russian"; and Zuckermann, Crimean Jew are in charge of Russia's Asiatic relations. To a Japanese (it is much easier for Orientals than for Westerners to see him) Stalin said, "Welcome! I, too, am Asiatic." "For some time to come," said the powerfully built Karakhan, moving panther-like about his office, "we will feel closer to Asia than to Europe. Of course we must always deal with both, as we must always be the merging ground of both." Under the Stalin régime, Russia will support Asia's revolt whether it takes a communist turn or not. Under Stalin the Asiatic, Russia's significance changes from that of the evangel of a strange new economico-political ideology in the world, to that of the more easily understood inciter of an Asiatic group of nations against the hitherto dominant Western group. A religious crusade simmers down to a political campaign, fervor cools into opportunism, sensationalism is superseded by safety, fanatic idealism practicalizes into self-interest.

MAHATMA GANDHI

MOHANDAS KARAMCHAND GANDHI

1876–

MAHATMA GANDHI

I

WHILE Kemal in Turkey is leading his religious-minded people from religious passion to national passion as a basis of society, Gandhi in India—only ten years, although we think of him as ages, older—is taking religion into social and political life, and building Indian nationalism upon it. "The idea-tight division of human activity into religious, social, and political compartments is the prime fallacy of the modern world—and the basis of Western hypocrisy," said the Mahatma to me as he sat on his rough stone floor at Sabarmati colony, his large eyes covering me and his sharp chin and long nose pointing at me with a gesture definite, yet delicate. "If religion is not needed in politics, where on earth is it wanted!" Of course he means personal religion, not clerical institutionalism.

Gandhi's task, like Sun Yat-sen's, of building into a nation a multitudinous Asiatic people of homogeneous culture, makes him important enough. When that task involves bringing into human sympathy and productive intercourse the votaries of two traditionally hostile religious and a dozen sects—cleft by age-sacred snobbery into hundreds of castes—it makes him not only famous but great. But his significance is beyond this, in that he carries on his tremendous task in a newly argued spirit of revolt against the accepted rules of Western civilization. His gospel, stark folly to the modern world at first sight, raises questions, awakens doubtful thought as to the fundamentals of human progress.

Gandhi's is the same problem of the restoration of racial dignity, beaten down by the rifle butts of the West, which we have encountered in the rest of Asia. But Gandhi's method of meeting it is different from those of Yamagata, Sun Yat-sen, or Kemal. It is not, as theirs, effective competition with the West in its own "game" of military and industrial prowess, nor, as Lenin's, excellence in this game by a different organization of its human pawns. Gandhi's is yet more original. It is to repudiate the game entirely and prove man's greatest and only permanent good is to be reached by an utterly different activity with an opposite philosophy. Of this, Gandhi would have India be the example. But like all great religionists, his outlook is more than national. India is to preserve the way of life which must be adopted by the "modern" world when its prosperity shall have crashed and its "progress" shall have led into a *cul-de-sac*. Then India, if she has been true to her own soul, shall automatically assume leadership of the world. She shall be its savior.

Gandhi would have India politically free, but not at the price of becoming idealogically enslaved. He would have India respected by the materialistic world, but not at the sacrifice of her own peculiar genius. He would have Indians well fed and adequately housed but not at the expense of coming to live more for the flesh than for the spirit.

Because he is the one Asiatic leader who gives these considerations logical weight, Gandhi is to hasty Westerners a little mad—or just pathetic. And yet, more than any of the new Asians, he disturbs us. In that he is the one Asian leader who sees beyond the rapidly approaching day when East shall challenge West on a basis of material equality, and endeavors to prepare against that day, he stands on a different plane from others.

Gandhi interprets the spirit of India to be other-worldliness. This spirit is to operate socially and politically through the power of love which Jesus talked about. Gandhi is the first leader to organize "turning the other cheek" as a weapon of nation-wide revolution. Ironically enough, he must use it against the British, who brought the Christian Gospel to him and his land —the British, nominally Christians, yet the most successful users of swift and scientific violence in world history. We have the spectacle of the world's greatest exponent of the "weapons of the flesh" against its thus-far greatest experimenter with the weapon of the spirit.

Because he is not content, like the rest of Asia (except the Russians) to take one step at a time, he may fail. But failure or messiah, or both, he stands as a seer among statesmen, a saint among heroes.

Of the six great Asian personalities portrayed in this

book, Gandhi alone has been set forth with a degree of adequacy to the English-speaking world. He has been presented—usually by men who have never seen him, as Romain Rolland—in the rôle of a saint, and as a rebel against Western culture, an Asian reactionary. These are fascinating sides to his character. But the line of my study requires me to chart the Indian leader's human development rather than exclaim over his mystic saintliness, and to uncover the truly significant Western influence in him rather than use him to prove the Kipling bromide that East and West shall never meet. For the Mahatma, at first glance exactly opposite in spirit and purpose to the other nation-makers of Asia, is found on close study to profit as they do by Western attainment and experiment in freeing the East from the domination of the West. Gandhi does it with the long vision of the saint rather than of the opportunistic and pragmatical lawyer-demagogue which his training might well have made him. His *Swaraj* is founded upon Asian culture, imbued with its spirit, and implacably opposed to industrial civilization and the Western manner of life, yet has the Western ideals of action, social equality, and economic prosperity as unmistakably as has Bolshevism. In addition its leader preaches mental independence.

I first approached Mahatma Gandhi in the company of Chin the Golden of Young China. As we drove at dawn in a miniature "double-ender" cart behind a speedy, trotting bullock over the bridge at Ahmedabad and up the Gujerat River, where below us on the sand-bars morning prayers, ablutions, burnings of the dead, and cloth-bleaching were proceeding, all watched by great cranes knee-deep on one leg in water looking transcendentally on, Chin said to me with Chinese prac-ticalness and suspicion: "If Mr. Gandhi is a holy man he will see our minds—that we come to try him out—and will not speak freely and act naturally!"

A first view of him dispelled any such fears. A gnomelike man with large ears and enormous nose and skeleton-like body clad only in a coarse white cloth from waist to knees sat with feet folded back beside his loins (they are twisted from this posture, which only skeleton-like legs could assume), chuckling joyously and unrestrainedly as a child, great brown eyes dancing under low upper lids. He was listening to a serious young lady disciple recounting misadventures on a recent mission. Soon she caught the spirit and laughed too. The visiting American and Chinaman joined in.

It was good, for one hears little laughter in India—in contrast to the sound forever on the ears among the sunny-tempered Chinese, Siamese, and Burmans. We were ready to regard Gandhi as a mystic. But we saw no kinship between him and the Indian fakir. With such an introduction we were bound to study him as a man, rather than as a god. I am of the impression that he prefers such treatment.

II

In 1869, only twelve years after that desperately violent Indian attempt to break the British clutch known as the Great Mutiny, Putlibai, young fourth wife of the *dewan* or prime minister of Porbandar, bore as her fourth son the one who through the mystical power of organized nonviolent resistance was to lead his people within reach of nationalism and freedom. She named him after her venerable lord and husband *Karamchand Gandhi*, prefixing *Mohandas*—"Servitor of the Great One"—an index of her intensely religious character.

The remote northwestern principality of Porbandar, whose limestone-built "White City" gleamed over the Arabian Sea, had been far to one side of the torrent of resentment, outrages, and reprisals encompassing the Black Hole of Calcutta. Yet the noble Gandhi family was far from untouched by the establishment of the white man's dominance. Dewan Kamarchand was not a man to truckle to any one, and his fidelity was ingrained. His father who had occupied his high office before him had been forced to flee from an unjust *rana* of Porbandar but had offered only his left hand to a temporary royal employer of Yanagat, declaring that his right hand still belonged to his original master. Karamchand, showing the hereditary spirit during service in Rajkot, publicly rebuked a British commissioner for speaking disparagingly of his none too defensible

prince. The affronted British over-government demanded through the prince an apology. The dewan
point-blank refused it. He was arrested, but that
brought no apology, and English prestige had to go un-
requited. Karamchand Gandhi took British suzerainty
as a matter of course and was loyal to the "raj," as
were the heads of other native administrations, but
stood firm on the point of native dignity. Starting
from that point, his son was to lead his people to
implacable opposition to the Westerner's assumed position in the motherland.

Mohandas Gandhi, before whom Brahmans were to
bow, ranked by birth after both this priestly caste and
the warriors. He was of the third or merchant group
of castes, a Banya. Both father and mother were devotees of Vishnu, most orthodox of Hindu cults, but
were much under the influence of Jains, puritans of
a reform movement twenty-four hundred years old,
claiming, like other Protestants, to go back to the early
authentic form of the faith.

The austere Karamchand's three first wives had gone
to swell the tremendous death rate of child bearers in
India. The upbringing of this fourth child of his fourth
family he left almost entirely to its young mother.
Frankness and executive integrity soon brought him,
as it had his father, into clash with a licentious rana.
He left the hereditary service, suffered distress for a
time, and then accepted high positions successively
under two other petty princes who appreciated honesty.

Through these vicissitudes the dignified matron Putlibai, draped in long robes and shawl, never failed to
gather her children about her on the cool floor, whether
it happened at the time to be of marble or clay trodden
by peasants' feet, and instruct them in the strictest precepts of *ahimsa*—the "nonkilling" doctrine, stressed by
the Jains, of truth-telling, chastity, and vegetarianism.

Then she would kneel with them in long prayer, and
they responded with childhood's ardent religiousness
and willingness to sacrifice. Frequently she fasted, and
her youngest son in particular was always ready to take
a vow with her. By intelligence, gentleness, and an
obvious capacity to suffer, she dominated her children
and determined their lives. If Gandhi's penchant for
politics came from his father, his religious conscience
was an endowment from his mother.

The lad had never been away from his mother's side
for even a few hours when he began to attend, after
many prayerful exhortations each day, the Porbandar
Primary School recently established by the British raj.
When he was seven, his father removed the family to
Rajkot. Here Mohandas continued an exotic education copied after the British public school system and
leading directly toward an English university, against
which he was to revolt so violently in adulthood.

"He was not known," says his secretary and co-
worker Krishnadas, to whom I am indebted for
authentic data on this portion of his life, "as a very
brilliant student, nor was he counted among the forward

boys." "During this short period," says the "Great Soul" in the autobiography of his "years of sin" just published under the title *The Story of My Experiments with Truth*, "I do not remember ever to have told a lie, either to teachers or schoolmates. I used to be very shy and avoided all company. My books and lessons were my sole companions. To be at school at the stroke of the hour and run back home as soon as school closed; that was my daily habit. I literally ran back because I could not bear to talk to anybody—I was ever afraid lest some one should poke fun at me."

This "inferiority complex" was a natural result of the extreme religious self-abasement his mother had instilled in him. A painful but eventually complete re-action from it makes an outstanding trait of his character. The lad who couldn't speak to anybody was to become the most fearless orator of India, and the boy who was deathly afraid lest some one should poke fun at him was to flout all accepted theories and manners of life, go publicly clothed only in a loin cloth, and unabashedly face trial and punishment as a felon.

It was not long before the inevitable youthful revolt against the restrictions of his life took place. His timidity kept him from making many friends, but he was excessively attached, as sensitive, shy children so frequently are, to the few companions he made. His self-consciousness he interpreted as cowardice, and his physical weakness galled him. "Look at these English-men," said his school comrade. "They have brawn and courage because they eat meat!" So the two boys surreptitiously took to eating the forbidden flesh to "make them men" in much the same spirit that many American boys have indulged in tobacco. But, as often in the case of the disapproved weed, Gandhi's indulgence brought him no pleasure. When he went into the temple courtyard and saw the heads sheared off of protesting sacrificial goats and their blood spurt into the dust, his stomach revolted against the dried meat he had purchased at the open-fronted shops along the narrow street. "I felt as if a live goat was bleeding and struggling in my stomach," he says. He came home and found that he could not eat the supper of pulse and rice rolled in thin pancakes for taking up in the fingers. His anxious mother questioned him closely. And the lies he had to tell her completed his nausea with the whole thing. "Let the Britishers have a monopoly on brawn," was his conclusion. "I will not dirty my soul for it."

He tried other "manly" sins, however, even taking up smoking. It became necessary to steal coppers to keep up the supply of cigarettes. These failing, and Mohandas being relied upon by his friend to settle their secret account, he stole a gold inset from the armlet of an elder brother.

Conscience worked the usual swift revulsion. Driven to confess, but unable to face his father in the enormity of his crime, the young Gandhi wrote out a confession, pushed it into the hand of the old gentleman who lay ill on his pallet, and drew back to await the thunder-bolt. The pious *dewan* turned to his son with deep distress showing in his features, and slowly tore the paper to bits. Not a word of punishment or rebuke came from his lips, although his illness appeared to have been greatly aggravated. Gandhi was over-whelmed. It seemed to him useless for such a de-praved creature as he to endeavor to live. He sought out his friend; they had one of the tragic conversations of youth and decided to commit suicide. This under-taking, the greatest possible sin to him who believes it is wrong to destroy an insect, was the furthest the future saint ever fell from the faith of his mother.

But the pair found, as has many a person, that it is not so easy for one to take his life. They collected poison *dhatura* seeds, but the initial dose griped them sufficiently to cause them to abandon the plan. And thus the supersensitive boy, who was to come to despise the body as a weight upon the soaring spirit,[1] wa. saved by the body to become one of the inspirers of the present world. A Chinese would quote the apt proverb: "More needful a saint on earth than another angel in heaven." To Mohandas his father's suffering was a converting example of the ideal Vaishnava (fol-lower of Vishnu) who, in the language of a favorite chant, "feels the suffering of others as his own suffer-

---

[1] "The body is the most perfect machine, but it, too, must be rejected, since it hinders the free flight of the soul."—Conversation with Rama-handran on machinery. Compare the ancient Jain precept: "Bring under thy body, afflict, weaken thyself, as fire eats away dry wood."

ing—knows neither passion nor wrath." The boy abjured all deceit for life, and transparent, even almost offensive frankness, was to become the key trait of his character.

He went through an experience when hardly twelve which showed in him the makings of a social revolutionary and religious transcendentalist. It was all through the accident of touching the scavenger who came to empty the family latrine. Doubtless thousands of Hindu boys accidentally touch this domestic member of the untouchable outcastes, perform the ablutions of ceremonial cleansing when told to do so, and accept the situation. Not so Mohandas. He washed, but asked his mother why. And he never became satisfied with her explanations. He protested the wrong in any one being cut off from human contact in the name of religion. "I told my mother that she was entirely wrong in considering physical contact with our faithful servant Uka as sinful," he says. If the Western reader feels at times that the lad was somewhat pathetically hedged in by his environment, he can still see that he submitted in nothing that did not appeal to his own reason. Here was mental independence for a child of twelve! To be sure, the Jain *shatras* might be interpreted to warrant the idea that the highest rank is open to one of any caste who would conform to the ascetic ideal—yet social self-respect demanded recognition of the Hindu class arrangements ordinarily. Never was a man more in awe of religious tradition than

Gandhi. But he was to shock the Brahman leadership of India with the noble challenge: "If I were convinced that the oppression of my brother was an essential part of my religion, I would give up my religion!" Creed could not overcome such a man. Rather it would be compelled to conform to his human sympathy.

As will be readily imagined, the sensitive lad with the overgrown head, flaring ears, and small, poetic face, with its strong nose, lush lips, and wide-set dreamy eyes, half covered by drooping upper lids, was high-strung sexually. Of all our six Asiatic leaders, he is the most adapted for a Freudian study. Sex was a problem for him from earliest childhood, as has indeed been the usual case with the world's great saints. And Gandhi in his autobiographical sketches is as frank as Augustine or Francis of Assisi about this important factor in his life.

Between twelve and thirteen he was married to Kasturbai, an attractive, lively, self-willed girl of the same age, partly because one of his elder brothers was to be married and the enormous expense of marrying off Hindu children could be lessened proportionately by a double wedding. Marriage at this age hardly meant more to the average boy, Gandhi himself tells us, than fine clothes, a rich banquet, and the joy of a girl playmate. But Mohandas took things more maturely and seriously and began reading everything he could get his hands on as to "what a young husband should know."

The conventional demand for lifelong fidelity particularly impressed him and he made it an ideal—fanatically fearing for vivacious Kasturbai more than for himself. "Two innocent children all unwittingly hurled themselves into the ocean of life," he was to say of the experience.

At thirteen the Indian girl was already a woman; her spouse had hardly reached active maturity. The inevitable reaction of his religious nature occurred: he became absurdly suspicious, and as he was to tell, violently jealous. This child husband made himself both utterly miserable and laughably ridiculous in his efforts to curb his young wife.

I had no reason at all for doubting the faithfulness of my wife, but jealousy does not ask for reasons. I thought that I must know every step she took, and I forbade her to go anywhere without my permission. Kasturbai was not disposed to submit to this; she insisted on going out whenever and wherever she liked. The more I tried to restrict her liberty the less she troubled about my orders, and this made me more and more furious.[2] Things came to such a pass that we two married children no longer spoke to each other. . . . Now I see it all clearly, but then I made desperate attempts to assert my marital authority.

While he quarreled with his girl-wife, her nonchalant air and well-turned body teased him, and he found himself compelled to war against excess in amorous pleas-

---

[2] This situation would not arise in the regions of former Muslem dominance, where women of quality are restricted to the *zenāna,* behind the *purdah* (curtain).

ures. Battling this distraction he went on, after a year's intermission, with high school, but his work suffered. His teachers tried to help him make up for the lost time by skipping him one class. Among results he had his particular difficulties with Euclid. An easygoing master obliquely suggested to the pupil that he get through an examination by cheating, "as everybody did," but this Gandhi ignored. Eventually he discovered how to apply his fine powers of logic to geometry, and after that it was a pleasure to him.

He was really single-mindedly devoted to Kasturbai, but not "according to knowledge." He was ambitious that she should enjoy the same mental riches that came to him and develop intellectually side by side with him. So he returned from school each day and painstakingly endeavored to tutor her in what he had learned. But she was interested in other things—domesticity and now motherhood. The session invariably ended in a quarrel with his unwilling and none too deferential pupil. Fortunately for both, she spent, according to custom, six months of each year with her parents and beyond his reach. "If, along with my devouring passion, there had not been in me a burning attachment to duty, I should either have fallen a prey to disease and premature death, or have sunk into a burdensome existence," he says. Very real was this crisis of puberty and from it his life philosophy grew.

When he was fifteen his father was taken with a fatal illness, and in addition to continuing his studies and keeping a young wife in hand he had most of the nursing to do. He happened to be on the hymeneal bed instead of holding his father in his arms when the angel of death called, and for that he never forgave himself, taking it as the rebuke of heaven for his carnality. He vowed never again to "let animal passion blind him," and set as his aim the Hindu ideal *brahmacharya*—absolute continence, in as well as out of marriage, commended for students and devotees.

In studies where he could reason he excelled, but pure memory work such as Sanscrit he found very difficult. He would have given it up had not its study been pointed out as a duty on the part of the son of a Vaishnava. He was to struggle at it for years, particularly utilizing his periods of imprisonment, and still to mourn his lack of facility in the sacred language.

At eighteen he passed his examinations for the university and began attending lectures in an Indian institution. An old Brahman who befriended the family following his father's death advised him to finish in London, and his mother consented after he had gone with her and sworn before a Brahman to abstain during his absence from wine, meat, and sexual intercourse.

Just before he departed a son was born to Kasturbai. Gandhi left her engrossed in her babe and took ship from Bombay. He was immediately confronted with the question of relations with Europeans. On shipboard they were friendly enough, although the patronage underlying their cordiality did not escape the sensi-

[396]

tive young man. Partly from dread of treatment as an inferior and partly from inborn bashfulness he kept to himself. Because, as he says, he did not know how to use a knife and fork, he took his meals in his cabin. How often the traveler sees Oriental students in the same distress of adjustment on Oriental liners, the trans-Siberian or elsewhere.

The Indian student arriving in London to-day is met by a committee of his fellow-countrymen and religion-ists and steered straight to congenial association and living arrangements in harmony with his customs, but it was not so in 1887. Gandhi found a lonely lodging, where he spent his days in homesickness and his nights in tears, and he starved to emaciation before he discov-ered a vegetarian cuisine in the land of the beefsteak. He was determined to remain true to his vow to his mother, and when, weak and emaciated, he happened into a restaurant established by the health reform branch of the Seventh-day Adventist movement of America, he put down the event in his notebook as truly a "dispensation of Providence."

His activities were always to grow out of his per-sonal sufferings, and right here he began his first public social work, as a propagandist for vegetarianism and simplicity in food. He gave up sweets and condiments and even eggs and milk, and made it a matter of boast that he could live on fifteen pence a day in London. Anglo-Saxon advocates of vegetarianism found in the cultured Hindu student an attention-attracter to their cause. The first public speech of a man to be one of the world's greatest orators was made in the vegetarian cause at Ventnor, England, while young Gandhi was spending a holiday with a friend. "I had ascertained," he says, "that it was not considered incorrect to read one's speech. I knew that many did so to express themselves coherently and briefly. To speak extempore would have been out of the question for me. I had therefore written down my speech. I stood up to read it but could not. My vision became blurred and I trembled, though the speech hardly covered a sheet of foolscap. Sergeant Mazumdar had to read it for me. His own speech was of course excellent and was received with applause. I was ashamed of myself and sad at heart for my incapacity."

He had not much improved at the end of his three-year stay in England. Of his public appearance on the eve of his departure for home, he says: "But this time too I only succeeded in making myself ridiculous. . . . When my turn for speaking came, I stood up to make a speech. I had with great care thought out one which would consist of a very few sentences. But I could not proceed beyond the first sentence. . . . My memory entirely failed me and in attempting a humorous speech I made myself ridiculous. 'I thank you, gentlemen, for having kindly responded to my invitation,' I said abruptly and sat down."

He had wanted to take up medicine in college, but his brothers had told him that his father had regarded

vivisection and surgery as practices in which a Vaishnava could not engage. The Brahman mentor therefore
had recommended law. The study of the law Mohandas had found easy enough, bringing to it the native
Oriental gift for comprehension of human relationships.
What had concerned him more was how to compete
with the assertive white man. He first decided to meet
him in his own style. He bought a silk "topper," had
a dress suit made in Bond Street, and sent home for
a heavy gold watch chain. He began lessons in dancing, French, elocution, and violin. Each morning he
spent ten minutes before his mirror parting his hair
and arranging his tie. This lasted about three months,
and then the emptiness of it revolted him. The crisis
came, as before, when he was offered the flesh of one
of his "little dumb brothers" at the table of hospitality
and mirth. He arose in nausea, went home and packed
away his dress clothes. Sitting in prayer, he took oath
to abandon forever the attempt to be Western—or
anything else alien to his nature and training. He
began the development which was to enable him, like
Paul, to declare: "By the grace of God I am what I
am," and to glory in it. "I wasted a lot of time and
money trying to be an Englishman," he was to say.

Strangely enough, it was in the Englishman's country that he grasped the profundity of his own background. As a child he had been taught the hymns of
Vishnu and had heard the religious epic Ramayana
sung by a noted Hindu scholar in his home. But now,

in England, and due to the influence of the Theosophist founders, Madame Blavatsky and Mrs. Annie Besant whom he met there, he made the acquaintance for the first time of the noblest of his own Indian scriptures, the *Bhagavad Gita*. He read it in free English translation by Sir Edwin Arnold, under the title *The Song Celestial*. Arnold's metrical life of the Buddha, *The Light of Asia*, also cast a spell over him. Then a London friend introduced him to the Christian scriptures. He had varied from the general Hindu tolerance toward other religions to entertain a lively prejudice against Christianity due to abuse he had heard meted out to Hinduism by Christian missionary street preachers in his own land. But he states that the Sermon on the Mount "went straight to my heart on the first reading, for I felt that it contained the truth that renunciation is the highest type of religion." He took it literally and seriously. "Although I chose a path which my Christian friends had not intended, I remain forever indebted for the religious quest they awakened in me." He had learned as a child from a Gujarati verse:

> But the truly noble know all men as one
> And return with gladness good for evil done,

the doctrine of returning good for evil. But it was from Christ's sayings that he conceived, he says, his strategy of nonviolent resistance to tyranny which he made his weapon for gaining equality for his people and terminating imperialism. "My heart leapt for joy as I realized the simplicity and yet infallibility of the method." Religion was always the decisive influence of Gandhi's life, and now that he had found his cause and his weapon he wavered no more. Another influence which strengthened him at this time was Tolstoy's. In the disillusioned older man's "passive resistance," insistence on living the Sermon on the Mount, and theory that all domestic disharmony comes of "men and women using each other as instruments of pleasure," he found formulations of opinions toward which he had been tending.

In June, 1891, Gandhi passed his examination for the bar, and two days later embarked for his own country. He was happy chiefly in the thought of seeing his mother again, but he landed at Bombay to be stunned with the news that she had died. His brothers had withheld it from him in the fear that it would prevent success in his examinations.

Thinking fondly of his mother's ceremonial exactitude, he made pilgrimage to a shrine where he might fulfill the ceremonial atonement required of Hindus who leave their holy land by crossing the "black waters." However, the future leader of India was not scrupulous enough in these matters fully to satisfy sticklers for orthodoxy in his own district. The shy young graduate, with drooping under eyelids and the beginings of a mustache above his wistful mouth, one side of his face feminine and poetic, the other with features obstinate and almost forbidding, had no heart to frequent the old home. He undertook rather to establish himself in law in Bombay, booming capital of new Indian industry. He soon came in contact with several outstanding older men who appreciated his quality and became mentors and comforters to him.

They were the "Father of Indian Nationalism," the Parsi, Dadabhai Naoroji, who first helped him apply "good for evil" in a public controversy; the jeweler poet and mystic, Rajachandra, whose understanding and poise calmed Gandhi's spiritual upsets, and the young Gopal K. Gokhale, three years his senior, who was to win fame as educational reformer and forerunner of the Indian independence movement. Gandhi adored these men, yet he did not choose any among them *guru* of his life—the spiritual guide every Hindu looks for. He demanded nothing short of perfection.

When the keen edge of his mourning wore off he sent for his wife Kasturbai and the child. At once they fell to quarreling. Though still in love with her, Gandhi sent her home to shame her as a rejected wife. "I did not take her back," he says, "until I had made her utterly miserable. Later I recognized and deeply repented my folly."

Conscientiousness gained him respect, even from enemies, and like Lincoln, he disproved the common saying that one cannot succeed in the law and be honest. It was his rule to abandon a case, perhaps abruptly in open court, if convinced his client had falsely represented it to him. In harmony with Jesus's recommen-

[402]

dation to forgive debtors, he declined to undertake prosecution for debt. Esteem and fame of a particular brand began to come to him.

A Hindu firm with interests in South Africa offered a one-year contract to conduct a case in Pretoria. Gandhi went with high hope, little realizing in 1893 the suffering that lay before him, or that his triumph over it would make him the *guru* of all his people.

In Europe he had suffered from white superciliousness and his own inferiority complex, but in South Africa, a hotbed of racial arrogance comparable only to America's southern states, he immediately came in contact with the savagery which the dominant race exhibits when its prejudice or fear is aroused. The surprised, offenseless Indian, much more cultured and of far more elegant speech than his persecutors, found himself thrown out of hotels, out of trains on which he had paid his fare, insulted on the streets, beaten and kicked. The Boers (Dutch pioneers) were more ignorant and fierce than the English—justifying the meaning that the word, spelled with a double *o*, has acquired.

Indians had been brought under contract as laborers to the tropical lowlands of Natal as early as 1860. Many had chosen to stay on, and had even been encouraged by grants of government land until now they were about as numerous as the white settlers in that colony. The latter, jealous of prerogative as conquerors, had no mind to risk the moral effect on the natives of excepting any colored race from the social tyranny they imposed. A policy of "encouraging" repatriation was adopted, stiffened by one legal device after another. Natal Indians began to migrate to the Transvaal and others followed from India. Especially strong feeling arose there. White colonists declined to allow Indians to come as freemen and add to their difficulty in building up a white civilization amid overwhelming numbers of blacks. The Indians, conscious of ancient traditions of civilization and, if not freeborn in Natal as many were, at least freemen of another British domain, were not willing tamely to submit. The uncompromising spirit of the whites aggravated the difficulty, tending to bring what they feared, more or less Indian-native solidarity.

At first the unreasoning injustice of the Indian's lot sickened Gandhi and left him with a feeling of helplessness. He won his corporation cases, drew his large fees, dressed immaculately, and waited for the end of his contract to get away. A veteran American consular official of the "hard-boiled" mentality usually thought typical, recalled to me that Gandhi was a "clever, dapper young fellow, well on his way to making a million out of the law—then he went nutty over religion and race-equality, changed to a breech cloth, and ruined a promising career." He was as ever interested in religion, pursuing earnestly the study of Christianity, giving special attention to the "crazy Russian," Tolstoy, as its interpreter.

The Russian eccentric's writings had fallen into his hands just before he left England, and he had written Tolstoy a letter, half timid, half impulsive, to which he received an exalting answer in Bombay. It was the beginning of a correspondence and destined to become a unique example of the international and interracial spread of ideas. In Bolshevik days, when official Russia was to guffaw at him and men were to tell him Russia was utterly materialistic and evil, he would say: "I knew Tolstoy."

The only members of the ruling race whom he found to possess a human feeling for his people were the Christian missionaries. "Fate," he says, "cast me into the midst of those very fine Christian friends who belonged to the South African General Mission, where I saw Wesleyans, Presbyterians, and others." He read some eighty books on Christianity that first year. But he never could feel satisfied that the Westerners had fully comprehended the meaning of religion—not even of the Christianity they claimed to interpret. He was impressed that the goal was something deeper than the surface of any religion, yet, perhaps, common to all religions, a matter for individual attainment.

Reading those things with the prayerful help of these friends, [he was to write in 1924], I went on, and they were pilots endeavoring to pilot me through all the shoals and dangerous rocks that lay ahead. They were always asking me, "Well, where are you now?" From that day to this day that question has been addressed to me time after time, "Where are you now?" I venture to say in the great words of the Vedas,

"Neti, neti," Not this, not this. I have been obliged to say, if this be Christianity "not this, not this," and the deepest in me tells me that I am right.

An opportunity to put some of this conviction into practice came to him as he was on the eve of leaving at the year's end, in the shape of a petition from the leaders of the Indian community in Durban that he would undertake their attack in the courts upon the discriminatory legislation that had been passed. The Dutch Transvaal would have shut them out entirely, but for fear of giving Britain and Cecil Rhodes a further excuse for the threatening war. Meanwhile Natal had followed withdrawal of the land grants by a three pound head tax levied on every man, woman, and child, prohibition of trade unless accounts were kept in English, and other annoying conditions.

As always, sense of duty and sympathy for his fellow men held Gandhi. His people were helpless. The young barrister, skilled in the white man's law, was their only hope. He took the case and made it more than "Asiatics versus the South African governments," to be fought on a legal constitutional basis. He made it "humanity versus social oppression." He knew full well that his weapon of reason would be largely futile. Sun Yat-sen, Ito, Kemal, or Stalin would have seen only one other way to fight—violence. But Gandhi had recourse to the weapon he had discovered in the Sermon on the Mount, sanctioned he felt also by the deeper meaning of his own religion.

[406]

While he contested the unjust laws in the courts, he began the long work of organization and discipline of his people for the struggle he saw before them. He assembled representative Indians of Natal, who founded the Indian Congress, giving the persecuted community their first group expression. Showing his early understanding of the necessity for constructive as well as purely combative measures and his feeling that cultural development ranks with political, he organized an educational association to provide schools for their children, entirely neglected by the state. He taught his people to petition, and collected signatures by thousands. After meditation and agonizing prayers he had stepped out into the controversial, necessarily sensational life naturally so repulsive to him, and the Indian community had recognized their leader.

He was, of course, accused of self-seeking, and wealth he might readily have had, for the Indians were able and willing to pay well for his legal service to their cause. Instead he refused fees and simplified his physical life to that of the *yogi*.

The principle of government return for Indians not willing to become reindentured was accepted by the Indian government in 1894. This was a step toward peace, but did not make it any easier for those already in the country on the old terms. Gandhi was effectively reënforcing the contention of a minority of whites that the Indians were essential to the prosperity of the regions that had been developed through their industry along the coast and entitled to fair treatment everywhere.

To strengthen his stakes and to get Kasturbai and the children (she had been fruitful and borne him two more sons, and his attitude toward her had changed) Gandhi went to India in 1896. His speeches there in widely separated cities aroused intense interest and sympathy for the plight of the emigrants. Garbled reports of his speeches, quoting him as abusing the people of Natal, raised such sentiment in Africa that upon return he and his party were detained thirty days aboard ship at Durban before it was thought safe for him to land. He finally insisted upon going ashore, only to be set upon by a mob of burly whites. He was saved from brutal death when the plucky wife of a British official, Mrs. Alexander, heroically sheltered his bruised body with her own.

Kasturbai now showed her ability to understand and enter into the spirit of his work, and this was the beginning of a real partnership in which she was to become the able commander of the women of his forces. However, they still had their very human quarrels until after the fourth son was born. Then Gandhi suggested that their relationship henceforth be that of brother and sister, according to strict *brahmacharya* and Tolstoy's "kingdom of heaven." "From that time all dissension ceased," the saint was to say in his *Adventures*. "I am credited with great energy and quick mind although neither my mind nor my body are free from disease, and for that celibacy must be thanked. But how much greater strength and acumen I should have brought to my work if the twenty years of indulgence had been avoided." Gandhi made *brahmacharya* an essential part of his message, and when years later, on taking up his work in India, he realized the necessity of population control in the betterment of that country, the religious argument was strengthened by the economic one. He could not but blame his physical frailness upon early overindulgence, and this made him regard all sex relationship as destructive only. He never envisioned the freshening of body and soaring of spirit, the softening of ambition and tenderness toward fellow man which can arise from ideal physical intercourse. In his lack of the riches a Browning possessed he was handicapped to guide humanity, although the soul's sweet qualities were gained, *Sufi* fashion, from the marriage with God. If the Indian saint had done more justice to his body, one feels, and dealt with it as understandingly as with his soul, he would have been neither so puzzled nor self-condemned over his reactions.

III

Those were years when the little Dutch republics were defying England, and winning the admiration of the world for their pluck, while many a subject people were ruefully comparing that example of valor with

their own passivity. But quietly and persistently
Gandhi taught his people that their hope of freedom
should rest in spirituality. This was not to mean lack
of organization or of bravery. For him "love your
enemies," nonviolence, was nevertheless an essential
of *Satyagraha,* insistence on justice, or perhaps more
literally truth-gripping. He taught his followers to
condemn fear, in order that tyranny, which succeeds
only because it utilizes fear, might no longer hold them.
Adults through his publications and speeches, youth
through his schools, were being built up in soul-force
to stand for themselves and show their worth and
find their place in spite of the scorn of whites and of
half-conquered natives. But he did not, like a Sun
Yat-sen or a Kemal, expect or plan a new era overnight. To the man of the spirit, time is an untroubling
factor, and he has supreme confidence in the success
of his methods if adhered to.

Now it seemed that the prospects were fair. The
announced war aims promised amelioration of the Indian status in the Transvaal under Britain, and the
victory was bound to be hers in the long run. Not
despising political acumen, Gandhi gave an active interpretation to his *Satyagraha* by aiding the government in
every nonmilitary way. And from the organization at
his back he recruited an Indian Red Cross service,
joined by nearly a thousand, and leading it himself
was cited for bravery under fire. Thus early he notably
exemplified his dissent from the merely passive con-

templation of religious themes. It is the pragmatism combined with principle which marks a man for leadership. Later it was to show in his Indian career. Long after at Sabarmati he would explain, "My oblations are services to fellow men."

With his compatriots, as he thought, fairly set on the way to peaceful progress, he turned to the homeland and took ship with Kasturbai and the children in 1901 after an impressive farewell. But in a few months they were again begged to return. The last embers of the war had not been quenched before it became apparent that the new arrangements would mean less and not more liberty for Indians. He had received his first betrayal at the hands of British opportunism. He would patiently suffer many more, and then he would turn utterly against white rule. Now his Indian community begged his aid in presenting their memorials to the government.

At once he assented and enrolled himself as a resident in Pretoria early in 1903. The first move in his campaign was the founding of an organ, *Indian Opinion,* which he edited in English and Gujrati. It was the forerunner of a tremendous volume of publishing. Then, in 1904, his eleventh African year, he founded his first *ashram,* or retreat, in the form of an agricultural colony at Phœnix, fourteen miles from Durban, Natal, putting into it all his wealth. There he came at intervals when the pressure of his duties which centered around Johannesburg would permit, and there he offered a home to any who would come and live, along with him, according to the vow of poverty and self-control. For himself he claimed but two loin cloths. He was bidding farewell to the pride of life. No more would he be known as the dapper dressed, the clever lawyer, or even the mere statesman of his people. They were to call him the Great Soul, the *Mahatma*.

His main occupation was organizing sentiment against new restrictions upon residence in the Transvaal that were preparing, to be imposed even on Indians there before the British came. They involved a principle of segregation and of degrading class restrictions injurious to the pride and harmful to the prosperity of his countrymen. A diversion came when bubonic plague broke out in the unspeakable slum which was their residence quarter in Johannesburg. Gandhi, disdaining red tape, turned a store that was standing vacant into a pest house, by his prestige enforcing isolation which effectively stopped spread of an epidemic.

In spite of all he could do, the laws restricting the liberties of Asiatics in South Africa were being made more stringent. Yet Gandhi so far demonstrated his good will as to provide a corps of stretcher bearers who served during the suppression of the black insurrection in the early part of 1906. It might seem he was aiding the tyrant against weak fellow-sufferers, but then Gandhi would have opposed violent resistance among his own Indians.

The whites had a strong suspicion that the registra-

tion laws were being evaded by Asiatics through imper-
sonation of legitimate certificate holders by impostors.
To meet this, it was decreed by the party in power that
all Asiatics were to register again, and this time leave
thumb prints for identification, and have them on their
certificates. "Like paroled prisoners!" they exclaimed.
Gandhi, to whom the dignity of his people was even
more important than their freedom, called for unfalter-
ing resistance by way of mass refusal. This was religiously vowed by him and his following in a mass
meeting at Johannesburg in September, 1906. He and
a Muhammadan, Ali, were sent to London to protest,
and obtained suspension of the ordinance until such
time as a constitutional government should again be established in the conquered Transvaal. But when that
came a little later, the same regulation was promulgated. Passive resistance started on a large scale the
latter part of 1907, and Gandhi, as its leader, was imprisoned two months. The authorities could not afford
to keep him long, either then or later, lest his followers
get out of hand and forget the passive basis of his
program. He was willing to go far to demonstrate
reasonableness and faith in the new British over-rule,
and accepted a compromise: that he would set the example of registering again, and the authorities on their
part would repeal some of the obnoxious laws which
the registry had been intended to help enforce.

As a result, on the way to the place of registry,
Gandhi was set upon and beaten almost to death by

former Muhammadan followers who maintained that he was violating them and betraying the vow by compromising on the issue. He insisted on being taken to the registry office, where he completed the formality before he fell unconscious. The people as a whole followed him in the compromise. The Musselman fanatic who delivered the almost fatal blow over the head was arrested by the British, and Gandhi was summoned to testify against him. Gandhi had fought for both sects without discrimination. Here was a fine opportunity for a split in the Indian community which would nullify his work. But he refused to swear a complaint or testify. "The man will yet be my friend and advocate our cause," he said. The less numerous but vigorous Muslim section of the community was deeply impressed with this saintly action, and here began the ordinarily despised Hindu teacher's extraordinary influence upon those of the rival religion.

But the government, now the people were registered, refused to fulfill its part of the bargain. In their wrath, the people burned up the new registration certificates. Gandhi justified them in this, and passive resistance was again the watchword, not only among Indians, but among Chinese, Malays, and the rest of Asia there. The Mahatma's little Asiatic league stuck together in a way that presaged how the continent of Asia now unites against the white man's oppression. Severe penalties were decreed. When the authorities began to seize and jail numbers of delinquents, Gandhi helped by recommending voluntary surrender. Men and women of all classes went in groups and requested to be jailed. Kasturbai was one of the first to respond to her husband's call. With some high caste women as companions she went and asked to be incarcerated. The authorities accommodated them for three months. But soon the jails were overflowing. The overflow of prisoners had to be put in open mine workings. There many died. Gandhi got two months, with hard labor this time, in the latter part of 1908. But always his authority was needed on the outside to restrain his people. The situation was becoming as embarrassing for an "enlightened white man's government" as it was distressful for the Asiatic victims and the government had not the religious exaltation they enjoyed, to bolster it up.

Released, Gandhi was again deputized to go to London and seek the good offices of the "home" authorities for relief. He landed in the middle of 1909 and devoted himself to securing what might be welcomed as an honorable compromise. As a result, advice from London in October the following year, to which the Transvaal government assented in principle, recommended repeal of the stringent amendments of the alien residence laws that had been passed. Gandhi was willing to consent to limitation of residence if it could be put on an equitable basis which would not single out his own countrymen as undesirables. A South African deputy was sent to India, and the question of treatment of expatriates took its place in Indian politics. Telegrams regarding the matter came from as widely separated places as Simla and Peking.

Attempts were made with education tests and "democratic country of origin" tests to exclude the type of person aimed at—but always there were border-line classes who took alarm: East Europeans, Levantines. The question, "Are Jews Asiatics?" was raised. And to the greater embarrassment of Gandhi's party it was recalled that large numbers of his protégés were "untouchable" in their own country—subject to far more galling restriction in India if they went back than what was proposed here. Gandhi would not admit that a wrong there justified one here. On the other hand, the white parliament, determined to favor an increase of white population with European standards of living, was pledged to restriction of Asiatics, no matter what London government or local executives might promise. It was glad to welcome a court decision that wounded the tenderest sensibilities of the Indians. The question had been raised as to whether Indian women might come in as wives of residents. The court decreed that since the rites of Indian marriage did not bind the parties to monogamy, it was technically polygamous (even though all save the Muslems were restricted to one mate) and so inadmissible. The decree legally voided the marriages of those women who were in the colony. These had always been as few as was natural among contract laborers—to the satisfaction of the whites, who were divided between a desire to have Indians to work and a determination not to be supplanted by them.

Gokhale came to mediate and received a verbal promise of repeal from the government. He returned to India confident of Gandhi's ability to "see it through." The two men were not to meet again.

But in 1912 and 1913, when the proposals for new legislation came out, it was seen that instead of giving relief they ratified old causes of complaint and made new ones. The standing grievance of the poll tax on nonindentured laborers and restriction on license to trade was perpetuated in aggravated form. There was a great outcry, both in Africa and in India. Strikes followed in every industry dependent on Indian labor, and the pocketbooks of the whites were hard hit. Gandhi gave shelter at his *ashram* to all strikers who wished to come. The government soon found it desirable to appoint a committee to negotiate. Gandhi remembered the end of the previous compromise. He determined to give the arrogant whites a convincing demonstration of the spirit of his people. He set under way a vast procession of protest toward the Transvaal. Its marching orders were "Johannesburg or jail." At first the comfortable white population scoffed at the motley stream of men, women, and children reverently making its way across the country behind its frail, loin-cloth-girded prophet. The numbers swelled with each step, and the interest of the world was concentrated on the scene. Children were born en route—mother and babe were hoisted in stretchers on the shoulders of fellow-pilgrims and carried along. A babe in arms died—its mother bathed the little body with her tears and left it by the roadside, marching on "for the cause." The London *Times* commented: "It was a most remarkable manifestation of passive resistance."

In its usual red-faced embarrassment the colonial government arrested Gandhi and clapped him in jail, thinking that with the leader gone the demonstration would cease, but it only grew—in turbulence as well as in numbers—and the Mahatma was released on bail. He quickly caught up with the procession and resumed his place again at its head. The government arrested the marchers wholesale and crammed the jails. Still the orderly thousands, chanting Vedic hymns, continued on their way. Finally in desperation the government surrounded the entire procession near the Transvaal border, sorted out the marchers according to district, put them on trains, and took them under arrest to their own doors. Some were held in jail, and Gandhi received a sentence of nine months at hard labor. However in two months all were out.

At this moment there came into the life of Gandhi two Englishmen who were to play large parts in his cause and become his interpreters to the Western world. C. F. Andrews and W. W. Pierson, young missionaries of nonconformist minds well versed in Indian culture and politics, had recently associated themselves with

[418]

Rabindranath Tagore's philosophy and university when Gandhi's spectacular march centered the eyes of the Indian world on him and South Africa. Gokhale, now head of the ultra-official Indian National Congress, called for some one to go and lead a second march when Gandhi was jailed, and with Tagore's approval these two Englishmen volunteered. They were welcomed at the Durban pier by a delegation of Indians. One "intelligent but modestly unprepossessing little man," as Andrews expresses it, was chatting with them about conditions when Andrews recognized a leader known to have been sentenced with Gandhi. "Oh, are you out!" he exclaimed. "Then possibly Mr. Gandhi is released also. Do you know where he is?" The unpretentious little man said quietly, "I am Gandhi."

British regard of world opinion had made it unnecessary for the two British idealists to lead the next Indian demonstration, but their services were abundantly useful in the negotiations. Public opinion was aroused throughout the world anent colonial tyranny. Some of the strike disorders had resulted in loss of life.

Difficulties of expatriates in Africa and Canada were adding greatly to the ferment which was threatening a general outbreak in India. Lord Hardinge, the viceroy, took the bold step in late 1913 of dealing with the African situation in a public speech in Madras, forcefully calling the attention of the Home Government. Upon invitation the Indian government sent a man to

[419]

coöperate with African authority in investigation of conditions, and a Royal Commission went out. Gandhi's position had been made clear. He wanted immigration laws to be put upon a nonracial basis, to secure the right of Indians born in Africa to visit India and return, abolition of the three-pound poll tax, rectification of the law about marriages, reform in method and spirit of administering the existing laws regarding residence, etc. Now he and his followers, in view of broken agreements in the past, disdained to coöperate with the investigation. However it went on without them, and the result was a series of recommendations to which even the extremely prejudiced General Smuts felt obliged to agree.

The terms were agreed upon in June, 1914, and Gandhi and a delegation waited patiently at the State House for General Smuts' signature. News came that Kasturbai, whose health had steadily failed since her release from prison, lay dying at the *ashram,* begging to see her husband. Andrews said: "You must go and leave this to me." Gandhi wiped the mist from his eyes and replied: "I must stay here until the agreement is signed. I must not risk another betrayal of my people. I entrust Mrs. Gandhi to God."

Andrews bethought himself of Smuts' habit of going to his office at six thirty or seven o'clock in the morning, and went there to wait for him. "I can't see you now —I can't see any one," was the Dutch general's annoyed greeting. Andrews overtook the premier at the door of his inner office. "Mrs. Gandhi is dying," he said in a low voice. "Oh . . . then come in!"

"Mr. Gandhi will not go to her side until the document is signed," persisted Andrews. The general pulled it out of his desk. "Will you assure me that everything is as arranged—that the government's interests are fully protected?" "Yes," said Andrews. Smuts signed without further reading and Andrews rushed with the document to Gandhi, who set off at once for his wife's bedside. Slowly she recovered. Andrews attributes a great deal of the honesty with which the agreement was kept to the dramatic conditions under which it was signed, and highly praises Smuts' graciousness. Possibly the idealism for which he was to receive credit following the World War was watered by contact with the spirit of the great Indian and his associates.

The government yielded concessions on the main points: Indian immigration in general was to be stopped, but migration among the different colonies permitted. (The government of India had stopped recruitment of indentured labor in 1912.) However, Indians were to be allowed to bring in wives, and polygamy was to be a question of number of wives, and not of the ceremony of the wedding. The three-pound tax was abolished. Separate educational facilities were to be provided. Thus the way was opened for the Indians to become amalgamated to the structure of the colony. They had learned the lesson that they were not helpless, that they had rights and could defend them with-

[421]

out wronging any one. Gandhi was satisfied for the time. Some of his followers would have been for keeping up passive resistance until they had gained their other aims: the franchise, freedom to own land, impartial granting of trading licenses. He was unwilling to take advantage of the violent labor troubles on the Rand at the time, and advocated advance step by step.

It was the fateful midyear of 1914 that the Mahatma, his stubbly hair by now sprinkled with white, thin as a mummy, felt he could leave Africa and give response to the tremendous demand which his work for the expatriates had created for him in India. A case of pleurisy was the immediate cause for his departure. His sons had long since gone to the Motherland to receive the best education obtainable, and the eldest had already attained note as a lawyer. Gandhi had disapproved. He had come to regard the legal profession as immoral. But the son, appealing to his father's example, had been permitted to work out his own salvation.

At the boat, Gandhi, Kasturbai, and several disciples who accompanied him were loaded down with presents by a grateful people. Not to discourage the good feeling of the moment, Gandhi received them, but en route to Bombay he insisted they be turned back to the Indian community for welfare work. Kasturbai is described as having handed over her necklace of gold, such as Indian women so love to wear on every limb and finger, in a torrent of tears. Gandhi, agreeing with the British

economists that the infatuation for hoarding gold is one
of the reasons for India's poverty, and having the more
important incentive of spiritual humility, could never
approve of his wife's wearing this trinket. And she
understood and wanted to support him, but—she was
still a woman. After this sacrifice she, too, became a
saint.

Gandhi was shocked to find new machine manufac-
tures ruining the home industry income of the homeland peasants, forcing them to the cities to live in even
greater poverty and squalor than the community with
which he had worked twenty-one years in South Africa.
Before beginning in his new field he thought it desirable
to renew his acquaintances and connections in England,
and there he went with Kasturbai. Suddenly the World
War began. He and his wife enrolled in a volunteer
service corps composed of the Indians in London. But
the climate was too damp for his weakened lungs and
the beginning of 1915 found him back again in India.
He was saddened by the death of his old friend and
mentor, Gokhale, but a great place was left vacant
which he was shortly to fill. Gandhi said of him: "He
seemed to me all I wanted in a political leader. He was
pure as crystal, gentle as a lamb, brave as a lion, and
chivalrous to a fault."

Gandhi's interests had been primarily social, but the
War created a tremendous need for him in the political
field. Forces for insurrection had been piling up. Terrorism had almost made an end of orderly government

in Bengal. More or less followed by the police, a revolutionary plot was maturing. It was too great an opportunity for the German enemy to miss. And it was their maladroit effort to establish a liaison that stirred the authorities to arrests.

Arms in India the plotters would have seized were shipped to the War area. So the country was spared what might or might not have gone down in history as a glorious revolution. It was all over so quietly that one of Gandhi's supporters could say later, "India had never dreamed of revolution," nor of "anarchical crimes," in spite of isolated instances of bomb throwing.

It was to this situation that Gandhi returned, and he embarked on a program of speaking all over the country that was to take him a year. The government rewarded his influence for peace and loyalty by conferring the *Kaisar-i-Hind* medal. Under the stern provisions of the Defence of India Bill, passed early in the year, and the conciliatory power of Lord Hardinge's government, the sporadic mutinies ceased and the country settled down peacefully to bear its share of the burdens of the War.

In 1916, as a center for his teaching, Gandhi established another ashram, not far from Ahmedabad in his home province, calling it *Satyagraha*—"Truthgrip." With that absence of demand for haste which differentiates the spiritual man from the professional reformer, he started a slow enlightenment of India from this center. There was much groundwork to be laid, in his opinion, before self-government could be claimed.

Periodical dissensions between Hindus and Muhammadans, involving some bloodshed, revealed the greatest weakness in his nation. He used his "soul-force" to mediate the difficulties between indigo planters and tenants in Bihar. He went frankly against the government at Kaira, when the crops failed, and the tax officials did not make humane allowance nor heed the peasants' petitions. Gandhi advised them to decline to pay taxes or utilize the administration in any way. They solidly endured a few months' persecution, ending with adjustment by the government. Gandhi's capacity to lead his people to victory against wrongs was established.

Regarding the European War, Gandhi accepted the orthodox Allied interpretation: that it was to establish justice and end war. He had such a desire to "play fair" with the British that he even advocated enlistment, up to the very time of its close. How, one may well ask, could a man devoted to the principle of nonvio· lence do that? For the deviation from principle involved in this recognition of violence "I was to be severely punished," he was to say later, referring to the trouble caused in India by the War and by Britain's repudiation of wartime promises to the Indian people. At the time Gandhi felt that "the mouse who does not resist the cat is not practicing virtue. Men should be able to fight, both in body and in spirit, and then controlling that ability they will have their greatest victory in passive resistance. But in the meantime those who have not yet had faith to comprehend this, and who still take pride in force might as well, might better, use that force on the side of justice." He had not yet given up hope of steady progress toward liberty in coöperation with the British, nor had he yet suffered the disillusionment which was to come to so many—that the winning side did not fight for virtue only.

Menaced by the Irish rebellion and Muslem disaffection, Lloyd George, fearing that a wavering Indian allegiance might turn the scales against Great Britain, promised through Montagu and Chelmsford a constitution for India that would provide a large share of home rule. The idea was uncompromisingly opposed by the civil service there, who not only saw their supremacy endangered, but looking with the usual Occidental disdain upon Asiatics sincerely believed that Indians are incapable of exercising the functions of government.

Meanwhile, more than a million of India's young men went into the War, in one capacity or another. A volunteer regiment was even raised in notoriously rebellious (and nonmilitary) Bengal. Indian capital to the amount of a hundred million pounds was subscribed to war loans. Indian industry enjoyed the stimulus of military patronage, and the cloth factories got permanently free from an abusive tax which had discriminated against them in favor of Manchester. In spite of danger along the northern border, Britain was able at one time to reduce her effectives in the country to only fifteen thousand men.

[426]

War prosperity went with increased cost of living, in spite of regulations to curb profiteering, and satisfied neither dealer nor consumer. The Muslems were anxiously watching the fate of their holy places and the Caliph, and anticipating with misgivings their future in a democracy where they would be outnumbered by rival religionists whom they had treated badly.

As the War ended, young Indians who felt their country had done its part were impatient for the reforms promised in 1917 and 1918. But manifestations of this feeling were drastically suppressed by the unsympathetic civil service, with no restraining hand from London. The British government was engaged in the most amazing imperialistic enterprise of its history. Lloyd George and Winston Churchill seemed carried away with the belief that with Germany defeated and Russia on her knees, British dominance could be extended indefinitely.

The voice for united Indian opinion was the National Congress, founded thirty years before by two liberal Englishmen who aimed to create a loyal politicalmindedness of progressive tinge among the natives. For many years previous to the War, Gandhi's old mentor, Gokhale, had dominated the organization, but a younger group had grown dissatisfied with his moderation. Leader of the extremists had been the rough old prophet, Tilak, credited with compounding the political watchword, *Swaraj*—from Sanscrit roots surviving also in the French words, *soi, regent*. Gandhi put forth intense effort to interpret it "self-rule" in the wide sense of Solomon's dictum: "He that is slow to anger is better than the mighty, and he that ruleth his spirit than he that taketh a city." He had a deep faith that the material victory would follow the spiritual. But he was destined to go far beyond Gokhale whom he endorsed.

Tilak was political-minded, though he found his appealing issues largely in the defense of social and religious prejudices. At the time of Gandhi's return he had just been released at the age of sixty-eight from six years' prison exile on the charge of editorial laudation of the young terrorist assassins who fought the partition of Bengal. Gokhale in his dying days had plead in vain that Tilak moderate his attitude—"be reasonable." Tilak had been pioneer in the use of boycott as a means of *swadeshi*, that is, industrial independence by rejection of foreign goods. Supporting Arubindo Ghose, chiefly concerned with native culture, he had favored the project of Indianizing education as an offset to the un-national British schools. His fervor to be first among those averse to England had not cooled by his imprisonment.

Gokhale had passed on leadership of the unofficial Congress to Satyendra Sinha (afterwards Lord and Governor of Behar) and his ability dominated the session at the close of 1915. But next year it was Tilak and Mrs. Besant who won the plaudits of the Congress at Lucknow. That versatile lady, Irish, born in London, long ardent in Socialism and Theosophy, had turned her energy to Indian politics and founded an Indian Home Rule League of her own. Her ability, following, and fame among the British united to make her acceptable as a leader, and next year she was rewarded with the presidential chair—woman and Westerner though she was. Without her influence, perhaps, the authorities would have looked less kindly upon the founding of a great Hindu university near Benares, which she pushed through.

Gandhi was to be hailed as successor to all these great names because to him it was given as to an authentic seer, to found the superficial agitation upon hitherto scarcely realized depths of principle. Swaraj, the protection and reinvigoration of native culture, nonviolent resistance combined in Gandhi's mind at maturity to produce the profoundest expression of the spiritual genius of India in modern times. He owed much to his predecessors, still more to the lessons of his experience in Africa. For the unselfish and truly spiritual personal quality with which he glorified his task, the world will not find a parallel since St. Francis of Assisi.

It is said that during the first year after his return he was deterred from expounding his program of passive resistance by a promise given to the dying Gokhale. The prolonged years of war and the moral issues thought to be involved bade him be patient. In the Kaira taxation affair he had shown what could be done, but in the main he stood for coöperation among the people and with the government. His voice was heard in this cause in many parts of the country, and fame and credit were his among whites and natives alike. Meanwhile his intimacy with the problems of India was becoming more complete, and the need of healing her divisions more clear.

His first great political stroke was the winning of the Muslem community by persuading the Congress to take as its own the defense of the Sultan as occupant of Muhammad's spiritual throne—the Khalifat (Caliphate) movement. The Muhammadan world outside of Turkey, which had failed to fulfill German expectations by uniting against the Allies, felt at this time betrayed by an ungrateful England, who, it believed, ignored war-time assurances and sided with France and America to ruin Islam by annihilating native rule in Turkey, Morocco, and Arabia. At the end of 1916 the Lucknow Pact defined the alliance between the Indian National Congress and the Indian Muslem League. The unrevenged blows he had borne at Musselman hands had come to fruitage.

Gandhi's association of Indian Independence and Hindu-Muslem unity with the Caliph's cause was to prove a dangerous policy, as well as one—the only one —to lay him open to an accusation of time-serving. But for several years it was to make him dictator of Indian opinion.

In the last year of the War two grave investigations were concluded. One of these was the inquiry on seditious crimes, dealing with the disaffection before the War; the other was the Montagu-Chelmsford survey on self-government, preparatory to fulfillment of England's promises. Its proposal of representative government in matters of chiefly social administration and crown control in those affecting political sovereignty was at once rejected by Indian extremists like Tilak. The angered British wondered whether his group favored agitation for the impossible as surest way to gain everything possible, or whether he was merely vexed, as an old man, to sense that full realization of his hopes could not come in his day. Those on the other side, as C. F. Andrews, were equally impressed with his nobility and devotion to principle. A large moderate element hailed the Montagu reform as very promising, and grouped themselves into a separate liberal Congress to criticize and make suggestions.

Somewhat aloof from Congress politics himself, Gandhi recommended coöperation. The new plan did indeed point to a future government, increasingly democratic and Western in form. Yet, "What of that?" some thought—"What has blood-draggled Western democracy that we should be content to see India on that road?" This was another kind of discontent, obsessed with nostalgia for half-mythical glories of ancient Hind, vaguely aspiring to find a purely Indian formula for their renewal. Gandhi thought he knew that formula, but would have worked it out while avoiding friction with other well-meant programs.

The crisis came when the haughty Lloyd George-Churchill government sought to repress with the one hand while holding out the bait of freedom with the other. Its first new Indian measures were based not on the Montagu-Chelmsford report but on the sedition inquiry, and were not the promised liberal constitution but the Rowlatt Acts—extending part of the war regulations over into peace time and suspending Anglo-Saxon fundamental rights of man which the British themselves had made a standard of justice in the country. The object was to prevent Indian barristers utilizing the loopholes of law in defending perpetrators and inciters of violence. Intense agitation followed, led by men who had acquired the Western viewpoint on liberty; by others, too, no doubt, who chiefly planned to renew the pre-War insurrection. Sentiment was worked up to the point of violent eruption among the benighted masses and the half-enlightened.

The Acts threw the whole country into a violent frame of mind which brought a crisis upon Gandhi's program of nonviolence. Gandhi's chief objection was the deep one of the defender of race dignity and equality. For himself the white man must have constitutional guarantees. He was willing to concede that government without them was good enough for his colored subjects.

The Mahatma saw the time for demonstrating on a large scale the power he had learned in Africa. The hope of being of spiritual benefit, of preventing violence while gaining justice, drew him into the political arena. From his Satyagraha Ashram in February, 1919, he proclaimed what he called the "Satyagraha Movement." Its essence was the right and duty of people to disobey an unjust law. He exemplified it by starting a paper, the *Satyagrahi,* which he refused to register under the objectionable press regulations. The British soon closed it down. It was his first personal clash with the government in India. The combined agitation and the arguments of Indian members of the legislative councils only availed to bring amendments limiting life of the obnoxious bill to 1922 and more closely safeguarding its application, and government-constituted majorities passed it in March.

Gandhi called for a strike or *hartal,* combined with prayer and fasting, for March 30 (generally postponed till a week later) which was to inaugurate a national program of nonviolent resistance. Rioters in Delhi tried to enforce this on the indifferent, and had a fatal clash with the interfering police. In dread of violence, Gandhi rushed to quiet his followers, but was not permitted to enter the Punjab. News of his detention added fuel to the fire. Hindus and Muhammadans, their differences temporarily forgotten, rose with one accord all over the Punjab and Bombay provinces and news of arson, plunder, and murder of Europeans crowded the wires.

Gandhi did important service in restoring peace and order in the Bombay Presidency, vehemently addressing his followers personally at Ahmedabad, metropolis of his home district. But his influence was not allowed in the north, and there the civil authorities called on the military. The great city of Amritsar was harried for days by a murderous mob of mixed religious complexion. The population of that city is mixed Hindu and Muhammadan, but it is a center and site of the famous "Golden Temple" of the Sikh sectaries, those virile religionists of North India, used by England as her most trusty fighters and policemen throughout her Asiatic possessions, yet now to appear as potential menace to her rule.

General Dyer was called to take charge, and issued orders against public gatherings of any sort. Three days later, a throng of between six and ten thousand gathered in a square, the Jallianwalla Bagh, destined to become the "Black Hole" of Indian nationalists, listening to speakers urging their just claim to government consideration. Many Sikhs present had come from out of town for a festival and did not know the rule that had been made. To Dyer it was an opportunity to demonstrate that orders are orders. He lined up fifty riflemen at the other side of the square from the speaker's stand and coolly opened fire without warning. The narrow entries, which alone had prevented bringing in the machine gun carriages, also prevented quick escape of the crowd, so the slaughter continued under his direction for ten minutes. When he marched his men back to quarters nearly four hundred lay dead in the square and about twelve hundred wounded were left to shift as they could.

It was one of those cruel and crucial mistakes which the dominating white man suddenly driven into "funk" is liable to make when he sees the overwhelming numbers against him. It was the same sort of thing which happened when Captain Everson fired on the Chinese students in front of Louza police station in Shanghai in 1925. Like that event it stands as the atrocity marking the beginning of the end of the white man's rule in its particular country.

Martial law was proclaimed, the censorship clamped tight, while a reign of terror ensued in the province. The military showed ingenuity in devising degrading and unusual punishments. There were floggings and enforced crawlings. Armored cars and bombing planes mingled the remains of guilty and innocent when involved in protesting mobs. Order by frightfulness had been attained by the end of April, before the news could leak out.

Gandhi had called for punishment upon Dyer. The Standing Committee of the National Congress appointed a commission of which Gandhi was a member to investigate the rumors. Horror and incredulity mingled in greeting their report, but the government ignored it in haughty silence for a time. Eventually, as world condemnation increased, Dyer was taken out of India— to be given a promotion and retired.

However, Gandhi did not give up expecting justice

from the government. In London the ponderous new Montagu-Chelmsford constitutional enactment advanced to second reading and debate in Parliament. India had almost forgotten it. After excoriation by every sort of public voice, in which Gandhi led, the Indian government took official notice of the Amritsar affair and appointed the Committee of Investigation (including a minority of natives). Long months of taking testimony over the massacre began.

Meanwhile old provocations rankled. The Rowlatt Acts stayed on the books, though destined never to be applied. Plague and cholera kept up their toll, and there were local famines. Worse than these, the influenza came, which affected half the population and killed more in a year than the plague had in ten (about thirteen million). The nation's nerves were on edge.

Muslem resentment over the predicament of the Sultan-Caliph at Constantinople increased. The leaders organized in November, 1919, an all-India Khalifat (Caliphate) Conference. Gandhi, Hindu, was invited to preside over the assembly. He had made himself responsible for India's hardest, most precarious task, unification of Muslem and Hindu partisanship into one nationalism.

Old Clive and Hastings had established hold on India by taking sides in the contests among Hindu princes and their rebellion against a decadent Muslem emperor. Her hold on the country still depended upon Hindu-Muslem schism. British civil servants would always fall back upon this as the great justification of British rule in India. If Gandhi's leadership could bring exchange of that enmity for united political sentiment, alien rule would be automatically brought to an end. "As soon as we shoe unity, the British will step out— they are sensible people," he said. "To paraphrase the saying of a rough British protagonist of the commoner's struggle in England: 'If we Indians could only spit in unison, we would form a puddle big enough to drown 300,000 Englishmen.' "

It has been popular to laugh at the apparent absurdity of his attempt, but his "aggressive saintliness" seemingly was to accomplish more toward that goal by 1922 than what we are wont to call civilized rule had done in a century. After that were to come dark deeds and doubtful moves.

The Musselmans, who had been the main reliance of the British, became for the time the most audacious adherents of Gandhi's noncoöperation. His strategy received its first public adoption in this Muhammadan Khalifat Assembly. It went beyond Gandhi and declared for the drastic means named long before, after British Captain Boycott by resentful Irish tenants, now become Asia's own weapon of nationalism.

Gandhi waited upon British justice until June. The anger of his people could be restrained no longer. He must either direct their action or withdraw cravenly and let it burst forth into futureless violence.

He who had been loyal to the British raj by tradition and experience assumed the headship of implacable opposition to it in a ringing challenge to the Viceroy. The letter sheds strong light upon Gandhi's character. It was followed by another in August. They contain the paragraphs:

> The only course open to me is either in despair to sever all connection with British rule or, if I still retain faith in the inherent superiority of the British Constitution to adopt such means as will rectify the wrong done and thus restore confidence. I have not lost faith in the superiority of the British Constitution and it is because I believe in it that I have advised my Muslem friends to withdraw their support from Your Excellency's government, and advised the Hindus to join them.
> It is not without a pang that I return the Kaisar-i-Hind Gold Medal granted to me by your redecessor for my humanitarian work in South Africa, the Zulu War Medal, granted in South Africa for my services as officer in charge of the Indian Volunteer Ambulance Corps in 1906, and the Boer War Medal for my services as assistant superintendent of the Indian Volunteer Stretcher-bearer Corps during the Boer War of 1899-1900.

But, he adds, after referring to the scenes that took place in the Punjab and the events back of the Caliphate movement:

> I can retain neither respect nor affection for a government which has been moving from wrong to wrong in order to defend its immorality. . . . The government must be moved to repentance.
> I have therefore ventured to suggest non-coöperation, which enables those who wish to disassociate themselves from

the government and which, if unattended by violence, must compel the government to retrace its steps and undo its wrongs.

The Viceroy, Lord Chelmsford, retorted by calling Gandhi's "the most foolish of all foolish schemes."

Hundreds of noted Indians followed his example. Sir Rabindranath Tagore turned back his knighthood with one of the most cutting letters that a King of England must ever have received. Gandhi proclaimed a *hartal*, or strike, for August 1 to inaugurate a definite noncoöperation campaign. He took careful count of details. "Complete order through complete organization" was his slogan. Instruction sheets were issued to all patriots which warned that experienced group leaders must be used, flag and whistle signaling be understood, patriotic slogans and songs used at certain times, and streets and stations kept clear. Noncoöperation included repudiation of titles of honor, resignation of office, nonsubscription of government loans, substitution of private arbitration for official law courts, a suspension of their profession by lawyers, boycott of the schools, and peaceful agitation for *swaraj*.

The further step which Gandhi called "mass civil disobedience," and which would involve refusal to pay taxes, with mass violation of all orders not involving moral principle, was to be taken as soon as the people had been disciplined through this.

Gandhi dreaded mobs; he would have preferred war

to unorganized violence. His motives were primarily moral, the political ones following as a consequence. His philosophy was first that India should through these campaigns be disciplined for her own good. The overcoming of British tyranny would follow automatically, but of more importance to him than the throwing off of despotism was the saving of the soul of India.

At the same time he was condemning the British government, Gandhi made a gallant appeal to the English people. He affirmed his faith in British bravery and sense of fair play, and asked the British people to make up for the perfidy of their government which had completely shattered the faith of its Indian subjects. "Bravery on the battle-field is impossible for India, but bravery of the soul remains open to us. Noncoöperation means nothing less than training in self-sacrifice. I expect to conquer you by my suffering."

Considering with perhaps an even greater discernment than our other makers of modern Asia the full implications of nationalism, Gandhi instituted a cult of the spinning wheel and the wearing of *khadi* (*khaddar*), or homespun cloth. It had both practical and symbolic value. No foreign machine industry had taken more wealth out of India or injured home industry more than the textile industry of England. Calico was named after the Indian city Calicut, and Europe at one time got many of its finest textiles from India. Now India was raising the cotton, selling it cheaply to England to be made up, and buying back the machine-made product. It seemed impossible for the peasant to maintain a decent standard of living through agriculture alone (indeed, this is increasingly a problem in America). Gandhi saw a combination of home industry with agriculture as the only hope for economic rehabilitation short of establishment of great industrial centers and the moving of the population to cities—the solution taken by Japan but opposed by Gandhi as ruinous to the native culture. Spiritually he believed that industrial work was necessary to the soul's health, and saw an opportunity to put all classes of his people at the exercise of spinning.

Socially a universal interest in spinning would break down caste barriers. Even the Brahman must spin the sacred cord which never leaves his neck and it is the only form of manual labor against which no caste can hold prejudice. Gandhi's spinning campaign comprised all the elements of the "love country cloth" put out in China following the student revolution of 1919, but it went much further than that. There was method in Gandhi's madness of the spinning wheel.

The true reformer seems to be happiest when he has taken on the most causes. In the midst of the political crisis the Mahatma led a campaign against drink and wine shops, and against opium dens. Even tea houses and betel nut chewing were included in his ban. India is naturally a prohibition country, wine being against the religious precepts of both Hindus and Muslems; nevertheless there was a government-licensed wine business. The Indian people took so vigorously to the suppression of liquors that Gandhi had to interfere to keep them from destroying the shops by mob action. "You must not try to compel another by physical force to become good," he told them—a statement of considerable interest to prohibitionists and their opponents in America, as well as his doctrine that it is right and dutiful to disobey an unjust law.[3]

Under such conditions, the new Montagu-Chelmsford constitutional experiment, popularly called the "dyarchy," went into effect. A voting constituency of 7 per cent of the population was to elect provincial legislatures and a national assembly, on a "balance system" specially protecting the Muhammadan minority. These representative bodies would ratify appointments of and provide budgets for ministers of education, sanitation, etc., while the raj kept control of finance, justice, and the military. "Noncoöperation" of course ignored the system entirely, Gandhi pronouncing any participation in the sinful British administration "contamination." The raj "saved face" by patronizing a very small constituency of Englishmen, Anglo-Indians, and Indian Liberals who were willing to profit by being the sole electorate and office-holding group.

In December, 1920, Gandhi was able to persuade the Indian National Congress, meeting at Nagpur, to incor

---

[3] I once asked the Mahatma in a light moment how this would apply to the situation in America. He replied: "If you conscientiously believe that deprivation of alcohol is destructive to individual, society and culture it would seem to me that you should disobey the prohibition law."

porate his nonviolent, noncoöperation policy in its very constitution. The Congress also constitutionally adopted representative election of delegates, with boycott and ostracism of native magistrates not living up to the program. Begun as an informal and unofficial body gathering somewhere in India in December of each year, the National Congress was now a state within a state, something like the Philippine National Independence Committee between 1922 and 1925.

The pot was boiling for a spill-over. Various agrarian uprisings took place. In February of 1921, the puritanical Akali Sikhs adopted Gandhi's method to gain control of Gurdwara Temple at Nakana Sahib. Two hundred unarmed resisters were voluntarily marched to a cruel death at the hands of Pathan temple guards, giving a thrill of martyrdom to the nation. The government, previously merely annoyed at what it believed would be a "five-minute enthusiasm" or a saint's vision, was at last thoroughly alarmed. In March it definitely declared the Congress and affiliated organizations to be seditious. Curiously enough this decisive step took place over the issue of government protection of wine shops. "It was not the first time for European civilization and alcohol to march hand in hand," remarks Romain Rolland. Thousands were arrested and penned, many were more brutally treated. Clashes with constables took place all over the land. Gandhi fasted and prayed and persuaded, to keep down the violence.

The next National Congress wanted to adopt the final step of mass civil disobedience. Gandhi prevented for the time. He launched a fervid unity campaign between the Parsis—who, he said, were "tainted with the spirit of Rockefeller"—Hindus, and Musselmans. Using the exultation of the crisis, he went further and asked Congress to declare that outcasts might enter schools and use public wells. Many supported him, including Brahmans, but others were offended.

Women came forward as the sex had never before done in India. Many distinguished women such as the poetess Sarojini Naidu underwent arrest and suffering for the cause. Gandhi declared yet more openly for liberation and equality.

His four sons, now grown, took active part in his movement, including the eldest, who, despite his father's disapproval, was in law. Two of his sons were imprisoned at hard labor for short terms. "How can you remain dry-eyed," asked the women who came to sympathize with Kasturbai when they were sentenced. "I have only two sons in prison," replied the graying woman who seemed to grow more straight and precise with the years. "I've no right to weep when thousands of India's sons are there."

By August, 1921, Gandhi, becoming more drastic, endorsed the burning of foreign manufactured goods in huge bonfires in the streets of Bombay. With religious enthusiasm the poor brought cotton and the rich, brocades and silks and cast them on the bonfire. It was a reflection of what had swept over China two years previously. Men like Rabindranath Tagore and C. F. Andrews protested. Tagore, who knew much of the West, saw no evil in European material standards of living, and Andrews suggested that the destroyed goods might have been given to the poor. Gandhi replied sturdily that it would be like offering jewels to a starving man, and that "it would be wrong to give these poisonous goods that were destroying India to the poor, for they, too, have their sense of honor." This was the true Oriental sense of personal dignity. Six hundred years before Christ, Confucius, moved by the same logic, said, "Many a man has starved of come-here-and-get-it food."

Tagore, India's second most famous citizen, had returned from protracted travels in Europe to be frightened by the mental domination of his old contemporary. He took an oblique view of Gandhi's movement which hitherto he had supported strongly. "We need all the moral force which Mahatma Gandhi represents and he alone in the world can represent. It is criminal to try to transfer moral force into physical force," he said. On his part Gandhi felt Tagore had been led into the fallacy of the West and had deliberately overlooked the spiritual basis upon which he was conducting his political and social relations.

The controversy between the poet, interested in the beauty or tragedy of the world as it is, and the social reformer, interested in a future state existing only in his mind, was inevitable. It has a most striking parallel in the controversy between Lenin and Gorky. Gandhi's answer to Tagore brought out the spirit of its author as strikingly as Lenin's retort to Gorky on his promontory in Italy that "it is a time for crushing of skulls." Said Gandhi:

I do not want my house to be walled in on all sides and my windows to be stuffed. I want the culture of all lands to be blown about my house as freely as possible. . . . But I refuse to be blown off my feet by any of them. . . . Mine is not a religion of the prison house. It has room for the least among God's creations. But it is proof against insolent pride of race, religion, or color.

We must not surrender our reason into anybody's keeping. Blind surrender to love is often more mischievous than forced surrender to the lash of the tyrant. There is hope for the slave of the brute, none for the slave of love.

When all about me are dying for want of food, the only occupation permissible for me is to feed the hungry. India is a house on fire. It is dying of hunger because it has no work to buy food with. Khulna is starving. The Ceded Districts are passing successively through a fourth famine. Orissa is a land suffering from chronic famine. India is growing daily poorer. The circulation about her feet and legs has almost stopped. And if we do not take care, she will collapse altogether. . . .

To a people famishing and idle the only acceptable form in which God can dare appear is work and promise of food as wages. God created man to work for his food and said that those who ate without work were thieves. We must think of the millions who to-day are less than animals, almost in a dying state. Hunger is the argument that is drawing India to the spinning wheel.

The poet lives for the morrow, and would have us do likewise. He presents to our admiring gaze the beautiful picture of the birds in the early morning singing hymns of praise as they soar into the sky. Those birds had their day's food and soared with rested wings in whose veins new blood had flowed the previous night. But I have had the pain of watching birds who for want of strength could not be coaxed even into a flutter of their wings. The human bird under the Indian sky gets up weaker than when he pretended to retire. For millions it is an eternal vigil or an eternal trance. I have found it impossible to soothe suffering patients with a song from Kabir. . . .

Give them work that they may eat! "Why should I who have no need to work for food, spin?" may be the question asked. Because I am eating what does not belong to me. I am living on the spoliation of my countrymen. Trace the course of every coin that finds its way into your pocket, and you will realize the truth of what I write. Every one must spin. Let Tagore spin, like the others. Let him burn his foreign clothes; that is the duty to-day. God will take care of the morrow. As it says in the *Gita,* Do right!

In May, 1921, twelve thousand coolies struck in the tea gardens of Assam. The government imported Ghurkhas, the primitive traditional enemies of the Hills, to take their place. Riots ensued and there was a rail-road strike in Bengal. Feeling, as always, that any violence would ruin his strategy, Gandhi conferred with the Viceroy, Lord Reading, on its prevention and also restrained the fiery and gifted Muhammadan leaders, the Ali brothers, from the extreme methods which they contemplated. Yet feeling was coming to its climax. Although he sensed that his people were not yet disciplined for it, Gandhi had to inaugurate his full program or let it drop in favor of violence. Like Kemal, he was compelled to take chances on undisciplined chiefs in a different type of warfare. In July the Caliphate Conference threatened to refuse military service and proclaim a republic if the British attitude toward the Turkish nationalists were not changed.

In an effort to veer public feeling, the British government decided the Prince of Wales should visit India. The patriots resolved upon noncoöperation in his reception and boycott of all British goods. In August a bloody outbreak of the fanatical Muslem Moplahs took place in Malabar against the Hindus. The British tried to pin the uprising on Gandhi. He immediately went to quiet it.

Gandhi showed the greatest sensitiveness at the slighting of the Muslem cause. When he heard the Ali brothers had been arrested, he called for noncoöperation as a spiritual duty, proclaiming that men should serve such a government neither as civil functionaries nor as soldiers. When the Alis were sentenced to two years' imprisonment, Gandhi called for mass civil disobedience and the All-India Congress ratified the move at Delhi on November 4. All registers were to take up spinning and the vow of nonviolence. They were then to refuse any longer to pay taxes. On November 17 the Prince of Wales landed at Bombay amid prayer and fasting proclaimed by the Mahatma. The populace were out with Gandhi, burning foreign cloth, but the rich members of the community, especially the Parsis, abandoned their *hartal* in the pursuit of social distinction and rushed to welcome the Prince. An enraged mob of twenty thousand lower-class members pillaged the homes of the wealthy "traitors," beating men, mistreating women, killing about fifty.

The "defection" wounded Gandhi "like an arrow in his heart." He rushed to the scene of violence, and was sick with humiliation when the naïve crowd cheered him, thinking he had come to lead them in their retribution for the sake of his country. Gandhi mounted a cart before the mob, fearlessly denounced it, and justified the Parsis. Immediately he suspended the order for mass civil disobedience and imposed a twenty-four-hour fast each week on himself as penance for the sins of his people.

However, the *hartal* worked silently well through the remainder of the country. On Christmas Eve of 1921 in Calcutta, the Prince of Wales passed through a city which might have been dead.

The National Congress met at Gandhi's city Ahmedabad and urged all Indians publicly to enroll as resisters and prepare for arrest against the prospect that delegates and committee would be incarcerated at any time. Gandhi was elected dictator with power to appoint a successor. "Violence if necessary" was with Gandhi's resistance voted down. The British responded by outlawing the Congress and the Caliphate organization and jailing twenty-five thousand men and women.

With Kemal or Lenin it would have been time to

risk everything on extreme action. Gandhi's word could have thrown the entire nation into active revolution. There was assurance that the native troops, especially the Sikhs, awaited his command to insurrect. He had the power of political dictator, saint, and to the humble people, God.

But he lacked the egotism of the fanatic and he would not appropriate God or claim visions. He was truer to the principles upon which he had started than to the opportunity. Then, too, he possessed what might be regarded as a sort of superhuman balance. "The British want us to put the struggle on the plane of machine guns," he said. "They have these weapons and we have not. Our only assurance of beating them is to keep it on the plane where we have the weapons and they have not."

So Gandhi issued his "declaration of war" to the Viceroy on that plane. The date of his open letter was February 9, 1922. It gave Lord Reading seven days to change the government's policy.

The letter had scarcely been delivered when an outrage took place at Chauri-Chaura in the district of Gorakror, which allowed the British to throw the stigma of "atrocity" back upon the Indians. Twenty-seven police who interfered with a nationalist procession were chased into their barracks and burned to death in them. They were not Gandhi's people, but as Rolland says, "He had really become the conscience of India." Immediately, in spite of what he called "Satan's forbidding," Gandhi retracted his ultimatum to the Viceroy and called off the campaign.

I know that the drastic reversal of practically the whole of the aggressive campaign may be politically unsound and unwise, but there is no doubt that it is religiously sound. The country will have gained by my humiliation and confession of error. The only virtue I want to claim is truth and nonviolence, for confession of error is like a broom which sweeps away dirt and leaves the surface cleaner and brighter. I feel stronger for my confession. Never has a man reached his destination by persistence in deviation from the straight path. Just as the addition of a grain of arsenic to a pot of milk renders it unfit as food, so will the servility of the rest prove unacceptable by the addition of the deadly poison from Chauri-Chaura . . . the bitterest humiliation was still to come. God spoke clearly through Chauri-Chaura. Nonviolent noncoöperators can only succeed when they succeed in attaining control over the hooligans of India.

I must undergo personal cleansing. I must become a fitter instrument able to register the slightest variation in the moral atmosphere about me. My prayers must have deeper truth and humility. For me there is nothing so cleansing as a fast. A fast undertaken for fuller self-expression, for attainment of the spirit's supremacy over the flesh, is a most powerful factor in one's evolution. . . .

He imposed upon himself a five-day fast as penance. In a further statement he said:

There is so much undercurrent of violence, both conscious and unconscious, that I was actually and literally praying for a disastrous defeat. I have always been in a minority. In South Africa I started with practical unanimity, reached a minority of sixty-four and even sixteen, and went up again to a huge majority. The best and the most solid work was done in the wilderness of minority. . . . I know that the only thing that the government dreads is this huge majority I seem to command. They little know that I dread it even more than they. I have become literally sick of the adoration of the unthinking multitude. I would feel certain of my ground if I was spat upon by them. A friend warned me against exploiting my "dictatorship." I have begun to wonder if I am not unconsciously allowing myself to be "exploited." I confess that I have a dread of it as I never had before. My only safety lies in my shamelessness. I have warned my friends of the committee that I am incorrigible. I shall continue to confess blunders each time the people commit them. The only tyrant I accept in this world is the "still small voice" within. And even though I have to face the prospect of a minority of one, I humbly believe I have the courage to be in such a hopeless minority. That to me is the only truthful position. But I am a sadder and, I hope, a wiser man to-day. I see that our nonviolence is skin-deep. We are burning with indignation. The government is feeding it by its insensate acts. It seems almost as if the government wants to see this land covered with murder, arson, and rapine in order to be able once more to claim exclusive ability to put them down.

For the first time, perhaps, talk like that of an old-fashioned "testimony meeting" was heard in high political discussions. Like Lenin, Gandhi had no fear of being in a minority, but in how different a spirit! He could not loose fury like Lenin. "We use violence to the end that violence may cease," said the founder of New Russia, but Gandhi stuck to the dictum of Christ: "They that take the sword shall perish with the sword."

These two drastically opposite viewpoints which have puzzled the intellects of mankind for centuries and lie behind all the argument over disarmament and perfect peace to-day, are being worked out for the eyes of this generation in two of the world's most populous nations on the largest scale in history. The patriots of India, who did not live on Gandhi's high spiritual plane, suffered intense disappointment. They did not repudiate him there nor at the next conference, but they did give him the feeling that they were looking elsewhere.

Gandhi had been under threat of arrest since 1920. All his affairs had been in order and he had printed instructions to his followers entitled "If I am Arrested." In this he told them that any violence of resentment would be to him a disgrace and a repudiation.

The Indian government, as the South African, had long debated the question of Gandhi's arrest. The Mahatma's influence had been needed to keep down violence, and it had not been considered wise to make a martyr. Now, taking advantage of his shadowed popularity and the general puzzlement, the advocate general of Bombay, Mr. Strangland, proceeded against him. Gandhi precipitated the government's move by strong reply to a telegram from the Birkenhead-Montague administration which to Indians was the acme of insult. In his paper he wrote:

How can there be any compromise whilst the British lion continues to shake his gory claws in our faces? The British Empire, which is based upon organized exploitation of physically weaker races and upon a continuous exhibition of brute force, cannot live if there is a just God ruling the universe.

. . . It is high time that the British people were made to realize that the fight that was commenced in 1920 is a fight to the finish, whether it lasts one month or one year or many months or many years. I shall only hope and pray that God will give India sufficient humility and sufficient strength to remain nonviolent to the end. Submission to the insolent challenges that are cabled is now an utter impossibility.

At the Sabarmati *ashram* he waited seizure. He even stated that he longed for imprisonment as a rest from his years of turmoil. And he wanted it as penance for the lapse of his people into violence. Squatting with his disciples on the sandbar in the Gujrati River, the Mahatma led his usual sundown worship, chanting to the two-toned strumming of the huge viol played by his giant musician, his departing hymn:

He is a real worshipper of Vishnu, who feels the suffering of others as his own suffering. He is ever ready to serve, and is never guilty of overweening pride. He bows before every one, despises none, preserves purity in thought, word, and deed. Blessed is the mother of such a son: in every woman he reveres his mother. He preserves equanimity and never stains his mouth with falsehood, nor touches the riches of another. The bonds of desire cannot hold him. Ever in harmony with reverent feeling for the sacred worship, his body in itself possesses all the places of pilgrimage. He knows neither desire nor disappointment, neither passion nor wrath. . . .

With his young editor, Banker, he was taken to the drab red-brick jail within sight of the ashram. Kasturbai and the disciples followed him to the gate, kissing his feet, but he spoke reassuringly to them and went behind the bars silently. "In the evenings the public assembled in large numbers at the Sabarmati Prison to do homage to their beloved leader; the masses stood before the prison as before a temple. When the bell rang to announce the hour of admission the sound was received with thrills of joy. Then the crowd of pilgrims approached their revered Mahatma; some threw themselves at his feet, others touched him with awe, others again showed their respect only by profound salaams. Mothers laid their infants in his arms and old women touched the ground before him to show their devotion." When he entered the court room of District Judge Broomfield of Ahmedabad, on March 18, 1922, the entire court stood in respect to the unusual prisoner. He plead guilty on every count and the judge wished to sentence him without the distress of further proceedings, but the pursuing, crude-speaking crown's advocate, Lloyd, insisted upon attack and rebuttal. In perfect equanimity, covered only by his loin cloth, Gandhi faced the bar and confessed considerably more than he was accused of. He took full responsibility for all the violence of his people and proceeded to an exposé of the amazing policy of perfidy which had turned him from staunch loyalist into an implacable enemy of British rule. He then told the judge he must either resign, dissociating himself from a law that was evil, or, upholding that law, pronounce a maximum penalty. The judge commented on the prisoner's "noble and

even saintly life." He asked Gandhi to name his own
punishment, suggesting that his forerunner Tilak's sentence had been six years. Gandhi expressed delight
that he might suffer the same penalty. "I cannot
refrain from saying," remarked the judge, "that you
belong to a different category from any person I have
ever tried or am likely to have to try."

Young Banker made the same humble yet accusing
confession as his master. The prosecutor declared that
the Mahatma must be buried alive in prison and no one
allowed access to him, or his cell would soon become a
Mecca for the whole world.

Gandhi and Banker were sent off to Yerawada prison
of none too savory reputation. Gandhi's letters from
prison revealed the art of living to which he had attained, both physically and spiritually. He wrote C. F.
Andrews:

My Dear Charley:
I would not expect to see you in jail—to be allowed a
visitor is a privilege and a civil resister (who has severed rela-
tions with authority) may neither seek nor receive a privilege.
With love,
Mohan.

On April 14, 1922, he writes an Indian friend:

Prisoners are allowed to have a visit once a quarter and
to write and receive one letter. This one I am going to write
to you. Banker and I were brought to the prison (Sabarmati)
on the 18th of March. Monday we were informed we were
to be moved to an unknown destination. The police escorted

us to a special train. The deputy police superintendent was instructed that I have goat's milk and Banker cow's milk on the journey. [The Hindu's religious scruples in eating were respected in Gandhi's case but not in that of his disciple, which caused the Mahatma more distress than if the discourtesy had been done to himself.] From Khirki a police van brought us to the prison. I had previously said to Banker that I would refuse food if they tried to forbid me to spin, for I had taken a vow to spin at least half an hour a day. I told him he was not to get excited if I had to adopt a hunger strike, and he was not to follow my example out of a mistaken feeling of solidarity. The director announced that as we entered the prison we must leave our spinning wheel and basket of fruit. At Sabarmati we had been allowed to sleep in the open air but here we could not hope for this favor either. Our first impression was thus rather unfavorable. I did not let this trouble me and moreover the fact that I had practically fasted for the last two days prevented me from being affected. Banker felt everything so much more. He is afflicted with nightmares and so does not like to be alone at night, besides this was the first painful experience of his life, whereas I was accustomed to the cage. Next morning the director appeared to ask how we were. I saw that my judgment of him, formed on first impression, had been a mistake, in any case he had been in a flurry on the night before. He gave the order that we were both to be allowed to have our spinning wheels again, also he no longer held out against the special food we asked.

The first days are of no account; relations are as cordial as possible between the prisoner and his warders. I see quite clearly however, that our prison system is almost devoid of humanity. The prison committee consists of the administrator, a clergyman and some others. I pointed out to them that Banker suffered from nervousness and for that reason should sleep in my cell. I cannot conceal the contempt and unfeeling indifference with which this request was treated.

What do they know of Banker and his position in life and the education he has enjoyed? An hour after this conversation a warder informed that Banker was to be transferred to another section. I felt like a mother who has been robbed of her only child; I had read to him from the *Gita* and he had looked after my feeble body. Banker had lost his mother only a few months before. She said that death would not be hard for her now that she knew her son was under my protection. The noble woman did not know how powerless I was to prove. Since then he has received permission to come to me for half an hour every day to teach me carding in the presence of the warder who has to see that we speak of matters only necessary to our occupation. I had to use all my ingenuity to get the privilege to keep seven books: five purely religious, an old dictionary, and an Urdu language manual. The use of a pocket knife presents another problem. I gave the superintendent the privilege of depriving me of bread and lemons or letting me have the knife to cut them with. After a great deal of fuss my own pen-knife was placed in the keeping of the warder and only handed to me when actually needed. A convict warder who was sentenced for murder has to watch me during the day, at night he is given an assistant. Both are very harmless fellows, they do not molest me in any way. One of my fellow prisoners in the same section is, I surmise, an Arabic state prisoner. A triangular space within the central block was formally divided by a chalk line I was forbidden to cross; thus I had a space of about seventy feet long for my exercise. When an inspection official was here recently, I drew his attention to this white line as a proof of the lack of human feeling in the orders of the prison administration, with the result that the whole triangle was made free to me.

I am in solitary confinement and may not speak to any one. Some of the great reformers are in the same jail with me. I do not see any of them, though I do not see how my society could do them any harm; they again could not harm me. Should we conspire for escape we should only be doing the government the greatest favor. If it is a question of protecting them from infection of my dangerous ideas, the isolation has come too late. They are already thoroughly infected. There is only one more thing I could do, make them still more enthusiastic about the spinning wheel. What I said about my isolation is not intended as a complaint. I feel happy, my nature likes loneliness, I love quietness, and now I have an opportunity of engaging in studies that I had to neglect in the outside world, but not all the prisoners enjoy solitary confinement. It is as inhuman as it is unnecessary. The director merely does his best to be just to their bodies and neglects their souls, hence it comes that prisons are abused for political end and therefore the political prison is not free from persecution, even within their walls.

I end with a description of the course of my day. My cell is, in itself decent, clean and airy. The permission to sleep in the open air is a great blessing to me who am accustomed to sleeping in the open. I rise at four o'clock to pray. I am not allowed a light, but as soon as it is light enough for reading I start work. At seven o'clock in the evening when it is too dark to read, I finish my day's work. At eight o'clock I betake myself to rest after the usual ashram prayer. My studies include the Koran [he was trying hard to find contact with the better side of Muhammadanism], the Ramayama, books about Christianity, exercises in the Urdu language, and much else. I spend six hours in these literary efforts, four hours I devote to hand spinning. To begin with I had only a little cotton at my disposal, but now the administration has given me sufficient—very dirty to be sure—perhaps very good practice for a beginner in carding. Please say to Moulana Abdul that I count on his keeping pace with me in progress in spinning. His good example will cause many to make a duty of this important work. You may tell the people at the ashram that I have written the promised primer and will send it to them if I am allowed. I hope it will be possible for me to write the contemplated religious primer and also the history of our fight in South Africa.

In order to divide the day better I take only two meals instead of three. For the last three days, the superintendent has let me have goat's milk and butter. Besides two new warm blankets, a cocoa mat and two sheets have been given me, and a pillow has also arrived since. I could really do without it. Up till now I have used my books or my spare clothes as a pillow. There is also a bathroom with a lock available which I am allowed to use every day. The sanitary arrangements have been improved.

So my friends may not be at all anxious about me. I am happy as a bird, and I do not feel that I am accomplishing less here than outside the prison. My stay here is a good school for me and my separation from my fellow workers should prove whether our movement is an evolving organism or merely the work of one individual and therefore transient. I myself have no fears. I am not eager to know what is happening outside. If my prayers are sincere and come from a faithful heart, they are more useful—of this I am certain— than any fussy activity. I am very anxious on the other hand about the health of our friend Das and have good reason to reproach his wife for not informing me how he was. I hope that Motilalaji's asthma is better.

Please try to convince my wife that it is better for her not to try to visit me. Devandas made a scene when he was here. The proud and sensitive boy burst into tears to see me standing in the superintendent's presence, and I had difficulty in calming him. He should have realized that I am a prisoner and as such have no right to sit in the superintendent's presence. Of course, Rajagopalchar and Devandas should have been offered seats. I do not think the superintendent is accustomed to be present at meetings of this kind (he must be forgiven for not knowing the rules of courtesy), but I should not like the scene to be repeated on a visit from my wife, and even less that an exception should be made

for me, and chairs offered. I can keep my dignity even standing, and we must have patience for a little until the English
people have advanced enough to extend on every occasion and
universally their lovable politeness with unforced cordiality
to us Indians. [This incident reveals the heart of Asiatic-
Western mutual scorn.] I hope that Chotani Nian has dis-
tributed the spinning wheels he has given among the poor
Muhammadan women.

With loving greetings to all fellow workers.

Describing this prison life later, he said, "I used to
sit down to my books with the delight of a young man
of twenty-four and forget my four and fifty years and
my poor health."

Gandhi was soon busy at his old occupation of fighting inequality by personal suffering, even in prison.
On May 1, 1923, he writes the governor of the prison:

You were good enough to show me the order to the effect
that certain prisoners will be assigned to a special section,
and inform that I was one of the number. Some of the prisoners condemned to hard labor as Messers K., J., and B. are
not worse criminals than I, besides they had probably a much
higher position than I, and in any case they were accustomed
to a more comfortable life than I have led for years. So
long as such prisoners are not also assigned to a special group
it is impossible for me, however much I might like it, to
avail myself of special prison orders. I would therefore be
very grateful if you would strike my name off the list of the
special section.

Yours obediently,

By November of that year a new governor had taken
charge and confinement was darker for the saint. He
writes:

At the time that you informed my comrade, Mr. Abdul Gani, that the prison rules did not allow you to grant him food which cost more than the official ration, I drew your attention to the fact that your predecessor permitted all my comrades as well as myself to arrange our own diet. I further informed you that it was very unpleasant for me to enjoy a favor denied to Mr. Abdul Gani, and that for this reason my diet must also be restricted to what is in accordance with the rules and what is allowed to Mr. Abdul Gani. You were good enough to ask me to accept the old rations for the time being, and to say that the whole question would be discussed with the general inspector, who was shortly to visit the prison. I have now waited ten days. If I am to keep a good conscience I cannot wait any longer, for I have nothing at all to discuss with the general inspector. I have no reason to complain to him of the decision you took in the case of Abdul Gani. I willingly recognize that you are powerless, even if you were inclined to help my comrade. Nor is it my aim to work for a change in the food regulations of the prison. I desire one thing only, to protect myself against any preferential treatment. . . .

I therefore ask you from next Wednesday to give me no more oranges and grapes. In spite of this my food will still be more expensive than the official ration. I do not know if I need four pounds of goat's milk, but so long as you refuse to reduce my food so that its cost is in accordance with the rules, I must, although reluctantly, accept the four pounds of milk.

I do not need to assure you that there is no question of dissension. . . . It is only for the sake of my own inner peace that I propose that you should restrict my diet, and I beg for your understanding and approval.

Yours obediently,

M. K. GANDHI, No. 827.

But Gandhi's six-year program of self-improvement

was interrupted by an illness to the death, which the
prison physician diagnosed as appendicitis. He was
asked to submit himself to an operation to save his life.
The British wondered if they would have trouble with
him in view of his writings, following the Tolstoyan
view, that

Medical science is the concentrated efforts of black magic.
Quackery is infinitely preferable to what passes for high
medical skill. We labor under the delusion that no disease
can be cured without medicine; this has been responsible for
more mischief to mankind than any other evil. For a diseased
man to take drugs and medicines would be as foolish as to
cover up the filth that has accumulated on the inside of a
house. Hospitals are institutions for the propagation of sin.
They seduce many to pay less attention to the warnings of
their body and to give themselves more and more to a life of
vice. I would urge students and professors to investigate the
laws governing the health of the spirit and they will find that
they will reveal startling results with reference to the cure
of the body. The man who lives in the proper spirit need never
get ill, but because modern medical science entirely ignores
this permanent spiritual element its activities are too restricted
to achieve real and permanent success.

The Indian community watched Gandhi in this crisis
and his followers looked to their Mahatma Guru to
escape contradiction of himself. He did so by saying,
"In prison I must accept the prison régime. It involves
medical supervision which now prescribes surgery; I
submit." Later when attacked by casuists who asked,
"Why did you go to the hospital?" he replied, more

simply, "Because I wanted to live." Some have made much of this, but Gandhi never claimed consistency. Rather he claimed honesty and ability to learn and change with experience. One who has perused the "ads" in any Indian newspaper and has gotten a glimpse into the growth of quackery there under the guise of Western medical science can understand the Mahatma's position on medicine and his feeling that it was important enough to demand the production of his volume titled, reminiscent of Mary Baker Eddy, *Guide to Health.* A large proportion of this quackery is concerned with aphrodisiacs, and nostrums for escape and cure from venereal infection: hence Gandhi's feeling that hospitals have encouraged sin. Be it said to his credit that since his own experience at the hands of British surgeons, he has been less condemnatory of medical science and has turned to it for aid in his recent paralytic strokes.

The doctors said he would die if compelled to remain in the prison. Consternation spread throughout the country. Hindus sent consecrated ashes and holy water from the Ganges. Muhammadans prayed to Allah for him, and Brahmans held intercessory services in their temples. Dark threats were heard among the lower classes. Both Indian leadership and British policy had "gone moderate" since the Mahatma's incarceration. There was no need to set India afire again by permitting the death in a British jail of its human god. On the recommendation of the judge who had sentenced him,

Gandhi was released on February 5, 1924, having served a few weeks less than two years.

A great impromptu feast of rejoicing was celebrated the length and breadth of the country. The news was announced with music and processions and mass gatherings in temples and mosques. Members of age-hostile religions, castes, and races crowded through streets and bazaars arm in arm shouting that Gandhi had come from God to destroy evil. Work and trade stopped in many places—even modern factories had to close down. The rich and, in many cases, sovereign princes and municipal government gave great feasts for the pariahs, distributing food, money, and clothing.

Meanwhile the subject of all this rejoicing was being assisted to his ashram incognito, announcing that he would remain in retirement. He waited for the young political chiefs to come to him. Chit Rangan Das and Motilal Nehru had turned Swaraj from a national movement into a political party. Under pressure of Muslims, whose more active nature chafed at complete noncoöperation, these Hindu leaders had veered patriotic sentiment to the idea of utilizing the new representative system to embarrass the government. From absolute nonparticipation in the elections, they changed strategy to election of a majority of the legislators, who would then noncoöperate from within—which they called "wrecking." It was carrying noncoöperation within the government's own lines, but it substituted active obstructionism for dignified aloofness and involved abandonment of the religious principle that the whole government, including its new representative machinery, was unholy. The young leaders had hoped that they would have the Mahatma with them. Muhammad Ali had gone so far as to assure them in a special conference that he had a telepathic message from Gandhi in prison authorizing the move.

In Bengal, a Swarajist victory at the election made Das majority leader in the legislature. By refusing ratification of all ministerial appointments and voting down all budgets, the Swarajists completely nullified the dyarchy plan both in Bengal and in central provinces, and the British responded by suspending home rule in these provinces. Nehru became the Swaraj whip in the National Assembly at Delhi where he united various sympathetic elements into what was termed the Nationalist Party, which, by stormy parliamentary tactics, monotonously demanded full responsible government.

The young leaders' first conferences with Gandhi confirmed a lurking suspicion that Muhammad Ali's message had been considerably garbled in transmission. The rock-founded old saint, always as unmoved by opinions of his followers as by those of his enemies, roundly condemned their abandonment of principle and the tinge of chicanery involved in "wrecking." He granted their privilege to pursue their strategy but demanded they separate themselves from the Congress. The matter came to issue at the Congress control com-

mittee meeting at Gandhi's city in June, 1924. Discussion showed that Swarajist participation in the elective system had gone too far for a return to the original
noncoöperation, and after a threat to separate himself
entirely from the Swarajist Party and form another
Congress, Gandhi compromised on making the program
of the Congress preëminently social-economic. Men of
activity primarily political were virtually barred from
membership by a new qualification requiring the spinning of two thousand yards of yarn a month by each
member.

There was to be staunch support of Hindu-Muhammadan unity, equal rights for pariahs, and development
of home industry symbolized by the spinning wheel. In
the following month Gandhi made his first public appeal
since imprisonment in the founding of the All-Indian
Spinners Association. Surely, thought the world, the
Mahatma would have abandoned his most visionary
enterprises such as the cult of the spinning wheel. But
practicality meant to him this, rather than "practical
politics." The *charka,* spinning wheel, was put on the
National Congress flag. By 1928 Gandhi was to be able
to preside over an exhibition of *khadi* (hand-woven
cloth) at Madras, ranging from floor coverings to em-
broidery. His spinners' association was to employ 750
educated young men in its organization and operate
166 production depots and 245 sales depots taking in
a million and a quarter dollars a year without reckoning the dyeing, printing, and charka-making industries,

contributing to the income of eighty thousand homes. Meanwhile Mrs. Annie Besant's National Home Rule League drafted a Commonwealth of India bill formulating a modified dominion status for India.

Swaraj participation in elections inevitably progressed to participation in administration. Motilal Nehru accepted a seat on a government commission to plan an officers' training school in India, and survived the storm of criticism. (Swarajists, opposed to violence on principle, nevertheless have steadily worked for an Indian "Sandhurst" as a means of "Indianizing" the army in India.) National Congress supported a bill for the protection of the native steel industry. But always, the reactionary British civil service was willing to spoil budding confidence and coöperation by an attempt to reintroduce the noxious suppression of civil rights which reminded of the Rowlatt Acts. Some degree of justification always existed in the influence from Russia, seen in the activities of a small but sinister group, chiefly young Bengalis, who advocated violent revolution. In October, 1924, the Viceroy Lord Reading promulgated a summary ordinance for Bengal. Popular resentment forced the Mahatma to admit greater stress upon political activity—seen in the modified ruling that the monthly two thousand yards of yarn could henceforth be bought and donated if Congress members lacked time to turn them out with their own hands. The Mahatma himself, however, the busiest man in India, never failed to turn in his stint. "Do you always spin

during interviews?" the writer once asked. "Yes," was
the reply, kindly and yet not without a "bite"—"thus I
can always feel that my time is not wasted regardless
of to whom I must talk. Besides, with my hands
engaged so actively, is there not less temptation to use
them on some vexing questioner?" In his whimsy was
indicated the deep relation between manual industry
and nonviolence in his philosophy of Swaraj.

Gandhi, Das, and Nehru issued a joint declaration
against the resumption of tyrannical methods by the
government, and the nationalist political aggregation in
the Indian assembly was recognized as the All-India
Congress delegation "at court." At the following Congress meeting at Belgaum (December, 1924), Gandhi
presided—his first great public appearance since 1922.
Before the next Congress, the vigorous, incisive Das had
suddenly died. He has been sorely missed. The following Congress, the first one presided over by a woman
—Sarojini Naidu, the fiery poetess—saw a fight between
orthodox noncoöperators and Nehru over office holding.
Gandhi remained aloof from this controversy. His
attitude was well known, but he busied himself with
the fundamentals, tolerantly leaving their application
to the politicos. And he was gathering strength for the
test year—the year of 1929 whose shadow was falling
over the land.

In that year the ten-year trial arrangement of the
dyarchy would be at an end. The English Parliament
would have to consider its workings and draft a system

to succeed it. The civil service, backed by the conservative government in power in England, demanded an end of this compromising with native truculence—a return to the dignity of unquestioned British dominance. India demanded the establishment of some régime which would grant the dignity of complete independence to home rule. Russia's encouragement of every element movement that embarrassed the British provided inspiration to native agitators, warning to British liberals, argument for yet sterner attitude to British tories. The radicalism and ruthlessness of the nationalist movement in China had weakened the confidence of British labor in its attitude of sympathy for colored races. It was a dark shadow, and the British raj was stalling for time rather than taking steps to make it less ominous. Spender remarked, "The whole method which keeps the date '1929' hanging over India and makes it a fore-ordained year of crisis and agitation is bad, and the proper way out of it is to get the Indians themselves to work on the problems which must be solved before there can be any considerable further advance toward responsible government."

It was popular among the British and Anglicized community to say that "old man Gandhi was a remarkable fellow, but that he was a dead dog politically." Or, that "he was finished physically and had gone home to die." Since these elements control all the news services, "Gandhi's finished, isn't he?" became the phrase with which the matter was dismissed in the conversation of the worldly wise of Europe and America. The wish was father of the thought and some Englishmen were frank enough to confess it. The journalist, J. A. Spender, describing an interview in 1925 says, "Garbed in a spreading loin cloth, he came in with a light step, almost running, a lithe and animated figure radiating cheerfulness and benevolence and sat crosslegged on the ground behind a low desk covered with books and pamphlets. The scene was the strangest mixture of the real and the impossible. Shutting one's eyes one could suppose one's self listening to a highly polished English politician; opening them one saw an Indian Guru nearly naked, surrounded by his disciples who plainly regarded every work that fell from him as inspired." Spender says his mind went back to a famous cartoon of the year 1896 picturing Mr. Gladstone holding a pen in his mouth, writing with another one, his eyes burning, every hair on his head on end, his desk strewn with papers, notes for speeches, advice to leaders, etc., while underneath was the caption "Politically dead." "There were cynics in England," says Spender, "who challenged Mr. Gladstone's sainthood; but no Indians who challenged the sainthood or political headship of Mahatma Gandhi." Spender tested the Mahatma's relationship to the younger men who had taken active headship of the party by questioning their recent policies. He found no opening for a knife edge. Had they made mistakes? Possibly, but politics were built up of mistakes. The *pandit* Motilal

Nehru, like his predecessor Das, was a very devoted and self-sacrificing man. He had given up great wealth, abandoned his motor cars, let his beautiful garden run to seed from pure zeal in the cause of India. The actions of such a man had value which placed them above ordinary criticism. If possibly he were wrong, he had earned the right of making his own mistakes. It is easy to see the Mahatma's hold even upon leaders whom he frankly opposes at principle's demand.

A vital threat to both his political program and more fundamental spiritual movement faced the aging leader in the cooling zeal of the Muslem community and the general breakdown of Hindu-Muhammadan unity. It had begun with the fiasco of the Caliphate cause due to the suppression of the Sultan-Caliph, not by Great Britain and the Western Powers, but by the Turks themselves. When the delegation of the Indian Caliphate Conference was refused permission to enter Turkey by Mustapha Kemal, Indian Musselmans not only found themselves out of face before the world, but suddenly without the special motive which had driven them into the Mahatma's nationalist fold. The defection from the faith in western Asia but made them the more sectarian. The application of representative government aroused in them deep fears for their safety as a minority of seventy million among two hundred and fifty million Hindus of various sects, which were stimulated by precautions on their behalf in the British gov-

ernmental scheme. C. R. Das had first struggled with
the difficulty of providing them extra-proportional
representation in Bengal. In a majority only in the
North, physically the more virile but behind the Hindus
in education and wealth, they saw representative government militating against them. In spite of Gandhi's
work, community interest ranked with them above
national interests. They began to be distinctly afraid
of Swaraj. The older Muslem Conference replaced the
defunct Caliphate Conference as community voice, and
drafted more and more exaggerated guarantees as the
price of adherence to the cause. Muslem participation
in the All-India Congresses grew more and more per-
functory.

There was a revival of the sectarian spirit on the
other side as well. A militant Hindu organization, the
Maha Subha, was organized to reconvert those popula-
tions forcibly inducted into Islam but not yet converted
at heart. It aroused a rival in the Muslem missionary
Tanzim movement. Such activities among priests and
scholars were immediately reflected in outrages by
ignorant votaries. The first was the Moplah outbreak
in which the aggressive tribe near Bombay fanatically
attacked their fellow residents. Bloody clashes occurred
in widely separated parts of India, usually over playing of Hindu processional music near mosques, slaying
of sacred cows by Musselmans, or recrudescence of the
rumor that Muslem Pathans (Afghans) were stealing
Hindu boys for sacrifice. The British said that Gandhi's

doctrine of putting a spiritual allegiance above that of obedience to the state was responsible for the outbreak of religious strife. In India "God and conscience," said they, "may be above Cæsar, but in India Cæsar is one while God is worshiped in many forms whose adherents dwell in mutual tolerance only through Cæsar's constraint." The Swarajists, including indeed many Muslems, maintained that the British secretly encouraged dissension. The exodus of the entire Hindu population from the town of Kohat following rumors of an impending *jehad* drove Gandhi to public action. He did not blame the British. "I blame no one," he wrote. "I blame myself alone. I have lost the power to make myself audible to the people; beaten and helpless I turn to God, who alone can hear me." He went to the Delhi home of his old Muhammadan friend Ali, and on September 18, 1924, publicly began a fast to bring the communities to spiritual unity. By the twenty-sixth, leaders of all sects of both religions had rushed to the Ali home and constituting themselves into religious conference, issued the following proclamation:

The leaders here present are profoundly moved . . . we impower the president personally to communicate with Mahatma Gandhi the solemn resolution of all those taking part to preserve peace and to announce to him our unanimous desire that he should break his fast immediately so that he may be present at the meeting and favor it with his coöperation, his advice, and his leadership. He himself shall select the means to be used to check the spread of the existing evil as rapidly and effectively as possible.

The result was a compact attacking the problem in such practical ways as specific agreements on cow-killing, music, calls to prayer, etc. Spender remarked: "Supposing it were announced in the newspapers that Mr. Baldwin had declined his food when the miners had threatened to go on strike, or Lord Birkenhead was making trouble in the cabinet—we should have the nearest parallel I can think of. . . . Gandhi's explanation of the spiritual effect was given in a purely matter of fact way as if the sequence of cause and effect were self-evident." Indians of course believe in the mystical effect of the vicarious penance of a *guru,* and they were cut to their hearts that they had endangered, through his self-martyrdom on behalf of their souls, the precious life of the Mahatma. Gandhi goes at fasting in a scientific way, as he does at turning the other cheek. His instructions to disciples on the hygienic precautions to be taken when fasting might come from Bernarr Macfadden. Nevertheless, several of his recent illnesses have been the effects of his fasts for the purification of his people. Fasting as practical politics sounds fantastic to the border of lunacy to Western ears. When I point out that it accomplished more than the police force of all India, Westerners will say, pursing their lips, "clever after all." Truth is, it is no more clever than the Cross of Christ. To Gandhi it is obvious, sure, honest. Mysticism is not mystical to the mystic. But then the world produces thousands of Baldwins and only a few Gandhis.

The South African situation had grown tense again. A Color Bar bill, designed to bring back the discriminations against which Gandhi had been promised would forever be dropped, was passed by the lower legislative house. General Smuts denounced it in words which might have come from his old opponent, the Mahatma himself, and which might well be the gospel for the dominant race at all its points of contact with other races in this age: "There is only one guarantee for the security of white civilization in South Africa: honest justice between man and man." Fortunately the bill was defeated in the Senate. In December of the next year another settlement was made between the Indian government and Premier Hertzog, which in sum provided that Indians in South Africa were either to conform to the Western standard of living or receive assistance to return to India. Gandhi called it "an honorable compromise."

It was a spiritual victory dependent on the awakened sense of justice of the ruling group. A greater victory of this same kind Gandhi first believed could be won in India, but experience has taught him that he had to rely upon force—*soul*-force—rather than appeal to conscience. An American missionary, Mr. Enoch, asked him why he was not more ready to enter a round table between Lord Reading and Indian leaders. The Mahatma's reply was one of the most significant statements that has come out of New Asia and one which is the key to many developments as far east-

ward as China and Japan and as far westward as Egypt
(and possibly the United States): "For twenty years
I worked on the presumption that white men would
deal fairly with colored people if the cause were presented to them properly, but I have come to the opposite
conclusion—that it is not in the nature of white men
to deal fairly with colored races, and that they would
never be satisfied to do so, and that here was a condition which nothing that could be done around a round
table could change."

Lord Reading was replaced by Lord Irwin, whose
first inaugural pronouncement was an appeal to end religious rioting—broken out afresh in spite of both the
prestige of the Mahatma and the strong arm of the
British police. Considerable advance was made by the
government in strengthening itself, through the unofficial and gorgeous chamber of princes at Delhi, with
the native princes who still hold semi-sovereignty over
one-third the area of India.

In the highly exciting Fall elections of 1926, the
Swaraj Party, while losing rather seriously in the Punjab
and United Provinces, swept the boards in Madras. It
came out with one-third of the membership in the Delhi
National Assembly—very good in that to a considerable degree the membership there is "protected" rather
than proportional. The Swaraj Party began to call
itself the Congress Party—indicative possibly of a nar-
rowing of Congress influence as well as Swaraj assurance. In any case certain confident British statements

that the Swarajists were "done for" were completely falsified. "This is my endorsement by my people," said Mr. Gandhi to the writer, who was at his ashram as the returns came in. "I will lead them forward now, if necessary, to the use of the ultimate weapon: mass civil disobedience."

Gandhi, in his fifty-eighth year, went out, and his lecture tour was abruptly ended by a stroke he suffered in a railroad train between Bombay and home. "Finished *now*," said the worldly wise. But the Mahatma's faithful disciples took him back to the ashram, where he got in touch with his spiritual source of healing. He attended the National Congress at Madras, in evident vigor and radiant cheerfulness. "Do you honestly believe that India would be happier if Britain got out altogether?" the *Times* of Ceylon asked him. "Yes," he replied, "I believe it is the only solution of India's problems—and not only the problems of India, but also those of Africa. There is no halfway house to that solution. It would be better, I admit, if the British remained as friends at the mercy of India—and did penance for their misdeeds—and they would have to be at the mercy of India if they remained without the bayonet which keeps them here now. I admit, too, that there would be strife if they went, internecine trouble, probably much innocent blood would be shed, but India ultimately would find herself."

"Why not reach your goal by coöperation?" they suggested.

"I am strongly against coöperation with any force that is evil. I realize that the individual, or the particular administration, is not to blame. I should not care whether the administration were British or, from viceroy to doorkeeper, Indians, if they represented a system which is evil."

"Is your National Congress so holy?" he was asked.

"Congress is not entirely good, but it does a certain amount of good and that is why I support it."

Attracted to a wider-than-Indian view by the progress of the nationalist movement, Congress in this session took its first cognizance of its relation to the general movement of the "snubbed" throughout larger Asia. "The time has perhaps come," said Chairman Srinivasa Aiyander, "for us seriously to think of a federation of the Asiatic peoples for their common welfare." Aiyander followed this up by a motion immediately upon the opening of the Delhi Assembly, questioning the government over the dispatch of Indian troops to China. The government disallowed the motion on the ground that it would embarrass conduct of foreign relations. Gandhi wrote about this time, "My mind goes to China. I wish I could help. Young China opposes any movement, action, or person interfering with Chinese self-expression. Chinese, even Christians, have begun to distrust the Christian endeavor that has come from the West into their midst." The Mahatma longed to preach victory over the domination of the West through nonviolence in China and greatly deplored the tendency to fight the West "with its own weapons" in that land. "In casting off Western tyranny it is quite possible for such a nation to become enslaved to Western thought and methods," he said. "This second slavery is worse than the first." For a time he thought of going to China at the invitation of Chinese student organizations. It was as well perhaps that the rising tides of events in India prevented, for he would have suffered heartbreak worse than that suffered by Tagore at the pragmatic mentality of new China.

Although the Congress renewed the policy of non-coöperation in office, sufficient participation came to permit the restoration of the dyarchy representative government in Bengal and central provinces. This was largely done through Muhammadan feeling. Gandhi fasted, prayed, and worked, but the strife between the two great communities had continued. The year ending April, 1927, showed forty riots and 197 persons killed. The collapse of the Afghan dictator Amanullah Khan, whom Hindu Muhammadans had come to look to in spite of his imitation of Mustapha Kemal as the one remaining hero in Islam, threw them into indecision and unrest, and whisperings of perfidy became Gandhi's greatest worry. Contemporaneously with the December, 1928, Congress at Calcutta, the Indian Muslem League had met at Delhi ostensibly to formulate a policy for dominion government in which Musselmans and Hindus could meet. They ended by declaring for enjoyment of Muslem majority position in the provinces where they outnumber Hindus, representation in excess of their proportion where they are a minority, thirty-three representatives in the Delhi Assembly, and a selfish share of administrative jobs. At the same time, however, Musselmans loyal to the Mahatma conducted a rival Muslem league at Calcutta, which supported the Congress. Belatedly taking action, Parliament in the Fall of 1927 had authorized a commission under Sir John Symon to proceed to India, investigate and report on the working of the dyarchy, and draft a plan to succeed it. All elements in India went into a passion of resentment when not a single Indian was appointed to the commission. The liberal Swarajists and more radical groups refused all coöperation with it in supplying information or opinion. *Hartals,* or prayerful boycotts, took place in Indian cities coincidently with the visits of the commission, and an attempt was made on the life of Sir John himself. The British explanation of failure to include a single Indian in a body to draft a plan for the government of India was explained with the arguments that this was a commission representing the British Parliament and to gather information from the government viewpoint, and that its findings after completion would be submitted to Indian as well as other opinion. Also that should the government appoint any Indian of either religion or any faction, all other groups would be outraged, and that to include a representative of each group would make a parliament or a mob—not a committee. Indian sentiment considered the first excuse lame, and the second further insult. The commission returned to England in February and sallied forth once again in November, 1928. This time it procured the assistance of a native committee constituted by the central Assembly at Delhi after a fight in which the Swarajists narrowly lost. It gave promise of making a report by November, 1929, in the face of the necessity of drafting a new government before the New Year! By this time the various factions had ceased to look to the commission's report for any fundamental change or real contribution toward solution, but had come to regard it, with apprehension or exultation as the case might be, as a date-setter for momentous events.

The Calcutta Congress had drawn up a "dominion status constitution" and adopted two resolutions inspired by Mahatma Gandhi. The first represents his compromise with the more radical younger element: that if complete home rule on dominion status were not granted by December 31, 1929, the Mahatma would lead India in a revolution of full noncoöperation and mass civil disobedience directed to complete independence. The second resolution embraced acceptance of his moral (or social) program for the year of waiting, which the leader who relied so strongly on spiritual force considers an absolute prerequisite for his "spiritual" revolution. Total abstinence from intoxicants and removal of caste untouchability are its two main planks. The venerable but still forceful Dr. Annie Besant, who

had merged her "constitution," which had gained a
reading on the floor of Parliament, in the Congress
constitutional scheme, wanted an active political campaign outlined by the younger Motilal Nehru, and expressed her disappointment by a somewhat disturbing
personal attack on Gandhi. He replied that, "It is by
applying ourselves to necessary reforms in the social
sphere that we acquire the power and momentum to
carry through a great political movement." The editor
of the Swaraj *Indian Social Reformer,* whose weekly
appears under the motto of William Lloyd Garrison,
"I will be as harsh as truth and as uncompromising
as justice; I will not excuse, I will not retreat a single
inch—and I will be heard," remarks:

> We are glad to find first place allotted to total abstinence
> against the organized material resources of political power of
> Western materialism. India can oppose to them nothing but
> the justice of her cause and the unalcoholized brains and
> muscles of her people. If the innate repugnance to drink of
> the Indian people breaks down, as it has been doing, it will
> not be long before the Hindus and Muhammadans of India
> go the way of the Maoris, the Red Indians and the Hotten-
> tots. The removal of untouchability is equally urgent in
> order to rally the full forces of Indian nationalism in the
> cause of freedom.

The Mahatma showed his usual critical freedom and
insistence on simplicity and sincerity by questioning
the reality of an independence demonstration to welcome the Congress staged by volunteers in European-
style uniforms. In his mouthpiece *Young India,* he

wrote: "If I had my way I should separate the deliberate portion from the demonstrative and spectacular. I should exclude visitors from the deliberative section, at least by a strong and elegant fence, holding meetings in the early morning hours and evenings under the open heaven." Younger men found fault with his stress upon asceticism and poverty, which they said was apt to foster a morbid pessimism which would lessen activity, and they begged him not to come to appear to his people as "the gloomy sage of Sabarmati."

The Indian ruling princes, meeting in their chamber in Delhi, indicated fear of what the crisis might mean to them by resolving that no proposals would receive their assent which did not "proceed upon the initial basis of British connection." These protected potentates, who rule one-fifth of India's people and one-third of her territory, are regarded variously by the patriots according to whether they have democratic and social tendencies, but likelihood of their survival with the British gone is hardly a question among the politicoes.

While the Congress passed its resolutions, peasants in Bardoli, Bombay Presidency, were conducting a desperate campaign against tax-paying, and workers in the cotton and jute mills of Bombay were striking. In both efforts the nonviolent principles of Mahatma Gandhi were followed, and both brought semi-success in their objectives. The peasants were well-nigh ruined by their victory, but contributions came from all over India toward their rehabilitation. Then the workers of the Burma Shell Oil Company struck. The management called in big Pathans from Afghanistan to break the strike. Hatred expressed itself in an absurd rumor that Pathans were kidnaping Hindu boys for human sacrifice. The result during the first two weeks of February, 1929, was 116 killed and 700 wounded, many houses burned, British military activities resembling war conditions in the streets, and small flare-ups in many cities. It was to be noted that the Hindu Musselmans did not as a rule join their fellow-religionist Pathans in the strife.

Mahatma Gandhi, passing through Calcutta en route to Burma, gave the tense populace an organized interest by inaugurating a campaign of foreign cloth-burning. He was arrested on the evening of March 5 for conducting a demonstration in a public square, and was held in jail overnight. The next morning he was released on bond. He promised the police commissioner that there would be no further public burnings, as these incited to violence, but called on all his people to continue their private collecting and burning of cloth. Subhas Bose, the Bengal leader, proclaimed that "the flame Gandhi had lit will not die out until it has destroyed the last vestige of foreign cloth in this land." Such a blow at Lancashire hits close to the political heart of England. On the other hand, if not followed through persistently, it but increases England's sales and India's tribute. Gandhi went on his way to Rangoon to exhort the happier populace to Burma to beware against a British "divide and conquer" policy, and its lord mayor, in the presence of the city corporation and twenty thousand people, welcomed Gandhi as "one who had given lifelong devotion to the cause of social, moral, and spiritual improvement of humanity, often against tremendous odds, and whose ideals of service and sacrifice served as a beacon light to guide the nations of the earth."

Gandhi, characteristically replying, said his visit was solely for business. Americans who read this dispatch possibly thought he meant private commercial affairs. But the Mahatma has no business other than that of "his Father" and his people. What he really meant was a rebuke: that the quiet, intense application to the "business" of preparing for a great "soul" crisis was more in order than flowery speeches and demonstrations of welcome.

To add to the tenseness of the year 1929, the government introduced into the Delhi Assembly a new bill recalling the Rowlatt Acts. Nationalists fought it bitterly, but a government-manipulated majority turned it over to a select committee for the government. And then came reactionism in South Africa with Premier Hertzog swearing that the Color Bar bill would be forced through the next legislature. There was no Smuts now to preach tolerance. And "honorable compromises," and all the suffering behind them, would be swept aside by arrogance and political opportunism.

As this crucial year wore on, punctuated by peasant

and industrial strife, communist outbursts and fanatical clashes, the mummified figure of the Saint of Sabermati dominated its momentous possibilities. One pictures him on the stone floor of his study writing the dialogue of which he is the modern master, for *Young India,* or engaging in the conversations that are almost debates with hyperbolic, sometimes mischievous wit, making no effort to be cryptic but provoking his hearers with strange phrases which may suddenly assume profound meaning when called to mind the next day. Or one sees him squatting on a bare platform erected high in the open air, ringed about by thousands of squatting Indians, the full-gowned Brahmans in front, bare-chested workmen in the middle, here and there a turbaned Musselman with turned-up shoes, and row on row, off to the rear, the women in their unbleached khadi like dandelion puffs settled on the ground, lifting the pointed chin which almost touches his huge nose, and opening his toothless mouth framed by the flaring ears to say in that deep, assured voice which penetrates to the bowing thousands: "We will go on now, to the use of our ultimate weapon, mass civil disobedience. Every regulation our rulers make save only those of moral connotation, ten thousand of us will break with fasting and prayer."

The program involves absolute refusal to pay revenues and unarmed mass movements for the occupancy of government houses. I have asked a British civil servant what answer the government could have for this. "Machine guns," he said succinctly. One shudders at the possibilities. There are still thousands of true Gandhists who will die cheerfully but will not pay. And there are millions of others in India in whom the more primitive emotions will rule. "Distraught human nature could stand no more," said Gandhi at the time of the Chauri-Chaura riots. Martyrs have a way, in this world, of inspiring crusades, and he who comes in peace of bringing the sword. Behind the Afghan ranges looms the figure of Lenin, saying: "Smash skulls. Shed blood that bloodshed may cease."

Indecision, such as has preceded the white man's most irretrievable mistakes and ruthless deeds in Asia, possessed the government. The Symon Commission knew not whether the report would have to be given to a conservative or a new labor Parliament. Political chiefs and officials were doubtful of their policies and fearful of their careers. Englishmen, even liberals, took the challenge of the Indian Congress with Anglo-Saxon recoil. A people not self-sustaining should receive from their rulers, not tell their rulers what they would have—and to them the Indian people were not self-sustaining. While Indian leaders claimed they were phrasing their program in Western constitutional language for unimaginative Westerners to understand, Englishmen accused them of being copyists from the West, phrasemongers not expressing the souls of their own people. And Indians said, in the words used by the world's greatest woman orator, Naidu, in New

York: "We ask for sympathy from no element in the West—we trust no element in England—not the most liberal element.—For the simple reason that England's labor, Liberal or Tory, cannot *afford* to let India go." S. K. Ratcliffe, veteran liberal, unconsciously gave basis for her opinion: "Any change of status must consider the problems of the rulers as well as of the ruled. King John's feelings when he received the Magna Charta were not referred to. This is the dark side of the picture. The hopeful side is well told in Spender's words:

Returning to India after fourteen years, I was most of all struck by the breaking down of the barriers between British and Indian, cantonment and city, which had seemed to be irremovable when I was there before. Men of both races were working intimately with each other in science, art, education, philanthropy, and a large part of the administration services.

The views of the die-hard will be heard saying "Are we to hold the cow while they milk it—to give them the protection . . . and at the same time leave them free to govern or misgovern?" This foolishness, as it seems to the Gentiles, is at the heart of the British system all over the world, and by general acknowledgment the secret of its endurance.

Thus are the lines drawn for the Mahatma's next great battle, and since it is not likely to be short and the ascetic warrior is sixty years old, may he not feel that wish is any father to our thought that it may be his last. Let us throw a few spotlights of his philosophy against his incisive, emaciated features, and leave him to the future which is to us always a matter of months, and ominous; but which he views as evolving æons, in perfect assurance.

Gandhi's life development is clear and straightforward. Spender's complaint that "No one could have been more friendly, but I bore away the impression of a mind working on a plane with which I could not establish contact," is as revealing of one side as the other. The combination of politician and saint is so unusual to our modern mind that M. K. Gandhi needs, nevertheless, the most elaborate interpretation. We could understand Tilak better, who said that politics was no field for saints, but according to the Mahatma, politics separated from spirituality degenerates into exploitation. "Jesus was in my humble opinion a prince among politicians. You tell me that Jesus refrained from interference in politics. I do not think so—but if you are right, the less Christian then was he. To-day government affects every phase of life; it may threaten our very existence. Interest in government must be regarded as religious interest and we must insist on our governors obeying the laws of morality." However, the daily job of the politician gives the Mahatma no thrill. "Most religious men I have met are politicians in disguise. I, who wear the guise of a politician, am at heart a religionist." And harking back to his conviction that in any campaign it is the underlying principle rather than the tactics that counts, he says: "My experiments in the political field have not had much

value." He has exercised what Woodrow Wilson recommended: open diplomacy openly arrived at. Gandhi's
own political life is an outstanding example of candor
and idealism. As Fülop-Miller says:

Never once in his whole life has Gandhi made use of secret
negotiations, misleading explanations, tactical subterfuges, or
surprise strokes. He has rather ostracized from political life
and stigmatized as disgraceful all this clandestine trafficking
hitherto looked on as indispensable.

Convinced that only questionable schemes need fear the light
of full publicity, he has always given his opponents notice
beforehand of every step he is going to take, published full
and truthful accounts of all deliberations, and never concealed
or even tried to make excuses for a failure. By this very
unconditional straightforwardness he has succeeded in disarming his enemies so that the Delhi Government finally had to
abandon as useless all supervision of his actions by secret
police.

Gandhi's theory of government approaches much
more nearly to that of ancient Confucius, who held that
the will of Heaven was the will of the people, and inspired the doctrine of the right of revolution (so sadly
overworked in China), or to that of Thoreau from
whom he got the term "civil disobedience" than it does
to the despotism of India's history. "The people," he
says, "must do away with error and injustice of a state
which are expressed in the form of bad laws by enforcing the repeal of these enactments through voluntary
acceptance of suffering." It is therefore, not only necessary to transgress an unjust law, but also to accept

the penalty which this transgression brings. Subjection to a rule which is founded on unjust premises he calls an "immoral barter for liberty," which must be opposed by "rebellion without any signs of violence."

Such rebellion cannot be accomplished until all fear of death has disappeared in the rebels; until, indeed, they have reached a state of spiritual exaltation where victory is hardly more consequential to them than death. Any tinge of the traditional revolutionary spirit, "It's your life or ours," means ruin to it.

The moment of victory has come when there is no retort to the mad fury of the powerful. We must, by our conduct, demonstrate to every Englishman that he is as safe in the remotest corner of India as he professes to be behind his machine guns. That moment will see a transformation in the English nature in its relation to India, and that moment will also be the moment when all the destructive cutlery in India will begin to rust.

"I cannot find it in my heart to hate any single Englishman," said Gandhi to the author in 1926. But it would seem that he has been somewhat disillusioned in his faith in the white man's sense of fair play. The mystic power of love, demonstrated in unresisting martyrdom, he believes powerful enough, however, to conquer even an Anglo-Saxon. He puts into effect the strategy of Christ—and the older Buddha: "Man shall conquer anger by love, evil by good, avarice by generosity, and the liar by truth."

[492]

MAHATMA GANDHI

In this spiritualization Gandhi sees sure protection against Bolshevism.

If anything can possibly prevent this calamity descending on our country, it is *satyagraha* (soul-force). Bolshevism is the necessary result of modern materialistic civilization. Its insensate worship of matter has given rise to a school which has been brought up to look upon materialistic advancement as the goal and which has lost all touch with the final things of life. If I can but induce the nation to accept *satyagraha*, we need have no fear of Bolshevik propaganda.

In fearlessness and restraint of even "righteous" anger Gandhi finds the superior qualities dignifying the physically helpless Indian and entitling him to assume the position of the forgiver of his tyrant. For,

it is only the stronger who can forgive the weaker. Strength does not come from physical capacity. It comes from indomitable will. We in India may in a moment realize that one hundred thousand Englishmen need not frighten three hundred million human beings. With a definite forgiveness must come a mighty wave of strength in us. . . . It may be that in other countries governments must be overthrown by brute force; but India will never gain her freedom by the fist. For the destiny of this country is different from that of the other great empires. India is predestined to exercise religious domination over the whole world. She needs no weapons of steel, she will win wholly and solely by soul-force. I want India to recognize that she has a soul that cannot perish, and that can rise triumphant above every physical weakness and defy the physical combination of a whole world. We have a message to give to the whole world. I would gladly use the British race to spread our ideas over the earth;

[493]

but this can only happen if we conquer our so-called conquerors by love.

It is in this wide sense—the sense of an Isaiah, not a Maccabeus or a Kemal or a Sun Yat-sen—that Gandhi supports nationalism. "I work for the freedom of India; I was born in India; I inherited its culture and was created to serve my country. But my love for my country has not only no desire to injure any other nation—it rather aims at serving as best it can all other nations in the truest sense of the word." In this interpretation of nationalism the Mahatma stands pretty much alone in to-day's nationalist-mad world. Such kinship as he does have is with a few liberated souls in Europe and America, and, in all the rest of Asia, with only the Christian Socialist Kagawa of Japan.

During most hectic political crises Gandhi could never forget that his prime purpose was cultural. In November, 1920, he founded the National University of Gujrat at his own home city of Ahmedabad. It combined Hindu and Islamic cultures as its foundation, was dedicated to preservation of the dialects of India and the Persian language and to carry out a "systematic study of Asiatic culture, ranking it as no less essential than the study of Western sciences. Every Asiatic nation faces the alternatives of reverting to the ancient agricultural basis, transforming into industrial society, or trying to find some new combination of the two. Gandhi's aim was that his university should "build a new culture based on the traditions of the past and enriched by experiences of later times." It was to be a tolerant and synthesized harmony of culture. Beneath the university Gandhi founded a system of contributory schools taught by his disciples on his self-sacrificing plan. The educational program was to exclude nothing except the spirit of exclusion.

Cultural breadth was to break down social arrogance. "There is nothing untouchable in humanity," said the Mahatma. As did Lenin, he believed that mass education would do away with caste feeling. Manual work—chiefly spinning—and student self-support as a matter of principal were policies of his educational system.

Rolland remarks that his institutions are more convents than schools. True—from our conception of schools. The model at Satyagraha Ashram requires the vows of absolute truth-telling and living, nonkilling, celibacy, appetite control, nonstealing (if one take more than the necessities of life he is stealing), nonuse of goods made by modern industry and of machinery, and fearlessness, even of criminals and wild animals. Pupils are entirely separated through a ten-year course from their families. A day and a half each week is given them for creative work according to their own genius. Regardless of caste, they take their turn at the humblest work. Lady Slade, daughter of the British Admiral once commanding in Indian waters, who had come back for spiritual mentorship to the people she had been taught in her youth to disdain and who was among the seekers of all races sitting at Gandhi's feet, was gladly doing her assignment of scavenger work when the author visited the ashram. The secondary language of Gandhi's schools is English, and he has scandalized native orthodoxy by requiring reading of the New Testament.

Gandhi's educational campaign is not confined to institutions. His four greatest books, published by the tens of thousands, are parts of a definite mass educational campaign. They are *Hind Swaraj,* his doctrine of individual and national self-rule, *Ethical Religion, Guide to Health,* and *Adventures in Truth.* His intense human sympathies and his religious theories meet in his care for the physical needs of his people. He is on perpetual crusade against dirt, and roundly condemns the British government, in spite of all it has done, for tolerance of conditions conducive to plague and famine. It would seem to have done much, but its own statistics are Gandhi's best argument: expenditure for military 30 per cent. of the yearly revenue; for general administration 5 per cent.; for civil works 5 per cent.; education 5 per cent.; irrigation 2 per cent.; forestation 2 per cent.; other 15 per cent.

One of his strongest denunciations is against conditions on third class railway carriages. He teaches from platform and through press that there must be ash-pails by every latrine, that food must be covered, that work is beneficial, that breathing should be done through the nose, that the upper reaches of streams should be for

[496]

drinking and the lower for washing and bathing, and
that food should be well chewed. He includes recipes
for simple and tasty food in his sermons and religious
and political magazines.

Gandhi, as every Indian, is not lacking in love of
beauty. He insists on the highest type sacred music
obtainable at his ashram. He will read and discuss
even the love poetry of Tagore with insight and delight.
But true social reformer that he is, he must, like ancient Confucius and recent Tolstoy, evaluate art primarily for its social, rather than its esthetic contribution. He condemned Oscar Wilde, during whose
sensational days Gandhi was a student in London, for
"not shrinking from glorifying the immoral" when he
could do so in perfection of form. One remembers
Wilde's "Happy Prince," and how he could be a poet's
very picture of Mahatma Gandhi. Or the humani-
tarianism of the "Ballad of Reading Gaol." Human
sympathy makes strange fellow workers in this world.

Gandhi's program of education is designed to perpetuate the best of the native culture. He makes no
claim to perfection in the native life. But he sees a
fundamental possibility of perfection in it, just as he
sees a fundamental hopelessness in machine-centric society. "Western civilization is godless, while Indian is
permeated with faith in God." He sums it up, "The
time will come when the West will say: 'Oh! what have
we done?'" Gandhi would have this culture perpetuated not only because it is Heaven's special gift to India

but pragmatically also because it is the only economic system fitted to India. Factory production breaks up the village industries, reducing the rural bulk of the population to poverty and vagrancy, while on the other hand Indians prove unable to compete in modern industry with other nationals, become a prey to foreign exploitation, and see steady exportation of their national wealth. It is necessary to reintroduce simple home industry applying to the vast majority of the people: hence the campaign for spinning.

In Gandhi's tilt against the machine he will certainly lose. Even now the great factory chimneys of Ahmedabad overshadow the thatched roofs of his ashram. And from encouragement of the *charka* Swaraj is turning to development of great steel, cotton, and wool mills and tariff for protection of home industry. The breakdown of the villages and industrialization of the cities must inevitably continue, as in every land on whose shores the all-conquering machine has gained a foothold. But possibly his protest will have made his people know that the machine is made for man and not man for the machine, and save that terrible experience preceding the humanizing of industry suffered by Western societies. And the campaign of the spinning wheel, in coördinating the economic activity of the nation to one end, may point the way to mass introduction of health information, improved agriculture, coöperative buying and marketing, and eventually, let us hope, population control.

There remain, too, the spiritual fundamentals of Gandhi's economic revolt, which may be found to apply even in a machine age, and for which he will be revered when the *charka* is forgotten: that welfare is not synonymous with profit, and that production, in filling the innate requirement of the human for expression through work, is more important than product.

The truest light on Gandhi's mind is his theological views. His childhood rebellion against the scripturally endorsed degradation of one-fifth of the population compelled him to adopt an eclectic attitude on "authority." His declarations would suit any Christian modernist:

My belief does not require me to accept every word and verse in the sacred writings as divinely inspired. I decline to be bound by any interpretation, however learned it may be, if it is repugnant to reason or moral sense. . . . I have no hesitation in rejecting scriptural authority of a doubtful character in order to support a sinful institution. Indeed, I would reject all authority if it is in conflict with sober reason or the dictates of the heart. The devil has always quoted scripture. But scripture cannot transcend reason and truth. It is intended to purify reason and illuminate truth.

Yet think not that this means Gandhi has the mind of the scientific modernist. It accepts "revelation" more devotedly than the most conservative Tennessee fundamentalist. Where such revelation clashes with his essential humanism Gandhi finds it unauthentic. He is an eclectic fundamentalist. Only Asia could pro-

[499]

duce such a phenomenon. The Western mind must be too pettily consistent.

So Gandhi, while supporting the Caliph and teaching the New Testament in his schools, remains a faithful Hindu.

I can no more describe my feeling for Hinduism than for my own wife. She moves me as no other woman in the world can. Not that she has no faults. I dare say she has many more than I see myself. But the feeling of indissoluble bond is there. Even so I feel for and about Hinduism with all its faults and limitations. Nothing elates me so as the music of the Gita or the Ramayana of Tulsidas, the two books of Hinduism I may be said to know. I know that vice is going on to-day in all the Indian shrines, but I love them in spite of their unspeakable failings. I am a reformer through and through. But my zeal never takes me to a rejection of any of the essential things of Hinduism. . . . My faith offers me all that is necessary for my inner development, for it teaches me to pray. I am here in all humility to tell you that for me Hinduism, as I have found it, entirely satisfies my soul, fills my whole being, and that I find a solace in the Bhagavad Gita and in the Upanishads that I miss even in the Sermon on the Mount. When disappointment stares me in the face and all alone I see not one ray of light I go to the Bhagavad Gita; I find a verse here and a verse there, and I immediately begin to smile in the midst of overwhelming tragedies—and my life has been full of external tragedies— and if they have left no visible, no unalterable scar upon me, I owe it to the Bhagavad Gita.

This is a profession of the faith which scores of thousands of educated Hindus would make to-day, and to them the preaching of the missionary who thinks of them as pagan idolaters or as heathen walking in darkness is very near an insult.

But I pray that every one may develop to the fullness of his being in his own religion, that the Christian may become a better Christian and the Muhammadan a better Muhammadan. I am convinced that God will one day ask us only what we are and what we do, not the name we give to our being and doing.

"I would go to America," Gandhi said to the author, "if I could go to help Americans rather than to be a show. Your people are very tragic to me. They will take the longest risks—exhibit the greatest heroism in the world in material adventures. But they want their spiritual experiments insured against loss beforehand."

"They are bewildered," I said. "Maybe they would follow the true religion if they were told what it is."

"Definition enough for any one is this," he replied, pausing with hand holding the spinning thread in mid-air, and laboriously bringing out the following phrases as he irregularly twirled the wheel: "the conviction that I shall always live, as truly as I live now—and that I can better my condition. Are the American people bewildered, or do they rather want spiritual attainment made easy for them as they are accustomed to have material attainment?"

So the orthodox Hindu Gandhi, while condemning untouchability, presiding at great banquets where men and women of all castes eat from common bowls, adopting scavenger and Muslim children at his ashram, and preaching that "our being treated as social lepers in practically the whole world is the spiritual consequence of our having treated a fifth of our own race as such (we have driven the pariah from our midst and have justly become the pariahs of the British Empire)," none the less upholds the Brahman doctrine of caste. The eighty-four classes and thousands of sub-classes will, he says, disappear with social pressure, but the four fundamental divisions must remain, although not involving nonintercourse. He takes issue with Tagore. "I am certainly against any attempt at destroying them. The caste system is not based on inequality; there is no question of inferiority." Caste is the projecton in this world of the underlying principle of reincarnation, and "nature will, without any possibility of mistake, adjust the balance by degrading a Brahman, if he misbehaves himself" in the next birth, or bringing back the good member of a lower caste into the next higher. His tenacity to this Hindu socio-theology appears the more striking and honest in that India's *guru* himself comes not from the highest caste and is reverent to the favored Brahmans who from the standpoint of character and accomplishment may be just brash on the world's forehead.

One wonders that this most tender of humanists can overlook the historic origin of caste: a system born of conquest—a "sanctified" way of keeping the conquered in subjection.

And Gandhi stands for cow protection! The writer

heard him promise devotees to procure Muslem assent
to a higher slaughter tax on beef (abattoirs being in
the hands of Musselmans) which the government, always seeking revenue, would be quick to endorse.
Consequently less beef-buying; *ergo* less killing of the
sacred animal which in India needs adaption to man as
much as the machine to us of the West. But Gandhi
would place the cow in which dwells divine life in the
category with man, rather than with machinery. And
he deepens and spiritualizes the issue with a profound
principle.

The central fact of Hinduism is cow protection; cow protection to me is one of the most wonderful phenomena in
human evolution. The cow to me means the entire sub-
human world. Man through the cow is enjoined to realize
his identity with all that lives. Why the cow was selected
for apotheosis is obvious to me. The cow in India was the
best companion. She was the giver of plenty. Not only did
she give milk, but she also made agriculture possible. This
gentle animal is a poem of pity. Protection of the cow means
the protection of the whole dumb creation of God. *Ahimsa*
[nonkilling—also nonviolence] is the gift of Hinduism to the
world, and Hinduism will live as long as there are Hindus to
protect the cow.

Even idols Gandhi finds place for as symbols. After
all, are not the cross of the Christian world and its
New Jerusalem glorified idols? he asks. Where these
exist, the minds of their worshipers still need them.
Such sides to Gandhi make him seem a little estranged

from us. In the same degree they make him nearer his own people, and that is the important thing.

We have seen Gandhi's resentment toward Christian mission activity as reflecting on the dignity of his race and culture—a feeling common to New Asians. He made a further criticism before a missionary conference in Calcutta in 1925: "You give statistics of so many orphans cared for, so many adults won to Christianity. . . . I do not feel convinced thereby that that is your mission. In my humble opinion your mission is infinitely superior. It should be to find the *man* in India, and if you want to do that you will have to go to the lowly cottages not to give them something but probably to take something. I miss that receptivity of mind, that humility, that will on your part to identify yourselves with the masses of India." Doubtless the missionaries have a good reply. And it is significant that Gandhi's European assistants have been drawn from the mission body into the humility he speaks of. Stanley Jones, in his *Christ of the Indian Road,* shows what tremendous influence Gandhi is having upon mission endeavor in India and all Christian evangelism.

Out of Gandhi's own experience comes his teaching as to sex. The ideal is uncompromising conquest of the instinct so that even married couples come to live as brother and sister. This *bramacharya,* in an atmosphere of freest social intercourse, is strictly enforced at his ashram. The spiritual principle has as always, he finds, its economic benefit, and the fundamental material necessity of population control he would bring entirely through spiritual means. "Is it right for us, who know the disease, famines, and pauperism of India, to bring forth children? We only multiply slaves and weaklings, until we have ameliorated India's misery and suffering." Every report of a birth affects him painfully, and he calls upon an entire nation to reduce its number of marriages, and, in marriage, to practice perfect self-restraint and cease to procreate for the time being. Here his social sense overrules the religious Hindu feeling that limitation of births interferes with the universal scheme of bringing souls back to earth to work out their salvation. Gandhi has four sons, but, as in other matters, he is not ashamed to confess the unfortunateness of his example. Will he, asks one, for the "weakness of his people," concede to scientific birth control? Not likely, but he prepares the way for that innovation which must be the answer to the East's prosperity and the world's peace.

On child marriage, like untouchability, he is not orthodox. "I loathe and detest child marriage. I shudder to see a child widow. I have never known a grosser superstition than that the Indian climate causes sexual precocity. What does bring about untimely puberty is the mental and moral atmosphere surrounding family life." His own childhood sufferings had brought the attention of India's saint to her most vulnerable point long before an American lady journalist made capital thereof.

He was nauseated and aroused by the picture of the life of prostitutes brought to him by a deputation of one hundred women from the brothels of Barisal, in Andhra Province. He says he was able to read in the eyes of the speakers more than they dared tell him. He consented to become their adviser and protector. Campaigning against prostitution he said, "The two hours I spent with these suffering sisters is a treasured memory to me. I bowed my head in profound shame at their degradation. I will far rather see the race of man extinct than that we should become less than beasts by making the noblest of God's creation the object of our lust. Of all the evils for which man has made himself responsible none is so degrading, so shocking, so brutal, as his abuse of the better half of humanity. The female sex is the nobler of the two, for it is the embodiment of sacrifice, silent suffering, humility, faith, and knowledge." We readily apprehend to what extent his remorse over mistreatment of Kasturbai underlies the last statement.

There are disturbing narrownesses in Gandhi. "We have nothing to learn from the foreigner. The traditional old implements, and plow and the spinning wheel, are our wisdom and welfare." The Mahatma often speaks in hyperbole, which those who see his smile can understand but his readers may take too literally. "I would have my windows open on the world," he told Tagore. Yet a Swarajist writer says: "It is wrong to import others' products and ideas and to export one's own." If Gandhi had never imported ideas—and never exported them (intentionally or otherwise)—he would not be the world's mahatma to-day.

Gandhi is very different from Sun Yat-sen, Kemal, or Ito who took from the West for their people. But he is equaly different from the traditional yogi or fakir of his own India. He is a product of Western influence on the East as much as his contemporary nation-makers in new Asia, but his eclectic mind chose differently out of the West's paradoxical civilization. His movement, as the able T. L. Vaswami defines, is "India's return to herself, to her own culture, her own civilization, her loyalty to the law of her own history, her genius, her own individuality, the God-given inspiration of her own life," but it is a reinterpretation of India's ancient theoretic idealism in terms of human welfare taken clearly from the practical-minded West. "To a people famine-ridden and idle the only form in which God dare appear is work and wages," is a startling addition to the sutras. It is of a part with the accusations of Westernized Kagawa and his "social Christians" in Japan: "the church says, 'we take responsibility for your future but cannot be concerned with your present.'"

India was floundering in the morass of her own traditions when Gandhi came. Out of these he has organized a coherent doctrine and a forward movement, salted with the definiteness of the Sermon on the Mount, applied with the pragmatism and vigor of the West, and inspired by his own sacrificing life. He has taught India what she wants in her inmost soul and what she must do to get it. Whether his method is followed and the ideal result is attained or not, he must go down as the creator of the Indian Nation that shall eventually emerge. He has made the masses of India a factor in the struggle. Politicoes could never reach them— that required a saint. Says the *Leader* of Allahabad: "The vast depths of immobility are heaving with life. The lesson of self-reliance has gone home and the whole nation has been taught that what it would have it will have to strive for and that nothing is worth having which has not been won by one's own efforts."

Even in his mistakes Gandhi succeeds, as Blanche Watson phrases it: "They have been few—and they, too, have 'worked.' A man who says that he would rather be 'right with God' though that meant wrong with all his friends, who seeks, and apparently receives, divine guidance, who is not afraid to retrace his steps —such a man cannot but succeed in the end." Of course it is a long end. "I can wait forty, or four hundred years—it is the same to me," he said to the author. "Life goes on forever—we all persist in some form and inevitably victory is ours." Here he is supreme over us of the West, who cannot wait, and to whom life is not forever, but a lifetime.

The Mahatma, says Tagore, "is the liberated ego which discovers itself in all other souls." —"I cannot say," says Gandhi in characteristic English argot, "that

the title has ever tickled me. I have felt sick at the
adulation of the crowd." But it is justified adulation.
C. F. Andrews, whose critical sense is not dim, ob-
serves: "Almost perfect selflessness enables Gandhi to
see more truly and clearly than other men and to realize his clear vision with unrivaled resoluteness." In his
later career he has lived up to the evaluation of Gokhale,
who passed to him the torch of Indian leadership: "He
is, without doubt, of the stuff of which heroes and
martyrs are made. Nay more. He possesses the mar-
velous spiritual power of turning ordinary men around
him into heroes and martyrs." His personal life is
nearer the standard of Him who challenged: "Who
among you convicteth Me of sin?" than any other seen
in our time.

This life will be for all men of all ages to come. Romain Rolland envisions a special contribution to our immediate post-war age: "The world is swept by the wind
of violence. Each people kills the other in the name
of the same principles, behind which all hide the same
covetousness and Cainish instincts. All, be they nationalists, fascists, bolshevists, members of the oppressed classes, members of the oppressing classes, claim
that they have the right to use force, while refusing
this right to others." Better force than cowardice, says
Gandhi, but force defeats itself. "Who will prove this
faith? And how, in an unbelieving world? Faith is
proved by action. Europe, bled by wars and revolutions,
impoverished and exhausted, despoiled of her prestige

in the eyes of Asia, which she formerly oppressed, cannot long resist on Asiatic soil the aspirations of the awakened peoples of Islam, India, China, and Japan. But this would mean little, no matter how rich and new might be the harmonies which a few more nations would bring to the human symphony; this would mean little, if the surging spirit of Asia did not become the vehicle for a new ideal of life and of death, and what is more, of action for all humanity. This is India's great message to the world. It is the clarification of the age's problem of the place of force." Blanche Watson, American interpreter, sees the same angle of Gandhi's work. "The political fortunes of the non-coöperation struggle will have their ebb and flow; battles will be lost and battles won. If Gandhi should be taken away the Gandhi idea will persist, and its constructive working out in different parts of the world will furnish the necessary counter-balance to the violence and blood-lust of the West!" I would add—of the lusty new East as well.

Gandhi is greatest of the makers of Asia, because, unlike the other makers, he would sacrifice his nation's hope of independence rather than commit one act of violence or chicanery to attain it. He is the world's unique leader, its modern prophet of the gospel of love, whose spiritual descent is through the Buddha, Mo Ti, Jesus of Nazareth, St. Francis of Assisi, and Tolstoy. Such men last longer than their immediate causes, and become a factor bearing upon every cause that stirs humanity after them. Gandhi may be the George Washington to the new Indian nation of the twentieth century, but long after this now precious hope shall have materialized, flourished, and slipped into the shadows like Asoka's empire, he will remain a Christ to peoples of many heritages—the Messiah of the Meeting of the Races.